I dedicate this book to the countless false confessors
whose personal experiences have informed
and inspired my research.

CONTENTS

PREFACE

Why I Wrote This Book

When I was in the sixth grade, Mrs. Avery was my teacher. Young and fresh off a stint with the Peace Corps in Uganda, she had slides to show class and stories to tell. Growing up in Brooklyn, I was mesmerized by her worldly experiences.

One of our first written homework assignments was to read a biography and write a book report. For me, the biographical subject was easy: Mickey Mantle.

Having become baseball conscious after the Dodgers left town in 1958 and before the Mets arrived in 1962, I was a Yankees fan (it didn't hurt that they were perennial World Series champions). Switch-hitting center fielder Mickey Mantle, wearing the number seven on his back, was my pinstriped hero. Somewhere, I might still have reel-to-reel tapes of his home runs as they were broadcast on the radio.

I read a biography, and then a second. I was only twelve but I liked to write (later that year, I wrote a short story, which I still have, about an inventor who patented a wristwatch that could regulate body temperature). The point is, this book report was to me a labor of love. Plus, I really wanted to impress Mrs. Avery.

It was a Friday afternoon when she returned everyone's graded handwritten papers. I was excited to get my grade. She called my name, then glared at me, and I looked down only to see an F circled and in red. I was stunned. I went up to her after class thinking it had to be a mistake. No mistake. She flunked me on the paper, she said, because I plagiarized it.

Mrs. Avery didn't *ask* if I plagiarized; nor did she try to get me to admit it. Very simply, she accused me and convicted me, both in the same sentence. End of conversation.

I don't remember what I said, if anything. All I can recall is the powerful urge to hold back tears. I was too old to cry with dignity—in front of her or in front of my classmates. So I walked out in silence trying like hell to keep it together. That stoic face lasted until I opened the door at home, saw my mother, and broke down.

My mother is my hero for what happened next—and, I will add, for so much more. She knew I'd spent a whole lot of time on that assignment. When I told her what happened, she bee-lined for Mrs. Avery, who assumed that I must have copied my report off a book jacket. She didn't have proof, she said—just the sense that the paper was too well written. I wasn't there, but my mother told her to find proof of plagiarism or apologize. She went to the library, apparently, found no proof, changed the grade, and apologized.

I tell this story because I will not forget my sense of helplessness at being accused of something I didn't do—and discerning no good way to defend myself. Add the highest of stakes to that experience, and you'll understand in part why the subject matter animates me.

* * *

Fast forward half a century or so. Over the course of my career, I have collected some shocking research data and I've witnessed some horrifying miscarriages of justice.

I've seen police extract confessions from young teenagers and other vulnerable suspects using jaw-dropping forms of deception and implied and sometimes explicit promises and threats.

I've seen police trick mothers out of their sons' interrogations, in one instance switching rooms after a bathroom break, not telling her where they moved, and inducing her thirteen-year-old son to confess.

I've seen police outright lie about evidence to break someone down into a state of despair—for example, telling a suspect, falsely, about his fingerprints on the weapon, his hair in the victim's grasp, an eyewitness's identification, or the results of an allegedly failed polygraph exam.

I've seen judges unwilling to serve as the gatekeepers they get paid to be by failing to exclude from evidence confessions that were quite clearly coerced, not voluntary.

I've seen prosecutors bend logic until it breaks, refusing to concede innocence despite DNA results that excluded the confessor, without doubt, and identified the actual perpetrator.

I've read contemporaneous newspaper accounts during trial that accepted the government's public relations spin on the case, hook, line, and sinker.

I've received heart-wrenching letters from countless prisoners, many of whom were later absolved, and desperate family members writing on their behalf.

I've been cross-examined by hostile prosecutors, one of whom, while seeking to re-convict an innocent confessor who had already been exonerated by DNA, referred to me on the record as the "insufferable Dr. Kassin."

I've done battle—in court, on stage, and in print—with those who train detectives in the kinds of trickery and deceit that con innocent people to confess.

I was berated and threatened by fringe bloggers belonging to an Amanda Knox hate group after writing in support of her ultimately successful appeal in Italy.

I've seen cases in which medical examiners literally rewrote their autopsy reports after police disclosed that a suspect had confessed. In each case, the pathologist appeared in court, adding "independent" medical corroboration for a confession that had corrupted their judgment.

In short, I've witnessed scandalous dirty little secrets that wind their way from the interrogation room, into the crime lab, the DA's office, and the courtroom, all of which can put you and your loved ones at risk—whether you did anything wrong or not.

I know what you're thinking: "I would never confess to a crime I did not commit." Don't tell that to Amanda Knox, the twenty-year-old American girl dubbed "Foxy Knoxy," who momentarily and "confusedly" confessed to killing her college roommate in Perugia, Italy. To this day, Knox struggles to understand what happened to her and what she was thinking at 5:45 a.m. on the morning she signed a confession.

Don't tell that to Peter Reilly of New Canaan, Connecticut; Anthony Wright of Philadelphia, Pennsylvania; Joe Buffey of Clarksburg, West Virginia; Wesley Myers of Columbia, South Carolina; Juan Rivera of Lake County, Illinois; John Kogut of Long Island, New York; Nga Truong of Worcester, Massachusetts; Huwe Burton of the Bronx, New York; or Chris Tapp of Idaho Falls, Idaho.

Don't tell that to survival-trained POWs throughout history who were coerced by the enemy and propped up on camera to confess to alleged war crimes neither they nor others in their platoon committed.

And don't tell it to the countless numbers of men and women who sign false confessions for stealing money or merchandise from their employers—which they are forced to pay back, which gets them fired, and which they had nothing to do with.

Citing basic psychology research, the Innocence Project and other cases on which I have worked, and quotes from individuals who confessed to crimes they did not commit, this book will tell the story of how this happens, how the system turns a blind eye, and how to make it stop.

This book is all about why innocent men and women, intensely stressed and befuddled by the promises, threats, trickery, and deception of a police interrogation, are duped into confession, no matter how horrific the crime.

It's about why innocents sometimes get so confused that they lose their grip on reality, as if brainwashed; internalize a belief in their own guilt; and confabulate false memories in the process.

This book is about how police come to identify innocent people as suspects because they think they can tell when someone is lying by looking into their eyes, observing changes in their facial expression or posture, or listening to their quivering voice.

Guess what: research shows that none of these behaviors signal lying versus truth telling. Police are not demonstrably better at human lie detection than you or I would be by flipping a coin.

Nor can police distinguish between true and false confessions. I should know. I went into a prison outside Boston and video recorded male inmates confessing to the crime for which they were incarcerated. Then I asked these same inmates to confess to a crime I knew they had not committed. When I later showed the tapes to college students and experienced police officers, neither group could tell the difference.

This book is about the fact that while common sense tells us that adolescents lack cognitive maturity and should not be treated as adults, John Reid and Associates—the Chicago-based firm that trains more interrogators than anyone else—now offers courses to educators on how to interrogate students in school using the same types of techniques taught to homicide detectives.

In a situation where *Miranda* does not apply, where parents are not informed, where students essentially are in "custody," and where disobedience evokes disciplinary action, this practice is perilous.

This book is about the paradoxical fact that innocence as a state of mind can be your worst enemy. Believing at the core that truth and justice will prevail, innocent people almost always waive their right to remain silent and have a lawyer present.

"When police accuse you, why didn't you lawyer up?" I'd ask one exoneree after another. With a shrug of the shoulder and a puzzled expression on the face, each would say, in almost identical words, "I didn't need a lawyer. I didn't do anything wrong."

This book will explain why, whenever someone confesses, everyone—prosecutors, judges, juries, and appeals courts—is duped into believing that the confessor is the perpetrator.

Video statements from actual cases are even more compelling. In tapes that resemble Hollywood trailers, even innocents will describe what they allegedly did, how, and why. They will tearfully apologize and express remorse. They may stand and physically reenact the crime. These statements are so compelling that I defy any judge or jury to see through the charade.

This book will explain why confessions trigger a self-fulfilling prophecy, making it almost impossible to reverse. Research shows that once a suspect confesses, an eyewitness is more likely to identify that suspect in a lineup; an alibi witness is less likely to vouch for his whereabouts.

Once a suspect confesses, the polygraph examiner is more likely to see deception in his charts. All of a sudden the handwriting on the bank robbery note, the footprints, and the bite marks all look a whole lot more like the suspect's. By the time a confessor goes to trial, there is a mountain of evidence—well, often nothing more than a house of cards corrupted by a false confession.

Finally, and most important, this book is a lesson in how to protect yourself and your family. You may never get trapped in the crosshairs of a homicide investigation. But one day your son or daughter may be in the wrong place at the wrong time.

Or, if you work at Macy's, Wal-Mart, Pizza Hut, Marriott, or Amazon, you may one day get called in to a supervisor's office and be accused of stealing from the company. "I did nothing wrong" is not a defense. To the contrary, this innocence mindset will lead you, blind, into the abyss.

Finally, it's important for me to make this point: invisible as they may be to us, false confessions are *everywhere*.

Granted, I am something of a magnet when it comes to drawing people with stories of false confessions. But this happens all the time. Wherever I go, whenever I speak, I am approached by men and women victimized by a system in which miscarriages of justice are too easily engineered by confession. Through all these stories, I have to say that, while the names, dates, and places change, the script is always about the same. And it needs to be stopped.

ACKNOWLEDGMENTS

Over the years, I have learned so much from so many people that it's hard to know where to begin. I will start with my academic mentors. I am deeply indebted to Arthur S. Reber, my undergraduate advisor, hero, and role model. Arthur had the audacity to study unconscious processes before the Zeitgeist allowed him to do so. I am also indebted to the late Charles "Skip" Lowe, my graduate advisor, who taught me all I know about attribution theory, and the late Lawrence Wrightsman, my postdoctoral mentor, a founding figure in psychology and the law and a good friend with whom I broke open the study of confessions.

All that I've learned, and this book, would not be possible without the many intensely dedicated thesis students at Williams College who took a chance on a new and scary topic. In particular, I thank Christina Fong, Christine Caveney Goldstein, Lindsay (Holland) Boeger, Katherine Lee Kiechel Koles, Karlyn McNall, Katherine Neumann, Rebecca (Norwick) Eyre, Marisa (Reddy) Randazzo, Samuel Sommers, and Holly Sukel. More recently, I have learned and benefited more than anyone can know from the graduate students at John Jay College and elsewhere who have populated my lab and have pushed the study of confessions into important new directions. In particular, I want to call out Fabiana Alceste, Aria Amrom, Sara Appleby, Stephanie Cardenas, Will Crozier, Linda Geven, Lisa Hasel, Johanna Hellgren, Kristyn Jones, Jeff Kukucka, Victoria Lawson, Timothy Luke, Stephanie Marion, Caroline (Crocker) Otis, Jennifer Perillo, Gabriela Rico, Lucrezia Rizzelli, Patricia Sanchez, Jenny Schell-Leugers, Laura Smalarz, and Brian Wallace.

Many friends and colleagues at other institutions have helped, directly or indirectly, to build a knowledge base on false confessions that did not previously exist. Over the years, I have leaned on and learned from so many scholars—including Ray Bull, Stephen Ceci, Itiel Dror, Brandon Garrett, Naomi Goldstein, Thomas Grisso, Gisli Gudjonsson, Charles Honts, Richard Leo, Elizabeth Loftus, Christian Meissner, Allison Redlich, Melissa Russano, Kyle Scherr, Laurence Steinberg, Aldert Vrij, and Gary Wells.

My own interest in the subject notwithstanding, the study of false confessions was shot out of a cannon by attorneys Barry Scheck and Peter Neufeld, the brilliant and passionate cofounders of the Innocence Project. Their foresight to analyze the causes of the wrongful convictions exposed by DNA, which unleashed the dirty little secret of false confessions, changed the conversation. I am indebted to them and their incredible staff—most notably, Rebecca Brown, director of policy, who knows more than anyone about reform efforts throughout the country; research analyst Vanessa Meterko, who has her finger on the pulse of the IP database; and attorneys Susan Friedman, Nina Morrison, and Vanessa Potkin.

I could not have written a book like this without the repository of wrongful convictions maintained by the National Registry of Exonerations, founded and scrupulously updated by Samuel Gross and Maurice Possley. The archive they have assembled, which I relied on throughout this book, is a gold mine. I am similarly indebted to Steven Drizin, clinical professor of law at Northwestern University School of Law, who founded the Center for Wrongful Convictions of Youth, and the center's codirector, Laura Nirider. No one knows more or fights harder on behalf of juveniles interrogated into confession.

More than anything else, I am indebted to the countless false confessors whose personal tragedies have informed and animated my research. I've worked on several of their cases; many have visited my classes and met with the students in my lab. For their time, their stories, and their research-inspiring insights, I want to thank in particular Kenzi Snider Brown, Joseph Buffey, Huwe Burton, Billy Wayne Cope, Jeffrey Deskovic, Gary Gauger, Adam Gray, Byron Halsey, Johnny Hincapie, Amanda Knox, Barry Laughman, David McCullum, Antron McRay, Alvin Mitchell, Wesley Myers, Peter Reilly, Kevin Richardson,

Juan Rivera, Yusef Salaam, Raymond Santana, Marty Tankleff, Malthe Thomsen, Korey Wise, and Anthony Wright.

Last but not least, I am fully indebted to my family, the backbone that has enabled me to take for granted my most important pillars of support. Beginning with my mother and blogger, Betty Kassin, who modeled strength and independence when I was a kid, and to this day; my wife Carol, who has accompanied, supported, and tolerated me on this entire journey; my children, Briana and Marc; their partners, Andrew and Malin; and their gifts, the magnificent grandchildren who now center my life—Jordan, Elle, Henry, and Hedda.

Part One

Introduction

I

THE PROBLEM IN A NUTSHELL

It was a September morning in 2002. I was preparing for a new semester of psych classes at Williams College, in western Massachusetts, when the phone on my desk rang.

"Professor Kassin, I'm a producer for ABC News. We're working on a story about an old case and wonder if you'd be willing to look at some videotaped confessions for us." Intrigued, I asked what case they were investigating. "I can't tell you," she said.

Scrambling to transition from summer to fall, and too busy to play games, I explained that I had no time to make a blank-check commitment to a new project. I repeated my question: "What's the case?"

Pushing back, she explained that they were working on an exclusive story about a highly visible crime from the past and did not want word of it to get out. "Can you keep this confidential?" she asked.

Sure, I said, no problem. "What case?" The producer paused—the kind of pause that's hard to interpret. "It's the Central Park jogger," she said.

Seldom in life am I rendered speechless. This was one of those times. I was disoriented. Taking stock, I said nothing. I just kept hearing the echo in my head: *Central Park jogger*.

On the night of April 19, 1989, a twenty-eight-year-old investment banker named Trisha Meili, a Wellesley graduate with two master's degrees who worked on Wall Street, was intercepted while jogging, violently beaten, dragged through grass into a ravine, raped, tied up with her own shirt, and left for dead in a puddle of mud inside Central

Park, Manhattan's rambling green wilderness. Her skull was fractured; her brain was swollen; her left eye was crushed; she had lost several pints of blood. When she emerged from a coma one week later, she had no memory of what had happened.

Coming at a time when crack cocaine had become epidemic, violent crime rates were soaring, and racial tensions were peaking, this incident marked an "enough is enough" moment in the city's history. Local papers were ablaze with headlines like "Nightmare in Central Park!"

Amid the uproar, NYPD detectives solved the crime, or so it seemed. Within seventy-two hours, they announced that five teenagers, ages fourteen to sixteen, of black and Hispanic descent, had confessed. Each boy implicated himself and the others; their stories were detailed; four of the confessions were on videotape for everyone to see. Case closed.

I had followed this story closely at the time. Hell, I am a native New Yorker, born and raised in Brooklyn, then in a beach town in Queens. Like everyone else, I grew up riding the subway into the Bronx for Yankees baseball and into Manhattan for everything else. For me, Central Park was a rectangular green oasis to escape the city grid for demonstrations, festivals, rock concerts, and the best hot pretzels in town.

I had left the city for graduate school at the University of Connecticut in 1974. But in the ensuing years, I went on to get my PhD in social psychology and develop a particular interest in the interrogation tactics that police use to get confessions—sometimes, shockingly—from innocent people. Four years before the jogger case broke, Larry Wrightsman and I wrote an article critical of these tactics and the hazard of false confessions. In fact, we proposed a taxonomy that distinguished between three different types of false confessions. More on that later.

This was who I was—New Yorker, research psychologist, and false-confession expert—when the ABC news producer rendered me speechless on the phone. Even after I regained my mental footing, all I could say was, "The Central Park jogger case, really? What about it?"

I'm not sure anyone on the planet is more inherently critical than I am of police-induced confessions. I am hardly naive. And I will admit that this case gnawed at me at the time. Something wasn't right. Then again, I thought, this was not a single isolated admission of guilt allegedly taken in some back alley by some small-town sheriff in the middle of nowhere when no one was watching. This was *five* detailed confessions, four on tape, taken in Manhattan in the Central Park Precinct, recorded by an assistant district attorney, at a time when the whole world was watching.

Based solely on these confessions, uncorroborated by any other evidence, and in fact contradicted by DNA testing of the rape kit, which excluded all five boys, Antron McCray, Kevin Richardson, Yusef Salaam, Raymond Santana, and Korey Wise were tried in 1990, convicted, and sent to prison. This horrific case was all but settled—not only as a matter of law but for the city's peace of mind.

All that began to unravel for me in the fall of 2002 when ABC disrupted my sense of balance with word that this case was coming back into the news. What happened at that time, thirteen years later, that no one saw coming, was that Matias Reyes, a serial offender known as the "East Side Rapist," stepped forward from prison. Serving a life sentence for three rapes and a murder committed after and near the jogger attack, Reyes contacted the DA's office out of the blue to assert that he was the Central Park jogger rapist and that he'd acted alone.

Some suggested that Reyes was just clamoring for attention—not an unreasonable hypothesis. Reinvestigating the case, however, the Manhattan District Attorney's Office questioned Reyes and discovered that he could recount accurate yet previously unknown facts about the assault.

Reyes was able to explain, for example, why the jogger had no keys to her locked apartment when she was found. Reyes said he took her keys, as he did with his other victims, so he could break into her apartment. Failing to get her address, he tossed the keys into bushes nearby.

He also said he was able to sneak up on her because she was wearing headphones and listening to music. Having suffered traumatic head injuries, the jogger was amnesic for the entire episode, so in 1989 no one knew to ask about this. After Reyes, the DA interviewed her, and she confirmed that she used to listen to music through headphones when she ran.

Then there was the DNA, the evidence that clinched it: the semen samples originally recovered from Meili's body, clothing, and socks—which had excluded the boys as donors—unequivocally belonged to Reyes. The only semen found on Meili was his.

I agreed to appear as an analyst on ABC's *Prime Time*, on one condition: I needed to see the entire case file, I told them, not just the videotaped confessions. Later that week, two large cartons arrived containing police reports, medical reports, trial testimony, and the like. Setting everything aside, I pored over the documents and played, rewound, and replayed the tapes over and over again. When I was done, I had no doubt. The five boys, now men, had not raped the jogger. That is pretty much what I said inside the ABC News studio, located, ironically, one block from the west side of Central Park.

The story aired on the night of September 26, 2002. Legal correspondent Cynthia McFadden interviewed Reyes from prison. His account was compelling and of course buttressed by DNA. There was no reasonable way to reconcile his accurate description of events with the 1989 confessions. Yet to my surprise, the city's newspapers were reluctant to reconceptualize what happened and embrace a wrongful conviction narrative of the original five defendants. Considering all the attention the crime got in 1989, the spotlight seemed awfully dim on this news flash. I wondered, What would the DA do?

On November 1, I published an op-ed in the *New York Times:* "False Confessions and the Jogger Case." In the allotted 1,059 words, and a fact-checking experience I won't soon forget, I tried to explain how false confessions come about, how they look and sound, why we are so easily fooled into believing them, and how all of that is relevant to this case.

On December 5, three weeks ahead of Christmas, and over protests from the NYPD, Manhattan District Attorney Robert Morgenthau followed the evidence and joined in the motion to overturn the defendants' convictions. In a fifty-nine-page motion that proved to be one of the most devastating deconstructions of a confession I had ever read from a DA's office, ADA Nancy Ryan wrote, "Perhaps the most persuasive fact about the defendants' confessions is that they exist at all." Two weeks later, New York Supreme Court justice Charles J. Tejada vacated the convictions.

Fast-forward five more years. I received an email from Sarah Burns. A new graduate of Yale, who majored in American studies, Burns first learned about this case while working on an undergraduate thesis on racism in media coverage. Now she was working on a book and had questions about the confessions. Could we meet? She lived in Brooklyn, and I had just accepted a position at the John Jay College of Criminal Justice in New York City, so we met in my office. It was clear right away that she had obtained information about the insides of the case that I did not know. I learned from her. What she could not fully grasp were the confessions.

As our meeting wound down, I asked Sarah about her timetable for completing the project and whether she had a publisher. She let me know that she was also contemplating a PBS documentary based on the book. In a tone that I meant as supportive, so she would not be discouraged, but which may have come across as patronizing, I said something like, "It's not easy to get a contract with PBS." Then she let me know that she was not worried, that her father had something of an arrangement. Her father? That was the moment I hit my head in embarrassment and realized that her father was Ken Burns, the greatest-ever documentarian of American history.

In 2011, Sarah's book was published, titled *The Central Park Five: A Chronicle of a City Wilding.* One year later, an award-winning documentary based on the book was released, directed by Ken Burns, Sarah Burns, and her husband, David McMahon. I could tell from my own family and friends that the film changed the conversation about this case in a way that the exonerations ten years earlier had not. Shortly thereafter, the city settled with the five exonerees for $41 million.

I open with the Central Park jogger case because of its historic and symbolic significance. Here was a crime and investigation that captured the world's attention. Not just one confession was taken, but five were alleged—four appeared on videotape for all of us to see. Race played a decided role, stoking archetypical fears of black- and brown-skinned

In 1989, Korey Wise (16), Antron McCray (15), Kevin Richardson (14), Raymond Santana (14), and, allegedly, Yusef Salaam (15) confessed to the infamous rape of the Central Park jogger. *Mugshots released to the public.*

Thirty years later, post-exoneration, Wise, McCray, Richardson, Santana, Salaam, and I posed for this selfie at the Innocence Project's 2019 gala. *Photo courtesy of the author.*

teen gangs. Just about everyone accepted the storyline of their guilt. And why not? "This is my first rape, and it's going to be last," said defendant Korey Wise on camera.

This story continues to be told. In 2019, Netflix released *When They See Us*, Ava DuVernay's miniseries docudrama about this case. I have to say, the blending of fact and fiction that characterizes docudramas in general makes me uneasy. In some ways, and especially in light of my obsession to distinguish fact from fiction in any false-confession case, this was no exception.

That said, this film has raised public awareness to yet a new level. I was lucky enough to attend the world premiere at the famed Apollo Theater in Harlem—the one neighborhood that never did believe the city's accusations against the five boys. The night was electrifying; the five exonerees, whom I have come to know well over the years, and their families, were in attendance.

The Central Park five is a case of historic significance. But it was not a unique, fantastical, a one-time-only incident. *It happens all the time.*

INNOCENTS WHO CONFESS—A COMPOSITE SKETCH

Whenever I lecture in public, I open with a PowerPoint slide that I call my "wall of faces," a glossy poster-sized copy of which hangs in my tenth-floor office. This wall presents a matrix of twenty-eight portrait photos that I update periodically. The pictures—and the stories they tell—are a varied lot. They are men and women of all races; children, teens, and fully formed adults; people from different ethnic backgrounds and countries all over the world. A quick glance would suggest that these individuals had little in common. Not so. Each and every one confessed to a theft, rape, murder, or other heinous crime they did not commit.

Some of these individuals implicated not only themselves but also innocent friends and acquaintances. And if a single false confession isn't inconceivable enough, there are a boatload of cases that featured multiple false confessions—as in the Central Park jogger case, noted earlier, and the Norfolk Four, the Englewood Four, the West Memphis Three, and the Beatrice Six, to name just a few others.

In some instances, serial false confessions to multiple crimes are taken from the same person—like Henry Lee Lucas, of Texas, who confessed to hundreds of murders in the 1980s, many of which were later discredited, and Sture Ragnar Bergwall, of Sweden, also known as Thomas Quick, who confessed to more than thirty murders committed in Sweden, Norway, Denmark, and Finland between 1964 and 1993. He was convicted for eight of these murders before being fully exonerated and released from prison.

Taxonomy of False Confessions

Forty years ago, within weeks of defending my PhD dissertation and getting married, I accepted a postdoctoral fellowship to study jury decision making with Larry Wrightsman at the University of Kansas. Almost

Hanging in my office at the John Jay College of Criminal Justice in New York are the faces of innocent individuals, diverse in backgrounds, who confessed to a horrific crime they did not commit. *Photo courtesy of Drew Gurion.*

immediately, I became curious and then intensely interested in confession evidence. After poring over the pages of legal history and searching for recent stories reported in books, newspapers, and TV documentaries, it was clear to me that police use interrogation tactics that are psychologically manipulative—enough to break innocent people down into confession.

Two experiences in tandem sparked my interest and concern. First, I could not help but notice in our early data collection with mock juries that confession evidence all but guaranteed conviction. Understandably, people instinctually trust confessions as a matter of common sense. Second, through a law course on evidence that I was auditing, I came across a footnote in the assigned casebook that cited Fred Inbau

THE PROBLEM IN A NUTSHELL

and John Reid's *Criminal Interrogations and Confessions*, a leading "how to" interrogation manual published in 1962. I borrowed it from the library and read all 214 pages. The social psychologist in me was horrified. I could not help but wonder what effects these tactics had on innocent people.

There was no science at the time and no area of expertise per se, so I had not yet become involved in an actual case. But in 1908, Harvard psychology professor Hugo Münsterberg published a controversial and prescient book, *On the Witness Stand: Essays in Psychology and Crime*. In an unnumbered sixth chapter titled "Untrue Confessions," he relayed a "sad story" about a young Chicago man named Richard Ivens, who was convicted of murder based solely on a confession to police. Münsterberg was troubled by the confession itself and how it was taken. Despite having alibis, Ivens was convicted in short order. Within the week, "he was hanged for a crime of which he was no more guilty than you or I."

Münsterberg grasped the commonsense potency of confession evidence in court, noting that "it would be inconceivable that any man who was innocent should claim the infamy of guilt." He also grasped that confessions were fallible. He speculated on why innocent people might confess, using words like *hope, fear, promises, threats, suggestion, cunning calculations, passive yielding, shock, fatigue, melancholia, auto-hypnosis, dissociation,* and *self-destructive despair.* Münsterberg's insights lay dormant for more than half a century. But he was right.

Looking backward, I found that the false-confession phenomenon occurs on a regular basis but with unknown frequency; that it can be found throughout history, as in the Salem witch trials of 1692; that it is universal, especially in some countries, wherever criminal justice records are kept; that innocent people confess not only in the world's criminal justice systems but also in military, school, and work settings; and that all this seems to happen particularly to some types of people and under certain types of circumstances.

Comparing and contrasting known instances throughout history, we found that false confessions could be sorted neatly into three piles, each representing a different type of false confession. So in a book we edited in 1985, *The Psychology of Evidence and Trial Procedure*, Larry and I introduced a taxonomy that distinguished three types of false confessions: voluntary, compliant, and internalized. To this day, scholars and the courts abide by this distinction.

A *voluntary false confession* is one in which people claim responsibility for crimes they did not commit without prompting or pressure from police. Baffling as this may seem, this type of false confession often occurs in high-profile cases. When Charles Lindbergh's infant son was kidnapped in 1932, an estimated two hundred people volunteered confessions. When "Black Dahlia" actress Elizabeth Short was murdered in 1947, more than fifty people confessed. In 2006, John Mark Karr confessed to the still-unsolved murder of young JonBenet Ramsey.

No one has systematically studied these types of false confessions, in part because they are often easily disproved at the outset by the confessor's ignorance and inability to furnish corroborating details about the crime. There are several reasons why innocent people might volunteer confessions. Some reasons are born of pathology—for example, to satisfy a compulsive need for attention or self-punishment; or in response to feelings of guilt or delusions. Other reasons seem rational—for example, the perception of tangible gain or the desire to protect a parent, child, or someone else.

By far the more common and problematic type of false confession is not spontaneous or self-initiated but, rather, induced by police. In these instances, an innocent suspect denies involvement when first questioned but is then transitioned from denial to admission through the process of interrogation. Two types of police-induced false confessions can be distinguished.

In *compliant false confessions*, the suspect capitulates to escape a stressful in-custody situation, avoid physical harm or legal punishment, or gain a promised or implied reward. Sometimes the incentives are pretty concrete, like being allowed to sleep, eat, make a phone call, go home, or, in the case of addicted substance abusers, feed a drug habit. This type of confession is an act of public capitulation by suspects who know full well they are innocent but are so desperate to gain the short-term benefits of confession that they lose sight of the substantial long-term costs.

This type of compliance was dramatically illustrated in the Salem witch trials, long before colonial Americans declared independence from England. In that year, 151 men, women, and children were accused of witchcraft. Sometimes blindfolded, shackled, stripped naked, prodded with pins, beaten, deprived of sleep, and publicly humiliated, 55 confessed. Twenty who did not confess were executed.

In Mississippi in 1934, three black tenant farmers were stripped, laid over chairs, and whipped with a buckled leather strap until they confessed to murder.

In the 1989 Central Park jogger case described earlier, five New York City teenagers were tricked into confessing after lengthy tactical interrogations, each claiming he expected to go home afterward. Innocent people, who know they are innocent, come to believe, under stress, that confession serves their self-interest.

The third type of false confession, which we called *internalized false confessions*, are the hardest to understand. In these instances, innocent but psychologically vulnerable suspects not only agree to confess as an act of compliance but become confused, lose their grip on reality, and come to believe that they committed the crime in question. Remarkably, sometimes these beliefs are accompanied by false memories. I hesitate to use the word *brainwashed* to describe this process because of the historical baggage linked to the term. But you get the idea.

The first time I encountered something like this was in reading two books about seventeen-year-old Peter Reilly, who confessed in 1973 to killing his mother, brutally, in New Canaan, Connecticut. Reilly was a good kid. But the transition of his mental state over the course of interrogation, especially after police told him that he failed an infallible polygraph exam, was chilling. At one point, he conceded: "This test is giving me doubts right now." Hours later, using the language of inference, not memory, he said, "Well, it really looks like I did it." Still later, he confabulated a false memory: "I remember slashing once at my mother's throat with a straight razor I used for model airplanes." Reilly was convicted but then exonerated after spending more than a year in prison.

For me, Reilly became the poster child for an internalized false confession. I have since seen the same process play out over and over again. The case of fourteen-year-old Michael Crowe, whose sister Stephanie was stabbed to death in the middle of the night while sleeping, illustrates the point. After being told that police had found blood, hair, and other evidence of his guilt, Crowe burst into tears: "I'm not sure how I did it. All I know is I did it." Eventually, police convinced him that he had a split personality—that "bad Michael" acted out of

jealous rage, while "good Michael" blocked the incident from consciousness. The charges against Crowe were later dropped when a drifter from the neighborhood was found with Stephanie's blood on his
clothing.

Demography of False Confessions

Diverse as it is in appearance, my wall of faces poignantly illustrates that
false confessions can happen to anyone. But this should not be interpreted to mean that all segments of the population are targeted equally
or are similarly vulnerable. Nothing could be further from the truth.

Juvenile Injustice

To start with, youth is a substantial risk factor. Statistics show that well
over 90 percent of juveniles whom police seek to question waive their
Miranda rights to silence and a lawyer. This is not surprising. Children
and adolescents are compliant, especially to adult figures of authority;
and they are naïve about the legal system. In fact, the presence of a
parent, guardian, or other "interested adult"—which many states require to protect young suspects—does not lower this waiver rate because adults so often urge their sons and daughters to cooperate.

It's not just about Miranda. No matter how you slice the data, once
juveniles waive their rights and enter the hall of mirrors of a police
interrogation, they are more malleable than adults. When the National
Registry of Exonerations examined nearly nine hundred wrongful convictions from 1989 to 2012, they found that 42 percent of all juvenile
defendants in the sample had falsely confessed, a far higher percentage
than adults. In the archives of the Innocence Project, roughly half of all
false confessors later exonerated by DNA were twenty-one years old or
younger at the time; roughly one-third were eighteen and younger.

These statistics are supported by years of research, in the laboratory
and in the field, showing that juveniles are more impulsive than adults,
more malleable, more vulnerable to manipulation, and at greater risk in
an interrogation.

In the context of developmental sciences, this vulnerability is not
surprising. In classic psychology experiments originating in the 1970s,
Walter Mischel introduced the "marshmallow" test. In these studies, a
preschool child is brought into a room and seated at a table in front of a

marshmallow or a pretzel. The experimenter tells the child that he has to leave for a while and presents this choice: "You can have this treat whenever you want, but if you wait until I return, you'll get two of them, not just one." Off into an adjacent room, the experimenter, stopwatch in hand, observes what happens through a one-way mirror.

In this predicament, some kids devour the solo treat right away; some wait the full fifteen minutes for the experimenter to return; most hold out for partial amounts of time before yielding to temptation. This may sound like a merely cute experiment (if you google the marshmallow test, you'll see entertaining footage of kids shutting their eyes and sitting on their hands to restrain themselves). But follow-up longitudinal studies have shown that kids who delayed gratification as preschoolers, compared to those who yielded, later performed better on other tests of self-control. They also went on to become more educated and successful adults.

What makes all this relevant is that while older children and adolescents have more self-control than preschoolers, they are not adults. In lab experiments involving hypothetical rewards, they are quicker to take a fixed sum of money now rather than wait for a greater amount in the near future. While individuals differ in this tendency to discount delayed outcomes, teenagers on average are more impulsive, focused more on here-and-now rewards and punishments than later consequences.

Neurological research reinforces the point that adolescence is a period in which the frontal lobes are not fully formed, creating an "immaturity of judgment" in decision making. It's why, twenty years ago, the National Institute of Mental Health referred to the teenage brain as "a work in progress." To the juvenile suspect too distracted to focus on long-term consequences, confession can serve as an expedient way out of a stressful situation.

I'll have lots more to say about children and false confessions later in this chapter and throughout the book. But let me be blunt about why a suspect's age is such an important demographic variable. The Central Park jogger exonerees were fourteen to sixteen years old when they were induced into confession. Peter Reilly was seventeen, Michael Crowe and Adam Gray were fourteen, Tyler Edmonds was thirteen, and Anthony Harris was twelve. All these cases were disturbing for the manner in which these children were questioned.

But it was a 1998 case that blew me away when it broke. Eleven-year-old Ryan Harris was sexually molested, beaten, and suffocated to death while riding her bicycle on the South Side of Chicago. Her body was found in an empty lot. Days later, two boys confessed to homicide detectives, independently, we were told, and with consistent details, before their captors took them by the hand and fed them McDonald's hamburgers.

The boys' appearance in court drew gasps from onlookers stunned by their smallness. They were barely visible from behind the defendants' table; their feet did not reach the floor as they sat. They were seven and eight years old. One month later, lab tests revealed traces of semen on the girl's clothing. Of course, these prepubescent boys were not capable of producing semen, so the charges were dropped. Shortly thereafter, the perpetrator was identified. He was a serial sex offender.

Vulnerable Adults

Although children are at risk merely by virtue of their youth and inexperience, certain adults are vulnerable because of cognitive limitations and mental health problems. As with juveniles, individuals with low IQ scores are overrepresented in the population of false confessors. Hence, in *Atkins v. Virginia* (2002), the U.S. Supreme Court explicitly cited the risk of false confession as a rationale for the decision to exclude this group categorically from capital punishment.

This risk was evident in the case of Earl Washington of Culpeper, Virginia. Reported to have a tested IQ of under seventy, which defines mental retardation, and interrogated for two days, Washington confessed to five different crimes, including rape and murder. Although parts of his confession were factually incorrect and he could not come up with some pretty basic details, Washington—who was highly suggestive and deferent to figures of authority—was convicted and incarcerated for eighteen years before being exonerated.

The diminished capacities that accompany a low IQ are substantial. Research shows that cognitively limited adults cannot adequately comprehend Miranda warnings, described by some in this context as "words without meaning." They are also highly suggestible. This vulnerability is easy to document objectively in the lab or clinic.

Individuals with mental health problems are also at increased risk during an interrogation. Psychological disorders are often accompanied by faulty reality monitoring, distorted perceptions, impaired judgment, anxiety, mood disturbance, poor self-control, and feelings of guilt. Clearly, for example, someone with severe anxiety will have a limited tolerance for stress as it intensifies over the course of an interrogation. Others may crack because they are substance abusers in need of a fix, or because they suffer from a delusional disorder, which makes it difficult to hold their grip on reality when confronted by a barrage of accusations. Again, the problem of suggestibility rears its ugly head in the context of an interrogation.

At about the same time that I was drawn into the social psychology of police interrogations, Gisli Gudjonsson, now professor emeritus at the Institute of Psychiatry of King's College London, had become interested in clinical and dispositional influences on false confessions. Born and raised in Iceland, Gisli started out as a police officer, then detective, in the capital city, Reykjavik. After a couple of years, and unlike his twin brother, who became a career officer, he went on to get his PhD in clinical psychology.

Gisli talks about the time he unwittingly took a false confession in Iceland without intense pressure or deception. What he did not realize at the time was that the suspect he was questioning had a history of alcohol-induced memory blackouts. Once confronted with an accusation, this suspect was quick to accept the belief that he must have committed the crime. As it later turned out, no crime had been committed.

In 1984, newly trained for clinical assessment and diagnosis, Gudjonsson developed what is known as the Gudjonsson Suggestibility Scale (GSS). To administer the test, he would read the subject a short story and later ask that subject to recall as much of it as possible. Next he would ask twenty questions, fifteen of which are suggestive of facts not presented in the story, and measure how often the subject "yields" in response to these questions. He would then give negative feedback in a "forceful manner," telling the subject there are errors in their account of the story and they must answer the questions a second time. At that point, he would record the number of times the subject "shifts" to new answers in response to this feedback.

The GSS shows that individuals differ in their dispositional levels of suggestibility, which means that some suspects are more vulnerable than others. Today, the GSS is used to examine defendants who had confessed and then recanted their confessions. More on this later.

Racial Bias

A third demographic variable to watch for is race—but for a different reason. According to the National Registry of Exonerations, nearly half of the more than 2,700 individuals whose wrongful convictions were overturned since 1989 were African Americans. The Innocence Project, which is involved in only DNA-based exonerations, reports that a shocking 60 percent of all their exonerees are black—regardless of whether they had confessed.

It is clear that race is a potent risk factor. But it's not because African Americans are more vulnerable once they appear in the interrogation room. The problem is bigger than that: Innocent African Americans are more likely to arouse suspicion in the first place because of their skin color and more likely, therefore, to find themselves in the crosshairs of a police investigation.

Time and again, statistical analyses of archival data and field studies have shown that minorities, particularly African Americans and Hispanics, are subjected to stops and searches by police at rates disproportionate to their number in the population and rate of offending. Racial profiling in the United States is widespread. On occasion, overt racism may play a role. More often than not, however, the problem is unconscious and inadvertent, a result of what social psychologists have called "implicit bias."

Demonstrations of implicit bias can be traced way back. In 1947, Gordon Allport and Leo Postman showed people a cartoon sketch of a train filled with passengers—including a dark-skinned black man dressed in a suit and a white man brandishing a razor. In a task modeled after the "telephone" game, one subject viewed the picture, then described it to a second subject, who had not seen it. The second subject described it to a third, and so on, through six rounds. In more than half of the chains of communication, the final subject misreported that it was the black man holding the razor.

Over the years, thousands of controlled experiments have revealed the subtle and not-so-subtle effects of implicit racism on judgments by schoolchildren, workers, patients, athletes, and others—enough to fill volumes. Fast-forward into the twenty-first century, and one finds psychology journals filled with more focused, more sophisticated studies relevant to criminal justice. Much of this research is described in *Biased: Uncovering the Hidden Prejudice That Shapes What We See, Think, and Do*, a book published in 2019 by Stanford University social psychologist Jennifer Eberhardt.

In one set of studies, Eberhardt and her colleagues used a "dot-probe" method of planting subliminal images into a visual array. She asked subjects, mostly white, to stare at a dot in the center of a computer screen while images of a black male face or white male face, or no images at all, flashed quickly off to the side for a fraction of a second. Then she showed a blurry image that gradually came into sharper focus over the course of forty-one frames. The subjects (who included both police officers and students) were instructed to press a key as soon as they recognized the object, and state what it was.

Some of the pictured objects that came into gradual view were crime related, like a gun or a knife; other were neutral, like a camera or a book. Consistent with stereotyping research in other settings, subjects who were "primed" with a subliminal black face were quicker to recognize the weapon than those who had seen a white face. Subconsciously, seeing a black face facilitated recognition of the threatening image, even though subjects were not aware of the subliminal faces that had flashed on the screen. The pattern of results appeared even among subjects who scored low on overt verbal measures of racial prejudice. The same pattern was then later found in a study of police officers. The mental association is automatic.

Nudging even closer to criminal justice relevance, Eberhardt worked with a Bay Area police department, analyzing twenty-eight thousand traffic stops for one year, using the forms that police fill out when they pull motorists over. As it turned out, 60 percent of the stops involved black motorists, even though they constituted only 28 percent of the city's population. Police were also more likely to search or handcuff black motorists.

The tone of these traffic stops also differed as a function of race. For hundreds of encounters spanning about a month, Team Eberhardt collected, transcribed, and analyzed body camera footage using a combination of human coders and machine learning algorithms. What they heard: police routinely used less respectful language when speaking to black motorists. No one uttered racial slurs and insults. But white motorists were more likely to hear "I'm sorry to have to pull you over," while black motorists were more likely to hear "All right, my man. Just keep your hands on the steering wheel real quick."

The race problem is not limited to our perceptions of adults. In a series of experiments published in 2014 and conducted in both laboratory and field settings, Philip Atiba Goff and is colleagues compared adult perceptions of black and white male children. Consistently, they found that people judged black boys to be older than they were and less childlike than their same-aged white peers. The implications are clear: in matters of criminal justice, black boys may not be afforded the "essence of innocence" that otherwise protects children. The consequences can be devastating.

Hitting the target of the problem, the starkest demonstrations of racial disparity come from shooter-bias experiments by Joshua Correll and others. In these studies, subjects are introduced to a video game in which they have to decide whether to "shoot" a male target who appears on the screen. Some of the targets were white, others were black. Some held guns, others held a cell phone, wallet, or another harmless object. If the target held a gun, the subject was instructed to shoot as quickly as possible—or be shot. If he held a harmless object, subjects were supposed to hit the "don't shoot" key as quickly as possible.

Consistently in these experiments, subjects are quicker to shoot the black target holding a gun and slower to "not shoot" the black target holding a harmless object. What's worse, subjects are more likely to mistakenly shoot an unarmed target if he was black than white. It's not too far a stretch to wonder if police are similarly prone to identify African Americans as suspects for interrogation, setting into motion the racial disparities that characterize wrongful convictions.

Frequency of False Confessions

In my initial explorations into how police get people to confess and how juries react to that evidence, everyone I spoke to said that while the idea of false confessions is interesting, if not outright fascinating, psychologically, it happens too infrequently to matter. "Once in a blue moon" is a phrase I heard more than once. Hence, some variant of an epidemiological question greets confession experts whenever we appear in court: "How many false confessions are there in the U.S.?" or "What percentage of all confessions are false?"

After reading the interrogation bible back in 1978, which laid bare the kinds of trickery and deceit that police are permitted to use, and with all of my training on the psychology of social influence, I just knew that the assumption of a near-zero baseline could not be true. I am now in possession of hundreds of heart-wrenching letters from prison to prove it.

The stacks of letters from prison were no joke. For me, the worst part was that at one point I started to receive so many letters that I could no longer open much less read them. Recently, having moved from Williams College to my position at John Jay, I took a day to clear all the files, books, tapes, disks, and whatnot out of my Williams office. In poring through an old box of letters, I came across an envelope with the name David McCallum in the return address, then a second envelope. That name felt awfully familiar, so I went to Google and discovered that McCallum was a fellow Brooklynite who was picked up at 16 years old, along with William Stuckey. They were both coerced into confessing to a murder, which they recanted. As it typical, both young men were convicted at trial. Stuckey died in prison; McCallum continued to fight, hence the letters.

In 2011, McCallum's attorney, Oscar Michelin, reinvestigated the case and came across DNA and other exculpatory evidence. In 2014, after 29 years, the Kinds County Supreme Court vacated the convictions of McCallum and Stuckey. McCallum was immediately released, and I had read about it in the newspapers, which is why I recognized his name. Shortly thereafter, I appeared on a panel at John Jay College in which McCallum and Michelin were presenters. It's the first time we had ever met; I greeted him with a profuse apology.

False confession is not a medieval, extinct, or once-in-a-blue-moon phenomenon. Innocent people can be induced to incriminate themselves even if they are not young, weak, or feeble-minded. It can happen to anyone. It can happen to you. I could populate a book with countless true stories of false confessions. But it's important to address the elephant-in-the-room question: How often do innocent people confess to bad things they didn't do?

Spoiler alert: It's not possible to pin a number on this problem the way an epidemiologist might calculate the *prevalence rate* of a particular disease in a specific population at a given point in time. No one knows how often innocents confess to police, only to have the charges dropped after the true perpetrator is identified. Nor does anyone know how many innocent confessors remain in prison because appeals courts do not take their claims seriously, sometimes even after DNA contradicts the confession. Nor does anyone know how often innocent people go on to accept a guilty plea precisely *because* they confessed, leading prosecutors to threaten the most serious possible charges and their own lawyers to fear conviction if they dared to go to trial. Once defendants plead guilty, in many states, they waive their right to appeal. Seldom are these cases ever scrutinized again.

But what we do know is that false confession is not a new or isolated phenomenon. The earliest explorations into wrongful convictions demonstrated a number of such instances. In a groundbreaking 1932 book titled *Convicting the Innocent*, Yale law professor Edwin Borchard presented a collection of sixty-five U.S. cases dating back to the nineteenth century, involving individuals who were convicted and later found innocent. What he did not see coming was that some of these individuals had actually confessed.

In the decades that followed, similar efforts exposed more cases. By 1987, Hugo Bedau and Michael Radelet published in the *Stanford Law Review* a compilation of 417 cases involving murder and other potentially capital crimes. By their analysis, forty-nine of these cases contained coerced and/or false confessions. That still doesn't answer the prevalence question.

In *Kansas v. Marsh* (2006), Justice Antonin Scalia estimated that criminal convictions in the United States have a total error rate of only .027 percent—or, as he put it, "a success rate of 99.973 percent." I don't know what is more absurd, the "score" he produced or the methodology he used to calculate it. Scalia derived his so-called error rate by taking the number of exonerations that we know about, most derived from murders and sexual assaults, and dividing that number by the total of all felony convictions, from drug possessions and auto thefts to tax fraud. Of course, this approach also presumes that all wrongful convictions are known to us, that what we see is not merely the tip but the whole iceberg.

THE DNA REVOLUTION

Then came deoxyribonucleic acid, otherwise known as DNA. Present in bodily fluids such as blood, saliva, sweat, urine, and semen, and in bone, skins cells, and hair follicles, DNA contains genetic information that is unique to each and every individual. Since no two people have the same genetic structure, except for identical twins, DNA found at a crime scene can be matched to the perpetrator, often with astronomical levels of accuracy. These molecules can be left on hard surfaces, clothing, bedding, fingernail scrapings, tools, weapons, glasses, cigarettes, toothbrushes; well, you get the idea.

In 1985, British scientist Alec Jeffreys developed DNA testing. One year later, this type of evidence was used for the first time to solve a homicide in England and then to link that same defendant to other unsolved rapes and murders. One year after that, a Florida man was convicted of rape through DNA in the first use of this technology in the United States. Shortly thereafter, federal, state, and city police departments started to obtain samples and assemble databases. The Combined DNA Index System (CODIS) is the U.S. national DNA database, created and maintained by the FBI.

Enter the Innocence Project. In 1992, in a historic milestone inspired by science, New York–based lawyers and law professors Barry Scheck and Peter Neufeld founded a small nonprofit legal clinic they called the Innocence Project (IP). If DNA can be used to identify the perpetrator, they figured, it can also be used to exclude an innocent suspect. Merging science and law in a novel way, their mission was to use this emerging DNA technology to examine prisoners' postconviction claims of innocence in crimes that contained testable biological evidence. And so it started, housed at the Cardozo School of Law, in the Flatiron district of Manhattan, and staffed by law students reading letters from prisoners pleading their innocence and begging for help.

As I now write, 375 people in the United States alone have been exonerated by DNA, including several who had served time on death row. The IP population is a "tight" group of exonerees—there is no serious dispute as to the *actual innocence* of these individuals. All the convictions were for murder and/or sexual assault, the up-close-and-physical crimes that leave DNA behind.

Barry Scheck and Peter Neufeld, who in 1992 founded the Innocence Project, initially housed at Cardozo School of Law in New York City. The Innocence Network now consists of sixty-seven organizations all over the world. *Photo courtesy of the Innocence Project.*

When Scheck and Neufeld reported on their first few DNA exonerations, they had the foresight to "autopsy" the case files to determine what caused these wrongful convictions. What they discovered was a predominance of mistaken eyewitness identifications, false confessions, informants who lied, and misapplications of forensic science. These factors were noted, archived, and posted on their web site. To everyone's astonishment, false confessions contributed to 29 percent of these cases. What's more, that number increases to over 60 percent in the IP's subset of homicide cases.

Let me stop here and elaborate on three points about these numbers. First, every DNA exoneration represents a mere fraction of the total of wrongful convictions. Most crimes do not leave behind testable traces of DNA; in those that do, often the samples are contaminated, destroyed, lost, tossed, or otherwise not accessible. Also, the vast majority of crimes are resolved by guilty pleas that steepen the uphill battle to get scrutinized on appeal. The point is, those individuals who are publicly exonerated by DNA represent the lucky tip of an iceberg the size of which is not known.

Second, I can attest to the fact that no one saw the false confessions numbers coming. I'd been studying and writing about false confessions for a decade when IP was founded. Larry Wrightsman and I had identified the three types of false confessions; I had scrutinized and begun to examine in the lab the components of a psychological interrogation. Yet the typical response from lawyers and psychologists was to concede that while the underlying psychology may be profound, innocent people just don't confess—and if they do, it's seldom.

The third point is, why would the incidence of false confessions more than double in homicide investigations? One can imagine an innocent person breaking under pressure to confess to petty theft or vandalism or some other minor crime. But murder? One would expect that innocent suspects would be more resistant, not less, to confessing to these most serious, often heinous, and consequential of all offenses.

This pattern seems backward until one realizes that homicide detectives are the all-stars of every police department. They gain fame and reputation, and are promoted, through their ability to close cases by confession; they are the chosen ones singled out for special training. This is mere speculation on my part, but it seems to me that homicide cases prompt interrogations of a whole different breed of trickery and deceit from all others. Hence, false confessions.

Back to the Innocence Project. What started in 1992, housed at a local law school, has since blossomed into the Innocence Network, consisting of nearly seventy independent legal organizations throughout the world. It has freed hundreds of innocent people from prison, altered public perceptions, galvanized scientists and legal scholars, and inspired reforms aimed at preventing future miscarriages of justice. This network has offices in cities and universities throughout the United States as well as in Argentina, Australia, Canada, Ireland, Israel, Italy, Japan, the Netherlands, New Zealand, Taiwan, and the United Kingdom.

In 1999, law professor Steven Drizin helped launch the Center for Wrongful Convictions (CWC) at Northwestern University School of Law. Ten years later, he went on to cofound the Center on the Wrongful Convictions of Youth, a nonprofit legal clinic dedicated to helping juveniles, codirected by Laura Nirider. Then in 2012, the CWC, along with University of Michigan law professor Samuel Gross and Chicago-based journalist Rob Warden, launched the National Registry of Exonerations—a database that archives detailed information about known exonerations in the United States since 1989. The registry is now housed at the University of California at Irvine.

Whereas the Innocence Project works directly on post-conviction claims that can be resolved by DNA, the registry archives a broader and more diverse sample of crimes and exonerations resolvable by all forms of new evidence. Sometimes the perpetrator is found as part of another investigation. Sometimes it turns out that the alleged crime was never committed. In the first documented wrongful conviction in the United States, for example, Vermont brothers Jesse and Stephen Boorn in 1819 confessed under pressure to killing Russell Colvin, their sister's vanished husband. Both were convicted, incarcerated, and sentenced to death—until the "victim" turned up alive in New Jersey.

As I write this sentence, the registry lists 2,809 wrongful convictions since 1989, resulting in more than 25,000 years lost to prison. Funded by charitable contributions, the registry keeps a running tally of wrongful convictions as they are reported. They also collect extensive details about each case from court documents and other sources, keeping track of the type of crime; year and geographical location; the age, gender, and race of defendants; and the factors that contributed to the wrongful conviction—including various forms of police and prosecutorial misconduct.

In its growing database—a treasure trove of heart-wrenching horror stories for scholars, the news media, and the lay public—NRE reports that 13 percent of individuals wrongfully convicted had been induced to confess (many others were convicted because of someone *else's* false confession). As in the IP sample, the false confession rate is more than double that percentage in homicide cases. It is not possible to extrapolate from all the numbers a statistical prevalence rate. Sadly, the NRE concluded in a 2017 report that "exonerations used to be unusual; now they are commonplace." And yet these known cases only scratch the surface.

Take the false confession problem as an example. The instances that are known do not include false confessors not prosecuted because their innocence was established; those who pled guilty to lesser offenses for a reduced sentence, thereby preempting critical scrutiny of their cases; or those innocent felons who remain in prison or whose records remain tarnished.

Most notably, perhaps, these instances do not include the countless false confessions taken in military settings, where prisoners of war, hostages, and other uniformed detainees have been coerced into obedience, or brainwashed into confessing, sometimes on camera for propaganda purposes, to war crimes that neither they nor other members of their platoon had committed. I've also had several conversations with U.S. Army defense lawyers, on bases all over the world, whose clients faced a court martial after confessing to a crime to a CID (Criminal Investigation Department) officer. Many of these defendants were young recruits who felt powerless to resist.

These instances also exclude unknown numbers of people who falsely confess to stealing money or merchandise in the workplace—ironically, in their minds, to save their job. Increasingly, in recent years, retailers have sought to recover losses from theft through internal investigations. Often that involves interrogating employees whom they suspect by deploying the same methods police are trained to use. I worked on one of these cases and was troubled by what I learned. I have no idea how common false confessions are in this environment. More on that later.

2

"OFF-THE-BOOKS" FALSE CONFESSIONS

"Once in a blue moon," they kept saying. It's not easy in life to know what you don't know. When it comes to the unthinkable, however, I have learned that false confessions are everywhere.

To illustrate the point that the official archives of false confessions don't begin to fully expose the problem, consider three nonconventional "off-the-books" cases from three completely different domains: the criminal justice system, the workplace, and schools. None of these cases has a home at the Innocence Project; none are archived with the National Registry of Exonerations; not one of these false confessors gets counted in the official tallies. And I'll describe others just like them throughout this book.

THE KILLING OF KITTY GENOVESE: THE INVISIBLE GORILLA

While many false confessions capture the spotlight of our attention, others remain hidden from public view (I worked on a case once in which the perpetrator was identified after police had taken a confession; the innocent confessor was then released and compensated in an agreement that contained a confidentiality provision). Yet history points to story after story after story. And for every one that is exposed for all to see, there are many others that remain unresolved and invisible to us all.

Utter the name Catherine "Kitty" Genovese, and people around you will know that she was the twenty-eight-year-old Queens woman who was stabbed to death on March 13, 1964, in a late-night attack. According to reports, she screamed for help but none of her neighbors came to her rescue; no one called the police until it was too late. In New York, this singular event inspired what became a new centralized emergency phone number, the precursor to 911.

In a front-page article in the *New York Times*, Martin Gansberg reported on March 27 that "for more than half an hour, thirty-eight respectable, law-abiding citizens in Queens watched a killer stalk and stab a woman in three separate attacks in Kew Gardens." Several months later, Abraham Rosenthal published the book *Thirty-Eight Witnesses: The Kitty Genovese Case*. All that remained was for someone to explain why so many of Kitty's neighbors failed to respond, not wanting to get involved, as if apathetic or, worse, callous. Within two weeks, this was the focal story that formed: On a cold, dark night, some number of neighbors in this middle-class urban community heard her screams and cries for help; many peered out their windows to the street below. But no one—not one person—called the police until she lay dead in a pool of blood.

For social psychologists, this event inspired the study of bystander intervention. Following a series of ingenious experiments described in the 1970 book *The Unresponsive Bystander*, Bibb Latané and John Darley coined the term "bystander effect" to describe the statistical fact that individuals are less likely to intervene when they're in the presence of others than when they're alone. This research trumpeted social psychology's situationist message: Kitty's urban neighbors were not apathetic, immoral, cruel, or monstrous. They were merely trapped in a socially induced illusion that their help was not needed. Specifically, they cited the dynamics of "pluralistic ignorance" (the sense that all is well because no one else looks alarmed) and "diffusion of responsibility" (the mistaken belief that others have already called for help). Followed by a constant parade of new horror stories, not just in Queens but all over the world, research on the bystander effect and how to mitigate it continues to this day.

Over the years, a controversy has simmered over the number of bystanders who actually saw or heard the attack and whether they tried to intervene. Did thirty-eight neighbors really witness what happened, as claimed, or was it thirty-nine, or as few as twelve, as some have argued? And did some neighbors try to intervene, as did a man who yelled out the window, causing Kitty's assailant to flee to his car temporarily before returning? With the spotlight shining on Genovese and her neighbors, very few Americans, or even New Yorkers, can tell you the name of her killer, Winston Moseley, how he was arrested, and the evidence used to convict him. In fact, that spotlight cast a shadow over another story—about a false confession closely linked to this event.

In a classic experiment, Daniel Simons and Christopher Chabris had research subjects watch a short video clip of six adults—three in white shirts, three in black shirts—passing a basketball to each other. Subjects were asked to count silently the number of times the players in white shirts pass the ball. That sounds simple enough. During the action, however, for nine seconds, an individual in a gorilla costume walks right through the room, faces the camera, and pounds his chest before leaving. When later asked about the clip, half the subjects tested were so focused on their task they did not even see it. As a result of "inattentional blindness," it was as if the gorilla was invisible (you can view this 1:22 clip on YouTube).

The bystander apathy story stole attention from a gorilla pounding its chest in Queens. For fifty-six years, while all eyes were focused on Kitty's neighbors, regardless of their number, another drama was unfolding, one that didn't quite make it into the history books but is glaringly relevant to the world we now live in. Twenty-five years before the infamous Central Park jogger case, Kitty Genovese presented a riveting story about a false confession.

Five days after stabbing Genovese to death, twenty-nine-year-old Moseley was arrested in a burglary and brought in by police for questioning. The evidence ultimately used to convict him was a confession, effortlessly taken, according to police—a confession amply corroborated by the fact that Moseley was able to lead police to Kitty's wallet and keys, which he had dumped outside his Mount Vernon workplace.

Moseley said he stabbed Genovese with a hunting knife twice in the back. He then fled to his car when someone yelled down through an open window. Convinced that no one would interfere, and driven by compulsion, he returned moments later because "I'd not finished what I set out to do." Following her trail of blood, he found Genovese slumped on the floor of a nearby apartment, stabbed her to death, and raped her.

Moseley seemed willing to answer questions, so detectives asked about other crimes. In response, he matter-of-factly said that he killed a young woman named Annie Mae Johnson one month earlier in South Ozone Park and then set her house on fire. "Anyone else?" they asked. "Yes," he said. He had also killed fifteen-year-old Barbara Kralik in her Springfield Gardens home eight months earlier, on a July night in 1963. Catherine Pelonero, author of a book on the murder of Kitty Genovese, described this last admission as a "bombshell."

Barbara Kralik lived with her family in a modest red-shingled three-bedroom house in Springfield Gardens. Shortly after 4 a.m., her mother heard a noise and called out to Barbara to see if she was okay. When Barbara did not answer, she asked her husband to check on her. But when he turned on the light, he found Barbara covered in blood from six stab wounds in her chest and side. Kralik was rushed by ambulance and regained consciousness in Queens General Hospital later that day, just long enough to say that she did not recognize her assailant. She died moments after making that statement.

Moseley later repeated these confessions to killing Genovese, Johnson, and Kralik with great consistency and detail, to his attorney, to a psychiatrist, and at his own trial. Detectives next pressed Moseley about the August 1963 murders in Manhattan of two young professional women named Emily Hoffert and Janice Wylie. These high-profile crimes, dubbed the "career girl murders" in the news, were still unsolved. But this time he denied any involvement. He had nothing to do with those killings and said so. Moseley was discriminating.

For police and prosecutors, Moseley's confession to the late-night Kralik murder in Springfield Gardens was inconvenient, to say the least. So they terminated questioning and took no formal statement. Why would homicide detectives turn their back on a self-initiated detailed confession from a possible serial killer? Here's one possible reason: months earlier, Queens detectives had taken a confession from a fair-skinned eighteen-year-old kid by the name of Alvin Mitchell, a high school dropout. At the time of Moseley's confession to Kralik's murder, Mitchell was sitting in jail awaiting trial.

Detective Frederick Lussen, who took Mitchell's confession, tried to explain to Bard Lindeman of the *Saturday Evening Post*: "We stopped asking Moseley about murders," he said, "because he might admit to anything." But that was not true. When asked about the career girl murders, Moseley shook his head and denied having anything to do with them.

Police had interrogated Mitchell seven times for over fifty hours, culminating in an all-night session that lasted nearly thirteen straight hours before he caved. He signed a statement written by detectives at 1 a.m., which he repeated in front of TV cameras in a staged perp walk the next morning. Mitchell immediately recanted the confession attributed to him, claiming he was threatened and physically abused— smacked in the head with rolled-up newspapers, an old "third degree" trick that left no visible bruises or cuts. His attorney was also vocal and animated as to his innocence. Still, he was set to be tried when Moseley blurted out his unwelcome confession to the Kralik murder. At least one of these confessions had to be false. But which one?

At the time, it was clear that Moseley had killed Genovese. He knew too much and was able to lead police to her belongings. It was less clear if he was credible in his two other blockbuster admissions. Determined to defend Mitchell's prior confession for killing Barbara Kralik, police were relieved when Moseley appeared to misstate how Annie Mae Johnson was killed one month earlier.

Moseley said that he followed Johnson to her home and shot her twice in the stomach with a .22-caliber rifle in front of her apartment. As she begged for mercy, he took her keys, rolled her over, shot her four times in the back, and had sex with her lifeless body. Then he dragged her through snow and into the house, up a flight of stairs, set her body on fire, stole about a hundred dollars, and ran out. It was an eerily compelling story but for one detail. The medical examiner had concluded that Johnson had been *stabbed* rather than *shot* and died of puncture wounds from an ice pick or some other sharp object.

Moseley was confronted with this disqualifying inconsistency but he stood by his story. Wanting to discredit him on Johnson, and thereby preserve the Mitchell prosecution, authorities flew to Johnson's home state of South Carolina, where she was buried, and had her body exhumed. Yet to everyone's astonishment, the local coroner confirmed Moseley's account. Johnson was shot six times with a .22-caliber rifle— just as Moseley had said. Four bullets, detected in X-rays, were removed from her body.

Remarkably, Moseley was never prosecuted for the Johnson murder. Yet his culpability was beyond dispute. In fact, the case was later cited by the Queens DA's Office in a letter opposing Moseley's applications for parole (Moseley was described in that letter as "delusional" and a "predator" with "an overwhelming compulsion to commit acts of violence"). Yet in the face of Moseley's newly demonstrated credibility (with confessions confirmed for both Genovese and Johnson, he was 2-2 in baseball terms), the already shaky case against Mitchell for the Kralik murder continued unabated.

True to our Sixth Amendment right to a speedy trial, and inconceivable by today's standards, the sequence of events triggered by the Genovese killing came quickly. On March 19, 1964, less than a week after killing Genovese, Moseley confessed to three murders. He was promptly indicted for the Genovese killing on March 23, pled not guilty by reason of insanity on June 8, was convicted of first-degree murder on June 11, and sentenced on June 15—all in Judge Irwin Shapiro's court. By sheer coincidence, his assigned counsel, Sidney Sparrow, had previously represented Genovese in a minor gambling offense for which she had to pay a small fine (the black-and-white portrait photo of her, the first image that appears in a Google search of her, was her mugshot).

The case against Mitchell, for the murder of Barbara Kralik, commenced immediately thereafter, also in Judge Shapiro's court. Why prosecute Mitchell after Moseley's confessions? Prosecutor Charles Skoller said he was persuaded by how closely Mitchell's confession aligned with a statement police took from a friend of his, sixteen-year-old George Borges, which implicated him. Borges allegedly said that he drove Mitchell to and from Kralik's house that night. But he later insisted that he was threatened and beaten and that this story was false. Upon reflection, Skoller would later write: "No police officer could coerce two boys to come up with stories as similar as these are in so many details."

I can understand where Skoller was coming from. Basking in hindsight, however, I could only fantasize the theatrical back-from-the-future moment wherein I return to 1964 to prophesy that in twenty-five years, in Central Park, New York City police will produce similarly *five* detailed confessions to the rape of a jogger from *five* teenagers, all of whom would later be excluded in DNA testing and proved innocent.

At Mitchell's trial, the prosecution relied on the defendant's recanted confession and the incriminating but also contested statement taken from his friend Borges. The defense sought to admit into evidence Kralik's "dying declaration." Before she died, Kralik said she did not know her assailant. Yet she and Alvin knew each other; he had dated her friend. The prosecutor objected that Kralik's hospital statement was hearsay, and the judge excluded it. The jury was never informed.

The defense centered on two witnesses. The first was an alibi witness who testified that he saw Mitchell hitchhiking, picked him up, and drove him home that night. This witness recounted where he picked Mitchell up and where he let him off.

The second witness was the newly convicted Winston Moseley. The links to Moseley were haunting. Kralik was stabbed in her bed at 3 a.m.—the very time that Moseley habitually felt the urge to prowl. In front of a packed courtroom, Moseley recounted in detail how he entered the Kralik house and walked upstairs, past other bedrooms, and into her room. She made a sound, so he covered her mouth with his hand and stabbed her with a small serrated steak knife. In fact, police had found a steak knife matching that description down the block from Kralik's house the next day—*a fact never released to the newspapers*.

Mitchell's trial ended in a hung jury: Eleven votes for acquittal, one holdout for conviction. Undeterred by the lopsided breakdown, spelling more than reasonable doubt, prosecutor Skoller convinced the Queens DA to retry Mitchell, which they did nine months later, in March 1965. In a self-congratulatory book about this case published in 2008 titled *Twisted Confessions*, Skoller wrote that the details provided by Mitchell were not consistent with innocence.

Ahead of Mitchell's second trial, the press was skeptical. In *Reading Eagle*, Ruth Reynolds asked, "Did the Boy or the Man Kill Barbara?" In the *Saturday Evening Post*, Bard Lindeman asked, "Who Didn't Kill Barbara Kralik?" But Skoller was determined not to repeat his past failure, and indeed this second trial would prove to be different.

First, he had Mitchell's alibi witness from the first trial arrested for outstanding traffic violations at the start of the second trial; sitting in a jail cell, this witness did not re-testify.

He did re-call Borges, Mitchell's friend who had recanted his incriminating testimony from the first trial. "Aided" by a polygraph test, and with a threat of charges pending, Borges agreed to testify again.

This time he did not waver (though he did admit that police had coerced him to implicate Mitchell and he could not recall whose car he supposedly had borrowed for the getaway that night).

As in the first trial, Skoller succeeded in convincing the judge to exclude Kralik's dying declaration that she did not recognize her assailant. She said this after regaining consciousness at the hospital just moments before she died. But the jury was never informed of this. Although relevant and exculpatory, this information constitutes hearsay, a secondhand account from a witness who is not present to testify. The law provides for certain exceptions to this hearsay rule. One is the "dying declaration" exception: any statement made by a dying witness while believing that death was imminent is admissible (the rationale is that someone who is dying and knows it has less incentive to lie; as a result, the hearsay statement can be considered reliable). At trial, the judge would not admit Kralik's statement because he was not convinced that she knew she was dying.

Perhaps most astonishing, Skoller brought in a brand-new eyewitness, a bus driver who testified that he recalled picking up a boy fitting Mitchell's description near Kralik's home that night—twenty months earlier. Called into the DA's office, the driver recalled nothing from the night in question. But then Skoller put him through a highly suggestive and leading set of interviews that both shaped his report and raised his confidence.

By any day's standards for how to obtain eyewitness identifications, it is clear that this eyewitness was tainted. What the record shows, without dispute, is that he went on to identify Mitchell—but not from a classic lineup containing a suspect surrounded by innocent foils, and not even from a single still photograph. Rather, Skoller shamelessly presented this witness with ABC TV news footage of Mitchell's early morning perp walk confession!

"Some prodigious tasks and feats of memory have been exhibited here," said Mitchell's attorney, sarcastically, at the start of his summation. Commenting on a motion for appeal later submitted, Judge Edward Thompson said: "Unquestionably the law is now well settled that a confrontation which is so unnecessarily suggestive and conducive to irreparable mistaken identification is a denial of due process of law."

Then there was Winston Moseley, a wild card, brought into court from prison. At Mitchell's first trial, Moseley recounted his depraved spree of violence—including the step-by-step account of the late-night walk through the Kralik house and murder. However, this time he refused to talk: "I didn't do it," he testified. "And I don't intend to go into any explanation why."

Mitchell could not catch a break. On March 12, 1965, after more than eleven hours of deliberation, at 1:35 a.m. (are judges allowed to compel a verdict by depriving juries of sleep?) the jury convicted Mitchell—not of murder, but of first-degree manslaughter. He served twelve years and eight months before being released. According to Mitchell, he was eligible for parole before that but was denied because he would not express remorse for the crime he insists he did not commit.

Why did Moseley, who had already recounted the Kralik murder in excruciating detail to Queens detectives, his own attorney, a psychiatrist, at his own trial, and at Mitchell's first trial, suddenly clam up? As I read through the record on this case, my head spun with questions. Did Moseley not want to perjure himself because he came to believe that his Kralik confession was not true? Or, was he threatened or incentivized in some way, and is that why the Queens DA's Office never prosecuted him for the shooting murder of Annie Mae Johnson?

In 2014, fifty years later, I tried to go to the source. Moseley was incarcerated at the Clinton Correctional Facility in upstate New York. Through a friend of a friend, I embedded two questions in a letter passed on to Moseley by a former inmate buddy of his. My two questions were: (1) Did you kill Barbara Kralik? and (2) why at Mitchell's second trial did you refuse to repeat the confession you had given before? Moseley's handwritten reply to his friend was short and to the point: "As for Saul Kassin, sorry, but I have absolutely nothing to say about Alvin Mitchell and the Barbara Kralik case."

In 2016, at the age of eighty-one, Moseley died in prison and quite literally took his answers to these questions to his grave. At the time of his death, he was the longest-serving prisoner in the state, prompting obituaries focused on the infamous rape and killing of Kitty Genovese. Yet one month earlier, he had raped and killed Annie Mae Johnson, a crime for which he was never prosecuted; he also confessed to killing Barbara Kralik, the crime for which Alvin Mitchell was prosecuted and convicted.

In 1968, Moseley escaped from Attica prison. He beat a guard sense-less, took his gun, and fled (he would later be captured in time to participate in the prison riot). During his escape, Moseley raped a wom-an and took hostages before having to surrender to federal authorities. Over the course of his life in prison, his request for parole was rejected eighteen times.

That brings me to Alvin Mitchell. He was released from prison in 1978. With help from a parole officer convinced of his innocence, Alvin found a room to live in and a job in upstate New York. Three years later, he wed the granddaughter of Julius Archibald, New York's first African American state senator. They were married for twenty-four years before getting divorced. Together, they had six children.

Today, Alvin lives in rural northern Vermont. Now in his seventies, he owns a home; works part-time for a security company; does volun-teer work in a local prison and homeless shelters; enjoys boating, fish-ing, and camping; and has a relationship with a woman who cares about him.

With help from an investigator who volunteered his time, I tracked Alvin down. I did not know if he would want to revisit this part of his life after so many years, and I was prepared to back off if he hedged. But he did not. We called and left a message; Mitchell called back and left this voicemail: "Yeah this is Alvin Mitchell. I just got your voice-mail. . . . I am very interested in what you were saying. . . . I would love to prove my innocence. I've been trying, wanting to do that for years. I appreciate you guys' concern. And hopefully we can do something there. Thanks a lot for getting in touch with me. Appreciate it. Definite-ly appreciate it."

I drove to northern Vermont in June 2014 to meet Alvin. In the backyard of his home, our meeting was an emotional one. While he struggled to recall the fine details of his three days of interrogations, and his two trials, he remembers threats and promises. He remembers being hit, starved, and deprived of sleep. He remembers the suggestion that he blacked out—not his fault—and being driven from one precinct to another for three days so his parents could not find him. I asked Alvin why he confessed. His reply was simple and to the point: "I would have confessed to killing the president because them people had me scared to death."

Two recollections in particular stayed with Alvin. He recalls that police took him to Barbara Kralik's house and into her bedroom and the horror that ensued. "Her mother was there. And the poor woman is pleading with me, 'How come you did this?'" The second memory was of his heart-stopping fear of death: "At one point, the paddy wagon stopped. The officer got out, opened up the back door and said, 'Run because I want to shoot you.'"

Alvin's memory was emotionally raw. He teared up and his voice cracked when he talked about how the case broke up his family, causing them to sell their home; how his sister and younger brothers had to be sent to live elsewhere; and how it destroyed his relationship with a girlfriend whom he had hoped to marry. "Like it was yesterday," he said.

Others I have interviewed about the case, insiders to the system, feel the same way. I talked to Judge William Erlbaum, who wrote a brilliant petition for appeal critical of the suggestive eyewitness identification in Mitchell's second trial. Erlbaum, who went on to become a State Supreme Court justice, insists that an innocent Mitchell was "targeted." Over breakfast at the Flagship Diner in Queens, he recalled this case as one of the two worst he had ever seen. Though cautious in his language, Judge Erlbaum went on to suggest that Mitchell was innocent and was critical of the case against him.

I also talked to Judge Joseph Lisa, then a young law secretary for Judge Shapiro in 1964. He went on to become chief of the Appeals Bureau of the Queens District Attorney's Office and a State Supreme Court justice. He continues to practice law. In court for much of the Moseley and Mitchell proceedings, Judge Lisa referred to Moseley's testimony as "riveting" and Mitchell's case as "highly unsettling." As he took me on a walking tour of the Genovese murder site in Kew Gardens, and the courthouse nearby where both Moseley and Mitchell were tried, Judge Lisa acknowledged that the Mitchell case haunts him as well.

Then there was Attorney Robert Sparrow, the son and then junior partner of Sidney Sparrow, Winston Moseley's lawyer. In preparation for Moseley's defense, Sparrow visited his client at the Kings County Hospital shortly after his arrest. With a reel-to-reel tape recorder in hand, he took Moseley's confession to the Kralik murder. "Chilling," "breathtaking," "emotionless," and "without remorse" were words he used to describe it. I visited attorney Sparrow in his home in Queens. Impressed by the richness of detail, he told me that Moseley's confession to Kralik's murder was "absolutely sufficient to persuade us." Sparrow died recently. The last time we spoke, he still had that tape.

I return to the invisible gorilla. Cognitive psychologists debate whether "attention-blinded" subjects don't see the interloper or see it but then quickly forget. Either way, and while the analogy to Kitty Genovese is admittedly a loose one, it makes a similar point: I am a New Yorker and a social psychologist. I study false confessions. I have been staring at this storied case for over fifty years. Yet like the gorilla pounding its chest in studies of inattentional blindness, the false-confession drama had never entered my field of vision. I had no idea.

Guess what. That gorilla did not just happen randomly onto the scene. Ten days after the Genovese killing, *New York Times* metro editor Abe Rosenthal had lunch with NYPD commissioner Michael Murphy. With Mitchell awaiting trial in the Kralik case, Moseley's blurted admission had stirred up a hornets' nest. Aware that Moseley had confessed to Kralik's murder and that Mitchell and his attorney were alleging coercion, the local papers were asking tough questions. Rosenthal wanted to talk about that. But in an exchange reported by authors Catherine Pelonero and Kevin Cook, Commissioner Murphy changed the subject. "Brother, that Queens story is one for the books. Thirty-eight witnesses . . . this beats everything." For the first time on record, Murphy injected that now-disputed claim into the story.

The seed of a new narrative was planted. Rosenthal put reporter Martin Gansberg on the story, who two days later confirmed the bystander report with the detectives who took Mitchell's confession. During this meeting, the detective expressed astonishing anger at Kitty's neighbors who did not intervene. On March 27, Gansberg's now famous article was published. His front-page headline read: "Thirty-Seven Who Saw Murder Didn't Call Police."

I cannot crawl into the minds of Commissioner Murphy or Mitchell's detective all these years later to know if changing the subject was a willful sleight of hand, a diversionary tactic aimed at moving the spotlight away from the Kralik confessions. Willful or not, that was the effect it had. Oh, one more thing. Those career girl murders that Moseley would not confess to—a few weeks later, the NYPD took a sixty-one-page confession from George Whitmore, a confession later proved false.

THE LOSS-PREVENTION GAMBIT:
FALSE CONFESSIONS IN THE WORKPLACE

I know what you're thinking. A false confession to a rape, murder, or other heinous crime is tragic. It wrecks the life of an innocent person and his or her family and friends; it leaves a violent offender free to harm others; and it utterly tramples our moral sense of what is right and fair. Mercifully, you figure, unless you're "struck-by-lightning" unlucky, stumbling in time and place into the crosshairs of an investigation is one of those things that likely won't happen to you. Think again.

According to a 2020 survey of the National Retail Federation, American retailers lose an estimated $61.7 billion a year in employee theft, shoplifting, cybercrime, and various types of e-commerce fraud. To help recover some of these losses, companies like Macy's, Walmart, Home Depot, UPS, and Marriott conduct in-house investigations through "loss-prevention" investigators trained in the same methods used by homicide detectives. In the case of employee theft, their objective is to identify suspects and get them not only to confess but also to reimburse the company for the stolen money or merchandise.

I became aware of this industry for the first time in 2006. I got a call from San Diego attorneys Sean Simpson and Charles Moore. They represented a client named Joaquin Robles, who had worked for Auto-Zone, a Memphis-based auto parts retailer. With over six thousand stores, AutoZone is the largest auto parts retailer in the United States and Mexico.

Robles, then twenty-six, had been working at a San Diego location for about a year. As part of his job, he often helped put store deposits into an armored truck. One day, the truck arrived at the bank with $820 missing. Octavio Jara, AutoZone's loss prevention manager, pulled Robles into a back room for questioning during his work shift. After several minutes of small talk, Jara told Robles there was a problem, that the bank had called after receiving an empty bag containing only a deposit slip. When Robles said he knew nothing about it, Jara accused him of stealing the money.

At first, Robles thought that Jara was asking for his help in finding the thief. He didn't realize he was under suspicion. Then, he recounted how Jara—following the company's recommended ruse of bringing in bulging files, videos, snapshots, and other props—brought into the room a black bag and pulled out of it a video camera and tapes that he said captured the theft. When Robles asked to see the tapes, Jara refused.

He continued to interrogate Robles in the room. For three hours, Robles insisted that he would not and did not take the money. He was adamant about it. Then Jara let him know that he used to be a cop. As Robles recalls it, Jara said, "All I have to do is give a phone call, and the police will be at the front of the store to pick you up, and they'll take you to jail because what you've done is a felony." Alternatively, Jara suggested, they could keep this matter in-house if Robles confessed and agreed to compensate AutoZone through payroll deductions from future paychecks.

This was a Hobson's choice, a no-brainer. So Robles handwrote a statement dictated to him. "I took the $820." He apologized, expressed remorse, explained that he had a family debt to pay, asked for a second chance, and signed a promissory note to pay back the money from future paychecks.

AutoZone promptly suspended Robles, withheld his next paycheck, and then terminated him. Because he was fired, Robles was unable to obtain unemployment insurance. Two weeks later, the bank called: The money presumed missing from the deposit bag was found; it had been misplaced through an accounting error, not theft. At that point, it didn't matter. Robles was denied his last paycheck and was out of a job.

It turns out that Robles had no outstanding debts at the time, nor did he feel mistreated because he thought Jara, a friend and ally, was helping him out of a jam. What a textbook illustration of trickery and deceit this was. Reflecting back on his decision-making years later, Robles said, "It makes me feel so naïve, so stupid." "I really hope that nobody goes through what I went through."

Robles hired attorneys and filed a complaint for damages. As soon as the complaint was reported in the newspapers, three other former AutoZone employees from San Diego stepped forward to say that they too were accused, threatened, and offered a false choice between calling the police and keeping the matter in-house via confession and payback. To compensate Robles, the jury at this trial awarded him $73,150 in damages.

In 2006, Robles was heading back to court for another jury trial, seeking to add punitive damages. Interested in learning about the loss-prevention industry as a venue for interrogations and confessions, I agreed to take the case. After reading Robles's confession and promissory note, and of course knowing that he had confessed to a nonevent, I scoured AutoZone's 200-page manual on how to interrogate employees.

This manual was eerily familiar to those I've studied on how to interrogate felony suspects—but without any checks and balances (most notably, the employee is not entitled to Miranda rights to silence or an attorney). Right away, I was struck by the rule that tape recorders are not permitted in the room. Make sure the employee does not have a recording device; do not allow the employee to tape the interrogation. Now ask yourself this question: Why the secrecy? If you are a loss-prevention manager and proud of how you solve your company's cases and recover losses, don't you want your supervisors to see and admire your work?

Next, I was struck by the antiquated, long-ago-discredited old wives' tales of lie detection that have no basis in science. In addition to the usual "If he can't look you in the eye, then he's lying" myth and the claim that "when a subject begins to slump, and his head droops, it means he is ready to admit guilt" (this is the subject of the next chapter), there was this horrifying nugget of wisdom: "Beware of too much respectfulness or helpfulness." God help the loyal, polite, cooperative employee who is brought into this situation.

Octavio Jara boasted in his testimony that he had conducted hundreds of loss-prevention interviews and posted a 98 percent confession rate. His boss characterized that number as "typical" (this compares to roughly 50 percent in the criminal justice system). Blithely, he added that a confession alone is proof of guilt—so no need for further investigation.

In contrast, I testified that the average person—including trained professionals—is only 54 percent accurate at distinguishing truth tellers from liars. Some may be slightly better. But even if Jara is among the best, do the math. To be sure, some workers, true to their confessions, do pilfer cash or merchandise from their employers. Unless Jara is a near-perfect mind reader, however, his 98 percent confession rate invariably means that he has taken confessions, money, and reputation from an awful lot of innocent employees. And if his numbers are "typical," then other AutoZone loss-prevention investigators have, too.

To counter the false imprisonment complaint, Jara pointed to the company's loss-prevention manual, which states that it is sufficient to ensure that the employee being interrogated has a clear exit path—in other words, access to the door. In response, I posed this question: How free, really, was Robles, an employee, to get up and leave the workplace, on a workday, during his own shift, without being fired? For all practical purposes, Robles was in custody.

After hearing from both sides, the San Diego jury awarded Joaquin Robles $7.5 million in punitive damages. Shortly after the verdict was reported in the *San Diego Union-Tribune*, and then drew a commentary from consumer advocate Ralph Nader, I received a spate of calls on my office phone from other former "AutoZoners" (the company word for its employees) who had similar experiences.

Ultimately, the courts reduced this award to $750,000. Still, one would think that AutoZone had learned from this experience. Or not. In 2014, Saul Elbein wrote an article in the *New York Times* titled "When Employees Confess, Sometimes Falsely," about an AutoZone case in Houston. And in 2019, I was asked to consult on yet another case, that one in Daytona Beach (I declined the request, as I most often do, even for cases of merit).

While the criminal justice system imposes constitutional constraints on the confession-taking process, employment venues are not similarly limited. I cannot quantify the problem; I have no idea how many employees have falsely confessed to stealing money or merchandise. But I do know that when I give public lectures, people come up to me all the time, sheepishly, to admit that they too once confessed to a workplace theft they did not commit because they thought it would spare a police investigation and save their job. That happened at a recent talk I gave at the University of Amsterdam. After the coast was clear, a psychology PhD student pulled me aside to let me know that this happened to her, too, before graduate school, and was personally devastating. Needless to say, Joaquin Robles is pictured on my wall of faces.

FALSE CONFESSIONS IN SCHOOL: PARENTS, BEWARE!

On October 31, 2005, photographer Teresa Halbach disappeared after a business appointment with Steven Avery at his salvage yard in Two Rivers, Wisconsin. She was twenty-five years old and grew up on a dairy farm near Green Bay. She had visited Avery's yard to photograph a car for *Auto Trader* magazine.

Twenty years earlier, Avery had been convicted of rape. After serving eighteen years of a thirty-two-year sentence, however, DNA testing proved he was innocent. His conviction was overturned, and he was in the process of suing the county and its former sheriff and district attorney for $36 million in damages.

Then came Halbach's disappearance. Within days, police found charred bone fragments in a bonfire pit outside Avery's garage, eleven shell casings from his .22-caliber rifle, and the victim's burned phone and camera in a barrel near Avery's trailer. Halbach's Toyota RAV4 was found nearby without its license plates. Bloodstains recovered from the interior matched Avery's DNA. Avery was arrested and charged with Halbach's murder, kidnapping, and sexual assault, and mutilation of a corpse.

To help build their case, police sought out Brendan Dassey, Avery's sixteen-year-old nephew, after Dassey's cousin told a school counselor that he had recently been crying. Brendan was a learning-disabled sophomore at Mishicot High School, where he received special education services. Police investigator Mark Wiegert and special agent Tom Fassbender went to the school, without a parent's knowledge or permission, pulled Brendan into a conference room and questioned him. Two days later, they returned at 10 a.m. and met with the dean of students, who summoned the boy to his office. Before Brendan knew it, he was in a squad car heading to the Manitowoc Police Department, forty-five minutes away.

If this case sounds familiar it's because it was the subject of a ten-part Netflix documentary, *Making a Murderer*, the award-winning true crime documentary written and directed by Laura Ricciardi and Moira Demos, which aired in December 2015 (a second season followed in 2018).

In one episode, Dassey can be seen sitting, passive and helpless, in the corner of an interrogation room. He was accompanied by Wiegert

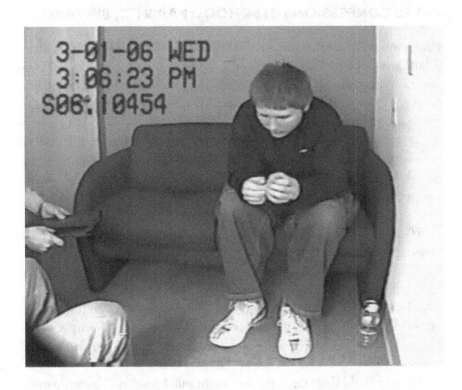

Sixteen-year-old Brendan Dassey, "costar" of Netflix's *Making a Murderer*, was interrogated for a total of forty-eight hours, culminating in a confession. In this frame, he was told for the first time that he was under arrest. Based solely on his confession, Dassey was convicted. *Permission to use video frame of interrogation granted by Dassey's attorney, Laura Nirider.*

and Fassbender, trained detectives trying to get him to implicate Avery in a confession. Dassey is perceptibly slow. With an IQ of 74, he did not trust his own assessment of reality. At one point, he says to his mother, "Mom, I'm stupid." After confessing, he tells her, "They got into my head."

It's bad enough that Dassey was young and learning disabled. Yet rather than compensate for his limitations, the police exploited him, using the kinds of trickery and deceit that were built for—and can draw false confessions from—fully functioning adults. In four interrogations that spanned a noncontinuous total of forty-eight hours, detectives accused Brendan and said that they already knew what happened and had physical evidence to prove it. That was untrue. They had no such evidence. Yet when Brendan insisted on his innocence, they sternly refused to accept his word, called him a liar, and threatened to arrest him.

The state of Wisconsin had just passed a law requiring that police record custodial interrogations. In this case, the tapes show that detectives offered Dassey a range of inducements. After accusing him of participating in the murder, they offered a lifeline by pretending to care for him as they would their own son. Using a tactic that the parent in me finds morally repugnant, Wiegert said, "I'm a father that has a kid your age," "I promise I will not leave you high and dry."

One can only imagine the psychological whiplash these alternating techniques can have on a person, especially one who is intellectually limited and under duress. This subterfuge set the stage for detectives to introduce calming "minimization" tactics. Feigning sympathy, they told Brendan that Avery, not he, was to blame. "It's not your fault, remember that," they said. "You've done nothing wrong." "Nothing wrong" means what: confess and all will be normal?

Eventually, Dassey succumbed and said that he assisted Avery in the murder. Moments later, in a jaw-dropping exchange that put on display how profoundly misled he was, Dassey asked whether he would get back to school in time for a project he had to present.

Using trickery and deceit was all part of the interrogator playbook. With Fassbender and Wiegert using the infamous Reid technique, to be described later, these interrogations featured two adult professionals doing tag-team battle with a child. Still, you may say to yourself, if that mismatch helps get a confession that exposes his guilt, solves a heinous crime, and gets justice for Teresa Halbach's family, so be it. So, did Fassbender and Wiegert get Brendan to describe the crime, with accuracy, and with detail that only a perpetrator could have known? Did they get Brendan to give a confession that led them to other corroborat-ing evidence?

The prosecutor in this case said yes. But not so fast. Brendan's "narrative" was riddled with factual errors. What's worse, Fassbender and Wiegert fed him information through a series of hints and leading questions. You can see it for yourself on the video recording. As in many proven false-confession cases, Brendan merely parroted the details of a statement authored by investigators.

Based on this confession, Dassey was convicted of first-degree murder and sentenced to life in prison. His appeals were denied; the

Wisconsin Supreme Court would not review his case. Dassey's appeals attorneys then filed a federal habeas corpus petition, setting into motion a dizzying chain of events.

A federal judge overturned Dassey's conviction in 2016, ruling that his confession was coerced. A three-judge panel later affirmed that ruling. But then by a four-to-three vote, the Seventh Circuit reinstated his conviction, and in 2018, the U.S. Supreme Court declined to examine the case. In 2019, five days before Christmas, Wisconsin's Pardon Advisory Board denied a clemency petition, which was signed by 250 national experts. At least for now and barring an extraordinary development, Dassey will remain incarcerated at least until 2048.

Over the years, the U.S. Supreme Court has sought to protect children, recognizing that they require "special care." In *Hayley v. Ohio* (1948), the court observed that events that might "leave a man cold and unimpressed" could "overawe and overwhelm a lad." In *J.D.B. v. North Carolina* (2011), the court stated that the "risk [of false confessions] is all the more troubling (and recent studies suggest, all the more acute) when the subject of custodial interrogation is a juvenile."

These risks are self-evident at every level of analysis. Looking at databases of wrongful convictions, one cannot miss the statistical fact that juveniles are far more likely than adults to be wrongfully convicted because of a police-induced false confession.

As noted earlier, research on human development explains how this can happen: Adolescents are more malleable than adults and more vulnerable to manipulation, especially when confronted by an adult authority figure. Universally, adolescents also exhibit an "immaturity of judgment" that leads them to make impulsive decisions—for example, deciding to break down and confess in order to escape an interrogator's bullying, without fully grasping the long-term consequences. Oh, and in case this is not clear: these limitations characterize adolescents in general—including those who would not harm a fly.

It's not just the community of scientific experts who understand the risks. Recently, the International Association of Chiefs of Police (IACP) published *An Executive's Guide to Effective Juvenile Interview and Interrogation*, in which they noted that "juveniles are particularly likely to give false information and even falsely confess when questioned by law enforcement." They went on to recommend some essential best practices—like ensuring the presence of a friendly adult, limiting the length and time of sessions, and avoiding the uses of deception.

If everyone gets it, then what's the problem? The problem is that not everyone gets it. Northwestern University Law professors Megan Crane, Steven Drizin, and Laura Nirider, co-directors of the Center on Wrongful Convictions of Youth, know this all too well (Drizin and Nirider represent Brendan Dassey). In an article titled "The Truth About Juvenile False Confessions," they presented a thought experiment:

Imagine you are a thirteen-year-old boy in middle school, and all of a sudden, the principal comes in, pulls you out, and takes you to a small room where three armed police officers are waiting for you. They sit you down, and you are surrounded. You have no idea what's happening until one of the officers reads your Miranda rights and then accuses you of inappropriately touching a three-year-old girl who lives next door to you.

The officer doesn't *ask* if you did it; she tells you they have proof. You might try to eke out a denial but the officers won't listen. You start to cry, but the officer tells you the only way to help yourself is to confess. Besides, she suggests, you were probably just curious—no big deal. You parrot back what you were told so you can leave. But then you are handcuffed, arrested, and charged.

The Crane team then reveals that this thought experiment is not a hypothetical. It was a real case involving a real boy named John. After two years of public humiliation, the charges against John were dropped. But what the hell were police doing in a middle school, interrogating John without first informing his parents? Surely they know that thirteen-year-olds do not comprehend their Miranda rights. And why didn't the school principal contact John's parents?

If you're a parent, be on guard. A few years ago, I received a plea-for-help email from the father of a fifteen-year-old high school boy. "I had the opportunity to attend your seminar at the College entitled 'Why innocent people confess' this past spring. I have a situation where my son falsely confessed to a bomb threat in our high school. Police used all the interrogation techniques you discussed. . . . Your HELP would be greatly appreciated."

The gentleman who contacted me was a systems engineer, and married. His son was an average student with no history of mischief. One day, someone at the high school scrawled a bomb threat onto a bathroom stall. The school was evacuated and searched for explosives. Nothing was found. Guided by surveillance footage of the entrance to this bathroom, troopers compiled a list of students to question. This man's son was on the list and was interviewed three times—first at school, then at the police station.

During the third interview, the boy agreed to take a polygraph (lie detector) examination. Five minutes later, the officer who administered the test, professionally trained in interrogation, told the boy and his parents that he "failed miserably." That's an old trick of the trade that often gets innocent people to confess to things they did not do. Hell, the polygraph charts, which present fluctuating graphics of heart rate, respiration rate, blood pressure, and other measures of physiological arousal, are presented as "medical" and "scientific." You can't argue with that.

In consultation with his shaken parents, and looking to cut his losses, the boy agreed to confess. In a written statement, he apologized, expressed his desire to remain at school, and offered to help repaint the bathroom. Almost certainly he believed that by agreeing to make amends, he was putting this trauma behind him. That's not what happened. Instead he was promptly expelled from school and lost his friends.

There was no physical evidence of guilt. No witnesses. No motive. Nothing in the boy's past suggested he would do something like this. The handwriting on the stall did not resemble, much less match, his penmanship. Yet this mismatch was not considered exculpatory. In fact, illustrating the kinds of confirmation biases that too often plague forensic examiners, the state's handwriting expert, fully aware of the confession, concluded that "the author made a conscious attempt to disguise his or her natural writing."

This boy was innocent. The case against him was later dismissed. But the confession he was induced to give derailed his teen life. The family filed a lawsuit against the school and state police. Repeatedly, they requested the alleged polygraph charts, but all requests were denied. Although the family was ultimately compensated through a lawsuit that was settled in their favor, that father, who had failed to protect his son from interrogation, wishes he knew then what he knows now.

I'd like to say that these stories are anomalous. But they are not. Despite increased awareness of the risks, a 2014 survey of hundreds of police officers nationwide revealed that they interrogate youth in the same manner as they do adults. This is not at all surprising. Other surveys have shown that the training is the same. In fact, the situation may be getting worse. In a troubling recent development, John Reid & Associates—a Chicago-based firm that created of the controversial Reid technique of interrogation—started to market special courses for school administrators all over the country.

There are some important lessons to be learned from this case. One is the shocking fact that the presence of parents in the interrogation room does not necessarily protect kids from the risks posed when they decide to waive their rights. Following from this fact, the second lesson concerns the importance of consulting with a lawyer. Analyses of juvenile interrogations show that kids are almost never accompanied by a defense attorney.

In part II of this book, I will describe the practice of interviewing and interrogation in grisly detail and the research that has exposed its archaic flaws. The Reid course purports to teach school officials how to know when a child is lying and then how to get that child to confess. In a 2016 *New Yorker* article titled "Why Are Educators Learning How to Interrogate Their Students?" journalist Douglas Starr quoted one course attendee who reported that on the topic of how to handle tears, the instructor, the president of Reid & Associates, advised: "Don't stop. Tears are the beginning of a confession."

For now, trust me when I say that if you are a parent, you do not want the principal of your child's school to interrogate students for theft, vandalism, and other acts of malfeasance, using the same psychological weapons that homicide detectives use. At a time when all experts agree that children should be protected from police trickery and deceit, in a situation where Miranda may not apply, where parents are not informed, where a student's presence is compulsory—essentially putting them in "custody"—and where disobedience evokes disciplinary action, interrogating school children using techniques built for adults should be stopped.

Part Two

Why Innocent People Confess

3

"LIAR, LIAR, PANTS ON FIRE!"

Police as Human Lie Detectors

Several years ago, I was at a law enforcement conference in Montreal, where Joseph Buckley—president of John E. Reid & Associates—lectured on the influential but controversial Reid technique of interrogation. I was sitting with Professor Gisli Gudjonsson, my longtime false-confessions colleague from King's College in London. Afterward, an audience member asked Buckley if he was concerned that his methods might at times cause innocent people to confess. His reply: "No, because we don't interrogate innocent people."

I've lost track of how many detectives I've heard say the same thing. To fully grasp this remark and why it is so troubling, you have to know that the highly charged process of *interrogation* is typically preceded by a "neutral" *interview*, wherein police determine on a hunch masked as science whether a suspect is lying or telling the truth.

In every false confession case I have reviewed, I ask, How did this innocent person become a suspect in the first place? Sometimes the answer is rationally rooted in a prior investigation: a witness misreported seeing the suspect at the crime scene; physical evidence or surveillance footage suggested the suspect's presence; or the suspect had a history of committing similar crimes, a contentious relationship with the victim, or a motive and opportunity. The husband caught cheating on his wife naturally becomes a person of interest if she disappears or is murdered. In the Central Park jogger case, NYPD detectives rounded up groups of kids who were running through the park that night, some of them assaulting bystanders.

Too often, however, police make a snap judgment based on an interview and a hunch. In San Diego, fourteen-year-old Michael Crowe was induced to confess that he stabbed to death his sister Stephanie. The charges were dropped weeks later when a local drifter was found with the victim's blood on his clothing. It seems that Crowe was targeted in the first place because detectives assigned to the case thought that he had reacted to his sister's death with too little emotion.

Then there was sixteen-year-old Jeff Deskovic. In 1989, in Westchester County, New York, his high school classmate Angela was raped and murdered. Deskovic attended her funeral and visited her wake three times, leading police to believe that he seemed overly distraught given his casual relationship to the victim. Deskovic too was interrogated until he confessed. In 2006, after sixteen years in prison, he was exonerated via DNA.

Then there was thirty-year-old Tom Franklin Sawyer of Clearwater, Florida, questioned for sixteen hours in 1986 until he confessed to a rape and murder he did not commit. The reason Sawyer became a prime suspect was that his face flushed and he appeared "embarrassed" during an initial interview, a reaction that police saw as proof of deception. What investigators did not know was that Sawyer was a recovering alcoholic with a social anxiety disorder that caused him to sweat profusely and fllush in tense social situations.

I could go on, and on, and on with stories of reflexive, mistaken, and—pardon my language—boneheaded judgments of deception, based on nothing more than a hunch, that set in motion catastrophic chains of events. Sometimes these judgments are based on a suspect's physical appearance. Sometimes they are based on a micro sliver of behavior.

Social psychologists know all too well that these hunches can be dangerous. I testified in a U.S. Army case several years ago, in Fort Drum, New York, where a CID investigator was asked why he targeted a young recruit for interrogation about a rape. He proceeded to describe how he "knew" that this recruit was not telling the truth: "He tried to remain calm but you could tell he was nervous and every time we tried to ask him a question his eyes would roam and he would not make direct contact, and at times he would act pretty sporadic. He started to cry at one time. We actually called it off because his breathing was kind of impaired. There had to be something wrong."

There had to be something wrong? A military investigator scares the hell out a young enlisted private, accusing him of rape, and then he interprets the man's anxiety attack as a sign of deception? Was that really the only way to interpret roaming eyes, impaired breathing, and tears? There was no evidence to support the prosecution, so this particular defendant was speedily acquitted at trial. But the story of how he became a suspect because of his demeanor repeats itself every day.

Where do police get these ideas—and, worse, their unshakable confidence in their lie-detection abilities? Part of the problem is that they are human. Whenever we meet someone for the first time, we form a quick impression based only on a "snapshot" of information. It happens fast and outside of conscious awareness.

In a lab experiment that illustrates the rapid-fire nature of this process, researchers Janine Willis and Alexander Todorov presented college students with photographs of unfamiliar faces for a mere one-tenth of a second. Even after this brief exposure, they found that the students formed impressions of how likable, trustworthy, and aggressive these individuals were. This tendency to infer personal traits from the face is early to develop: Children as young as three and four are quick to judge someone as "mean" or "nice" based on a brief exposure.

Apart from the empirical fact that people, including police, are not adept at distinguishing truths and lies on the basis of a person's demeanor, there is the problem of implicit stereotyping and bias. Suspects vary not only in their demeanor but also in their age, gender, skin color, hairstyle, and cultural and ethnic heritage; they may be tall or short; well dressed or shabby; they may or may not be fluent in English. All of this comes across in a glance, only to activate cultural stereotypes regarding criminality. Read *Biased*, by Jennifer Eberhardt, or *Blind Spot*, by Mahzarin Banaji and Anthony Greenwald, two recent books on the subject, and you'll see exactly how a detective's determination that a suspect is lying or telling the truth can unconsciously be tainted by the suspect's appearance.

Finally, while hampered by their humanness, many police detectives also take quickie courses in the Reid technique, Kinesic interviewing, micro-expression training, behavior analysis and interviewing techniques, and the like. More on these pseudosciences later.

THE PSYCHOLOGY OF LYING AND DETECTION

Reading people can be tricky because we often try to hide or stretch the truth about ourselves. Poker players bluff for money, police lie to suspects who in turn lie to police, politicians make campaign promises they know they can't keep, job applicants self-present in overly positive ways, and friends and acquaintances are often too generous with compliments just to be polite. At times, every one of us tells something less than "the truth, the whole truth, and nothing but the truth."

Let's step it back for context. The animal world is full of guile and deception in the service of survival. Insects like the praying mantis rest motionless like a dry stick; crocodiles camouflage themselves as driftwood to avoid scaring off prey; nesting birds like the mourning dove and snowy owl perform distraction displays or feign broken wings to divert predators from a vulnerable nest. To scare off rivals and attract mates, gazelles, howler monkeys, bats, and other creatures vocalize with deep sonic frequencies that create the illusion that they are larger animals. Animal behaviorists have observed that, further up the evolutionary ladder, primates hide a food source from others of their own species or turn away while reflexively baring their teeth—which signals fear—in battles for dominance with a rival within the group.

No psychologist would use the word "lying" to describe camouflage, distraction, and other adaptive animal displays. *Lying* is a term used to describe a form of deception that is intentional, not just a mistake; deliberate, not mindless or unconscious; and tactically motivated—in other words, a verbal or nonverbal behavior that one uses, successfully or not, to mislead another person about something.

"Thou shalt not bear false witness against thy neighbor." Despite what the Bible's ninth commandment implies, deception is not inherently immoral. I can still recall the times my then–three-year-old daughter, and later her daughters at that age, would react with great enthusiasm to a birthday gift someone handed them—even before they fully unwrapped it and realized what it was. That's what it means, I mused with pride, to become kind, civilized, and adapted to interpersonal life.

Of course, people lie for self-serving purposes, too—and that includes young children. In a pioneering 1989 study often replicated, Michael Lewis and others introduced what they called a "temptation resistance" paradigm in which they told three-year-olds not to peek at a toy when the experimenter left the room. This temptation was so hard to resist that most kids peeked. Then the experimenter returned and asked each child if they peeked. You can appreciate the conflict posed by this set-up. It turned out that among the three-year-olds who peeked, 38 percent confessed, 38 percent lied about it, and the rest did not respond. In a more recent paper titled "From Little White Lies to Filthy Liars," developmental psychologists Victoria Talwar and Angela Crossman note that the older children are in this situation, the more likely they are to peek and lie.

Just as deception has adaptive value, so too does the ability to detect lying in others—which explains why people all over the world, throughout history, have sought creative methods for doing it. In China, dating back to 1000 BC, someone suspected of lying was asked to chew a mouthful of dry rice and then try to spit it out onto a sacred leaf. If grains of rice stuck to the suspect's tongue and palate, he or she was judged guilty. The theory underlying this "test" was simple: lying (versus telling the truth) makes people fearful and anxious, which impacts their physiological functions—in this case, decreased salivation and a dry mouth. Centuries later, Erasistratus, a Greek physicist and physician, tried to detect deception by measuring the pulse. Across other cultures, physiological signals used to diagnose deception have included sweating, heavy breathing, and trembling.

THE PSYCHOPHYSIOLOGY OF LYING AND DETECTION

Enter the polygraph. If lying triggers fear, which increases involuntary physiological arousal, and if that arousal can be objectively measured, then boom—a polygraph can become a lie-detector test. In the United States, it made its first appearance in the early twentieth century, and in one form or another, it is still used today.

The polygraph itself is nothing more than an electronic instrument that simultaneously records multiple channels of physiological arousal. The typical signals are picked up by sensors attached to the body. Rubber tubes are strapped around a suspect's torso to measure respiration, blood-pressure cuffs are wrapped around the upper arm to measure heart and pulse rate, and electrodes are placed on the fingertips to record sweat-gland activity, or perspiration. These signals are then boosted by amplifiers and converted into a dynamic visual display. You've seen it dramatized on TV and in the movies. The conventional polygraph, large and bulky or folded into a portable suitcase, would produce a continuous moving chart on paper that shows how these bodily signals fluctuate in response to questions and answers. Today, all polygraphs are computerized, digital, and use laptops.

The apparatus itself becomes a lie-detector test only when paired with a set of questions for analysis. Here's how the test proceeds. First, the examiner conducts a *pre-test interview* of the subject to attach the wires, establish the questions to be asked, read the subject his or her rights, record baseline levels of arousal, and convince the subject that the polygraph works. Many polygraph examiners will go out of their way to explain to the subject, even if it's not true, that they are not affiliated with law enforcement, that they are neutral and objective seekers of the truth, even it that means proving the subject's innocence. Invariably, the examiner will try to demonstrate that the polygraph is infallible. This last process is fascinating. Many examiners do it through trickery, by asking the subject to pick a card from the deck and then to lie or tell the truth in response to a question about that card. Using the con of marked cards, the examiner gets to impress the subject with an accurate true-false judgment.

The pre-test interview is followed by the *examination* itself, formatted in a series of yes-no questions. The structure of this test is a perennial focus of controversy and development. The earliest examiners used what is known as the relevant/irrelevant test. Imagine you are wired up and the examiner asks you two questions: "Is your name Alex?" and "Did you rob the bank?" If your body becomes more aroused when you deny robbing the bank, you'd be diagnosed as deceptive. Test failed. I don't think it takes a rocket scientist to intuit the inherent flaw in this pairing of questions. Whether you're guilty or innocent, it's obvious that the second question is all that matters. That high-stakes question will trigger more arousal than the first, whether you stole the money or not.

Over the course of the twentieth century, centered largely in Chicago, the polygraph grew into a profitable industry with competing factions. This is where Fred Inbau and John Reid started, architects of a psychological approach to interrogation that I'll describe later, and founders of John E. Reid & Associates.

John Reid's most notable contribution was to construct an alternative to the flawed relevant/irrelevant type of test. Instead, he recognized the need for better comparison questions. In what he called the "control-question test," he would compare how subjects react to arousing crime-relevant questions ("Did you steal the money?") and control questions that are arousing but not relevant to the crime ("Did you take anything that did not belong to you when you were younger?"). In theory, only suspects who are guilty, and whose denials are false, should be more aroused by the crime-relevant questions. This offered a marked improvement over the relevant/irrelevant test, but it is still, to this day, controversial.

There is nothing inherently wrong with using a polygraph to measure arousal if it is accompanied by appropriate comparative test questions and an understanding that arousal is not a perfect proxy for deception. In 2003, the National Research Council concluded that under pristine conditions—for example, when the suspect is naïve, the examiner is both competent and objective, and the charts are numerically scored—it is possible to achieve levels of accuracy that exceed the known capabilities of human judgment.

Looking for physiological alternatives, other researchers have been experimenting with the measurement of electrical activity in the brain, blood oxygen levels, pupil dilation, reaction time, thermal imaging that detects changes in skin temperature, and microphones that can detect changes in the frequency, intensity, pitch, and micro tremors in the voice, which are thought to indicate stress.

According to a 2008 study funded by the National Institute of Justice, the most popular Voice Stress Analyzer (VSA) programs used by police departments all over the country produce results that are no better than flipping a coin. Yet I have lost count of the number of times I have seen the VSA used as a prop to leverage confessions.

The Abusive Post–Polygraph Test Interview

There is a third phase to just about every polygraph examination I've seen administered to crime suspects: the *post-test interview*. Once the test is complete, the examiner leaves the room only to return some time later to deliver the bad and disheartening news: "You failed the test." This feedback transitions and blurs the line between using the polygraph as a purportedly objective test and as a prop aimed at leveraging a confession. What does this post-test interview have to do with lie detection? Nothing.

Let me describe the problem through a case study I call "The Polygraph Abuse of Peter Reilly." The first time I read about a post-test interview, it was in a 1973 case in Connecticut. Eighteen-year-old Peter Reilly, of New Canaan, returned home one night to find the body of his mother, Barbara Gibbons, naked, savagely beaten, and mutilated on the floor. For no good reason, state police identified Reilly, a high school senior, as their suspect. Reilly had no history of violence, no mental illness, no conflict with his mother. To all of Reilly's friends and neighbors, the idea was inconceivable.

Still, Sergeant Kelly accused him. After hours of interrogation and denial, he offered Reilly a lie detector test, which the boy naïvely agreed to take. It was an amateurish, horribly formed relevant/irrelevant test. Yet afterward, they lowered the hammer: "Pete, we go strictly by the charts. And the charts say you hurt your mother last night."

The subject of two books—Joan Barthel's *Death in Canaan* and Donald Connery's *Guilty Until Proven Innocent*—the Reilly case was so eye-opening that my mentor, Larry Wrightsman, and I used it in 1985 to illustrate what we called an internalized false confession. This is a type of confession in which the innocent person not only agrees to confess but also shockingly comes to believe in his own culpability.

The transition of Reilly's mental state was chilling to hear in the audiotapes of his interrogations. At one point, he conceded, "This test is giving me doubts right now." Sergeant Kelly, relentless, suggested that Reilly must have blocked the whole thing from his mind. That's why he has no memory. Hours later, Reilly mentally capitulated: "Well, it really looks like I did it." Later still, Reilly fully embraced the guilty hypothesis he was persuaded to accept: "I remember slashing once at my mother's throat with a straight razor I used for model airplanes. . . . I also remember jumping on my mother's legs."

Reilly spent a little over a year in prison. Connecticut-based playwright Arthur Miller— the same Arthur Miller who wrote *The Crucible* and *Death of a Salesman*—mobilized a rescue effort. Others followed. Then independent evidence revealed that Reilly could not have committed the murder and that the confession even he came to believe was false. Reilly was released and never retried.

On September 29, 1973, eighteen-year-old Peter Reilly found his mother lying in a pool of blood in their home. She was the only parent he ever had. After Connecticut State Police led him to believe that he had failed a polygraph, Reilly said, "I definitely did what happened to my mother last night." Reilly was found guilty at trial, but his conviction was soon overturned, and he was released. *Photo licensed from Alamy Images.*

One witness reported seeing Timothy and Michael Parmalee, brothers who lived next door, run out the front door that night. Another witness came forward to say that Tim Parmalee, whom this witness lived with, had confessed to her (his fingerprint was also lifted from the back door of the Reillys' house). Police badgered this witness with a polygraph and threatened to charge *her* with perjury. To this day, no one has been charged.

I have to take a moment to digress. Thirty years after Reilly's release, in 2006, I invited him, along with author Don Connery, who wrote about his case, to visit my psychology-and-law class at Williams College in western Massachusetts. It was about a two-hour drive from his home in Connecticut.

We had never met before. He and I are about the same age, but of course his life was knocked off course in a way that mine was not. He was accused of murder while I was applying to graduate school. He had since bounced from one odd job to another, was married and divorced, left the state and then returned. Understandably, he was bitter—not only about what police and prosecutors did to him but that they never later owned up to their mistake.

Reilly's visit to my class was riveting. For me, in the 1970s, his experience proved eye-opening for what it showed about lawful misuses of the polygraph and internalized false confessions—an unimaginable concept I had not conceived of until 1985. His story became the prototype of other internalized false confessions that followed. Meeting him and watching his emotional scars opened up in a classroom, thirty years later, was a whole other more personal experience.

Peter and I have spoken recently by phone. He still lives in rural Connecticut, just a few miles from the university in Storrs where I went to graduate school. At the height of the coronavirus pandemic, we were both laying low. Together, he and I fondly recalled the historic appearance of the Beatles on the *Ed Sullivan Show* and the effect it had on our love of music and bands like the Grateful Dead. I play piano, badly these days; he plays guitar in three or four rock bands. He was still in close touch with Don Connery. In January of 2021, Connery died at the age of ninety-four.

This post-test interview gambit in which police pit allegedly infallible scientific charts against a suspect's memory is common and continues to this day—and it works on all types of suspects, young and old.

"You can't argue with medical evidence," suspects are told. "This is science."

In one particularly pernicious case, in 1996, Christopher Tapp of Idaho Falls was coerced into a false confession to the murder of Angie Dodge after sixty hours of interrogations. During that time, police staged seven sham polygraph exams and told Tapp that he failed each one. In each instance, the objective was to bring his story more into line with newly discovered evidence. In 2019, Tapp's conviction was vacated when DNA identified the killer through a genetic genealogy site.

Over the years, I have referred many such cases, which resulted in wrongful convictions, to Charles Honts, a psychophysiologist and lead-ing polygraph expert at Boise State University (he worked on Tapp's vacated conviction). Sometimes Professor Honts has been critical of how a test was administered; often he has found that negative police feedback was false—that a numerical scoring of the charts revealed a passing grade, not a failure.

Countermeasures: Polygrapher's Nemesis or Paranoia?

There's yet another complication to the myth that polygraph exams offer a golden pipeline to lie detection. The complication has to do with the possibility that suspects use *countermeasures* to defeat or distort a polygraph test.

Countermeasures can be mental (like counting backward by sevens to force an "arousing" level of concentration during control questions), or physical (like pressing your toes or biting your tongue, also to in-crease arousal during control questions). In a classic 1994 experiment, Honts and his collaborator John Kircher trained research subjects first to identify control questions (the baseline non-crime questions) and then to use countermeasures that pump up their physiological arousal to those questions. By raising the baseline in this way, the added arousal elicited by the crime-relevant questions is muted. Among subjects trained in countermeasures, 59 percent defeated the test—and examin-ers found it difficult to detect their usage.

In May of 2017, I gave a guest lecture on false confessions to an advanced undergraduate class at John Jay College. Afterward, a young African American woman named Kayla came up to me to ask if we could talk. After the room cleared, she told me, tearfully, about a recent experience. She was raised, an only child, by her mother in Brooklyn and was enrolled in the college's Honors Program. She was as bright as can be. Her career goal was to become an FBI agent.

Earlier in the year, she had applied for a summer internship at the FBI. She submitted her transcript and résumé and filled out the necessary security-clearance forms. To her delight, she received a call for an in-person interview. That's what she wanted to talk about. "The circumstances of my interrogation differ greatly from the cases you talked about during class," she said. "However, the experience, I can assure you, was just as traumatic."

Kayla and I met privately in my office. At that point, she let it all out. She had appeared on time for the interview only to learn that she would be administered a polygraph exam. "I was held for a marked period of time and strapped to a chair with numerous sensors," she recalled. Several minutes into the test, the examiner stopped, fell silent, and asked if she was using countermeasures. The answer was no, and Kayla said so. The examiner continued to query her, and she repeatedly denied trying to cheat the test in any way. Eventually, the examiner's question morphed into an accusation. The test was over, she said, and Kayla would no longer be under consideration for the internship.

The examiner suggested the possibility of a retest. But first Kayla had to admit to using countermeasures. The examiner pulled out a confessional statement and she signed it. She recanted moments later. "I lost something precious that I will never attain again: my dream of being an FBI agent," she said. "My chances have been obliterated since I signed a confession. I have many unanswered questions that I feel you have the answers to. If you'd be willing to sit down and talk with me, it would be greatly appreciated."

Kayla's story puzzled me. Why would a polygraph examiner accuse a nineteen-year-old woman, a college honors student, of trying to cheat on a test she had no reason to fear? And then why would that examiner trick her into signing a confession that barred her from an internship and now stains her government file? Nothing about this story made sense until I learned that polygraph examiners are hypersensitive to this issue because research shows—and they know it—that countermeasures work and that they cannot identify their usage. Add this to the list of limitations with polygraphic lie detection.

To digress a bit more, I am pleased to report that Kayla now is very much on track. She took her experience and converted it into a master's thesis. For one full year, in collaboration with two other graduate students, she ran a laboratory study in which an experimenter purportedly administered a polygraph examination and then accused subjects of using countermeasures to beat the test. After subjects denied the accusation, the experimenter randomly delivered positive feedback ("Based on what you're saying and your behavior, I think you are being honest") or negative feedback ("Based on your behavior, I don't think you are being honest") and continued to press.

Kayla was curious to know: How would outside observers view the subject in these situations? Would they take their cues from the interviewer? The answer was yes. Independent observers who later watched negative- rather than positive-feedback videos believed that the subject had used countermeasures and then lied about it. As I write, Kayla's goal is to apply to PhD and PsyD programs in forensic and clinical psychology.

HISTORICAL CONTEXT: LIE DETECTION IN POLICING

Up through the 1930s, American police occasionally deployed "third-degree" methods of interrogation to extract confessions. They used *physical violence* (punching, kicking, or mauling suspects, or hitting them with a rubber hose or phone book, which seldom left marks); *torture* (simulating suffocation by holding a suspect's head in water, or putting lighted cigars or pokers against his body); *deprivations* (denials of sleep, food, water, and bathroom breaks); and extreme *sensory discomfort* (for example, forcing a suspect to stand chained to a wall for hours). According to the Wickersham Commission Report of 1931, these barbaric tactics were "widespread throughout the country."

Shortly thereafter, the U.S. Supreme Court began to refuse third-degree confessions as a way to deter these practices. In Brown v. Mississippi, in 1936, a case that concerned three black tenant farmers, accused of killing a white farmer, who were whipped, pummeled, and tortured until they provided detailed confessions, the court unanimously reversed all three convictions and held that confessions obtained through physical abuse and torture were coerced, not voluntary. Not only were such confessions not to be trusted, as the Supreme Court had previously ruled, but they also violated the due process clause of the Constitution.

With third-degree confessions no longer accepted in court, police had to shift to methods that were more psychologically oriented. To meet this challenge, a first generation of interrogation manuals came to market. In 1940, Berkeley police lieutenant W. R. Kidd published a pocket-sized book titled *Police Interrogation*, specifically aimed to professionalize police work. In 1942, Reid and Inbau published *Lie Detection and Criminal Interrogation*, in which they sought to establish a scientific approach, beginning with use of the polygraph. Other books followed, including Harold Mulbar's *Interrogation* (1951) and Charles O'Hara's *Fundamentals of Criminal Investigation* (1956, currently authored by Devere Woods and in its ninth edition), and Arther and Caputo's *Interrogation for Investigators* (1959).

It is within this context that Fred Inbau and John Reid took center stage. Born in New Orleans, Inbau graduated from Tulane University Law School. He then moved to Chicago, where he directed Northwestern University's Scientific Crime Detection Laboratory, later bought by the Chicago Police Department. While there, he promoted the polygraph as a lie-detection tool and met Reid, who joined the lab in 1940. He spent most of this career as a law professor at Northwestern. A staunch law enforcement advocate, and a critic of Miranda, Inbau urged police to use all manners of deception to get confessions. When he died in 1998, the *New York Times* wrote that "he helped elevate trickery and deceit to a high art of police interrogation."

John Reid got his law degree from DePaul University. In 1936, he joined the Chicago Police Department, then accepted a position in its Scientific Crime Detection Laboratory. Reid trained there with Inbau as a polygraph examiner, used it in his work, and testified often as a polygraph expert. In 1947, he founded John E. Reid & Associates, a company that trains more interrogators—including police detectives, private security guards, and the military—than any other company in the world. Reid died in 1982.

In 1962, Inbau and Reid published *Criminal Interrogations and Confessions*, which described their approach in 214 pages. They revised this manual in 1967, in light of the Supreme Court's ruling on Miranda rights. They revised it again in 1986, 2001, and 2013, with Joseph Buck-

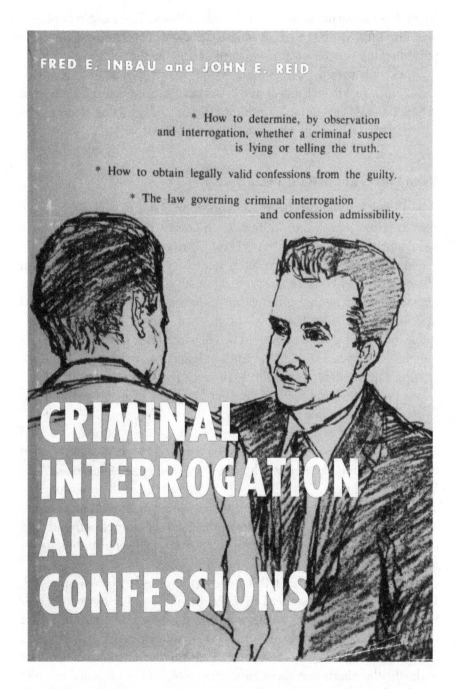

FRED E. INBAU and JOHN E. REID

* How to determine, by observation and interrogation, whether a criminal suspect is lying or telling the truth.

* How to obtain legally valid confessions from the guilty.

* The law governing criminal interrogation and confession admissibility.

CRIMINAL INTERROGATION AND CONFESSIONS

Fred Inbau and John Reid established John Reid & Associates in 1947 in Chicago. Training investigators in the Reid technique, they published this first edition of their popular handbook in 1962. *Photo courtesy of the author.*

ley and Brian Jayne as third and fourth authors. The most recent edition, the fifth, is 469 pages in length (at a lower price, they have also published briefer "Essentials" versions of the manual).

Buckley is president of Reid & Associates. He graduated from college with a major in English and holds a master of science degree in "Detection of Deception" from the Reid College (this degree was awarded to graduates of a six-month course of instruction).

Twin Pillars of the Reid Technique

When I saw Joe Buckley brush off a question about false confessions by asserting that "we do not interrogate innocent people," I had already lost count of the number of times I had heard that line uttered.

To appreciate this remark, it is necessary to understand the twin pillars of the Reid technique. First, a person of interest is identified for questioning in a neutral information-gathering interview largely rooted in Inbau and Reid's 1940s use of the polygraph. This is called the Behavioral Analysis Interview (BAI). The aim of this process is to determine if the suspect is telling the truth or lying. To do this, the interviewer asks nonthreatening and subtly provocative questions and then observes not just what a suspect says but how they look and sound while saying it—the so-called behavioral symptoms of deception.

This is a calm, non-accusatory process. A suspect can be questioned anywhere—at home, in the office, or on a park bench. If this happens in the police station, the door to the interview room can be left open. The flow and rhythm at this stage tends to be one-sided: The interviewer asks unstructured questions aimed to get the suspect to do most of the talking. In the process, the interviewer tries to schmooze, befriend, and establish a rapport, gaining the suspect's trust for the confrontation that may follow.

When I first read about this two-step approach, I was impressed. How careful and deliberate, I thought, to vet potential suspects rather than haphazardly tossing everyone into a full-blown interrogation. But then I examined the BAI alongside decades of research on people's ability to distinguish truth and deception. And then I took a closer look at the off-the-charts accuracy claims Reid & Associates was making, and I realized that a vetting process is great if it can truly separate the truth tellers from the liars. But if it does not make detectives more accurate, while filling them with false confidence, well, that can unleash the most fatal of outcomes.

Beware of the BAI. Throughout their manuals, Reid & Associates assert that these so-called body language indicators are based in science. They assert that they can train investigators to become highly exacting human lie detectors. These claims are not valid. In fact, research shows that the BAI codifies commonsense *mis*conceptions and is wildly *out of step* with the science. They are aware of this research.

There are two reasons why a hunch-masked-as-science judgment at Step 1 can set an investigation off course, often with devastating consequences. First, when detectives who fancy themselves human lie detectors are convinced that a suspect is lying or is telling the truth, that initial judgment becomes a pivotal choice-point in the life of that case. The "truthful" suspect is sent home; the "deceptive" suspect is held and advanced to Step 2—interrogation.

What's worse, it means that the process of interrogation becomes by its very nature guilt-presumptive and hell-bent on confession. Here's my formal definition, as published in the *American Psychologist*: "A guilt-presumptive process is a theory-driven social interaction led by an authority figure who holds a strong a priori belief about the target and who measures success by his or her ability to extract a confession."

The consequence of this mindset is that a detective—now tunnel-visioned by a strongly held belief—will unwittingly ask leading and provocative questions, reject the suspect's denials, and ratchet up the pressure, in turn making the suspect more anxious and the detective more determined to get a confession. This chain of events can create a feedback loop known as a self-fulfilling prophecy.

Reid-trained investigators cringe at the term "guilt-presumptive" and insist that the goal of interrogation is not to produce a confession but to get at the truth. My first response to that defense is to note that the title of the manual exposes their ultimate purpose: Criminal Interrogation *and Confessions*. As for aiming to get at the truth, as an objective fact finder might do, that ship had sailed with the unvalidated claim that the BAI produces high levels of accuracy, and the manual's advice that "the successful interrogator must possess a great deal of inner confidence in his ability to detect truth or deception." This appeal to closed-mindedness is unfounded and dangerous. This too is basic psychology.

For suspects who do not survive the BAI, Step 2 is the infamous nine-stage Reid technique of interrogation. This is where the detective launches into accusations, trickery, and deceit, all aimed at extracting a full confession. Although an interview can be conducted anywhere, the suspect of an interrogation should be isolated in a private, bare, windowless room, preferably soundproofed—a "controlled environment" free of all distractions.

Anyone who questions the guilt-presumptive nature of this process need only run down the list of tactics the Reid-trained interrogator is taught to use, starting with (1) the positive confrontation, a no-nonsense accusation of guilt, then (2) psychological "themes" that justify or excuse the crime the suspect is presumed to have committed, and (3) interrupting the suspect's denials and protestations of innocence. Several years ago, I spent $500 on a training CD produced by Reid to show to my class. At one point, to punctuate the necessity to prevent a suspect's denials, Buckley said: "If you let him talk, he'll tell you he didn't do it. And the more often he says I didn't do it the more difficult it becomes to get a confession." If these first three steps do not reveal the closed-mindedness that comes with a presumption of guilt, I don't know what does.

I'll return to the minutiae of the nine steps of interrogation in chapter 4. For now, let's ponder the friendly pre-interrogation interview, the underlying psychology, and the vetting accuracy with which it separates offenders and innocents.

From the Charts to Behavioral Analysis: Reid's Misstep

In 1905, Sigmund Freud, the founder of psychoanalysis, famously said: "No mortal can keep a secret. If his lips are silent, he chatters with his fingertips; betrayal oozes out of him at every pore." Freud, beware: in 1991, David Simon published his bestselling book *Homicide: A Year on the Killing Streets*. After shadowing homicide detectives in Baltimore, he captured the essence of the problem with this approach: "Nervousness, fear, confusion, hostility, a story that changes or contradicts itself—all are signs that the man in an interrogation room is lying, particularly in the eyes of someone as naturally suspicious as a detective. Unfortunately, these are also signs of a human being in a state of high stress."

The polygraph exam is premised on the age-old theory that lying provokes anxiety that can be measured through bodily arousal. One can't "see" internal changes to a suspect's blood pressure, respiration, or electrodermal response; that's where the instrumentation comes in. John Reid's insistence on a control-question test that compares responses to crime-relevant and arousing non-crime questions was a giant step forward. But then, as if he had Freud's quote ringing in his head, he took a wrong turn. John Reid & Associates has been doubling down on this mistake ever since.

Reid's wrong turn was to expand his analysis—to consider not only objective physiological responses, but snap judgments based on observable behavior—the so-called behavioral symptoms. This is the touchstone of the BAI: clinical hunches masquerading as science. In one fell swoop, John Reid, a law school graduate, self-educated in matters of behavioral science, anointed himself a mind reader. This new focus can be traced to a paper he wrote in 1953 with his protégé Richard Arther. The paper was titled "Behavior Symptoms of Lie-Detector Subjects."

In that paper, Reid and Arther reported on opinions they formed at their Chicago PD laboratory. Over the course of five years, Reid and Arther observed subjects' behavior and took notes, which they inserted into the case files. Then they compared their perceptions of subjects whose guilt or innocence was later verified. Through these comparisons, they determined that a suspect's guilt can be observed while administering the polygraph. "Once in the examining room, the guilty person looks very worried . . . having an extremely dry mouth, continually sighing or yawning, refusing to look the examiner in the eye, and moving about." And fasten your seat belt for this diagnostic insight on he who lies: "Sometimes he is too friendly or too polite."

As a trained behavioral scientist, this methodology leaves me shaking my head. Let's start with this: Reid and Arther "verified" for themselves which suspects were actually guilty and which were innocent—not based on objective and independent evidence but on whether the suspect had confessed after the polygraph exam! In light of what we know today about false confessions, and especially the fact that countless suspects made false confessions after receiving negative polygraph feedback, the carousel-like logic of using "confession" as a proxy for guilt should be self-evident.

This problem is especially acute in the venue of polygraph examinations. Reid and Arther tested suspects whose case files were already known to them. Whether they realized it or not, they formed hypotheses, expectancies, and beliefs. Then they constructed the test questions, conducted all facets of the interview, observed the "behavioral symptoms," read the polygraph charts, and rendered a diagnosis, which they often communicated to the suspect. And then, lo and behold, they perceived their two self-created groups differently.

In psychological research, the need for "blind" testing is basic—and has been ever since Robert Rosenthal published his work on experimenter expectancy effects. In a classic 1963 study, Rosenthal and Kermit L. Fode asked two groups of students to train albino rats to run a maze. Some students were told their rat was bred to be "bright"; others were told that their rat was bred to be "dull" (in fact, all rats were drawn from the same population). The results showed that the so-called bright rats learned the mazes more quickly. Somehow, the students had influenced the performance of these animals, depending on what they were led to expect.

A few years later, Rosenthal, along with Lenore Jacobson, published *Pygmalion in the Classroom*, a study in which they told elementary school teachers at the start of a school year that certain students were on the verge of an intellectual growth spurt. These "select" students were actually chosen at random. Yet by the end of the year, they had outperformed their peers on academic tests. Whether training rats or teaching students, people unwittingly act upon their beliefs in ways that produce a self-fulfilling prophecy.

The experimenter expectancy effect is why research psychologists routinely ensure that any experimenter they use to code people's behaviors must be "blinded," not informed, about the individuals they are coding. To ensure that an experimenter's perceptions are not purely subjective, research psychologists also try to ensure that at least two individuals independently code the behaviors in question. In this way, their perceptions can be compared and the "interrater reliability" of their codings can be calculated. No coding of a behavior—whether it's a smile, frown, facial gesture, or eye contact—is worth a damn if different examiners disagree.

To appreciate why this need for blind testing is essential to the polygraph business, consider this published study out of Israel. Eitan

Elaad asked polygraph examiners from the Israeli Police Force to evaluate and interpret charts previously deemed inconclusive. By random assignment, some examiners were told that the suspect had ultimately confessed; others were not presented with this contextual detail. Sure enough, those in the confession condition rated ambiguous charts as significantly more deceptive than those in the control condition.

Other research has exposed the same type of result when it comes to interpreting nonverbal behavior. In one study, Timothy Levine and his colleagues led observers to believe that a speaker they were watching was either lying or telling the truth. When later asked about that speaker's behavior, these observers overestimated the amount of gaze aversion the liar had actually displayed. It's an old but still true adage in psychology. Ambiguous information is like an inkblot: people see in it what they expect to see.

At the time, John Reid leaped uninformed into a domain of psychology that was not yet fully formed. His methods were flawed, his results could not be trusted, and most professional polygraphers have since distanced themselves from the analysis of behavioral symptoms. We now know that lie detection in the criminal justice domain can have foreseeable and catastrophic consequences—not just for the average cop, but for the likes of John Reid himself.

In a must-read 2013 article published in the *New Yorker*, Douglas Starr told the true story of a high-profile case with a twist. In 1955, in Lincoln, Nebraska, twenty-five-year-old Darrel Parker stopped at home for lunch one day, only to find his wife, Nancy, bound, raped, and strangled in their bed.

Several days later, police asked the distraught Parker to help with the investigation. When he arrived, he was taken to a windowless interrogation room where a polygraph examiner from Chicago hooked him up to the apparatus and asked questions. Each time Parker denied knowledge or involvement, the examiner, watching the movement of needles on a paper chart, would tell Parker he was lying. This back-and-forth soon morphed into a full-blown interrogation. After nine hours, Parker confessed. He recanted the next day but a jury found him guilty of first-degree murder. The polygraph examiner who so artfully elicited this polygraph-induced confession was John Reid. Starr notes that Reid's work on this case boosted his reputation and brought business to his company.

Fast-forward to 1970. Parker appealed his conviction on the ground that his confession was coerced. The U.S. Supreme Court agreed and granted Parker a new trial. In response, the state of Nebraska agreed to parole him for time served. Then in 1988, an inmate named Wesley Peery died in a Nebraska prison—but not before he confessed to killing Nancy Parker (Peery was an early suspect, questioned and released; he went on to reoffend, committing an armed robbery, a rape, and a murder). In 1991, Parker was pardoned; in 2011, the state's attorney general, Jon Bruning, publicly apologized and blamed Parker's false confession on John Reid's "questionable high-pressure tactics that led to numerous false confessions." Parker was granted $500,000 in damages. "Under coercive circumstances," Bruning said, "he confessed to a crime he did not commit."

"BEHAVIORAL ANALYSIS INTERVIEW": OLD HUNCHES MASKED AS SCIENCE

Today's BAI is an offshoot of Reid's earlier work. When polygraph charts indicating physiological arousal are numerically scored, the process, though controversial, offers some semblance of objectivity and increased accuracy. The analysis of *behavioral* symptoms, however, has been repudiated by today's better-informed polygraph community.

Still, this approach is alive and well in the pop-psych paperback world with titles like *Spy the Lie* and *How to Tell When Someone Is Lying to You*. It's also still alive and well at the Reid group. For the interested reader, I would recommend Buckley's 2012 commentary titled "Detection of Deception Researchers Need to Collaborate with Experienced Practitioners."

In support of the claim that training in the BAI can produce exceedingly high levels of accuracy, Reid & Associates like to cite a single fatally flawed study published in 1994 in which Frank Horvath and his Reid-affiliated colleagues selected sixty interview tapes from their home office collection, the ground truths of which could not be established with certainty. Then they edited the tapes in a manner that was not specified, showed these edited tapes to four experienced in-house staff employees of their training, and concluded from their judgments that the Reid technique produced high levels of accuracy. What's worse, no comparison group of untrained or lay evaluators was tested to ensure that BAI training had anything to do with the accuracy rates obtained.

The BAI contains two components: (1) a set of *questions* aimed at provoking different verbal responses from guilty and innocent suspects, and (2) a set of *behavioral symptoms* that interviewers should observe that indicate leakage of truth versus deception.

Behavior-Provoking Questions

The BAI protocol consists of fifteen or sixteen special questions. According to the fourth edition of the Inbau manual, "Research has demonstrated that innocent subjects tend to respond differently to these specialized questions than do deceptive subjects." No publications, peer reviewed or otherwise, were cited for this statement. So what are these special questions—and what evidence supports the proposition that a suspect's answers to them can be used to differentiate between offenders and innocents?

The query begins with a question about the *purpose* of the interview. This is followed by a *history* question that the investigator asks: "Did you have anything to do with this crime?" According to the manual, "this direct question often catches the deceptive suspect off guard" and sets off nonverbal alarm bells like crossing legs. Whereas the innocent person emphatically denies involvement, saying, "No way, I had absolutely nothing to do with it," the offender says, "Honest to God, I didn't—I swear." Just so you know, I have pulled these quotes right out of the manual. I would imagine that this question at the outset will catch the innocent suspect as off guard as the offender and set off the same nonverbal alarm bells. And why exactly is the "Honest to God" denial less emphatic than the "No way"? If you're confused, welcome to the club.

The list also includes crime-specific questions about *knowledge* ("Do you know who did this?"), *opportunity* ("Who would've had the best opportunity to do this if they wanted to?"), *motive* ("Why do you think someone did this?"), *punishment* ("What do you think should happen to the person who did this?"), and a *second chance* ("Do you think the person who did this should be given a second chance?"). For each question, Reid & Associates has determined that offenders, as opposed to innocents, will bob and weave; feign ignorance of all facets of the crime, who might have committed it, and why; and waver on the question of punishment and forgiveness.

In principle, it is entirely possible that the content of a suspect's answers to select questions can distinguish offenders and innocents. Over the years, I have written extensively about what I call the "phenomenology of innocence," the idea that innocent people exhibit no consciousness of guilt and, therefore, an openness to disclosure. This fact should provide a basis for a set of diagnostic questions—starting with: Would you be willing to waive your Miranda rights, or take a lie-detector test? Data from the lab and the field show clearly that innocent suspects are naïvely more willing to waive their Miranda rights—and other rights, too. That's a good start.

As for the BAI, there is no evidence that answers to these behavior-provoking questions are diagnostic. In a 2006 study that targeted this question, Aldert Vrij, a professor of social psychology, and his colleagues, assigned some subjects, but not others, to steal money from a wallet in a busy public setting. In this way, they knew for sure who was guilty and who was innocent. Financially incentivized to evade detection, these subjects were then interviewed using the Reid protocol. Analyses of these interviews revealed that responses to the behavior-provoking questions did not, as predicted, distinguish between truth tellers and liars.

Behavioral Symptoms Analysis

To this day, Reid & Associates touts their training in human lie detection. Their instructors travel the country offering workshops to law enforcement officers, loss-prevention managers, security guards, school administrators, and anyone else willing to pay for them.

In these workshops, and accompanying manuals, police are let in on the secret that deception can reveal itself nonverbally. Beware of deception, trainees are told, when a person appears too nonchalant, looks down, looks away, looks right, looks left, stares, blinks too much or not enough, freezes in his chair, slouches, slumps, shrugs, turns to the side, folds his arms, clenches his hands, crosses his legs, leans away, fidgets, squirms, sweats, hesitates to respond, or flashes a muscle twitch in the face. As one detective facetiously put it, "You can tell if a suspect is lying by whether he is moving his lips."

Over the years, I have funded and sent doctoral students from my lab to get trained in the Reid technique when its two-day course came to New York. Each and every one has returned in shaken disbelief over the claims made. "I thought my head was going to explode," said one former student who is now a psychology professor.

My students react with disbelief because they know that fifty-plus years of research in laboratories all over the world shows that laypeople are incompetent at lie detection; that trained professionals are only slightly better, if at all—though they are far more confident; that there are no behavioral cues, like Pinocchio's growing wooden nose, that reliably signal deception; and that an 85 to 90 percent accuracy claim would substantially exceed human lie detection performance achieved anywhere, ever, under controlled conditions.

To date, hundreds of experiments involving thousands of human subjects have tested people's ability to spot lies. In all of this research, one group of subjects makes statements known to be truthful or deceptive, while another group reads the transcripts, listens to audiotapes or watches videotapes, and then tries to judge the statements. Consistently, results show that people are only about 54 percent accurate in judging truth and deception.

Let's pause for a moment to assess what this means. Fifty-four percent may not sound dangerously low, but these are binary judgments, which means you can score at 50 percent just by guessing or flipping a coin. As to why people barely if at all exceed chance performance, research exposes two problems: (1) people tend to accept what others say at face value—a tendency referred to as "truth bias," and more importantly, (2) the cues people use to determine that someone is lying are *only weakly or not at all* diagnostic of lying.

The average Joe can't distinguish truths and lies, but what about experts specially trained to make these judgments for a living? When it comes to a nonskilled task like this, apparently, practice does not make perfect. In the first study of its kind, published in 1991, psychologists Paul Ekman and Maureen O'Sullivan administered to professional groups the kinds of materials used in testing laypeople. In light of the high-stakes judgments these professionals make, the results were jarring. Compared to college students, who averaged 53 percent (pretty much the baseline in the lay population), police investigators were at 56 percent, and so were polygraph examiners. Trial judges were at 57 percent and psychiatrists at 58 percent. At the top end, U.S. Secret Service agents averaged 65 percent (a result that has not since been replicated). What's worse, subjects rated themselves as confident regardless of whether they were accurate. They didn't know what they didn't know.

The problem, it turns out, is simple: the facial expressions and body language cues that people use do not actually signal deception, or the signal is so faint it is not practically useful in making individualized judgments. Here's a terrific illustration of the problem. In a survey of over 2,500 adults in fifty-eight countries, an international team of researchers found that roughly 70 percent of respondents believed that liars tend to avert their eyes—and that this was the best "tell."

That seems to be the common sense. Yet many researchers, over the years, have painstakingly coded the behavior of speakers as they lied or told the truth. When social psychologist Bella DePaulo statistically combined the results of 116 studies, she found that looking away, breaking eye contact, or averting a gaze, however you describe it, is not associated with deception any more than it is with truth telling. It's a common misconception, a myth still touted in the business. In fact, DePaulo found no support for other pop-psych BAI claims that people squirm, stutter, fidget, shift their posture, slouch, turn to the side, fold their arms, or groom themselves when they lie (for other comprehensive overviews, see Timothy Luke's *Lessons from Pinocchio* and Aldert Vrij's *Detecting Lies and Deceit*).

The literature on behavioral lie detection consists of hundreds of studies conducted by multiple researchers, using different methods and testing different subject populations all over the world. In science, this constitutes strong proof of convergent validity. Yet advocates of the Reid technique argue that the lab experiments are poorly constructed, not forensic enough, and not engaging enough. Besides, none of the subjects in these other studies were specially trained.

I sought to put this alleged limitation to the test. In 1999, Christina Fong and I recruited student subjects and asked them to sign an informed consent to participate in a project in which they might be asked to commit a mock crime. Once we lined up sixteen brave and willing souls, we randomly assigned each student to commit—or not commit—

one of four mock crimes: vandalism (pick up a piece of colored chalk, scrawl an obscene message on a campus building, drop the chalk, and leave), shoplifting (enter a local gift shop, steal jewelry or a stuffed animal, and walk out), breaking and entering (climb through the window of a campus building that houses answer sheets to an exam, which will set off an alarm), and computer hacking (on a terminal in a computer lab, log into a specific account and read a confidential email). Afterward, a uniformed security guard would apprehend them leaving the scene; this same guard would apprehend innocent subjects, too, once they arrived.

This was not a comfortable situation for anyone. The sixteen suspects were forewarned that they would be arrested and questioned about their activities—and that they should deny involvement. Their interviewer, they were correctly told, will know what crime was committed but not whether they were guilty or innocent. To incentivize their interview denials, we told all suspects that if the interviewer determines that they are guilty, they will be escorted across campus to Security and detained for a period of time. If he believes they are innocent, they will receive a five-dollar bonus and immediate release.

Enter "Detective McCarthy," a forty-eight-year-old financial advisor, white, clean shaven, dressed in civilian clothing, and holding a clipboard containing a Miranda rights form, interview questions, and a confession to be signed. After the suspect had waited five minutes, he entered the small interview room minimally furnished with two straight-back chairs and a table, a one-way mirror facing the suspect, and a clock on the wall behind the suspect. McCarthy formally introduced himself, turned on the camera and microphone, Mirandized the suspect, and proceeded to ask open-ended questions before refusing to accept the suspect's denials and making an accusation. Each session closed with McCarthy's request that the suspect sign a confession, and the suspect's refusal to do so.

When these sessions were completed, we were armed with sixteen videotapes that depicted brief interviews and denials by research subjects who were truly guilty or innocent of committing one of four mock crimes. We took these tapes to a neighboring town and recruited a new group of adult subjects to watch and render judgment. But first we presented the Reid technique training video on behavioral symptoms analysis, which I had purchased, to half of these observers, accompanied by the written course materials. We then tested their proficiency to ensure that they learned the content. The other half were not similarly trained; they were left to their own intuition.

Each subject watched eight interviews—four showing suspects who were guilty of each crime and four who were innocent of those same crimes. As in past studies in non-forensic settings, observers were not proficient at differentiating between truthful and deceptive suspects any better than would be expected by chance. But the differences between groups were even more telling. On average, naïve control subjects were 56 percent accurate, consistent with most studies. On a ten-point scale, their average level of confidence was 5.91. In contrast, Reid-trained subjects were less accurate at 46 percent and more confident at 6.55. When asked about what cues they used, Reid-trained subjects listed more cues, most of which they derived from the training. Putting the pieces together, we found that Reid training in behavioral symptoms analysis made people more confident and more articulate—but less accurate.

Perhaps this study was limited by the fact that the observers were laypeople, not law enforcement agents, whose training was condensed, not part of professional development. Can professionals better distinguish between the denials of guilty and innocent suspects? To find out, Professor Christian Meissner and I presented the exact same videos to forty-four North American police investigators. The results revealed a trifecta of risk to the innocent: (1) The police accuracy rate was 50 percent, the equivalent of a coin flip; (2) the police were more confident than anyone else we had tested; and (3) they were more likely to mistake truths for lies than the other way around. It's no wonder Darrel Parker, in 1955, didn't stand a chance when John Reid polygraphed and interrogated him into prison for a crime he did not commit.

THE STATE OF THE SCIENCE, FOR ANYONE WILLING TO LISTEN

Throughout history, people have assumed that the way to spot liars is to watch for outward signs of anxiety leakage. To be sure, crime perpetrators feel more nervousness than innocent suspects about being grilled. Yet in important real-life situations—from a high-stakes poker table, to the TSA screening area of an airport, and onto the hot seat in a police interrogation room—innocent truth tellers will also exhibit behavioral signs of stress.

Reporting on his experience at Reid training, Douglas Starr recalled that his instructor asked the group at one point, What's more important—verbal or nonverbal behavior? Intuitively the group chose nonverbal. The instructor's response: "Yeah, that's the whole ballgame right there." Well, he was wrong. This anxiety-leakage approach does not work.

Social psychologists interested in human lie detection have not only dispelled BAI-like myths but have also sought other ways to boost accuracy. To do this, a new theoretical model was needed to replace the ancient obsession with anxiety—which can afflict the leaky liar and truth teller alike. At the University of Portsmouth, Aldert Vrij has suggested an alternative approach: *Cognitive Load Theory*. This theory is built on the fact that it's more difficult to lie than to tell the truth. When you construct a false narrative, and want to be believed, you need to invent a story and then monitor yourself as you speak to make sure it's plausible and consistent with things you've said before—all while trying to *look* believable. For these reasons, lying stretches your cognitive resources thin in ways that truth telling does not.

With this difference in cognitive load as a starting point, Vrij and others reason that anything an interviewer can do to make the task more difficult should disrupt and expose the liar more than the truth teller, in turn, making it easier for observers to discriminate between the two groups. The interviewer's goal, says Vrij, is to challenge suspects and force them to think harder.

In one study, he asked subjects to recount true or false stories either normally or in reverse chronological order. This requirement made truth telling more difficult. But it disrupted lying even more so. As a result, observers who later watched these video presentations were more accurate at distinguishing between truths and lies in the reverse-order condition than in the control condition. Reversing order exposed the liars.

Other experiments have since showed that observers are more accurate at making truth-or-lie judgments when the speakers were forced to maintain eye contact with their interviewer, which was distracting, or when speakers were asked the kinds of unanticipated questions they could not have planned for. The more cognitively challenging the interviewer, the more exposed the liar appears relative to the truth teller.

Another way to outsmart the liar is through the strategic use of evidence, a technique that Maria Hartwig and Pär-Anders Granhag developed at the University of Gothenburg in Sweden. Suppose a wallet is stolen from a briefcase left in a coffee shop and another customer's fingerprints are lifted from that briefcase. That customer is now called in as a suspect in a police investigation. Many interviewers in this situation would walk in, toss the folder of prints onto the table, and confront the suspect. Forewarned, that suspect would be in a position to fabricate a story consistent with this evidence ("I was in the coffee shop at that time, I picked up the briefcase to move it away from my chair").

But what if the interviewer withheld the print evidence while asking the suspect to recount his or her whereabouts? In this situation, the suspect might tell an alibi story that denies any presence in the coffee shop at that time. Boom. Later confronted with the fingerprints, the guilty suspect will have been trapped in the lie. As in the cognitive load studies, observers become more accurate lie detectors when the interviews they watch use the strategic use of evidence technique rather than a flat-out confrontation.

WHAT NEXT?

The BAI is used to divine truths and lies. It is not confrontational; it's often friendly and conversational in tone. In fact, the interview presents an opening opportunity for police to establish a rapport with the suspect. How detectives do this is a matter of style and the situation. They can offer the suspect a cup of coffee, or water; make small talk about sports; establish a common bond ("Hey, I grew up in that neighborhood, too"); or offer up a personal disclosure—which begets a reciprocal disclosure. The key is to make it seem natural and organic, not contrived and tactical.

The point is, establishing a rapport may accompany the BAI, but it is a precursor to the more confrontational process to follow. Friendly as the interview may seem, the stakes are deadly serious. If a detective determines that a suspect is telling the truth, that suspect is sent home. However, if the detective thinks that a suspect is lying, an error made in almost all false-confession cases I've seen, fasten your seat belt. The process of interrogation is about to commence.

4

PSYCHOLOGICAL INTERROGATION

Getting Inside Your Head

In January 2018, at the invitation of Professor Oren Gazal-Ayal, dean at the University of Haifa Law School, I trekked from New York to Israel for a series of lectures, meetings, and conversations with criminal justice officials. Starting behind a law school podium and finishing inside offices at the Supreme Court in Jerusalem, I had a busy week. Three weeks before I was scheduled to arrive, the Israeli newspaper *Haaretz* blared this headline: "Israeli Court Blasts Shin Bet: Interrogation Tactics Led to False Confession."

Well, that's timely, I thought. But before I could read up on this case, my host alerted me to an award-winning Netflix documentary called *Shadow of Truth*. The subject? The murder of Tair Rada, a thirteen-year-old Israeli girl, and a confession by Roman Zadorov, a young Ukrainian immigrant living with his wife and son in the Golan Heights. Released in 2016, and over the course of four episodes, it's a riveting, twisting-and-turning whodunit, if you have the stomach for it.

The story begins with the brutal murder of Tair Rada in a girls' restroom at school. After ten days of police interrogations, Zadorov confessed. The people of Israel and the courts were steeped in controversy. Zadorov was found guilty and was sent to prison, but the victim's mother to this day does not believe he is the killer. Everywhere I traveled within the country, everyone had an opinion. This case arouses intense emotion.

That is what preceded me. Although I had a full schedule lined up, my host asked, "Is there anyone in particular you'd like to meet when you're here?" "Yes," I said. "I would like to meet Avi Shai, the chief of police in the Zadorov case, who appears in the film—oh, and Zadorov's lawyers."

And so I did. I was staying at a beachfront hotel in Haifa, which is less tropical than it sounds in January. Shai was my first meeting, in the lobby. He was open and welcoming. We chatted a bit—small talk, comparing notes about what it's like to be a grandfather. Then with the sound of crashing waves outside the window, the whiff of salt in the air, and espressos in hand, we sparred about the Zadorov case for over two hours.

We sparred over the fact that Zadorov went to the police station to help in the investigation and had no idea he was a suspect until he was arrested and held incommunicado.

We sparred over the fact that Zadorov was interrogated on and off, relentlessly, for ten days. He was not accompanied by a lawyer; he could not see his family.

We sparred over the fact that detectives repeatedly and outright lied to Zadorov about DNA, fingerprints, a polygraph, and other evidence.

We sparred over the fact that when Zadorov wasn't being interrogated he was in a jail cell with an undercover agent posing as a criminal. "Are police allowed to lie about the evidence?" Zadorov asked his confidante. "No. This is not Russia," he assured him. "This is Israel. They're not allowed to lie."

And we sparred about how police guided Zadorov's alleged reenactment when they took him to the scene of the crime and had to steer him when turned the wrong way.

Right away, I could tell this was going to be a fun, insightful, and combative week.

THE PROCESS OF INTERROGATION— SOCIAL PSYCHOLOGY ON STEROIDS

I can still recall like it was yesterday my introduction to the Reid technique. Here's some background. I was born and raised in Brooklyn, then in Rockaway Beach, New York. I am a baby boomer at my core—a child of JFK, the Beatles, the Rolling Stones, Dylan, and Vietnam. I spent three years at Brooklyn College at a cost of fifty-three dollars per semester and graduated in 1974. After publishing over thirty letters to the editor of the city's newspapers while in high school, I thought I'd major in journalism until I discovered psychology—and Stanley Milgram's new, profound, and highly controversial shock experiments on obedience to authority.

Entering my third and final year, Professor Arthur Reber, a cognitive psychologist who pioneered the study of nonconscious or "implicit" learning, invited me to help run an experiment in his lab. What an electrifying experience it was to watch college students, one after another, being influenced without awareness by slides of letter strings we had flashed at them.

Knowing what I wanted to do for a living, I went straight into graduate school at the University of Connecticut, where I got my PhD in 1978. At UConn, I was lucky to have scored as an advisor social psychologist and teacher extraordinaire Charles "Skip" Lowe. Lowe studied attribution theory, which was founded by Vienna-born Fritz Heider, author of the classic 1958 book *The Psychology of Interpersonal Relations*. The subject matter: how people perceive and explain other people's behavior.

From UConn, I moved to Lawrence, Kansas, home of the KU Jayhawks. I went thanks to an offer of a postdoctoral research fellowship with Larry Wrightsman, an eminent social psychologist, newly interested in law, and boundless in curiosity. He also had funding for research on jury decision making—the perfect fit, I thought, for someone like myself, interested in how people make attributions. In the fall of 1978, at twenty-five, I was gearing up to study juries when two things happened.

First, I started to collect data. To run controlled experiments, Wrightsman and his students were searching for moot court videos, transcripts, and case summaries that we could present to mock juries. Ideally, we needed cases that were ambiguous—not slam-dunk convictions or acquittals. As results from pilot testing came in, I could not help but notice that in cases with confessions in evidence, just about every mock juror voted guilty and cited the confession as the reason. No one had ever systematically probed the effects of confession evidence on juries, but this pattern was predictable from Heider's attribution theory so it made sense to me. I will return to this issue in chapter 8.

The second experience arose out a KU law school class I was auditing, on the rules of evidence. If I was going to study criminal trials, I had to know something about evidence and trial procedure. Sandwiched between chapters on direct and cross examination, competence, burdens of proof, hearsay and its exceptions, and the like, was a chapter on confessions. Somewhere in that chapter, I spotted a footnote to Inbau and Reid's *Criminal Interrogations and Confessions*. This being the pre-internet Stone Age, I went to the library and checked out the book. As I read through it, the social psychologist in me was stunned. "Holy shit," I said to myself. "This is like Milgram—but a whole lot worse."

Background Primer on Social Psychology

Although born helpless, human infants are equipped with reflexes that orient them toward people. They are uniquely responsive to human faces, they turn their head toward voices, and they can mimic certain facial gestures on cue. Then within a few weeks, they flash the first smile, to the delight of parents all over the world. The newborn seems an inherently social animal.

Adults too are drawn to each other like magnets to iron. We work, play, and live together, and often make lifetime commitments to grow old together. People need people—which is why we are vulnerable to subtle, reflex-like influences, yawning when we see others yawn and laughing when others laugh. As Roy Baumeister and Mark Leary put it, the need to belong is a "basic human motive," a pervasive drive much like the needs for food, water, and sleep.

That is why people become distressed when they feel neglected, rejected, excluded, stigmatized, or ostracized from a valued group—a form of "social death." It's why people worry so much about their public persona, live and online, that they suffer from social anxiety disorders. And it's why socially connected people are happier, physically healthier, and less likely to die a premature death. The need to connect is about survival.

The consequences of the human social response can be seen everywhere. In one study, paid confederates stopped on a busy street in New

York City, looked up, and gawked at a window of a nearby building. There was nothing to see. Yet a camera stationed behind the window showed that 80 percent of passersby stopped and gazed up, too.

In another study, subjects in a lab were set up to work with a partner who had a habit of rubbing his face or shaking his foot. Hidden cameras revealed what is called "the chameleon effect," as subjects, without realizing it, mimicked these motor behaviors, rubbing their face or shaking a foot to match the partner's behavior.

Of course, sometimes social contagion can prove hazardous, as when people join mobs that spiral into violence, or insurrection, exhibit the symptoms of a "mass psychogenic illness," reenact copycat or hate crimes, or commit suicide while under the influence of a fanatical cult.

People's inherently social nature serves as an implicit and explicit backdrop for understanding interrogation and its devastating range of effects. Classic research shows that the tendency to affiliate with others for social-support purposes is particularly apparent when people are under stress. Sixty years ago, Stanley Schachter theorized that an external threat triggers fear and motivates us to affiliate, particularly with others who face a similar threat. In a laboratory study that demonstrated the point, he led some subjects, but not others, to expect that they would receive painful electric shocks as part of the experiment. He then gave them a choice of waiting alone or with another subject in the same situation. Most chose to be with this other subject even though that other person was a stranger.

It's also clear that people derive physiological benefits from social support. In *Annals of Behavioral Medicine*, Matthew Roberts and others reported on a study in which they directed female college students to immerse one hand into a container of ice water for up to three minutes. Try it, and you'll see that it's painful and not that easy to endure. Throughout the session, blood pressure and heart rates were recorded. Levels of cortisol, a stress hormone, were taken from saliva samples after the session.

Here's the interesting part: Some subjects were accompanied in the room by a supportive fellow student who was actually a paid confederate. Others were accompanied by a neutral confederate or no one at all. The benefits of social support were clear: Subjects who were accompanied by a supportive confederate, relative to all others, reacted with lower blood pressure, a lower heart rate, and lower cortisol reactivity, and they rated the experience as less painful.

It is both axiomatic and empirically well documented that because human beings are inherently social, they are needy if not at times desperate for acceptance and approval. This neediness lurks as a motive that renders us vulnerable to the social influences I will sum up with this acronym: COP (compliance, obedience, persuasion).

Compliance researchers test ways to increase an individual's willingness to succumb to requests for money, votes, personal favors, or a confession. Over the years, Robert Cialdini and other social psychologists have learned from the masters of influence in sales, advertising, and politics, and put their strategies to the test. In *Influence: Science and Practice*, Cialdini described over a hundred colorfully named methods of influence that have been tested—like the *foot-in-the-door technique*, the *door-in-the-face technique*, *lowballing*, the *dump-and-chase technique*, the *but-you-are-free technique*, and the *disrupt-then-reframe technique*.

The foot-in-the-door technique is a particularly relevant example. In sales, folk wisdom has it that one way to get a person to comply with a sizable request is to start small and get your "foot in the door." Break the ice with a small initial request that a customer can't easily refuse, and that customer is more likely to succumb to a second, larger request. Research is unequivocal; the technique works. In the first-ever study of it, in 1966, Freedman and Fraser presented themselves as a consumer-survey company and contacted housewives with an outrageous request: Would you let us bring a handful of workers into your home for two hours to inventory your household products? Not surprisingly, only 22 percent consented. But if the company representative had called three days earlier with a smaller request, for a brief phone survey, the rate of compliance more than doubled, to 53 percent. This basic result has been repeated over and over. People are more likely to donate time, money, food, blood, use of their home, and other resources after first getting roped in with a small initial request.

Whereas compliance research aims at changing behavior, the study of *persuasion* focuses on how to change people's inner beliefs and attitudes. Motivated by the propaganda battles of World War II, Carl Hovland and other social psychologists in the 1940s founded the Yale Communication and Attitude Change Program. Their focus: how to create, frame, customize, and deliver persuasive appeals.

For maximum impact, the goal is to ensure that the message captures the subject's attention, for information-processing purposes, and heightens the subject's motivation. To achieve all of this, the source should come across as knowledgeable and trustworthy, the arguments should be airtight and hard to counter, and the subject should be induced into a receptive frame of mind. Emotional appeals can be particularly potent—especially messages that arouse fear, an early warning system that signals danger in response to pain, threats, and noxious substances. Arousing fear to facilitate persuasion is common—as when certain religious cults use scare tactics to indoctrinate new members. It's also frighteningly effective.

Of all topics in social psychology, the study of *obedience to authority* is the most spot-on relevant to the process of interrogation. Taught from birth to respect legitimate forms of leadership, people are reflexively docile—sometimes to a comical fault. This was demonstrated in an old study titled "The Social Power of a Uniform," in which Leonard Bickman had a male research assistant stop passersby on the street and order them to do something unusual. In some instances, he pointed to a paper bag on the ground and barked, "Pick up this bag for me." At other times, he pointed to an individual standing near a parked car and said, "That guy is overparked at the meter but doesn't have any change. Give him a dime." When the bossy assistant was dressed in street clothes, only a third of bystanders stopped and followed his orders. But when he wore a security guard's uniform, nearly nine out of every ten obeyed.

If people are willing to take orders from a total stranger, one can imagine how far they will go when the figure of authority has power and the stakes are high. Certainly, the pages of history are sobering. From the monstrous events of Nazi Germany, wherein executioners morally disengaged in their own defense ("I was just following orders") to more recent acts at the behest of terrorists, ruthless regimes, and seditious ex-presidents, obedience is a force of human nature to be reckoned with.

Enter Stanley Milgram. In the early 1960s, at the time that Adolf Eichmann stood trial in Jerusalem for Nazi war crimes, Milgram, a young professor at Yale University, commenced a dramatic series of nineteen experiments involving hundreds of adults, mostly men. The first was published in 1963; except for one he did not publish, the rest were reported in his 1974 book *Obedience to Authority.* Milgram did not realize at the time—and neither did his research subjects—that they were about to make history in one of the most famous psychology programs ever conducted.

The first experiment set the tone. Forty men from the New Haven area, aged twenty to fifty, whose jobs ranged from unskilled to professional, answered a newspaper ad offering $4.50 for their time. Once they arrived in the basement laboratory at Linsly-Chittenden Hall, they met two men. One was the experimenter, a stern young professional dressed in a gray lab coat and carrying a clipboard. The other was a middle-aged gentleman named Mr. Wallace, an accountant with a pleasant demeanor who was utterly average in appearance. After quick introductions, the experimenter explained that he was testing the effects of punishment on learning. By supposedly random lots, the sub-

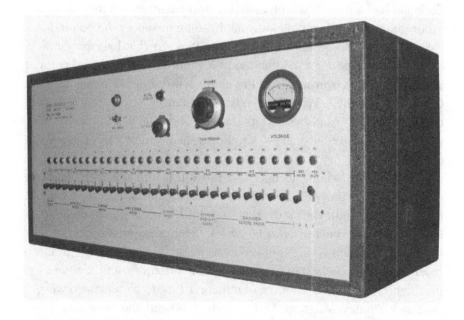

For his classic experiments on obedience to authority, Stanley Milgram created a shock generator with switches ranging from 15V to 450V. This machine still exists and can be seen in the Archives of the History of American Psychology at the University of Akron. *Photo used with permission of Milgram's estate.*

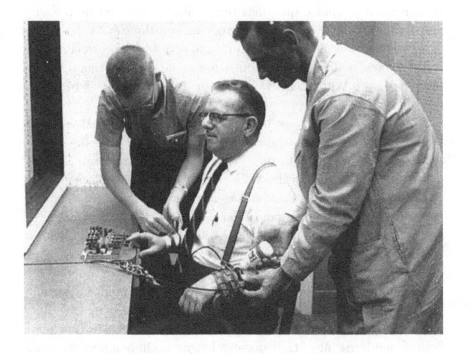

The subjects in Milgram's studies believed they were shocking Mr. Wallace, the man who appeared to be strapped into his chair before each session. *Photo used with permission of Milgram's estate.*

ject was assigned to serve as the teacher and Wallace the learner. So far, so good.

Then the situation took on a more ominous tone. The subject was told this his job was to test the learner's memory and administer electric shocks of increasing intensity whenever he made a mistake. The subject was then escorted into another room, where the experimenter strapped Wallace into a chair, rolled up his sleeves, attached electrodes to his arms, and applied "electrode paste" to prevent blisters and burns. Wallace expressed concern but the experimenter reassured him that although the shocks were painful, they would not cause "permanent tissue damage." The experimenter then took the subject back to the main room and seated him in front of a "shock generator"—a machine with thirty switches that increased from 15 volts, labeled "slight shock," to 450 volts, labeled "XXX."

At that point, the experiment began. First the subject read a list of word pairs to Wallace through a microphone. Next he tested his memory with multiple-choice questions that Wallace answered by pressing one of four switches. After each correct answer, the subject moved on to the next question. After each error, he announced the correct answer and delivered a shock, setting off a menacing buzzing sound in the learner's room. With each wrong answer, the intensity was to be increased by fifteen volts.

Subjects were not aware that the experiment was rigged and that Wallace was a paid confederate who was never shocked. As the session proceeded, however, the learner made more and more errors, leading the subject up the shock scale. At 75, 90, and 105 volts, Wallace grunted in pain. At 120 volts, he shouted. At 150 volts, he cried out, "Experimenter! That's all. Get me out of here. I refuse to go on!" Screams of agony and protest continued. At 330 volts, he fell silent and failed to respond, not to be heard from again.

Along the way, subjects, wary of increasing the shocks, turned to the experimenter for guidance. Many subjects were tormented and pleaded with the experimenter to check in on Wallace. Some of them trembled, stuttered, groaned, bit their lips, and dug their fingernails into their flesh. Some burst into fits of nervous laughter. On one occasion, said Milgram, "we observed a seizure so violently convulsive that it was necessary to call a halt to the experiment."

In response to each and every subject, the experimenter—cold in tone and seemingly unmoved by the learner's distress—systematically prodded subjects to continue, the fourth and final prod being an unambiguous command: "You have no other choice; you must go on."

Milgram described the procedure to psychiatrists and laypeople and asked them to predict how they would behave. On average, these groups estimated that they—and others—would call it quits at the 135-volt level. Not a single person thought they'd escalate to the highest shock. The psychiatrists estimated that only one out of a thousand people would exhibit the full measure of obedience. Everyone was wrong. On average, subjects administered twenty-seven out of thirty possible shocks. Twenty-six subjects out of forty—that's 65 percent—delivered the ultimate punishment of 450 volts.

After this inaugural study, Milgram went on to observe the same pattern of results in an experiment with forty women. Others reported the same basic effect in different populations and in other cultures. No psychologist can fully replicate this study today because of more stringent ethics rules aimed at protecting human subjects. But recent partial efforts have shown that nothing has changed (for overviews, I would recommend Arthur Miller's *The Obedience Experiments* and Thomas Blass's *The Man Who Shocked the World*).

On October 26, 2013, to commemorate the fiftieth anniversary of his classic paper, Yale Law School hosted a one-day conference on the legacy of Stanley Milgram. I was invited to speak; the title of my presentation was "The Role of Situational Forces in Shaping Police-Induced False Confessions." To me, as I noted, the most remarkable aspect of Milgram's findings is that an experimenter in a lab coat is a relatively weak figure of authority. At most, he wielded $4.50 over his subjects. Unlike homicide detectives, military superiors, employers, or school administrators, Milgram's experimenter could not ultimately enforce his commands. And yet subjects surrendered . . . which brings us right into the bowels of the interrogation room.

The Reid Technique: Nine Steps into the Abyss

I don't think it takes a rocket scientist to understand how someone can be broken into submission by having their head shoved into a vat of water, simulating suffocation; or getting smacked repeatedly with a rubber hose, which hurts without leaving visible marks; or being chained to a wall overnight, forced to stand for hours on end. But after the U.S. courts declared in the 1930s that police could no longer extract confessions by third degree, they forced a paradigm shift in police work. Psychological gaslighting tactics were needed instead to get under a suspect's skin and inside the head. Hence the processes of trickery and deceit—coercion replaced by the dupe. The Reid technique was not the only approach used early on—and it's not the only alternative today. But it is the most common and has had a deep-seated influence on law enforcement agencies, whether they are formally trained in it or not. (For a terrific account of the history of interrogations in the United States, I would recommend Richard Leo's 2008 book *Police Interrogation and American Justice*.)

In the two-step approach of the Reid technique, police pivot from interview to interrogation as soon as they decide that their suspect is hiding something. There's no getting around it. This means that interrogation is *by definition* a guilt-presumptive process of influence aimed at producing a confession. As for specifics: the Reid technique calls for one precondition and nine steps, which unleash three processes, all laser-focused on producing one or more admissions of guilt followed by a full confession.

First, the precondition. The interrogator should place the interrogation suspect alone, without friends or family members, into a special room. That room should be small (recommended ten feet on all sides), windowless, preferably soundproofed, and far removed from familiar sights and sounds, people, phones ringing, wall hangings, or other sources of distraction. The room should be furnished with two or three armless straight-backed chairs and a desk. Ideally, the room should contain a one-way mirror, enabling a fellow detective to observe the suspect for signs of fatigue, anxiety, and withdrawal. You may get by in life "with a little help from my friends"—but not in this situation.

Against the backdrop of this isolating physical environment, the Reid interrogator launches into a nine-step attack designed to overcome the suspect's resistance both by punishing denials and rewarding admissions. This attack begins with the "positive confrontation," which means flat-out accusing the suspect, doing so with certainty, and citing incriminating evidence—whether it exists or not (Step 1). The interrogator then develops sympathetic "themes" that help to minimize, morally justify or excuse the crime, or externalize blame (Step 2); interrupts and rejects the suspect's attempts at denial or claims of innocence (Step 3); overcomes the suspect's factual, moral, and emotional objections (Step 4); ensures that the suspect, if seeming dazed, passive, and confused, does not withdraw (Step 5); shows sympathy and understanding and urges the suspect, if showing signs of resignation, to "tell the truth" (Step 6); poses the "alternative question" that offers a choice between a morally reprehensible versus sympathetic explanation for the crime (Step 7); gets the suspect to make an admission of guilt (Step 8); and converts that admission into a fully detailed written or taped confession (Step 9).

Although I have seen hundreds of Reid-inspired interrogations, I've never seen one play out according to the orthodoxy of this sequence of steps. But they all do involve *isolation*, a necessary precondition; the dual processes of *confrontation* and *minimization* aimed at eliciting an admission of guilt; and the *production* of a full narrative confession. Each of these components has been documented in real-life observations and in surveys of police. Each enables police to break a suspect down and shape his behavior, like a lab rat in a Skinner box—whether that suspect committed the crime or not.

As an undergraduate psychology major, I was required to induce a hungry white rat to press a bar attached into the wall of a Skinner box. Once the rat presses the bar, a food pellet is released through a food dispenser tube. The food pellet reinforces the act of pressing the bar, which increases the behavior. This naïve rat has never been in the box before, so it sniffs around, pokes its nose through the air holes, grooms itself, rears on its hind legs, and so on. You can wait and hope for the rat to happen upon the bar for the first time, or you can speed up the process. If the rat turns to face the bar, you deliver a food pellet into the cage. Reinforcement. If it steps toward the bar, you deliver another pellet. If the rat moves closer and touches the bar, you deliver yet another one. Once the rat is pawing at the bar, you withhold the next pellet until it presses down, which triggers the feeder. Before long, your subject is pressing the bar at a rapid pace. By reinforcing "successive approximations" of the target response, you will have shaped a whole new behavior.

Shaping is the procedure that animal trainers use to get circus elephants to walk on their hind legs, bears to ride bicycles, chickens to play a piano, squirrels to water-ski, and dolphins to jump through hoops. The dolphin trainer at Sea World begins by throwing the dolphin a fish for turning toward a hoop, then for swimming toward it, swimming through it underwater, and finally jumping through the hoop held many feet up in the air. This same process applies to people, especially those who are confronted under pressure with the strongest of rewards and punishments.

Perils of Interrogation: Structural Considerations

Before addressing the perils of individual tactics, it's important to recognize two structural "macro" flaws inherent in this interrogation paradigm. The first is that interrogation is at its core a guilt-presumptive process. The second goes to my early "holy shit" realization that this highly scripted Milgramesque process of gradual escalation aims to break the suspect down, step-by-step, fifteen volts at a time.

Interrogation Is Guilt-Presumptive

As punctuated by the opening salvo of the Reid technique, the direct positive confrontation, interrogation is a theory-driven social interaction led by an authority figure who has formed a strong belief in the suspect's guilt and single-mindedly measures success by confession.

Proponents of the Reid technique recoil when I use the term *guilt-presumptive* to describe their interrogation process. But there's no getting around it. The goal of interrogation, they insist, is not to produce a confession but to get at the truth. Fair enough in words. But the title of their manual does expose the ultimate purpose: *Criminal Interrogation and Confessions*. Even more telling is the language they use. I own all five editions of their handbook, and they continue right up though the fifth and most recent edition, published in 2013. Starting on the opening page of the chapter on the nine steps, they use the words "suspect" and "offender" interchangeably—as if they are one and the same.

Think about this. The offender is a proven criminal; a suspect is a mere hypothesis. To toss these words around as if synonymous betrays in language what they won't admit in words: once a suspect is identified, that suspect is in their mind the offender. The process is so presumptive they don't even realize it. "It is a capital mistake to theorize before you have all the evidence," wrote Sir Arthur Conan Doyle, who in 1887 created the character of Sherlock Holmes. "It biases the judgment." I would add to this pearl of wisdom that presumptions bias not only judgment, but also behavior.

So what? you might ask. If a suspect is innocent, who cares what the interrogator presumes? Here's the problem: social psychologists have long observed that first impressions are quick to form and hard to break. Once we form a belief about someone—that they are good, bad, warm, cold, competent, inept, guilty, or innocent—we lose interest in new evidence and, worse, we interpret contradictory information in light of that first impression.

When told that a good person is described as "calm," we assume that means gentle, peaceful, and serene. When a cruel person is said to be calm, that same word means cool, shrewd, and calculating. Based on your first impression, the word "proud" can mean self-respecting or conceited, "critical" can mean astute or picky, and "impulsive" can mean spontaneous or reckless.

The most pernicious reason first impressions are hard to break is that once formed, they create a self-fulfilling prophecy. In a classic experiment in 1978, Mark Snyder and William Swann asked pairs of subjects, strangers to each other, to engage in a getting-acquainted conversation. In each pair, one participant was supposed to interview the other. But first, these interviewers were led to believe that their partner was either introverted or extroverted (actually, the partners were assigned to these conditions on a random basis).

Interviewers prepared for the session by selecting questions from a preset list. Some of the questions presumed introversion ("What do you dislike about loud parties?" "What makes it hard for you to open up to people?"), others presumed extroversion ("How do you liven up a party?" "In what situations are you most talkative?"). Sure enough, subjects who thought their partner was introverted chose introvert-oriented questions; those who thought their partner was extroverted asked extrovert-oriented questions. Everyone unwittingly sought out evidence that would confirm their expectations.

Here's the most concerning part of the results. By asking one-sided questions, which their partners dutifully answered, the interviewers actually created a reality that supported their false beliefs. This self-fulfilling prophecy was so clear that neutral observers who later listened to the interviews were left with the mistaken impression that the partners really were introverted or extroverted, as the interviewer had presumed.

This experiment may seem only remotely linked to guilt-presumptive interrogations. Not so. This phenomenon is strong, pervasive, and highly relevant. In 2003, my colleagues and I modeled a study after Snyder and Swann involving fifty-seven pairings of mock interrogators and suspects. First, we induced some suspects but not others to steal a $100 bill from an empty room, after which interrogators questioned them via headphones from a separate location.

Before starting, we led interrogators to believe that most mock suspects in the study were guilty or that most were innocent. Note for a moment how mildly we varied the interrogators' presumption. We didn't vilify the suspect or suggest we had hard evidence. We merely altered the baseline probability of guilt and innocence.

Yet the vicious cycle of events unleashed by the presumption of guilt was unmistakable. Interrogators who presumed guilt chose to ask more incriminating questions, conducted more coercive interrogations, and tried harder by all accounts to get their suspect to confess. In turn, this more aggressive style made the suspects sound defensive and led observers who later listened to the tapes to judge them as guilty, even when they were not. It gets worse. The most aggressive confession-driven interrogations occurred when guilt-presumptive interrogators questioned innocent suspects whose vehement denials frustrated their efforts.

These types of results have been replicated in other labs and in a recent study at Uppsala University in Sweden involving sixty police officers. The effect is powerful, consistent with basic research on confirmation biases, and on target as a criticism of the Reid technique.

This is not a mere laboratory phenomenon. To this day, I am haunted by the South Carolina case against Wesley Myers, an innocent man badgered and brainwashed into confession by detectives who formed a baseless first impression so strong that they rendered themselves oblivious to all signs of his innocence. I served as an expert for Myers and testified at his trial. But he was convicted in 2001 and spent seventeen years in prison before his conviction was overturned and he was released. You can watch the story of what happened in Season 1 of Kelly Loundenberg's Netflix series, *The Confession Tapes*.

On March 13, 1997, thirty-six-year-old Teresa Haught was killed while closing up the Mill Inn, which she managed, in North Charleston, South Carolina. A single mother of four, she was dating Wes Myers. Whoever killed her set the bar ablaze afterward. For no good reason, police lasered in on Myers as their suspect. The morning he learned of Teresa's death, said Detective Tetanich, "something was wrong with him . . . he was acting funny." Acting funny? He'd just learned that the woman he was dating was killed. Did you expect business as usual? It's hard for this psychologist to overstate the absurdity of this remark.

Wesley Myers was questioned, fingerprinted, tested, searched, and interrogated by multiple investigators. His interrogation was an ongoing ordeal, not a single event. The day after Teresa's murder, Myers was questioned by polygraph examiner Lieutenant McHale. For three days, he gave a consistent and uncontradicted account of his relationship with the victim and his whereabouts the night of her murder. "You willing to cooperate?" "Anything you want. I'm trying to tell you, I have nothing to hide."

Myers was emphatic and cooperative, and no evidence linked him to the crime. In fact, he should have passed the BAI with flying colors. He non-defensively embraced the proposition that hair found in Teresa's grasp would identify her killer; he eagerly agreed to take a polygraph and was visibly disappointed when the test was postponed; he consented without hesitation to searches of his parents' house, his room, and his car; he was confident that all evidence would exonerate him, and speculated when asked about who the culprit might be. When McHale asked whether the killer should be punished, Myers got choked up and said, "Whoever done this needs to pay for it."

That Myers lacked a consciousness of guilt was beside the fact. "He looked funny," and that alone set off a relentless tunnel-visioned drive toward confession. Trapped in a classic guilt-presumptive interrogation, there was nothing that Myers could say or do to make it stop. Resorting to the controversial bait question, McHale led this exchange:

Q: Can the hair be yours?

A: No.

Q: If it was?

A: I'd freak.

Q: How would you explain it?

A: I couldn't, no way.

Q: Assume the hair is yours . . .

A: No way . . . my hair is not going to show up there . . . you'll be able to clear me.

Q: If a witness says he saw you at the bar 1–3 a.m. . . . .

A: Then he's a liar. He didn't see ME. I wasn't there.

In what followed, Detectives Clayton, Tetanich, and Cumbee combined forces in a psychological attack. Detective Cumbee staged a phone call from SLED (South Carolina Law Enforcement Division) and reported that the hair in Teresa's grasp belonged to Myers. This was not true. It belonged to someone else. Yet this disclosure—plus the lie that witnesses saw Myers in the bar that night—disoriented Myers and led to his eventual capitulation.

Although the confession-taking session was not recorded, the lone video of McHale's pre-polygraph "interview" plainly shows the development of a minimization theme ("It's so easy to kill somebody when you're angry"; "Sometimes you don't know how strong you are"; "If you're guilty and it's an accident . . ."). At one point, McHale explicitly distinguished between first-degree murder, which brings a life sentence, and involuntary manslaughter, which brings a three-year sentence in South Carolina, maybe even "four months and you're out."

Later in this chapter, I will make the case for why U.S. courts should ban police uses of the false evidence and minimization ploys. For now, the point is that police presumed Myers guilty, blinded themselves to all innocence cues, and mentally broke him down, suggesting at one point that he blacked out. Eventually, a confused Myers relented: "I must have done it," he said. After taking a written confession, detectives told the local press that they would be escorting Myers to the county jail in a "perp walk." On camera, on local TV, Myers said he was sorry.

Myers retracted his confession and went to trial. Juries are typically bowled over by confessions. In this case, this South Carolina jury sent a note to the presiding judge, Edward Cottingham, during deliberation, saying "We are hopelessly deadlocked." The judge then met with jurors, off the record, without Myers or his attorney present. I have no idea what was said, but this deadlocked jury went on to deliver a guilty verdict. When this off-the-record meeting came to light, and DNA tests revealed another male's DNA mixed in Teresa's blood, Myers's conviction was overturned. In 2015, after fourteen years, he was released from prison.

This case illustrates what it means to give an internalized false confession during a Reid technique interrogation—to become so vulnerable in grief and so confused by false evidence that when police insist that you don't recall the crime because you'd blacked out, you have almost no cognitive choice but to accept that version of reality. In an interview shown in *The Confession Tapes,* Myers put it this way: "They mind-raped me and made me believe I killed someone I loved. It was all a setup."

Interrogation Is Like Milgram—But Worse

A second striking feature of interrogation concerns the "Milgramesque" nature of the process itself. In 1963, Milgram published his first classic obedience experiment, in which 65 percent of subjects obeyed an experimenter's commands to deliver up to 450 volts of electric shocks to a hapless confederate. The parallels between police interrogations and the protocol Milgram had established to elicit obedience are striking.

In both venues, the subject is isolated, without access to friends, family, or other means of social support, in a specially designed space, whether the laboratory or an interrogation room. The subject is confronted by a figure of authority—a psychology experimenter with minimal sway or a detective with power. The subject then engages a contractual agreement with that authority figure to proceed—volunteering and receiving payment in advance of participation in Milgram's paradigm, signing a waiver of Miranda rights in the interrogation setting.

Once the structure of these situations is in place, the authority figure uses deception to reframe the purposes and consequences of the subject's actions. In Milgram's experiments, subjects were led to believe that the objective was to test the effects of punishment on a learner through the administration of shocks that may be painful but do not cause harm. In an interrogation, suspects are led to believe that confession serves their personal self-interest better than denial.

In both venues, the authority figure then proceeds to make a series of unwavering and relentless demands. Milgram used four scripted prompts and prods (ranging from "Please continue" to "You have no other choice, you must go on"); the Reid technique offers a series of nine steps (beginning with the "positive confrontation" and culminating in "converting the oral admission into a written confession").

Two additional similarities are notable for the protections they afford. The first concerns questions about ethics. In social psychology, controversy erupted after the publication of Milgram's first article and continues to exert influence over present-day institutional review boards (IRBs) in the behavioral sciences. Today, no institution or funding agency would approve this experiment as originally conducted. The stress inflicted upon the subjects, not to mention the self-insight concerning what they did, is over the top. In law, similar questions are typically framed within a rubric of concerns for the "voluntariness" versus coercion of a suspect's confession and hence its admissibility as evidence at trial. In my view, today's IRBs protect human subjects a whole lot better than the U.S. courts protect crime suspects.

The second point of similarity concerns the necessity of recording. When Milgram's first paper was published, it was hard for anyone to fathom the results. "What was wrong with those forty guys in New Haven?" was one common expression of disbelief.

Then in 1965, Milgram released a black-and-white documentary titled *Obedience*, which contained footage from his experiment. This film, shown in Psych 101 classes all over the world, enables the viewer to observe the structure, protocol, and power of the situation that elicited his published results. Although I am aware of no data that surgically address the impact of the film on people's attributions for the behavior of obedient subjects, Martin Safer reported that among his students, those who saw the film, compared to those who did not, later overestimated the amount of shock that subjects would administer. Watch the film, and you'll grasp the power of the situation Milgram had created to command obedience.

For exactly this reason, I have been urging the mandatory recording of interrogations since 1985. Personally, I don't see how a judge is competent to determine whether a confession was voluntary without watching the interrogation process. Nor do I see how a jury is competent to determine if a confession can be trusted as true without seeing that same eliciting process. Yet even today, almost half of all states in the United States still, inexplicably, do not require police departments to video record interrogations from start to finish.

The Milgram-Reid paradigms share one final structural commonality that helps to explain the devastating power they exert. In both venues, full obedience is achieved through gradual escalation, culminating in 450 volts in Milgram—and, of course, a full confession in the interrogation room. First have the suspect place himself at the scene of the crime, advised Inbau and Reid in 1962; then get the suspect to admit seeing what happened; then get a partial admission to playing a minor role; then a larger role; then ultimately a full admission of guilt supplemented by details.

The case of Melissa Calusinski of Lake County, Illinois, illustrates the point. A story featured on two episodes of CBS's *48 Hours* reported that Calusinski was a twenty-two-year-old assistant teacher at a day care center in an affluent suburb outside Chicago. One day in 2009, sixteen-month-old Benjamin Kingan fell unconscious, foaming at the mouth, with no pulse. Two hours later, Melissa and others on the staff were informed that Ben had died. The next day, a forensic pathologist concluded from the autopsy that the boy had a fresh skull fracture and had died from blunt-force trauma to the head. Because Melissa was present at work that day, homicide detectives brought her in for questioning. "Do you think you're in trouble?" they asked. Visibly distraught, she said "No, because I didn't do anything."

Seated in the corner of the interrogation room, pinned between two walls, two detectives, and a table, and cut off from any means of exit, Calusinski—a gentle soul who was "slow" in school and never in trouble before—had no idea what she was in for. More than once she told detectives she was claustrophobic. She used the word "scared" over and over again to describe her emotional state. None of that mattered. "We're not going anywhere until we get the facts here," she was told.

As with Wesley Myers, it's not clear what Calusinski could have said or done to stop what happened next. Detectives asked if she would take a lie detector test. Without hesitation she said yes; it would show she was telling the truth. What about talking to other children in the class who can talk, would that be a good idea? Yes again. And what about talking to other teachers in the class? Again, Calusinski showed no fear of incrimination. She showed no signs of a guilty conscience. Yet they plowed on.

Over seventy times (yes, I counted), often while crying, Calusinski adamantly denied doing anything to harm the child. But her captors would not relent: "We're not going anywhere till we get to the bottom of this." She informed the detectives that Ben had been sick. Earlier in the week he threw up; the next day, he did not come in. On the day Ben died, she called for help as soon as she noticed that he was unconscious.

None of what she said had any effect. At various points, detectives yelled at her, cursed, and slammed their fists on the table. The interrogation was recorded; you can see it for yourself.

None of this was a problem, argued the state's attorney's office. Calusinski was not even in custody. Really? Every time detectives left her alone in the room, they locked the door. If that is not a textbook criterion for custody, I don't know what is.

Then detectives lowered the boom: This was a homicide. Ben's skull was fractured—and that's a "medical certainty." Proof of homicide, they said, was "definite," "substantial," "scientific." The only question to be resolved was whether it was an accident or intentional.

"Accidents happen every day," she was told. "You're a good person." After telling Calusinski that the facts contradicted her story, detectives deployed Step 7 of the Reid technique: The alternative question: You're either a witness or a murderer. "That's what it's coming down to."

Twice the detectives suggested that Calusinski could not trust her own memory. "We've had incidents in which people just flat out black out."

After four hours, Calusinski the witness "admitted" that she saw Ben fall back and hit his head.

At six hours, she said she dropped him—an act of negligence, an accident.

At nine hours, after being warned that this was her last chance, Calusinski confessed that she threw Ben to the ground in frustration—a script her interrogators had cultivated.

The children had been acting up, they suggested to her, which was frustrating ("frustration" is a common minimization theme). She then became angry with Ben, a suggestion she picked up on, and threw him to the floor. She said she saw his head bounce.

At fourteen hours, for good measure, detectives handed Calusinski a plastic doll to demonstrate. She dropped it. Not good enough, they said—not hard enough to account for the child's injuries.

Moment later, this time holding the doll with two hands, she dutifully re-reenacted how she slammed the boy to the ground. Game, set, match.

Calusinski had been broken down into a state of full compliance. "I'm trying to make it sound right," she said at one point. "I want to help you guys so much."

Having fully surrendered in the final demand for a physical demonstration, Calusinski asked how much longer it would take "because I just want to go home and spend time with my parents and my puppy." Then she asked, "Is this going to be on my record?"

As detectives moved this young woman from 0 to 450 volts in fourteen hours, she had no idea that she might not see the inside of her home ever again.

Enter Dr. Thomas Rudd. I first became acquainted with this case while lecturing at the 2015 Annual Meeting of the American Academy of the Forensic Sciences. The meeting was held in Orlando, and the title of my presentation was "Confessions in Context: Why Confessions Corrupt Forensic Perceptions and Judgments." Held in a hotel ballroom, the session featured a handful of high-profile speakers cautioning about cognitive bias in the forensic sciences.

After my presentation, a gentleman stepped up to the microphone. I was half expecting a critical remark about how trained forensic professionals are immune to bias. Instead, he introduced himself as Thomas Rudd, Lake County coroner, and his first words were, "I just want to say that everything Dr. Kassin said about confessions and forensics is right."

Dr. Rudd and I talked after the session. He told me about the Calusinski case. When the boy died, the autopsy physician concluded that his death was caused by a skull fracture resulting from blunt-force trauma to the head. That set into motion a homicide investigation.

Three years later, after Calusinski was convicted and sentenced to thirty-one years in prison, Rudd assumed the position as Lake County coroner, reviewed the case file, and was dumbfounded by what he saw: Scabbing and scar tissue in the boy's skull from an old and massive head injury. There was no evidence of a fresh skull fracture. The result was conclusive. He checked with a colleague, who agreed. Pediatric records confirmed it. The original pathologist admitted that he missed it and submitted an affidavit to that effect.

In 2015, the year we met, Rudd changed the cause of death from homicide to "undetermined" and urged that Calusinski be released and that "the State's Attorney needs to do his duty." His conclusions were backed by histology slides and x-rays not presented at trial. None of it mattered. Calusinski had confessed, which apparently was sufficient to uphold her conviction on two state appeals—regardless of what ambiguities existed in the medical evidence.

PSYCHOLOGICALLY COERCIVE TACTICS THAT SHOULD BE BANNED

After years of examining police-induced confessions, I cannot help but notice that the processes by which *false* confessions are taken are eerily, and not coincidentally, similar. Sometimes it feels like I'm watching a rerun of an old bad movie. The names, dates, and places may change, but the script is always about the same.

Overall, 50 to 60 percent of all interrogations in the United States (and in the UK) yield admissions and confessions. In the vast majority of these cases, the session lasted from thirty minutes to up to two hours. This range can be derived from observations of live and recorded interrogations, interviews with suspects, and surveys of police—who estimate that their longest interrogations last an average of about four hours.

Then there's the population of false confessions. In 2004, law professors Steven Drizin and Richard Leo compiled an archive of 125 proven false confessions and found that 34 percent of interrogations lasted 6 to 12 hours; 39 percent lasted 12 to 24 hours—the average was 16 hours! This is not surprising. Especially under stress, and in a hostile environment, people who are isolated for a prolonged period of time desperately crave the company of significant others for the psychological and physiological benefits of social support. Prolonged isolation constitutes a form of deprivation much like hunger, thirst, and the need for sleep.

But that's not all. The six to twenty-four hours of custody are not filled with meditative silence, chill music, and quiet contemplation. At worst, the conditions are physically uncomfortable and abusive. At best, the time is partially or continuously filled by a relentless barrage of guilt-presumptive questions from which there is no escape, and an array of gaslighting tricks that the average American assumes to be unlawful.

Watch any of these sessions, and you'll see that the detectives do most of the talking to a silent and bewildered suspect. By my count, Melissa Calusinski denied harming Ben seventy-five times in nine hours. Once repeated denials of wrongdoing failed to win her release, and as she became more and more desperate to go home, what were her options?

The amount of time police can grill a suspect is one problem. But the kinds of trickery and deceit the courts permit are psychologically coercive and need to be stopped. It does not have to be this way. In particular, the research community and I point a finger at two tactics that put innocent people at risk: The false-evidence ploy and minimization themes that communicate leniency.

The False-Evidence Ploy

When I lecture to public audiences, I often ask: By a show of hands, how many of you think American police are allowed to lie to a suspect about evidence? Usually about a quarter of audience members raise their hands. And how many of you think police are *not* allowed to lie about evidence? Usually about half or more raise their hands in agreement and react with shock when I reveal that they are wrong (predictably some don't respond one way or the other).

In 1969, in *Frazier v. Cupp*, the U.S. Supreme Court made it lawful for police to elicit confessions by outright lying to suspects about evidence. "The victim's blood was found on your pillow." "You failed the polygraph." "Your fingerprints were on the knife." "Your hair was found in the victim's grasp." "Your friend said she wasn't with you." "Surveillance footage puts you at the scene." "We have a witness who identified you." These are common examples of the brazen lies police have told during an interrogation.

There appears to be no limit to the creativity, type, or magnitude of deception that is permitted in the United States—even to an anxious and unwary teen suspect who just found his parents bludgeoned and unconscious.

Marty Tankleff

In 1988, seventeen-year-old Marty Tankleff set his alarm and woke up at the crack of dawn for the first day of his senior year at high school. All the lights were on in his family's large home in Belle Terre, Long Island. Concerned, he looked for his parents and found his mother in bed, motionless, in a pool of blood, and his father in his study, slumped in his bloodied chair, gurgling air but unconscious. Tankleff called 911.

Detective James McCready arrived, determined that Tankleff was not showing enough emotion, and labeled him a suspect (for starters, I don't know what this detective was thinking; Marty's tone in his 911 call was one of hysteria). While his parents were taken to the hospital, and in the absence of any evidence, or a violent past, McCready and his partner hauled Tankleff into the local police station and interrogated the boy for nearly six hours.

Tankleff, whose state of mind I cannot even imagine, repeatedly and vehemently denied the accusation. Over and over again, he told the

On June 28, 1990, four months later after being convicted, Marty Tankleff was sentenced for the murder of his parents. After seventeen years in prison, he was released when his conviction was overturned. He went on to attend college and law school. *Photo courtesy of Ken Korotkin / New York Daily News.*

same story about the morning and night before. Then McCready told Tankleff that his hair was found on his mother, which was a lie that confused the boy, who did not touch his mother, as far as he could recall.

Then McCready disclosed that a "humidity test" indicated that Tankleff had showered before calling 911, which would explain why he was clean in the presence of two very bloody crime scenes—also a lie.

Then in the coup de grâce of lies, McCready walked out of the room and left the door open. The phone rang in the squad room. It was a staged call. When he returned, he told Tankleff that he called the hospital and had good news and bad news. The good news was that his dad had emerged from his coma and was conscious. The bad news: his dad said that Marty was his assailant. Both of these news flashes were lies (his father never regained consciousness and died shortly thereafter).

Disoriented, Tankleff wondered if he had blacked out, broke down, and accepted the confession narrative McCready had started to draft.

Ultimately, Tankleff did not sign the statement that, I should note, turned out to be a wholly inaccurate description of the crimes. Yet solely on the basis of that confession, he was tried and convicted in 1990. Thanks to new witnesses and evidence, his conviction was vacated in 2008. At that point, he had spent more than half of his life in prison.

Marty Tankleff has lived a remarkable life. The week after his release, I invited him to join me in a talk I was already scheduled to give at the New York Legal Aid Society in Brooklyn. He had written to me from prison in the 1990s; years later, I submitted an affidavit on his behalf. But that was the first time we would meet. We decided to keep his appearance a surprise. With my daughter Briana in attendance, I opened my talk in a way I never did before: "I can't give you a firsthand account of why anyone would give a false confession," I started. "But I know someone who can."

Tankleff's case was well known throughout the New York City legal community. Sixty former prosecutors had signed a petition urging his release. So when I announced his name to a room full of defense lawyers, there was an audible gasp. As he approached the podium, he received a long, warm standing ovation.

Marty and I have appeared together in several classes. He was gracious enough to attend my last-ever psychology-and-law class at Williams College before I left for John Jay, where he is now an honorary member of my lab. After his release from prison, Tankleff went to college at Hofstra University, graduated from Touro Law School, and passed the New York State bar exam. On February 5, 2020, he was sworn in to practice law. He is now also an adjunct professor and advocate for criminal justice reform who has helped to exonerate other innocents who were wrongfully convicted.

Pardon my digression. I cannot resist an inspirational twist and turn in the life of someone so flagrantly mistreated by the legal system (I only scratched the surface; for a jaw-dropping account of the Tankleff saga, I recommend *A Criminal Injustice* by Richard Firstman and Jay Salpeter).

To get back on point, how can the courts of the United States permit detectives to lie, not once but three times, to a seventeen-year-old boy traumatized by a fatal attack on his parents, and citing the boy's father, whom he trusted more than anyone else, as the source of the biggest lie of all? Setting aside how morally reprehensible this is, it should not take

On February 5, 2020, Tankleff was sworn in as an attorney and signed the official state roster. *Photo courtesy of Marty Tankleff.*

a PhD in psychology to understand how lies of this number and magnitude can put an innocent suspect at risk.

Malthe Thomsen

Born and raised in Denmark to a family of educators, twenty-two-year-old Malthe Thomsen was a soft-spoken student on a semester-long teaching internship at IPS, a private New York City preschool, in 2014. Assigned to the "Blue Room," he worked with four- and five-year-old children alongside the head teacher and two assistants.

One day, a young assistant working in the room lodged a complaint that Thomsen was molesting children in the classroom. This assistant was a chronic troublemaker. In constant conflict with coworkers, she had filed several complaints against other teachers. She supplied no evidence of her allegations, stating that her word was her evidence (she had secretly recorded Thomsen with her cellphone; others would later describe the video as "unremarkable" and "of no investigatory value"). The school conducted an internal investigation, cleared Thomsen, and fired the assistant.

This assistant went on to report her complaint to the NYPD. Although she presented no proof, sex crimes detective Nela Gomez decided to interview Thomsen. On June 27, without warning, Gomez and another officer woke Thomsen up at 6 a.m., took him into an interrogation room at the police station, locked the door, and Mirandized him. Gomez then questioned Thomsen for four hours, off camera, before delivering him to ADA Rachel Ferrari for an on-camera confession.

According to Thomsen, Gomez told him that surveillance videos showed him touching children sexually and placing their hands on his genitals. That was a lie. No such footage ever existed. When Thomsen refuted the allegation, she suggested the possibility that he might have engaged in this conduct "without knowing it."

Thomsen had no idea that a police officer could misrepresent evidence in this way. This type of deception is not permitted in Denmark—or in most other countries. When Gomez said she had video footage, "my head like exploded," Thomsen would later recount. Trusting the authority of police, he said, I did not know "why she would lie about something like that." So Thomsen began to doubt his own memory. "I couldn't remember having done it, but if it's on video, then it would have to be true."

Gomez told Thomsen that she would wait all day until he admitted to abusing children. By minimizing the charge and promising leniency, she convinced him that it was in his best interest to cooperate.

Thomsen was cooked. Gomez told him to handwrite a confession, which he did. Then he amended it on cue and signed. Then he agreed to repeat the statement on camera to Assistant District Attorney Rachel Ferrari. "This morning, I had a rude awakening," he opened. "I realized that I had taken a kid's hand to the genital area of my shorts, and taken something good from it."

Thomsen was arrested, charged with sexually abusing thirteen children, and sent to infamous Rikers Island. He was incarcerated there for two weeks before posting bail (after receiving threats from other inmates, he was placed in solitary confinement). New York's *Daily News* put him on the cover accompanied by his Facebook profile picture with his niece on his shoulders. The headline read: "Sex Monster."

In November 2014, after a thorough investigation of Thomsen's phone and computer (as well as interviews with IPS personnel and children) drew blanks, the DA's office dismissed the charges. Thomsen returned home to Denmark. The city compensated him with an undisclosed sum of money.

Thomsen later appeared in Katrine Philp's 2018 documentary from Denmark, *False Confessions*. Traumatized by the experience, he seemed depressed and found it hard to smile. He gained weight and never did become a teacher. On January 19, 2019, he died of a blood clot in his heart. He was twenty-seven years old.

The Proof Is in the Science

England. France. Germany. Spain. New Zealand. Australia. Japan. Taiwan. All of Scandinavia. Police are not permitted to lie to suspects about evidence in any of these countries. Yet in the United States, this tactic is used and justified. John Reid & Associates to this day claims that this ruse does not put innocents at risk. On this point, they are both ignorant and incorrect—and just about every research psychologist knows it.

I offer four levels of proof for the proposition that the false-evidence ploy can lead innocent suspects to confess. The first comes from the real-life tragedies inflicted on the likes of Marty Tankleff and Malthe Thomsen. Or Chris Tapp, Michael Crowe, Gary Gauger, Daniel Andersen, Adam Gray, Keith Bush, John Kogut, Barry Laughman, Peter Reilly, Byron Halsey, Marcellius Radford, Calvin Ollins, Adrian Thomas, Juan Rivera, Michael Saunders, and Wesley Myers—to name just a few whose cases I happen to know well. The nefarious effect of false evidence is not a mere theoretical proposition. It's a police tactic that destroys innocent lives and allows the actual violent perpetrators to roam free and re-offend.

The second level of proof comes from basic Psych 101. Across the domains of human nature, it is clear that misinformation renders people vulnerable to manipulation. In both laboratory and field settings, experiments have shown that false information—presented through lying confederates, counterfeit test results, bogus norms, false physiological feedback, leading questions, and the like—can substantially alter a subject's visual perceptions, beliefs, self-assessments, motivational and emotional states, behaviors, eyewitness accounts, and memories for autobiographical events.

Even physiological functions in the body can be manipulated by misinformation. This is seen in the classic placebo effect, the well-established medical phenomenon whereby patients show improvement when given an inactive drug, or placebo. Somehow, this misinformation leads patients to believe they will improve, which can help make it so. That's how faith healers, shamans, and witch doctors all over the world have been known to perform "miracle cures" with their rituals.

The third level of proof comes from a relatively recent body of controlled experiments specifically aimed at confession. Drawing on our observations of actual cases, Katherine "Lee" Kiechel, my long-ago undergraduate thesis student at Williams, needed to devise an ethical paradigm for eliciting false confessions. Lee was a smart student, an All-American track and field athlete. While she didn't know it the time, she was heading toward a PhD in industrial/organizational psychology.

Lee and I theorized that the presentation of false evidence would lead innocent people to confess in an act of compliance. Inspired by the most inconceivable mind-numbing stories involving innocents who even internalize the belief in their own guilt, we also sought to measure both types of confession.

After extensive pilot testing, we recruited seventy-nine pairs of college students to work on a fast- or slow-paced computer task. One subject would read a string of letters timed to a metronome; the other would type them on a keyboard. Then the two would reverse roles. In fact, Lee played the role of the subject assigned to read first.

Before they began, the experimenter—seated across the table, facing the computer screen—cautioned the subjects not to hit the ALT key; because of a quirk in the program, it would cause the computer to crash, causing a loss of data. Everyone nodded that they understood. At that point, the experimenter set the metronome and the task was started.

The opening moments were uneventful. At sixty seconds, however, the experimenter, a male student named John, erupted and asked the subject if he or she hit the Alt key. He then grabbed the keyboard, tinkered with it, confirmed that data were lost, and accused the subject of causing the damage by pressing the key they were instructed to avoid. All subjects were innocent; no one had hit the Alt key; all at first denied the charge.

At that point, the experimenter turned to Lee, the confederate posing as the second subject and asked if she saw anything. Lee was well cast for this role. She had a disarmingly angelic appearance and was the kind of person you would not hesitate to trust. In half the sessions, she said no; in the other half, however, she offered up false evidence, claiming that she saw the subject hit the Alt key. At that point, as if betrayed, the blood drained from each subject's jaw-dropped speechless face.

Regardless of the condition, the experimenter then pulled out a blank sheet of lined paper and handwrote an apparently off-the-cuff confession ("I hit the Alt key and caused the program to crash. Data were lost. My fault"). He then pushed the paper across the table and asked the subject to sign it—the consequence of which would be a phone call from his professor, the principal investigator.

The results were clear on three fronts. Demonstrating the process of compliance, subjects were twice as likely to sign the confession handwritten by the experimenter when they were confronted by the false witness than when they were not. The accusation and witness report were upsetting. We learned over time to tone down the experimenter's expressions of distress after the first two subjects we ran could not hold back tears. Still, many students, just like many innocent suspects, signed the confession because they could not get out of the lab fast enough.

Further demonstrating the process of internalization, a sizable subsample of subjects who confessed later "admitted" guilt to a stranger (also a confederate) after the study was supposedly over and the two were alone. After subjects exited the lab into the waiting room, they encountered a supposedly naïve fellow student who was waiting for the next session. That student, working for us, leaned into the subject and asked, "I heard a commotion. What happened in there?" We secretly recorded the subject's response to that question. If the subject said, "I hit a key I wasn't supposed to hit," "I broke the experimenter's computer," or anything else that unequivocally indicated a belief in their own culpability, that form of "internalization" was noted.

And that was not all. The experimenter returned to the waiting room to let the waiting student know that they would have to reschedule the next session because of an equipment malfunction. At that point, he asked the subject to return to the lab. "If you don't mind, I'd like to

In the first experiment to produce false confessions in a lab, subjects (right)—
accompanied by a confederate (left) and an experimenter (bottom left, out of
view)—were tasked with typing on a keyboard, when the computer seemed to
crash. The experimenter accused the subject of hitting the Alt key, which they had
been instructed to avoid. All subjects were innocent. Yet many of them signed a
confession after the confederate claimed she saw them hit the forbidden key.
Some subjects even came to internalize the belief in their guilt (Kassin & Kiechel,
1996). *Photo courtesy of the author.*

reread the letters you typed as you sit at the keyboard. Perhaps you can
reconstruct how and when you hit the Alt key."

At this point, we were looking for evidence of something I've seen in
cases involving internalized false confessions. We were looking to see if
subjects would confabulate a false memory to support their newly
formed belief. Sure enough, a subsample of those who internalized a
belief in their own guilt did just that (for example, "Yes, stop, right here;
I hit it with the side of my right hand right after you called out the A").

The hierarchy of results formed a clear pattern. Overall, 69 percent
of subjects signed the confession as an act of compliance; 28 percent
internalized the belief in their own guilt; 9 percent confabulated false
memories to accompany that belief. Consistent with our hypothesis,

subjects were substantially more likely to exhibit these effects when confronted with the false witness report.

In 2006, ABC News' *Prime Time* sent a camera crew into my lab at Williams to replicate the study for a story titled "Inside the Box." I brought in two new students to play the roles of experimenter and confederate; we recruited new subjects; cameras were concealed from view. When I explained to the producer how the sessions would unfold, she was skeptical that the false witness would get anyone innocent to sign on the dotted line. Yet as we watched the first subject from behind a one-way mirror, we saw that subject not only sign the confession but also apologize profusely for damaging the computer.

These computer-crash findings have been replicated all over the world. One follow-up study conducted in the Netherlands went on to get the effect even when the confession meant the subject would have to pay for the damage. Other follow-up experiments showed that the false-evidence effect was particularly strong among children and juveniles and among adults who had been sleep-deprived for one night in the lab.

The false-evidence effect has also been produced using vastly different methods, leading innocent college students to confess to cheating, which violated their university's honor code; stealing money from the "bank" in a computerized gambling experiment; and recalling past transgressions they did not actually commit, including acts of violence.

In one particularly interesting experiment, published in 2009, British researchers Robert Nash and Kimberly Wade created a gambling task in which subjects took payment from the "bank" after winning rounds, but not after losing rounds. After the sessions were over, later in the day, the subjects were brought back into the lab. Half were told, falsely, that video recordings of the session showed they had stolen money during a losing round. The other half were shown digitally edited videos that fabricated a sequence in which they took money in a losing round. In both groups, false evidence led subjects to sign a confession. In the fabricated video condition, many of them also believed that they had stolen the money.

Let me take a quick detour at this point. You may be thinking that no police officer would ever doctor visual evidence in this way. It certainly is not a common form of subterfuge. Then again, there was this case I worked on in Chicago. On January 19, 1980, two pedestrians found the body of twenty-year-old Cathy Trunko on the sidewalk, a block away from her home. She had been stabbed to death. The next day, a kitchen knife was found under a bush not far from the crime scene. Police assumed that this knife, which had blood on it, was the murder weapon.

Five days later, at 2 a.m., police hauled in nineteen-year-old Daniel Andersen, a friend of the victim's, for drunk and disorderly conduct. Without any factual basis for suspicion, Andersen was taken to the homicide division for interrogations that lasted through the night and next day. For sixteen hours, Andersen was deprived of all food, drink, sleep, and access to a restroom. During that time, Detective James Higgins came in and offered Andersen a lifeline—sympathy, under-standing, friendship, and protection from other officers.

These hours of interrogation were not recorded, so it's not absolutely clear what happened. But this undisputed fact is revealing: Andersen wrote on a chalkboard in the interrogation room, "Need a friend, call a cop." He wrote this, he said, because he trusted Detective Higgins. But then Higgins exploited that trust. With Andersen repeatedly proclaiming his innocence, he switched gears: "Word on the street is that you did it," he said. He told Andersen they found blood on his clothes, which was not true.

In what proved to be the most devastating ploy, Higgins next showed Andersen a photograph of the knife that was recovered days earlier. Andersen said he did not recognize it. According to Andersen, Higgins next showed him a photo of the same knife alongside two work gloves from his car *that he recognized as his own*. With Detective Higgins insisting that people can commit horrible crimes without remembering, Andersen became disoriented: "Stuff like you dream about it. You have blackouts. Did I do this? And I thought, Oh my God. I could kill some-one and not remember doing it? Why would I kill anybody?" This "realization" prompted Andersen to confess. As soon as he was arrested and realized he was duped, he recanted the confession, pled not guilty, and went to trial.

I should note that this controversial photograph is in dispute. When asked about it in 1982, Detective Higgins equivocated. "I don't know," he said. "I don't recall." When asked again thirty-five years later, after an exonerated Daniel Andersen had filed a lawsuit again the Chicago Police Department, Higgins emphatically denied the claim.

Andersen's description of the doctored photograph, and the effect it had on him, cannot be overstated. In 1982, he was convicted of rape and murder, for which he would spend twenty-seven years in prison. In 2014, DNA testing on the knife conclusively excluded Andersen as the assailant, so his conviction was vacated and the charges were dismissed. One year later, without opposition from the state's attorney's office, the Circuit Court of Cook County granted Andersen a Certificate of Innocence.

There is a fourth level of proof for the fact that the false-evidence ploy is perilous and should be banned: The scientific community is in near-unanimous agreement. In 2010, the American Psychology-Law Society (AP-LS) published a white paper that was highly critical of the false-evidence ploy. In 2014, the American Psychological Association passed a resolution "recommending that law enforcement agencies, prosecutors, and the courts recognize the risks of eliciting a false confession by interrogations that involve the presentation of false evidence."

Recently, my colleagues and I published in the *American Psychologist* a survey of eighty-seven PhD confession experts from all over the world. Overall, 94 percent endorsed as reliable enough to present in court the proposition that "presentations of false incriminating evidence during interrogation increase the risk that an innocent suspect would confess to a crime he or she did not commit." A full 100 percent (an almost inconceivable number for so large a sample) endorsed the proposition that "misinformation about an event can alter a person's memory for that event."

What Do Practitioners Think?

Imagine a pyramid of knowledge. At the base are the long-standing principles of psychology, all of which point to the perils of misinformation. One step up are the experiments specifically demonstrating the false-evidence effect on confessions. Yet another step up are the opinions of scientists reflecting this research literature. At the very top of the pyramid are the real-life anecdotes from actual cases. This four-tiered pyramid of knowledge is all the evidence the courts should need to ban the use of this psychological "stun gun."

You might think that the entire law enforcement community disagrees. Not so. In January of 2021, a bill was sent to the New York State

Legislature that would ban this sort of police deception (this bill was first introduced in 2019 but was derailed by the coronavirus). The International Investigative Interviewing Research Group (iiiRG), a Europe-based network of law enforcement practitioners and academics, voiced its support in no uncertain terms: "The use of deception in obtaining confessions has been shown unequivocally by an extensive international body of research to result in an increased likelihood of inducing a false confession, particularly with vulnerable detainees." Then the iiiRG added, "Sanctioned deception by an investigator [also] serves to undermine the legitimacy of the court and wider principles of justice."

Closer to home, there is Wicklander-Zulawski & Associates (WZ)—the second largest law enforcement training organization in the United States. WZ has trained over 200,000 investigators, including in 34 of the 50 largest police departments in the country. Homegrown and based in Chicago, WZ also unequivocally supported the proposed ban. As its president, David Thompson, put it: "The false evidence ploy, explicitly misrepresenting the facts, is an unnecessary tactic and is destined to result in contaminated statements from the guilty party or false confessions from the innocent." In the United States, WZ offers an attractive viable alternative to Reid.

Then there's the U.S. government's High-Value Detainee Interrogation Group (HIG), a three-agency entity (FBI, CIA, and DoD) that brings together intelligence professionals to conduct interrogations that strengthen national security. Susan Brandon, HIG's research program manager from 2010 to 2018, wrote in support of the ban, that "research thus strongly supports the notion that lying about evidence is unnecessary."

Colonel Steven Kleinman, an experienced investigator retired from the U.S. Air Force, could not be clearer in his support for this ban: "While this tactic might appear benign at first glance, it has proven to be insidiously problematic as a factor in generating false confessions nationwide." Then he added, "As a former intelligence officer who has interrogated foreign military officers, terrorists, and violent extremists, I have learned that the truth is something to be leveraged not hidden."

This support comes from an impressive group of professionals who study, practice, and train in the methods of interviewing and interrogation. But not everyone is on board. Joe Buckley, president of John Reid

& Associates, was asked if he would support the ban. Unlike the others of his cohort, he declined. Instead, he released a public statement titled "Should Investigators Be Allowed to Lie about Evidence to a Subject During Interrogation?" Citing *Frazier v. Cupp* and other opinions, his defense is not that it's moral and without risk to innocents but that the courts allow it, that the confessions thereby produced are admissible at trial. We lie about evidence *because we can.*

In a section titled "Don't Be Fooled by 'the Research,'" he characterizes the evidence through a pinhole and tries to pick apart two studies. *Two studies* out of a body of knowledge consisting of thousands of basic psychology research studies, dozens of false-confession experiments, near-unanimous consensus among scientific experts, and God knows how many false-confession tragedies caused by interrogators using this ploy—including John Reid himself.

Minimization—Promises Unspoken but Implied

In addition to thrusting the suspect into a state of despair by the processes of confrontation, which may include presentations of false evidence, interrogators are trained to minimize the crime through the development of "themes" that offer moral justification or face-saving excuses.

Precipitated by expressions of sympathy and understanding, a detective might downplay the moral seriousness of an offense by suggesting to a suspect that his or her actions were spontaneous, accidental, provoked, seduced, peer pressured, alcohol or drug induced, caused by stress or raging hormones, or otherwise justifiable by external factors. At times, detectives not only "minimize" the crime but "normalize" what they allege the suspect to have done by suggesting that they would have behaved in the same way.

Different themes are recommended for different types of crimes. Arson, burglary, cybercrime, identity theft, shoplifting, stalking, vandalism—each type of investigation triggers its own themes. For a sex crime: "Joe, no woman should be on the street alone at night looking as sexy as she did. Even here today, she's got on a low-cut dress that makes visible damn near all of her breasts . . . it's too much of a temptation for any normal man." For a theft in the workplace: "Man, how in the world can anybody with a family get along with the kind of money they're paying you? . . . Anyone else confronted with this situation would do the same thing. Joe, your company is at fault."

Cases in which minimization tactics seduced innocent but beleaguered people to confess are found everywhere. In the Central Park jogger case, every boy gave a false confession that placed his cohorts at center stage and minimized his own involvement. Sixteen-year-old Korey Wise said he felt pressured by his peers. Each defendant thought he would go home after cooperating with police.

In North Charleston, South Carolina, Lieutenant McHale started to shape a theme for Wesley Myers even before interrogation had formally commenced: "It's so easy to kill somebody when you're angry," he said. "Sometimes you don't know how strong you are." He even went so far as to plant this seed: "If you're guilty and it's an accident . . ."

In Manitowoc County, Wisconsin, Brendan Dassey's interrogators let him off the moral hook in no uncertain terms. After befriending Dassey, feigning sympathy, and offering the assurance that "I promise I will not leave you high and dry," Detective Fassbender said that Avery, not Dassey, was to blame: "It's not your fault, remember that. You've done nothing wrong."

In Lake County, Illinois, detectives crossed the line from inference to assertion when they said to Melissa Calusinski: "We're not here to condemn you, we're not here to put you in jail." "Show us how angry you were . . . and let's just get this over with and move on."

In Myrtle Beach, South Carolina, a homicide detective accused Renee Poole of killing her husband and questioned her for some twenty-four hours. She was emphatic: "I swear to God, get me a Bible I will swear to God I did not know he was at that beach." No matter. The detective used minimization techniques to imply to Poole that her involvement was minimal, maybe even excusable. "The only reason you did it," he suggested, "was because you didn't know what you were doing." He later peddled this mitigation theme even more profusely, implying self-defense: "You couldn't get out, he's pushing you, he's threatening you."

Then there was a case in Sioux City, Iowa, where police officer John Kayl interrogated eighteen-year-old Juan Macias for allegedly fondling a three-year-old girl in the day care center where he worked. After informing Macias that he had failed a polygraph (which he had not),

Kayl launched into an interrogation couched in sympathy and understanding.

At one point an exasperated Macias said to Kayl, "You're trying to
convince me of something I didn't do." But eventually he buckled and
said he touched the girl inappropriately one time. "I just wasn't thinking. It just happened." I've never seen an interrogation quite like this
one. Kayl jumped from one theme to another, waiting, I guess, for
something to stick. At various times, he suggested that Macias did not
start off to hurt anyone, it started accidentally, he made a mistake, he
got caught up in a hormonal rush, his hands slipped, this was a onetime
thing, it was a mere curiosity thing, and he did this because he was
under great stress.

Several experts testified that Macias was coerced. The judge agreed
and ruled to suppress the so-called confession. Lacking any other evidence, the prosecutor dropped the charge.

As for what minimization themes sound like, you get the idea. For
suspects who are trapped in a lengthy interrogation and cannot seem to
extricate themselves by denial, minimization themes offer an escape
hatch—a way to get out now and cut their losses. Consistent with claims
made by the Reid technique, I think it is fair to assume that criminal
offenders will take comfort in confessing in response to these tactics.
But two core areas of psychology compel the conclusion that this tactic
may also lead innocent people to confess.

The first concerns the age-old principle of *reinforcement*. For over
one hundred years, generations of behavioral scientists such as Edward
Thorndike, John Watson, and B. F. Skinner have found that people are
highly responsive to reinforcement and the perceived consequences of
their behavior. Later studies of human decision making added that
people are particularly influenced by outcomes that are immediate
rather than delayed. Now is worth more than later.

The second core principle at work in this situation concerns the
cognitive psychology of *pragmatic implication*. When we read text or
hear someone speak, we tend to process information "between the
lines," fill in the gaps, and recall not what was stated per se, but what
was pragmatically implied. In one study, for example, subjects who read
that "the burglar goes to the house" often mistakenly recalled later that
the burglar actually broke into the house. In another study, those who

PSYCHOLOGICAL INTERROGATION

heard that "the flimsy shelf weakened under the weight of the books" often recalled that the shelf actually broke.

These findings show that pragmatic inferences can change the meaning of a communication, leading us to infer something that is neither explicitly stated nor necessarily implied. This research is directly applicable to the suspect being lulled by minimizing themes.

In an article published in 1991, Karlyn McNall and I wondered how suspects interpret an interrogator's minimizing remarks. The courts don't have too many objective rules as to what constitutes a coercive interrogation. But there are some: police must apprise suspects of their Miranda rights and may not take confession through physical force, threats of harm or punishment, or promises of leniency. Fundamentally, the courts understand that even innocent people, if desperate enough, would confess if they thought they would escape punishment.

We tested the hypothesis that minimization remarks depicting a crime as spontaneous, accidental, pressured by others, or otherwise excusable would lead people to infer leniency in punishment as if a promise had been made under the radar.

Basically, we had subjects read the interrogation of an actual murder suspect. The transcript was edited to produce three versions: one in which the detective made an explicit promise of leniency in exchange for confession, a second in which he made minimizing remarks by blaming the victim, and a third in which neither statement was made. Each subject read one version and then estimated the sentence they thought would be imposed on that suspect. The result: compared to the no-techniques control group, subjects who read the minimization transcript had lower sentencing expectations—as if an explicit promise had been made.

Other researchers went on to find not only that minimization communicates leniency but also that it facilitates the innocent person's decision to confess. In one classic experiment, Melissa Russano and colleagues paired college students with a paid female confederate for a problem-solving exercise and instructed them to work alone on some problems and jointly on others. In some sessions, the confederate appeared to struggle and sought the subject's help on a problem that they were supposed to solve alone, causing the subject to cheat. In other sessions, the confederate did not make this request to induce the crime.

The experimenter soon "discovered" a similarity in their solutions, separated them, and accused the subject of cheating. The experimenter then tried to get the subject to sign an admission through an explicit offer of leniency (e.g., "Things could be settled pretty quickly"), minimizing remarks (e.g., "I'm sure you didn't realize what a big deal it was"), both tactics, or neither tactic. Mirroring real life, subjects who cheated were more likely across the board to sign a confession than those who did not. But even though the cheating was defined as a violation of the university's honor code, the number of innocent subjects who signed a confession increased from a baseline of 6 percent in the no-tactics control group up to 18 percent in response to minimizing remarks. In fact, minimization has exactly the same effect on innocent suspects as an outright offer of leniency.

Joe Buckley is not fond of these results. More than once, I've heard him say that interrogators cannot be held responsible if a desperate suspect engages in "wishful thinking" by hearing leniency in minimization. In fact, in an April 4, 2007, report on behalf of *State of Wisconsin v. Brendan Dassey*, he wrote that the various uses of minimization— some of which bordered on explicit ("Get it out today . . . this will all be over with")—"do not constitute impermissible promises of leniency but rather sincere interest in working with Brendan to tell the truth."

Historically, U.S. courts do not accept confessions extracted by promises of leniency because of the risk to innocents. If police are free to hint at a promise, unspoken and under the radar, they are essentially circumventing the law's intent. And the wishful thinking interpretation makes no sense. One might try to prop up this type of blame-the-victim explanation in actual cases but it does not explain why minimization has the same effect on neutral observers in a psych lab, who have no skin in the game and no reason to think wishfully. The U.S. courts have been wrong on this issue and should reexamine the perilous tactic.

Mr. Big Technique: Go Tell It to the Boss

On June 22, 1990, nineteen-year-old Kyle Unger attended a rock concert at a Canadian ski resort near Roseisle, Manitoba, his hometown. The following day, sixteen-year-old Brigitte Grenier was found dead in a creek in a heavily wooded area of the concert grounds. The crime was horrific. She had been beaten, bitten, and strangled; sharp sticks had been forced into her vagina and anus.

Grenier was a high school classmate of Unger's. She was last seen leaving the concert area with seventeen-year-old Timothy Houlahan. When Houlahan returned in the early morning hours, he was covered in mud and had scratches and blood on his face. When asked about it, he claimed he had been beaten by an unknown male. His statements notwithstanding, the physical evidence was strong: The victim's blood was found on Houlahan's running shoes; his hair was found on her clothing.

When questioned by the Royal Canadian Mounted Police (RCMP), Houlahan gave two statements. In the first, he said he and the victim had consensual sex in the woods that night, but then he was attacked and left unconscious by an unidentified man. In his second statement, Houlahan directly implicated Unger as that person and killer. He said he then helped Unger move the victim's body out of fear for his own safety. Suspicious but needing more evidence, the RCMP then took a highly controversial approach: the Mr. Big technique.

Mr. Big is a Canadian-born sting operation aimed at producing a confession and/or generating new evidence. For high-profile investigations that have stalled, undercover police officers will identify a target, research that target's friends and interests, and then pose as members of a criminal organization led by the all-powerful "Mr. Big." They will then approach, befriend, and gradually ensnare him into the fictitious network. Operatives socialize and incentivize the target, offering the possibility of membership, the trappings of a lavish lifestyle, and protection from police. In a scheme that can last for months, operatives gain considerable control over the target. To demonstrate the potential, they may even pay large sums of money for odd jobs like delivering packages or retrieving luggage from a bus station.

The scheme climaxes in a meeting with the kingpin. In that meeting, Mr. Big may tell the target that he is under police suspicion for a crime, which may threaten the organization's security. Mr. Big can thwart the police but only if he knows the details. Alternatively, he may tell the target that because he is familiar with the organization's activities, he himself needs to disclose his own criminal history as a form of "insurance." Disclosing details of a past crime demonstrates trust and loyalty.

Of course, once the target confesses to Mr. Big, he is arrested and charged.

This is what happened to Unger. Based on Houlahan's statement and a single hair found on the victim that was considered consistent, the RCMP approached Unger on June 13, 1991. Two undercover officers staged a breakdown of their car near where Unger lived, befriended him, and told him about an opportunity to join their organization. On four occasions during that first week, Unger told one of his new "friends" that he had been wrongly jailed for a murder. The officer never asked him to elaborate. Nine days later, Unger met with "Mr. Big" for what he believed to be a job interview. "Larry tells me that you whacked somebody. That's fine with me. That's, that's fuckin' excellent," he said. "That's the kind of person I'm looking for."

None of these conversations were recorded, but Unger is said to have confessed in order to come clean; he said he was acting to please his new boss. In subsequent conversations, Unger contradicted his own account. Still, he was arrested. Although he pled not guilty, he and Houlahan were both convicted in 1992 of first-degree murder. Thirteen years later, DNA testing indicated conclusively that hair found on the victim that was attributed to Unger was not his. In 2009, his conviction was overturned.

The Mr. Big technique was created in the 1990s to sidestep Supreme Court of Canada rulings that guaranteed a suspect's right to silence and counsel and limited the kinds of interrogation techniques that can be used against suspects who are in custody. In Mr. Big encounters, targets are not aware of who they are dealing with, so they are free to leave and hence not in custody. At that point, threats, inducements, and deceptive tactics that would otherwise not be permissible can be deployed.

This controversial approach is used on a regular basis in Canada. Timothy Moore and other Canadian research psychologists are quick to note that the inducements that undercover agents offer in exchange for confession can be substantial. For Unger, the promise of a social network and income accompanied by a hint of protection for a crime for which he was a suspect made it worth confessing to a murder he had nothing to do with. In other Mr. Big operations, fear and protection from violence have been used to induce confessions.

No systematic research exists on the effects of Mr. Big. According to a 2018 article by political science professor Kate Puddister, Mr. Big has been used hundreds of times at an estimated cost of over $150,000 per investigation. Statistics suggest a "success" rate of between 75 and 95 percent, where success is defined by the conviction or affirmative exclusion of the target. The problem is, sheer conviction cannot be taken as a metric of success when some unknown number of these cases yield the ultimate in failure: the colossally wrongful conviction.

In 2014, in *R. v. Hart*, the Supreme Court of Canada overturned the conviction of Newfoundland resident Nelson Hart. Hart had confessed in a Mr. Big sting to killing his three-year-old twin daughters, both of whom had drowned. With Hart living in poverty and in isolation, the Supreme Court found his confession unreliable because the promises made to him were too enticing. After nine years in detention, Hart was released. In its opinion, the court stated that confessions obtained through the Mr. Big technique would be subject to a high level of scrutiny. Importantly, the court formulated a new common law rule: that Mr. Big confessions will be presumptively inadmissible unless the government can demonstrate that the probative value of the statement outweighs its prejudicial effect.

Asserting an intention to set this high bar on Mr. Big confessions is a well-intended step, but one, I would argue, that is not easy to implement when it comes to long-term sting operations, which are not recorded, where judges are not privy to context, and where they cannot observe the tens of hours of influence, words spoken, information communicated, and the threats and promises made or implied. Seeing only the target's final recorded confession to the boss, it is not possible for judges to provide serious oversight or make sound judgments of voluntariness and reliability.

PUTTING THE PIECES TOGETHER: INTERROGATION WHIPLASH

I've always described the Reid technique as highly effective—if everyone interrogated is the offender. But that is not the case. The BAI is flawed, police are too confident, they lack accuracy, and too often they bring innocents in for interrogation.

As a precondition, police demand and exploit a home-field advantage. They bring suspects into a private room in their "house"—a small room, windowless, soundproof, and bare in furnishings. Suspects are isolated, alone, and helpless to control even the simplest of functions, like a visit to the restroom, without permission. In this closed situation, all information flows from police to suspects.

What follows is guilt-presumptive and highly stressful, especially to the many suspects who voluntarily entered the situation to help in the investigation. The session opens with an accusation, stated with certainty. As one false-confession case after another shows, there's almost nothing an innocent person can say or do to stop the process or slow the momentum once identified for interrogation.

As the process unfolds, denials are punished and demeaned. "You're a liar." This can go on for hours, making you wonder what if anything you can do to get out or call for help. The more you claim innocence, the more hostile your interrogators become. Your offer to take a lie detector test will be rebuffed or used against you.

Police let you know that they have evidence of your culpability. "We've got you whether you cooperate or not." If they don't have evidence, they will pretend, or manufacture an outright lie, or two or three, something you didn't realize they could do. That false presentation of a phony witness, surveillance footage that does not exist, or your fingerprints can stop you in your tracks. Some suspects know these claims are lies, but they fear they are being framed, set up, and in need of escape. Others, more profoundly affected, become confused, disoriented, and lose their grip on reality, wondering if it's possible, why they have no memory, and whether they blacked out.

Juxtaposed with these processes of confrontation is the soft touch, whereby the interrogator or a second detective turns on a dime to offer sympathy and understanding and gain the suspect's trust. This pretense aims at setting up the minimization themes that suggest moral justification, excuses, and an offer of an escape. It's no big deal, suspects are told. It's no wonder so many innocent confessors are surprised when they are handcuffed and arrested. In their minds, they had cooperated and will get to go home.

At a macro level, the interrogator's goal is to increase the stress associated with denial, while reducing the stress associated with confession. Those words come right from the Reid manual. Whether we use the words *reward* and *punishment*, the carrot or the stick, or confrontation and minimization, the suspect is badgered by a two-pronged attack sure to produce psychological whiplash.

As the hours wear on inside an American interrogation room, the suspect is set upon by stress, fatigue bordering on exhaustion, a heightened need to touch base with a loved one, and in some cases, deprivation of food, water, sleep, a cigarette, or other needs. Under these circumstances, human beings find it hard to make a rational, future-oriented decision.

Further compounding the human tendency to do whatever it takes to escape physical or psychological pain, and to make short-term decisions under stress, police often press for an immediate now-or-never decision in response to a last chance "exploding offer." Time is pressured; no time to think. Help yourself now, or we can't help you later.

Women, men, and children alike, the average person is overwhelmed by this tactical assault on their senses. It can get so intense that some innocent people are pushed not only to confess to things they didn't do but also to internalize the belief in their own guilt. In essence, they are brainwashed, at least momentarily, yielding internalized false confessions. They transition from "I wasn't there" to "I guess I did it" to "This is what I did, and how I did it. Where do I sign?"

Judges in the United States should educate themselves on the psychology underlying the process of interrogation. The courts view the process through a narrow, classic if not archaic, conception of what coercion is. Looking through this lens, the Reid technique may not appear coercive to the naïve observer, or to the professional jurist, when the detective doesn't yell, pound the table, get in the suspect's face, or make threats of harm or punishment.

That is not the only way false confessions happen. In countless cases that I have seen, the detectives used trickery and deceit to lull the innocent suspect into a false sense of security and then dupe that suspect into confession. The courts seem to miss this distinction. The con is produced not only with classic coercion aimed at breaking a suspect's will but also by altering the suspect's cognitive grip on reality.

5

HOLLYWOOD CONFESSIONS

Lights, Action, Camera

Presuming guilt and wearing blinders, interrogators doggedly aim to get suspects to make an admission of guilt. Sometimes in the lopsided battle between the professionals and naïve suspect, innocence cannot rescue the innocent. No matter how small, partial, inculpatory, or credible the first admission, it serves as a springboard for the production of a full narrative confession.

You might think that even if interrogation is psychologically coercive, pressuring innocent people at times to confess, such errors would ultimately be detected by authorities and corrected—like a built-in safety net. I've lost count of the times I've heard a cop or prosecutor reassuringly assert that "I'd know a false confession if I saw one." But can police distinguish between true and false confessions? What about the rest of us?

"I'D KNOW A FALSE CONFESSION IF I SAW ONE"

The claim that one can identify a false confession brings me back to the literature on deception detection, which shows that people, including trained professionals, cannot reliably distinguish between truths and lies. Perhaps an oral confession is special, and somehow more transparent? It's an easy claim to make. But how do they know?

In July 2000, Rebecca Norwick Eyre, my former Williams student, and I decided to test this hypothesis in a two-phased study. After graduating, Becca was accepted into the social psychology PhD program at Harvard (she is now on the research staff at the Federal Judicial Center). Through a friend of a friend, I gained access to the Essex County Correctional Facility (ECCF) in Middleton, a medium-security prison for men, forty minutes north of Boston.

We packed my then-heavy video equipment into the car and headed to ECCF to recruit inmates for the first phase of the study. Offering twenty dollars for thirty to sixty minutes of their time, we had no shortage of volunteers. Once there, we set up shop in an empty room, sparsely furnished. I sat behind a table facing an empty chair; over my shoulder, Becca managed a VHS video camera set on a bulky tripod. We also placed an audio recorder on the table.

One by one, inmates who volunteered came in and sat opposite me, facing the camera. Their task was twofold: (1) "Give me a full confession to the crime for which you are serving time," statements we later verified by each inmate's records, and (2) "I'm going to tell you about a crime that you were not involved in. I'd like you to imagine yourself doing it and make up a confession as if you did." We based these latter events on a prior inmate's true confession. By a flip of the coin, we asked some subjects for their true confession first; others gave the false confession first.

To ensure that all confessions contained the same basic ingredients, each free narrative was followed by a standardized set of questions that probed for who, what, when, where, how, why, and other details ("Had you planned to do it?" "Did anyone see you?" "Afterward, what did you do and where did you go?" "Did you tell anyone about it?").

After two days, we left with tapes in hand; on average they were five minutes in length. We then created a master videotape and a corresponding audiotape that depicted ten different individuals, each confessing to one of five crimes: aggravated assault, armed robbery, burglary, breaking and entering, and automobile theft and reckless driving. Five were the actual culprits of these crimes; five gave false confessions.

To give a sense, here's the main portion of one confession: "I saw a kid walking down, uh, my street, Nichols Street in Lawrence and, uh, he was walking around like he was a big shot, a hot shot, and I noticed that he had a nice gold chain around his neck. I can get money for that, so I, I went and took it from him. Plain and simple. I just. . . . He was walking with a friend of his. I had a knife at the time, so, I always carry a knife with me for, in case of emergencies anyways, so I ran up to him and . . . bumped him, then he turned around and looked at me and was like, 'yo, what's your problem?' and then I didn't hesitate, I went real quick and put the knife to his throat and like, 'what's the problem?' I ripped the chain off his neck and I'm like 'that's the problem. Is there any more problems now?'" This particular confession was false.

In Phase 2 of our study, we showed groupings of tapes to lay adults. Knowing that people would intuitively trust all confessions, we let them know in advance that some of the statements they would see were true and that some were false. First, we tested sixty-one male and female college students who took part in exchange for extra course credit. Then with help from cognitive psychology professor Christian Meissner, we tested fifty-seven federal, state, and local police investigators from Florida and Texas recruited through personal contacts. As a group, the police averaged eleven years of law enforcement experience. Six out of ten had received special training in the Reid technique and other methods of interviewing and interrogation.

Three results proved striking. First, across observers, the overall accuracy rate was an unimpressive 54 percent. In keeping with most studies of truth and lie detection, our subjects had accuracy rates so low they may as well have guessed or flipped a coin. Second, the college students outperformed our police investigators—59 percent to 48 percent, but the police were more confident—averaging 7.35, versus 6.21 for the students, on a ten-point scale. Third, within the police sample, those specially trained at interviewing and interrogation were no more accurate than the others. In fact, despite high levels of confidence, they were more likely to make what psychologists call "false alarm" errors, which means judging false confessions to be true.

This is an astonishing result, important enough to warrant additional research. So in 2014, Charles Honts, Ronald Craig, and I wondered what would happen if we elicited true and false confessions from juveniles as opposed to adult inmates. In a study that modeled the same procedure, twenty incarcerated juveniles, all seventeen- and eighteen-year-old males, were video recorded reciting two confessions—one to the crime for which they were incarcerated, the second to a crime they had not committed. We then showed the tapes to four hundred college students and found that on average they were only 53 percent accurate. There was one interesting wrinkle to this result: subjects tended to believe the confessions, so were better at judging true confessions than false confessions.

Honts later showed these tapes to eighty-three practicing polygraph examiners attending a continuing education seminar. Within this elite professional group, only 55 percent of their judgments were accurate, though they were confident. This study revealed two interesting wrinkles. First, while the examiners correctly judged 62 percent of true confessions, they mistakenly *believed* 52 percent of the false confessions. Second, those trained in the Reid technique were particularly biased in this way. Conclusion: "Our results suggest that Reid training is detrimental when assessing the credibility of juvenile confessions." So much for the first layer of that safety net.

Innocence Deniers

Once police take a confession, they present the suspect to the district attorney's office, where an additional statement is sometimes taken and where the prosecutor determines if there is probable cause to charge the suspect. I don't know of any empirical studies that have tested the prosecutor's ability to identify false confessions. I do know this, however: I've seen time and again prosecutors adhere to a confession as an act of faith even in the face of overwhelming contradictory evidence that unequivocally excluded the confessor.

The Philadelphia-area case of Bruce Godschalk illustrates the point. Godschalk had served fifteen years in prison for two rapes to which he had confessed, when DNA tests indicated he was not the rapist. Yet in 2002, Montgomery County district attorney Bruce Castor Jr. inexplicably refused at first to accept the lab results. When asked why, he said to *New York Times* journalist Sara Rimer, "I have no scientific basis. I know because I trust my detective and his tape-recorded confession. Therefore the results must be flawed until someone proves to me otherwise." Godschalk was eventually exonerated. I had no idea at the time that DA Castor would nineteen years later represent former president Donald Trump at his post-insurrection impeachment hearing.

This is not an isolated incident. In a 2011 article titled "The Prosecution's Case against DNA," *New York Times* writer Andrew Martin lifted the veil on district attorneys who concoct implausible and far-fetched theories to counter the DNA exclusion of suspects who had confessed.

This article featured the case of Juan Rivera, of Lake County, Illinois, who was convicted for the rape and murder of an eleven-year-old girl after he confessed—even after DNA testing of semen at the scene excluded him. I consulted on Rivera's case and was appalled by the state's attorney's dual theory of why someone else's DNA, and not Rivera's, was found inside the victim. His new theory was that the young girl had prior consensual sex with an unknown male (even though her twin sister said she was not sexually active), after which time Rivera raped her and failed to ejaculate. She then made fun of him, and he killed her.

Three days after Martin's article was published, an editorial appeared in the *Chicago Sun-Times* titled "The Evidence Is In: These DNA Theories Are Just Stupid." Two weeks later, the Illinois Appellate Court described the state's new theory as "highly improbable," expressed remorse for Rivera's "nightmare of wrongful incarceration," and overturned his conviction. It later turned out that the DNA was matched not to a "consensual sex partner" but to a convicted violent felon serving a life sentence for another crime he went on to commit.

In some delusional-prosecutor cases, the DNA not only excludes the confessor before trial but also identifies the perpetrator. The 2004 case of South Carolina against Billy Wayne Cope is one such example. I testified at Cope's trial; his was one of those cases that will always haunt me. Cope woke up one morning to find his twelve-year-old daughter strangled to death in her bed. On a mere hunch, police identified Cope as the perpetrator and interrogated him for several stressful hours using an array of disorienting trickery and deceit. After two days, Cope agreed to confess in a statement filled with factual errors.

Shortly thereafter, an autopsy revealed that Cope's daughter was also sexually assaulted, which was not part of his confession. Subsequent DNA tests revealed that the semen and saliva found on the girl's body was not a match to Cope, but they were a match to James Sanders, a serial sex offender in the DNA database who was out of prison and had broken into other homes in the area as well.

One would think from this series of events that Cope would have been released from jail, freed, and compensated. Instead, the prosecutor—armed with a confession that did not match the facts of the crime and with absolutely no evidence to link the two men—theorized that Cope had pimped his daughter out to Sanders (the jury in this trial was not informed that Sanders was awaiting trial for two other rapes). On the basis of this evidence-less theory, the jury convicted both Cope and Sanders.

Cope's conviction was affirmed at the state level; in 2014, the U.S. Supreme Court refused to grant his request for an appeal; in 2017, he died in prison, prompting his prosecutor Kevin Brackett to say: "Billy Wayne Cope was a cruel and selfish individual who elevated his own sick desires above the welfare, happiness and ultimately the life of his own daughter."

I offer one more illustration from my files. In a 2001 rape case in West Virginia, DNA testing not only excluded confessor Joseph Buffey but also matched a convicted sex offender. Yet rather than agree to vacate Buffey's conviction, the prosecutor's office proposed the new theory that Buffey and the sex offender were co-accomplices. This theory flatly contradicted the confession extracted from Buffey, which made no mention of an accomplice, and it contradicted the victim's own lucid account of a harrowing and protracted ordeal involving a single perpetrator.

Having consulted in the Rivera, Cope, and Buffey cases, and others like them, I keep a running list; I call it my Hall of Shame, representing the most absurd prosecutor theories ever. In a 2018 *Slate* article, Lara Bazelon referred to these officers of the court as "innocence deniers." Suffice to say, so much for the second layer of that safety net.

In all of these cases, the million-dollar question is, Why was the confession so irrevocably persuasive that nothing else mattered? What is it about these statements, in print, or audio, or video, that blinds authorities to all other evidence that follows? Spoiler alert: It's not just that the defendant admitted guilt. It's that the admission was accompanied by a narrative sure to dupe any fact finder, whether it's a prosecutor, judge, jury, or appeals court.

Two cases illustrate the irrevocable effects on an innocent person who is incentivized by captors to confess—and to make it convincing in the process.

The Story of Huwe Burton

Just before New Year's 2018, Barry Scheck, cofounder of the Innocence Project, called me. Alongside his cofounder Peter Neufeld, Scheck is among the most brilliant and passionate voices for justice I've ever known. He and I had worked together on a number of cases. The reason he called was that he and colleagues at the Innocence Project, Rutgers Law School, and Northwestern's Center for Wrongful Convictions had spent nearly a decade reinvestigating the 1991 conviction of Huwe Burton in the Bronx, New York. They were now working with the Bronx district attorney's Conviction Integrity Unit (CIU).

In 1989, at the age of sixteen, Burton had confessed to killing his mother. He recanted his confession and pleaded not guilty but he was convicted at trial and sentenced to fifteen years to life. He was released on parole in 2009, but his life was forever limited by parole restrictions, the threat of re-incarceration, the effects of conviction on employment and housing, and his desperate need for closure both to clear his name and identify the person who had killed his mother.

After interviewing witnesses and scouring thousands of pages of documents and photographs, they were convinced that Burton was innocent. They had presented their case to the CIU, which joined in the investigation, hoping that they would recommend that Burton's conviction be vacated. The CIU, headed by ADA Gina Mignola, fully appreciated the problems but could not get past the confession. Scheck's request was that I meet with the group in person to present the recent science that explains how a *false* confession can ring so *true*.

On July 2, 2018, in the shadow of Yankee Stadium, we met in a large conference room at the Bronx County DA's Office. Mignola and her team sat on one side of a rectangular table, Scheck and his team sat on the other, and I sat at the corner head near a large screen. I was asked to speak for up to an hour. I came armed with PowerPoint slides that linked relevant research to the facts of the case. Within a few minutes, CIU members started to ask questions—really good questions. My "presentation" morphed into a "conversation" that lasted nearly two and a half hours.

Here is the Burton story in a nutshell and why it was so hard to see past his confession. Burton lived with his parents, Raphael and Keziah Burton, in a three-family house they owned in the Bronx. The Burtons were hardworking immigrants from Jamaica. Raphael was there, in Jamaica, visiting family for two weeks.

On January 3, 1989, at 5:30 p.m., Huwe returned home and found his mother facedown on her bloodied bed, naked from the waist down, with her legs hanging off the edge. A blue telephone cord was wrapped around her right wrist; a knife lay on the floor, behind the bed. The contents of her cashless purse had been dumped onto the living room floor.

Burton called 911 immediately, in a panic-stricken voice. Over the next day or so, police interviewed the boy on site, at the precinct, and again at the house for hours. Then on January 5, Detectives Sevelie Jones and Frank Viggiano brought Burton in at 5:30 p.m.—for a polygraph, they told him. That did not happen.

But he was interrogated for hours, during which detectives deployed a playbook of threats and promises. On the one hand, they threatened that if he did not cooperate, they would send him to Rikers Island for statutory rape—for having sex with his thirteen-year-old girlfriend. On the other hand, they promised that if he did cooperate, he would be tried in family court, where his mother's death would be treated as a mere accident. When I talked to Huwe about his expectation, he said it was explicitly stated and clear: "You'll go to family court and your dad will pick you up there."

Those were his choices. And he was alone. Throughout the night, Huwe repeatedly asked to speak to his father, who, in turn, was frantically calling the detectives to see his son. The detectives never told Huwe about his father's inquiries; they told Mr. Burton that Huwe did not want to talk.

Burton dutifully handwrote a confession at 11:15 p.m. Four hours later, he was taken to an assistant district attorney to repeat that confession on camera, which he did. It was this fifteen-minute performance that persuaded the grand jury that indicted him, the judge who ruled the confession voluntary, and the trial jury that voted for conviction. It was this confession that the CIU could not overcome twenty-nine years later.

As the video opened, Burton could be seen dressed in a light button-down shirt, seated in the corner between a desk and a gray steel locker. He looked tired but ready to perform. To his left, an old-style analogue clock displayed the time—3:20 (the uninformed viewer would not real-

In 1989, at 3:20 a.m., sixteen-year-old Huwe Burton confessed in painstaking detail that he killed his mother in the heat of an argument. Additional evidence soon suggested his innocence. Still, he was convicted and spent nineteen years in prison. *Photo released to the public and used here with permission from Huwe Burton.*

ize that it was late night/early morning). To his right but off camera stood Detective Jones, one of his interrogators. A stenographer and a video technician were also in attendance. Once the ADA Mirandized Burton, he was off to the races. In the space of six minutes and seventeen seconds, he uttered a 944-word narrative chronology, uninterrupted, before the ADA had a chance to ask her next question.

He opened by saying that he and his mother had an argument the night before that she continued the next morning. When Burton woke up, he said, he was "stimulated" on drugs and "didn't really know what I was doing." He got a knife from the kitchen, which his mother noticed. She tried to smack him, causing him to move. At that point . . .

"I stabbed my mother in the neck. She fell onto the bed. . . . I went into the bathroom to wipe the knife off. . . . Put the paper in the toilet. Flushed the toilet. Came back in and . . . dropped the knife. I tried to make it seem as if it was a rape or something else. . . . So I removed her bottom garments. And I wrapped a blue telephone cord around her right wrist." He then went on to state that he took the keys to the family's Honda Accord because he owed $200 to his crack dealer, "Bugs." He then proceeded to school as if nothing had happened, visited his girlfriend, returned home, and called the police.

The ADA asked Burton if he had anything else to add. A careful viewing reveals the minimization-based promises that were made to Huwe in his prior interrogation. "I didn't mean to do it," he said. "It was an accident." "You know, any help I can get. Help me start over again, it would be appreciated. . . . You know, start myself over again. Think I can make it better this time."

Burton had been duped. Early the next morning, he was charged, booked, photographed in a "perp walk," and transported to Rikers. Local papers were ablaze with headlines like the *New York Post*'s "Crack-Crazed Teen Stabs Mom to Death." In that article, Detective Viggiano vilified Burton: "This is a new one on me—that someone would degrade their mother to that degree."

Then a few days later, on January 11, police in Mount Vernon, just north of the Bronx, stopped a car late at night for running a red light. They called in the plates and discovered that the car, a Honda Accord, had been reported stolen. The owner: Huwe's mom, Keziah Burton.

They looked up the driver. His name was Emanuel Green. At twenty-two years old, Green was a violent felon with a troubled psychiatric history. He had already been incarcerated for a forcible rape and an attempted armed robbery with a steak knife. He was out on parole.

And here's the clincher: one month earlier, Green and his wife, Stacey, moved into the downstairs apartment in the Burtons' building. In that brief period of time, there was conflict between the Burtons and their new tenants. Although Stacey Green had told police she left for work early that morning, that was a lie. She never showed up that day.

As it turned out, Burton's confession—that he stabbed his mother once, with a serrated knife, which he dropped near the bed, early in the morning—was what police believed at the time but was wrong on important details. The autopsy and forensic testing later showed that she was stabbed twice, not once; with a blade that was smooth, not serrated; and that the knife found under the bed had no traces of blood and was not the murder weapon. The medical examiner estimated the time of death to be about noon, when Huwe was in school. The so-called facts that appear in Burton's confession were incorrect. To all this I will add that Burton was not, and never had been, a crack addict, and there was no dealer named Bugs to whom he owed money.

At this point, you would think that Burton's detectives would hit the reset button on this investigation, or at least pause to consider this most obvious rival hypothesis. Instead, Detectives Jones and Viggiano drove up from the Bronx, interviewed Green, and walked away with a statement in which Green claimed that Burton killed his mother and then turned to him, a stranger, to help cover it up and sell the car.

Although this statement seemed to implicate Burton, it also contradicted Burton's earlier confession. Green was arrested and held without bail until he testified at Burton's grand jury hearing, at which point he was released on his own recognizance without charges. (Green was killed in an unrelated "love triangle" shooting before Burton's trial about a year later.)

Defended by famed attorney William Kunstler, Burton went to trial in 1991 based only on his confession and Green's statement. What Kunstler did not know, and what the judge and jury therefore did not know, was that detectives in Burton's case had taken proven false confessions in the Bronx just two and a half months earlier, from two boys, one of them named Dennis Coss.

Burton was convicted and sentenced to fifteen years to life. After the jury announced its verdict, he cried out, "I didn't kill my mom. I didn't do it. Didn't . . . . How can you do this to me?" Even after the jury was excused, he screamed in disbelief, "How can they do this? Oh, no, no. I didn't kill my mom. Where are they going?" Burton was so devastated he had to be removed from the courtroom.

I asked Huwe about this moment. He remembers the shock like it was yesterday. After seeing the jurors in court every day, he figured they would see the truth through all the smoke and mirrors. "When I heard the verdict, my legs buckled; I just collapsed. It was the first time I ever saw my father cry."

For eighteen years in prison Burton maintained his innocence. When he first became eligible for parole, he was denied because he proclaimed his innocence and steadfastly refused to accept responsibility and express remorse—which is what parole boards typically demand as a precondition for release. "They tricked me into confessing when I was sixteen," he told me and the graduate students in my lab. "I wasn't going to let them do it to me again at thirty-two."

Burton's father, older and less healthy than he used to be, then visited Huwe in prison ahead of his next parole hearing and urged him to cooperate. "Huwe, we all know you didn't do this," he said. "Just tell them what they want to hear so you can come home." In 2009, twenty years after his mother was murdered, Huwe was released on parole. Sadly, his father had died before he was freed.

January 24, 2019, was one of those magical days that don't come around often enough. Two days earlier, the Bronx DA's CIU issued a recommendation for dismissal. "After reviewing the weight of the evidence the jury heard, as well as the new scientific and scholarly evidence on the risk factors that contribute to false confessions, the information about the false confessions in the Coss and Parker cases, and additional detail about Green's prior criminal history, the District Attorney no longer has confidence that Huwe Burton's confession is reliable."

That morning, forty-six-year-old Huwe Burton, dressed in a navy blue suit and a light-blue button-down shirt, appeared in Judge Steven Barrett's courtroom. Also in attendance were Burton's dedicated team of attorneys: Barry Sheck, Steve Drizin, Susan Friedman, and Laura Cohen; Gina Mignola and her CIU team; friends, family, journalists, and news camera crews. I didn't realize it at the time, but I sat next to Huwe's girlfriend, Schaunta. The courtroom was packed; a live feed of the event was transmitted to the courtroom next door.

After the two sides spoke, all in agreement, Judge Steven Barrett officially vacated Burton's conviction. Using the word "tragedy" to describe his twenty years in jail for a crime he did not commit, Barrett said, "For this I apologize on behalf of a system that failed him." Then Burton stepped up to the microphone to speak. Fighting back tears, he said, "It's been a long, long journey and I'm thankful I've reached this point. I stand here for that sixteen-year-old boy who didn't have anyone to protect him."

After a press conference that followed this at once somber and joyous event, several of Burton's friends and allies came together for a celebratory lunch at the Red Rooster in Harlem. Seated in a private room, around tables filled with internationally tinged soul food and

Thirty years later, Huwe Burton was fully exonerated, and in 2021 the city awarded him $11.5 million. *Photo courtesy of Sameer Abdel-Khalek.*

drinks (I highly recommend the fried chicken with hot sauce), everyone took a turn to speak.

I met someone for the first time at this lunch whom I quickly came to admire. His name was Dennis Coss and he entered with his wife and three children. In October 1988, Coss and a friend were interrogated by the detectives investigating Burton's case for a murder/robbery at a Key Food supermarket. Independently, both were tricked into confessing. Both said that they served as a lookout for a third accomplice; both named the same accomplice. Yet the person they were induced to name was in custody at the time and could hot have committed the crime. Their confessions were false, and they were acquitted within ten minutes of the jury's deliberation.

When the two sides reinvestigated the Burton case, they discovered that the prosecutor had not disclosed that the detectives had previously taken these two other false confessions (using the same tactics, I might add). But because those prior defendants were juveniles at the time, their records were sealed and could only be unsealed with their consent.

Coss had moved on, was married, and had children. In order to consent to unseal the case file, he would have to sit them down and disclose this unhappy episode from his past. He did not have to consent; he did not have to make this very personal sacrifice. But on behalf of Huwe Burton, a stranger, he did. I learned this story after Coss walked into the Red Rooster flanked by his family, when a speaker stood and said, "I'd like to toast Dennis Coss's children. . . . You should know that your dad is a hero."

I know that I've digressed from the question of why it's so hard for police and prosecutors to see past a videotaped confession. But wrongful convictions are human stories with long tentacles that should not be hidden from view. Lots of innocent people are touched, including citizens later victimized by the perpetrator who got away with murder while police zeroed in on the wrong person.

I would offer up three reasons why the grand jury, trial judge, jury, and DA's office could not see past Burton's videotaped confession. First is the appearance of voluntariness. At the outset, the camera technician scanned the room, showing and introducing everyone present. A clock on the table was in full view (the 3:20 on the face is a.m., not p.m.); Burton showed no bruises, cuts, swelling, or black eyes; and the ADA dutifully read him his rights.

The second compelling aspect of Burton's confession is that he launched into a nine-hundred-word statement without prompting, assistance, interruption, or interference. He exhibited full cognitive command of his narrative in which he detailed what happened before, during, and after the crime.

Third, Burton did not get emotional or cry, while matter-of-factly describing how he allegedly killed his mother and covered it up. Anyone prone to presume his guilt may well interpret his demeanor as that of a cold-blooded killer. To me, he looked like a kid in a daze.

To understand how a false confession can appear so compelling it's important to understand the underlying theatrics. Let's zoom in on the Bronx, where the practice of videotaping confessions began. Beginning in 1975, Bronx County DA Mario Merola initiated a program to do just that. After police convinced a suspect to confess, they would take him to the DA's office for an on-camera confession. Compared to the lifeless recitation of written statements reread in court, the theatrics were riveting; the effect was potent. In 1983, Merola said, "We get a conviction in virtually every case."

This practice of videotaping confessions was adopted in short order throughout New York City, in Chicago, and elsewhere in the country. Working for the National Institute of Justice, William Geller surveyed U.S. police agencies in 1990 and found that one-third of all large departments were videotaping interrogations and confessions, in whole or in part.

Here's the rub. If you've seen the 2012 documentary *The Central Park Five* or Ava DuVernay's 2019 Netflix docudrama, *When They See Us*, about the same case, you'll recall that interviews with the actual defendants or scenes that dramatized police badgering the five teenage boys (four into false confessions) were intense and at times hard to watch.

Yet those scenes did not depict word-for-word what happened. That was impossible because no video footage ever existed. Detectives interrogated the boys, on and off, for fourteen to thirty hours. None of it was recorded. It was only after the boys broke down and confessed that they were taken to an assistant district attorney to record their prepared statements *on camera.*

One of my ongoing mantras in life is "it's important to know what you don't know." Without a recording of all pre-camera transactions between police and a suspect, it is not easy to piece together how a narrative confession was formed.

In Huwe Burton's case, detectives said he spontaneously confessed without guidance. Burton testified that once they threatened to send him to Riker's Island for statutory rape, and promised that confessing to an accidental killing would yield absolution in family court, he fell into a state of compliance and concocted a story that detectives helped him script and refine ("Was it an accident?" "Did you have a fight the night before?"). "It was totally rehearsed," he told me. "Over and over and over again."

Before he appeared on camera, at approximately 2:00 a.m., police called Burton's godmother, Elise Gilmore, with whom he was close, and told her that Huwe confessed. She rushed to the 47th Precinct, where the detectives brought her upstairs to the interrogation room. Huwe "didn't look like himself, he looked—he looked real frightened," she later testified. "His eyes was all, you know, I can't explain it . . . it

was like he'd seen a ghost or something. . . . He didn't look right to me."
As soon as Gilmore urged Huwe to tell her what happened, Detective
Jones interrupted and directed Burton to "tell her just like you told us."

I asked Huwe what this was about and why police involved his godmother. "It was a dry run, a *test run*," he said. "Make sure you tell her
like you told us." "So I kept looking over her shoulder at Detective
Jones to make sure I was getting it right." It was a dress rehearsal; he
was ready for his big performance.

Next up, Burton was fed and given time to rest. Jones, who was in
the room for the videotaping, reminded Burton to repeat his earlier
story, which he did using words and phrases that sounded more like
police jargon than a teenager's street talk. He said he used crack "for his
own personal use" and that it "stimulated" him; that he "proceeded" up
the road and traveled "northbound." Describing how he sought to
create the impression that his mom's murder was a sex crime, he said he
removed his mother's "undergarments."

Psychologically whiplashed by big threats and even bigger promises,
Burton was a prepared and motivated performer, no different from a
Hollywood actor.

The Story of Daniel Andersen

Sometimes the pre-video phase of interrogation in which the admission
of guilt is converted into a narrative confession is even more explicit.
Consider the case of Daniel Andersen, already discussed in chapter 4.

In January 1980, twenty-year-old Cathy Trunko was found on a sidewalk near her home, stabbed to death. Over the next five days, the
Chicago Police Department conducted an investigation and retrieved a
kitchen knife from under a bush one thousand feet from the crime
scene. This knife, which appeared to have blood on it, was assumed to
be the murder weapon. Shortly thereafter, late at night, police picked
up nineteen-year-old Daniel Andersen for drunk and disorderly conduct. He and the victim were casual friends.

At the station, Andersen was confronted by numerous investigators
and interrogated for sixteen hours. During that time, he was deprived of
food, drink, sleep, and access to a toilet. Also during that time, he was
confronted with one of the most egregious and disorienting presentations of false evidence I have ever seen—a photograph of the knife

found in the bushes near the crime scene next to work gloves he recognized as his own, which he had left in his car.

Andersen's reaction to the photograph was classic. He became confused, wondered about what he may have done, and inferred the worst. "I asked him, I says, when I had that fear in my heart that I was like delusional, blackout, whatever you want to call it, and I asked him, 'Are those my gloves?' And he says, 'You tell me.' And I says, 'Did I do this? Oh, my God. You know, I don't want to get emotional, but did I do this.' He said, 'Yeah, Dan, you did.'" In disbelief, Andersen started to cry. Finally, "I remember telling him, I said, 'If I did this, I don't remember it.' 'Well,' he says, 'how would you do it? Just go outside your mind and say how you would do it.' And then I came up with a story."

I should mention that none of this interrogation was recorded, and no such photo was ever entered into evidence. When asked about this ploy at the time, Detective James Higgins testified, "I don't know. . . . I don't recall." Recently, as a defendant in a civil suit, he has emphatically denied using the ploy: "There was never, ever a photograph with gloves and the knife ever."

Juxtaposed with the accusation of guilt, Andersen reported that Detective Higgins promised he would go home soon and offered him a ride on his boat (Higgins flatly denied this but it turned out he was one of the few Chicagoans who did actually own a boat). "We are friends for a long time," Andersen recalled Higgins saying. Before leaving, Andersen wrote on a chalkboard in the interrogation room, "Need a friend, call a cop."

Eventually, Andersen confessed on camera in a question-and-answer session with an assistant state attorney. As in Huwe Burton's case, this was not a private session in which the ASA might lean in, privately, to confirm the voluntariness of the statement he was about to take. In addition to a court reporter, Detective Higgins monitored the proceedings from inside the room.

Andersen went on to recite a story in which he left a bar after heavy drinking; needed sex; went home to get an old "navy knife," which he put in his boot; returned to his car to get gloves to avoid leaving fingerprints; and headed to the victim's house. The two engaged in some conversation, they kissed, he fondled her breasts, he said he loved her and wanted to have sex. She refused and tried to scream, at which point he stabbed her three times in the chest. On his way back home, he tossed the gloves and the knife.

According to Andersen, Higgins asked for his assistance in solving the murder. Unwittingly digging his hole even deeper, Andersen complied. He supplemented his confession by drawing a map of the neighborhood for Higgins on which he marked the spots where the victim was attacked and the knife was tossed. Trying to get inside the mind of a killer, Higgins then led him step-by-step in creating a "list" of actions in which he speculated how he *would have* committed the crime.

On the basis of these confessional elements and nothing else, Andersen was convicted and sentenced to prison. Fast-forward thirty-five years. DNA testing of the knife that Andersen cited as the murder weapon in his confession was excluded. The blood on that knife was not the victim's. In 2015, Andersen's conviction was vacated and all charges were dismissed. The Circuit Court of Cook County then granted him a Certificate of Innocence, which the state's attorney did not oppose.

With the benefit of hindsight, you're probably wondering, as I did: How did the innocent Andersen's confession performance come about? What process transitioned him from the "realization" (inference) that he must have committed murder to a full-blown narrative confession detailing events before, during, and after? And how did he know how to map the crime scene?

In 2005, drawing on an abundance of false-confession cases, I likened the confession-taking process to a Hollywood production: "Scripted by the interrogator's theory of the case, shaped through questioning and rehearsal, directed by the questioner, and enacted by the suspect." I have never seen this metaphor played out as explicitly as in this case.

In 1982, long before the publication of research on false confessions, and over twenty years before I proposed the Hollywood metaphor, Andersen testified that Detective Higgins created a "script" and that "we went over it for hours," culminating in a "dress rehearsal" in preparation for his on-camera appearance with the assistant state attorney. In fact, Andersen said that he was literally groomed for his performance: "He took me into the bathroom, made me comb my hair, wash up, straighten out my clothes . . . they had pizza waiting for me."

THE CONFESSION—A CHRONOLOGY OF WHO, WHAT, WHERE, WHEN, HOW, AND WHY

In *Miranda v. Arizona* (1966), the U.S. Supreme Court warned that even without using third-degree tactics, the psychological interrogation advocated by the Reid technique and others can compromise individual liberty and "trades on the weakness of individuals." This comment was accompanied by a single footnote signaling the risk of a false confession. That footnote cited a then-recent New York case involving a nineteen-year-old African American man, five-foot-five and skinny, named George Whitmore Jr.

On August 28, 1963, two young professional women living in an Upper East Side Manhattan apartment were killed—twenty-one-year-

In April 1964, George Whitmore Jr. (center) was picked up on a Brooklyn street for questioning in the career girl murder case. After twenty-six hours of unrecorded interrogation, he allegedly produced a detailed, sixty-one page confession that later proved false. *Photo courtesy of Tom Cunningham / New York Daily News.*

old Emily Hoffert and twenty-three-year-old Janice Wylie. Several
months later, with this high-profile career girl murder still unsolved,
Brooklyn homicide detectives picked up and questioned Whitmore.

After twenty-six hours of unrecorded interrogation, they took him to
the assistant district attorney for what would become an exquisitely
detailed sixty-one-page confession to both murders, to a third murder,
and to a rape as well. The NYPD announced that Whitmore's confessions contained details that only the murderer could have known.

Chief of Detectives Lawrence McKearney laid it out at a press conference: "He wandered to the apartment on 88th Street. . . . He found
the door cracked . . . stabbed the girls repeatedly after binding them
with a sheet. . . . Then he calmly washed his hands and left." Whitmore
signed the statement attributed to him, but he later recanted it. He said
he was coerced and had not even read the statement he was pressured
to sign.

Ultimately, it turned out that Whitmore had a solid, if not ironic,
alibi: On the day of the murders, he was 160 miles away in Wildwood,
New Jersey, a boardwalk beach town with an amusement park on the
Jersey Shore. At the time of the murders, he was perched in front of a
black-and-white Motorola TV, watching Reverend Martin Luther King
Jr.'s historic "I Have a Dream" speech in front of the Lincoln Memorial.

After spending nearly three years in jail and a decade on bond,
Whitmore was exonerated. At that point, nobody disputed his inno-
cence. The actual perpetrator was later identified, prosecuted, and con-
victed. Whitmore's false confessions were historic in their significance.
This case is described in Fred Shapiro's 1969 book *Whitmore* and T. J.
English's 2011 book *The Savage City*.

Contamination: Details Only the Perpetrator Could Have Known

What shocked the conscience about Whitmore's false confession was
that it contained surprisingly specific, accurate, rich details about the
career girl murders that were not known to the public—the kinds of
facts, we were told, that "only the perpetrator could have known."
What's shocking, actually, is how often this happens and how blinding it
is even when the confessor claims innocence.

In a groundbreaking 2010 article published in the *Stanford Law Review*, Duke University law professor Brandon Garrett pored through thirty-eight Innocence Project case files containing police-induced false confessions. Each of these cases involved murder, rape, or both; in each, the confessor was exonerated by DNA.

By examining the content of each confession and comparing it to the then-known facts of the case, Garrett found that thirty-six of the thirty-eight false confessions contained crime details that were spot-on accurate, often exquisitely precise, and not in the public domain. In most of these cases, the defendant's apparent knowledge of these facts became a centerpiece of the prosecution's case at trial. After all, according to the detectives who testified, these were facts that only the perpetrator could have known. Five years later, Garrett expanded his sample in the light of twenty-eight additional false confessions and found that sixty-two of the sixty-six contained accurate details not publicly known.

In these cases, DNA is a crystal ball that tells us that these confessors were factually innocent and had no basis for firsthand guilty knowledge. Since the facts they disclosed were not known to the public and did not appear in the newspapers, that leaves only one other secondhand source: the police who conducted the interrogations. Purposefully or inadvertently, through leading questions and assertions, exposure to photographs, or escorted visits to the crime scene, police contaminated a whopping 94 percent of false confessions by communicating crime details to the suspect. Of course, no judge or jury would dare to acquit a defendant who exhibits guilty knowledge.

To their credit, John Reid & Associates and others have interrogation manuals that urge readers and trainees to purposefully hold back crime details from the media and from the suspect to ensure that the suspect's guilty knowledge is based on firsthand experience—not details acquired through exposure to news accounts, leading questions, photographs, visits to the crime scene, and other secondhand sources. So why is it that so many false confessions were contaminated by facts fed by police to the suspect? This can happen in two ways—inadvertence or something more nefarious.

Sometimes police can contaminate a confession without intent or awareness. It just happens as a natural part of having a conversation. In a 2007 article titled "I Took a False Confession—So Don't Tell Me It Doesn't Happen!" retired DC Metro police detective James Trainum told the story of a homicide investigation in which he and his partner interrogated a female suspect named Kim Crafton, on camera, and took what he thought was a rock-solid, fully detailed confession. After a lengthy interrogation, she told him that she and two men had kidnapped a man, used his ATM and credit cards at multiple locations, then beat him to death and dumped his body near the Anacostia River. She was arrested and charged with robbery and first-degree murder.

Crafton later recanted her statement. Trainum later discovered to his own surprise that she had an ironclad alibi. The logbook of a homeless shelter she was living in supported her alibi that she was there at the time. After ten months, she was released from jail, and the case was dismissed. On his end, Trainum pulled the videotaped interrogation from the shelf, watched it, and was horrified by what he saw. "We had fallen into a classic trap," he realized. "We believed so much in our suspect's guilt that we ignored all evidence to the contrary. To demonstrate the strength of our case, we showed the suspect our evidence, and unintentionally fed her details that she was able to parrot back to us at a later time. It was a classic false confession case, and without the video we would never have known."

Jim and I have spoken often since this episode. I know him to be the kind of person who would never callously pursue a case against an innocent person. He visited with me and the students in my lab shortly after writing about this experience. He is now a fierce advocate for recording interrogations from start to finish and a harsh critic of the Reid technique. In 2016, he published a book titled *How Police Generate False Confessions: An Inside Look at the Interrogation Room*.

Jim's experience tells us something about ordinary human social interactions. Language philosopher Paul Grice notes that people in general try to establish a common ground and tailor their speech to match what they think their conversation partner already knows. If the process of interrogation is guilt-presumptive, as I've argued, then an investigator may well share critical nonpublic crime details, believing that the suspect already has access to this information.

In real-life cases, where police may act not only on their beliefs but also their motivations, it's hard to disentangle benign inadvertence and purposeful contamination. But what if laypeople who are not paid to close cases exhibit this same tendency?

As described in an article published in 2020, Fabiana Alceste and Kristyn Jones brought fifty-nine subjects into our lab to play the role of a suspect. Half of these subjects were directed to break into a room in the lab; find a key hidden in a cup; and use the key to open a filing cabinet drawer, which contained the combination to a briefcase behind a partition, which contained a folder, which contained an envelope, which contained a $100 bill. The other subjects were not similarly instructed and knew nothing about the incident. They spent the time on an unrelated innocent task. All suspects were instructed not to confess if questioned about the crime.

Paired with each suspect, a second subject was instructed to play the role of an investigator. These investigators were taken through the various steps of the crime scene, then they interviewed a suspect in an adjacent room via a Skype audio-only connection. These investigators had no idea if their suspect was guilty or innocent. Half were incentivized with an offer of bonus cash to get the suspect to confess; the other half were not.

In Experiment 1, mock investigators communicated crime facts to both guilty and innocent participants at the same rate, demonstrating that contamination occurred naturally in the information-gathering interview. They over-shared information even though suspects steadfastly denied the charge. Alceste and Jones reported two key findings. First, investigators leaked crime details to suspects regardless of whether they were incentivized to get a confession. Overall, the questions they created contained an average of 3.94 out of 9 key crime details (for example, 78 percent disclosed the presence of a briefcase). Second, many of these leaked details found their way into all of the suspects' statements—including those who were innocent and had no firsthand guilty knowledge.

To sum up: naturally and without evil intent, mock investigators communicated crime facts to both guilty and innocent mock suspects who, in turn, inserted these facts into their statements. The risk of inadvertent contamination is clear.

Is Contamination Purposeful or Inadvertent?

Sometimes police contaminate confessions, despite training, in a manner that "feels" more purposeful than inadvertent. I am not a mind reader and cannot divine a detective's motives and intentions. But in some instances, the contamination of an innocent suspect's confession seems so oddly rich, and so egregious, that it's hard for me to sustain an inadvertence hypothesis.

In Detroit, exoneree Eddie Joe Lloyd had allegedly recounted the crime and victim in lurid detail, noting that the victim wore Gloria Vanderbilt jeans and half-moon earrings; that she was threatened with a red-handled knife; that she was strangled with long johns; and that a dirty green bottle was inserted into her rectum.

In Nassau County, New York, exoneree John Kogut allegedly gave detailed descriptions of his victim's "maroon or black pocketbook with a strap," "white high-top sneakers," and "gold colored chain with what looked like a double heart on it with a piece broken off of it." That's more perceptive about a woman's attire than I would ever be.

In Lake County, Illinois, exoneree Juan Rivera correctly stated that the victim's back door was damaged with a mop; that she wore "black stretch pants with stirrups on the bottoms and a multi-colored shirt"; that the knife was taken from the kitchen, broken, and found in a nearby backyard; that the victim had cuts on her legs and arms; and that she was both vaginally and anally penetrated.

Among many, the case of Barry Laughman well illustrates the point. One August evening in 1987, neighbors in Adams County, Pennsylvania, discovered the partially nude body of eighty-five-year-old Edna Laughman in her home. Investigators presumed that she had been killed the previous night. The neighbors, including twenty-four-year-old Barry Laughman, a distant relative, were interviewed.

A few weeks later, with the case still unsolved, Pennsylvania state trooper John Holtz called Laughman back for questioning at the State Police barracks in Gettysburg. Holtz asked the questions, and allegedly Laughman gave the answers. Although a tape recorder was available, the session was not taped. Instead, Holtz's colleague, trooper Donald Blevins, took verbatim notes by hand. The troopers reported that Laughman confessed after two hours. At that point, the handwritten statement was recorded in a process I'd never seen before: Holtz read both his questions *and* Laughman's answers.

Say what? With both a tape recorder and a suspect in the same room at the same time, why read Laughman's answers for him? Why not insist that Laughman speak for himself in his own voice? This procedure—which is not recommended in any interrogation manual I've seen, and which rendered Laughman conspicuously absent from his own confession—should by itself arouse suspicion that something was off.

Maybe what was off was that Laughman was intellectually impaired. IQ tests administered over the years indicated that he had an intellectual disability; he scored in the lowest 1 or 2 percent of the general population. Or maybe what was off was that Laughman suffered from severe anxiety disorders that were apparent to everyone who knew him. Or maybe . . .

I can imagine only two possible reasons for this odd departure from normative practices: (1) Laughman did not author the statement, which was, therefore, not in his own words, and/or (2) troopers Holtz and Blevins were aware of Laughman's cognitive limitations, believing him unable to repeat the answers that were prepared. Either way, trooper Holtz, when asked why he chose not to ask Laughman to repeat his own answers on tape, responded: "I'd be taking a whole new statement if I did that."

Setting aside the interrogation tactics used on Laughman, which were not recorded, the confession attributed to him contained some strikingly precise details about the crime scene and victim, that an innocent person could not have known or produced. According to Holtz, Laughman disclosed information that only the killer could have known.

Among these details were that the victim was found lying on her bed; she was faceup; she was on a pile of clothes; she was injured from a blow to the head; her arms were bruised from being gripped; her bra was pulled up to her neck; her mouth was filled with pills; there was semen in her vagina; there was a little blue bag with money missing; there was a pill bottle in her right hand; there would be no fingerprints on the bottle; there were four or five Marlboro cigarettes smoked in the house; one cigarette was put out on a chair near the bed; the front window was open; and a folding chair was placed up against a door.

How could anyone but the perpetrator know these things? Trooper Holtz testified at trial that Laughman was the source and that he and trooper Blevins were careful to withhold information "that only the person responsible would know."

That was not how Laughman remembered it. He repeatedly said at trial that Holtz put words in his mouth:

Q: "What did he say about the pills?"

A: "He said that I put them in her mouth."

Q: "Who was the one who started talking about cigarettes?"

A: "Trooper Holtz."

Q: "Who talked about the fact that there was sex with Edna?"

A: "Holtz."

Q: "Who talked about a blue bag?"

A: Holtz."

Q: "Do you remember . . . and you answering because I could never get a girl."

A: "*They* said I could never get a girl."

Q: "How did you know Edna had a bump on her head?"

A: "They were explaining it."

At trial, Holtz also gave theatrical testimony of the process by which Laughman had come to confess—an account of not just *what* he said but *how* he said it: "Barry stated he wanted to tell us something. You could see it was bothering him greatly. He grabbed the arms of the chairs. He raised in his seat no more than six inches, said he would like to tell us something but he asked us not to tell his parents."

Also compelling is that the confession Holtz and Blevins attributed to Laughman allegedly contained these five powerful indicators of credibility:

- Vivid sensory details about *how* the victim was killed (Laughman said "She was making funny noises like gagging sounds").
- A physical reenactment (Laughman demonstrated "how he had the nose pinched to hold the mouth open").

- Expressions of shame, regret, and remorse ("He asked us not to tell his mother or father"; "He then said that he did a bad thing . . . he knew it was wrong and wished he had not done it").
- A description of how he tried to mislead investigators (to conceal his identity, "he wiped his fingerprints off the bottle with the rag" and to make it look like a robbery, "he took four hundred dollars").
- Motive statements, indicating *why* he raped and killed the victim (he went to the victim for sex because "he could never get any girls" and later killed her because "he knew she would tell on him").

Whether by design or not, investigators also obfuscated Laughman's statement by concocting a nonsensical and, I think indefensible, procedure. By taping their own reading of questions and answers without Laughman, they added nothing to the written document on which the tape was based. As a result, troopers Holtz and Blevins ensured that no judge or jury could later scrutinize Laughman's level of comprehension, anxiety, or voluntariness, or his ability to recount the crime facts without prompting.

As in most trials that pit police officers versus the defendant, the officers prevailed. This one in particular was a slam-dunk conviction. In fact, the theatrical confession overshadowed the lab result presented at trial, which identified the rapist as a blood type A secretor. Laughman's blood type: B. In 2004, DNA testing on the semen found inside the victim conclusively excluded Laughman. After sixteen years in prison, he was exonerated and released.

CONFESSION AND THE ART OF ILLUSION

Professional interrogators are trained not just to dupe suspects into increasing degrees of admission but to produce oral and even demonstrative proof of guilt that will later dupe fact finders. They are trained in the art of creating illusions.

The final Hollywood product, scripted, rehearsed, and ready for prime time, is a statement sure to sell in court—even when it lacks corroboration and even when it is contradicted by other evidence. And if the storyline itself is not compelling enough, many false confessions feature additional con artistry aimed at making the admission of guilt believable.

In their manuals, Reid & Associates advise police to ask suspects crime-irrelevant autobiographical questions—like where they grew up or went to school, and where they live—and to incorporate the answers into their statement. At first glance this may seem superfluous. But here's the rationale, drawn directly from the manual: "At trial, the offender may allege that the confession represents only what he had been told to say—that the investigator put the words into my mouth." The presence of these irrelevant but accurate details will help to offset the claim that the statement as a whole is false.

There's even more to the illusions that make false confessions hard to detect. In 2013, researchers Sara Appleby and Lisa Hasel analyzed the contents of twenty known false confessions. They found that every single one contained visual and auditory details about the crime and the crime scene ("There was blood all over the walls," "As I ran out I heard the neighbor's dog barking"). All referenced the victim and described the victim's behavior before, during, and afterward ("She tried to run away," "Her body rolled out of the blanket").

Ninety-five percent of the statements referenced co-perpetrators, witnesses, and other actors ("Dennis, as John's driving around, says to the girl, 'You want to party?'"); 80 percent described what the victim said ("Then she said, 'Leave me alone, let me out'"); 75 percent described aspects of the victim's appearance ("She had dark hair, medium long. She had on a blue denim dungaree jacket, I think a dark top, dark pants, and white high-top sneakers"); 45 percent described the victim's mental or emotional state ("She was scared, she could hear me coming"); and 40 percent expressed sorrow and remorse or heartfelt apologies for the crime they did not commit. "This was my first rape," said sixteen-year-old Korey Wise of the Central Park Five, who was innocent, "and it's going to be my last."

The list goes on. Many of the false confessions articulated a motive and a minimization theme that justified, excused, mitigated, or externalized blame (for example, claiming the crime was spontaneous or accidental or blaming alcohol, peer pressure, or provocation). Still others contained explicit assertions that the confession was voluntary, "illustrators" such as a hand-drawn map or physical reenactment, or deliberately inserted errors allegedly corrected by the confessor.

Practice Makes Perfect—the Effects of Rehearsal

Earlier, I described the confession of nineteen-year-old Dan Andersen. Five days after a young woman was found stabbed to death, police arrested him for drunk and disorderly conduct. The next night, after sixteen hours, he recited a confession to the assistant state attorney. His statement contained crime facts that were accurate, though all of these facts were known to police. At trial, Andersen testified that the lead detective literally created a sexual assault and murder "script" and that "we went over it for hours," culminating in a "dress rehearsal" before his session with the assistant state attorney. Thirty-four years later, as a result of new DNA testing, Andersen's conviction was vacated and he was granted a Certificate of Innocence. In June 2021, a jury awarded Andersen $7.55 million in a lawsuit he filed against Chicago police.

In 1990 and a thousand miles away, sixteen-year-old Huwe Burton could also be seen on video describing how he killed his mother in the Bronx (described earlier). In footage that is stunning yet hard to watch, Burton recited a nine-hundred–word story, apparently without prompting or guidance. Stoic and unencumbered by emotion, he recounted in a chronological narrative what he did, how and why, before, during, and after he supposedly killed his mom. This performance seemed so voluntary and so compelling that it stymied the DA's Conviction Integrity Unit thirty years later. It turns out that the detectives questioning Huwe coached him and even took him through a "dry run" before putting him on camera with an assistant DA.

We've all heard it; we all know what it means. The expression "Practice makes perfect" describes the well-known phenomenon that repetition improves learning and memory. Hermann Ebbinghaus, a German psychologist who conducted the first-ever controlled experiments on human memory, at first using himself as a subject, introduced this concept as well as the learning curve and the forgetting curve. In 1885, he published *Memory: A Contribution to Experimental Psychology*. In that classic book, he reported on controlled experiments showing that the amount of information subjects retain improves as a function of the number of times they review it.

What Ebbinghaus and his progeny did not examine, then or now, was whether repetition changes the way *other people* perceive the person who recounts information—like an event from the past. So let me switch gears here. People cannot discriminate between truths and lies at high levels of accuracy—neither you nor I, nor the so-called experts who pitch themselves as human lie detectors. It's a daunting task. But one way to improve performance is to focus less on whether a speaker seems *anxious* (consistent with the flawed belief that lying increases anxiety in perceptible ways) and more on how much *effort* a speaker is exerting (consistent with the finding that it is cognitively more difficult to make up a false story than to recount a true one).

In general, people become better at detecting lies when focused on effort. But what if someone who is lying has practiced the falsehood, making it easier to tell? In a study published in 2019, researchers recruited people to describe on camera something they saw or did—or to make up a story about something they did not actually see or do. Some of these subjects told their true or false story only once; others did so three times. Then observers were brought in to view either the once-told stories or the rehearsed versions. At this point, you can probably anticipate the result. When observers watched unrehearsed statements, they were moderately accurate at distinguishing the truths and lies. But when they watched the rehearsed statements, their "discrimination accuracy" deteriorated. Observers are naturally misled into believing others who deliver a rehearsed and fluent false statement.

You can see where I am going here. What if the speaker is an innocent crime suspect, and the rehearsed lie is a false confession? The experiences of Daniel Andersen, Huwe Burton, and so many others certainly suggest an answer. To test the hypothesis in a controlled situation, Fabiana Alceste and colleagues brought college students into our lab and asked half of them, but not the others, to commit an elaborate, step-by-step mock crime—stealing a $100 bill that was hidden in an envelope inside a locked briefcase.

We forewarned each subject that an investigator would question them about the theft of $100 and that they should deny any knowledge or involvement, which they did. Then we flipped the incentive switch, something that happens in real interrogations. The experimenter returned and incentivized subjects to cooperate with the investigator by confessing. The investigator then turned on a video camera and said,

"Tell me everything." When the subject was finished, the investigator prodded the subject: "I need you to tell me a more complete story of what happened." After the second iteration, the investigator elicited a third ("Tell me again") and a fourth ("I think you'd better tell me everything just one more time").

Enter Phase 2 observers. An independent group of subjects watched one of the four iterations. When asked if they thought the confessor was guilty or innocent, they exhibited a predictable tendency to see guilt. But compared to their perceptions of the first iteration, where they exhibited at least a modest ability to distinguish true and false confessions, the more rehearsed iterations led almost every observer to believe the confession—even when the confessor was innocent. It's no wonder Andersen's jury, and Burton's jury, and so many others, could not see past these "Hollywood" productions.

The Error Correction Trick

One surefire way to create the illusion that a suspect has a perpetrator's guilty knowledge is to use the *Error Correction Trick*, as I call it. Over the years, many of the cases I have worked on contained confessions in which the suspect corrected and initialed minor factual errors before signing. Not all the detectives in these cases were formally trained in the Reid technique. But error corrections have seemed ubiquitous. The first couple of times I saw this, the error corrections weighed on my judgment; at the very least, they showed that the suspect read the statement carefully and was able to spot the error. Then I came across more and more instances, also containing error corrections, in which the confession was proven false and the suspect was innocent. How can that be?

Again, I turn to the Reid technique manual for insight. "It is good practice to purposefully arrange for the inclusion, on each page of the confession, of one or two errors, such as an incorrect name of a person or street, which will be subject to later correction by the confessor. When confronted at the trial . . . the confessor will encounter considerable difficulty in denying having read the document before signing it." It's something of a diagnostic check indicating that the suspect proofread the statement carefully and corrected what was wrong, thereby vouching for everything else. So far, so good.

But wait. The next paragraph continues: "When the previously described intentional errors are reached, the suspect will usually call them to the investigator's attention. *To play it safe, however, the investigator should keep the errors in mind and raise a question about them in the event the suspect neglects to do so*" (italics added). This explains why so many innocents who signed confessions appeared attentive if not outright cooperative. This is the sleight of hand behind the police-induced illusion that this trick creates. Only this time, it affects the judge and jury.

By the way, judges (and, I'd bet many prosecutors, too) are not aware of this trickery. Over the years, I've spoken to groups of judges in a handful of states. "By a show of hands, how many of you have ruled on written confessions while on the bench?" would be my first question. Everyone had. "And how many of you have seen confessions in which the defendant handwrote corrections to the statement?" To this question, most hands would go up. Third question: "How many of you know that many police are trained to deliberately insert errors for the defen-dant to correct?" At most a hand or two would go up. Then I read the italicized passage above from the Reid manual and many in the audience gasped. Judges who had assessed the credibility of confessions, and whose assessments may have been influenced by the presence of corrected errors, had no idea.

Sometimes this trick is deployed to an absurd degree. In Lake County, Illinois, exoneree Juan Rivera was interrogated relentlessly and without sleep for twenty-four hours. During the last night and into the morning, he sobbed so hard that his clothes were wet. He banged his head against the wall, squatted in the corner of the room, lay in a fetal position, hyperventilated, and pulled his hair out. He was transferred to a padded cell and put on suicide watch.

Yet according to the officers who took the confession that landed Rivera in prison, Rivera read the statement they had prepared aloud that morning and without assistance and made and initialed fifteen corrections to phrasing, spelling, and grammar.

According to these detectives, Rivera changed "North Chicago" to "Waukegan"; deleted "named Holly"; replaced "gollowed" with "followed"; changed "come" to "keep her company"; deleted "I wanted to take her virginity because I have done that before"; changed "I had her lick my penis" to "She licked my penis"; changed "stuck my finger in her pussy" to "played with her pussy"; replaced "croutch" with "crotch"; changed "stabbing" to "struggling with"; changed "dripping off" to "on"; replaced "stonach" with "stomach"; deleted "and some dropped on the floor"; corrected the spelling of "bhehind" to "behind"; replaced "whcih" with "which"; and crossed out a letter attached to the word "off."

In my report on this case, I wrote: "It may seem extraordinary that, after nearly twenty-four hours of interrogation—during which time a sleep-deprived Mr. Rivera suffered a severe mental breakdown that led to his transfer to a padded cell and suicide watch—that he would have proofread his statement so carefully as to spot and correct fifteen substantively insignificant errors."

The Letter of Apology

In the case described in chapter 4, Wesley Myers was badgered and brainwashed into confession. He killed his girlfriend in a fit of jealous rage, he said, and then set the bar she was working in ablaze. He spent seventeen years in prison before his conviction was overturned and he was released.

Myers didn't just admit guilt accompanied by a detailed narrative. After he surrendered his grasp on reality, his interrogating detective offered him an "opportunity" to apologize to the victim's mother. He said yes, they brought her in, he told her he was sorry and that he lost control and killed Teresa.

That wasn't enough. After Myers was arrested, the detective called the local news media to let them know they had had made an arrest and would be escorting the suspect to the county jail. The detectives testified that they advised Myers not to talk to the media. That's not how Myers recalls it. And why call the news media and stage the perp walk in the first place? In an appellate opinion, a state judge commented: "Such actions were improper and reflect poorly on the professionalism of the department." Nevertheless, Myers emerged into the light of day, in front of cameras, and declared, "I want to tell the world how sorry I am."

The presence of apologies and expressions of remorse within or outside the body of false confessions is all too common. It's part of the art of illusion. After getting a suspect to confess, police may use the pressure of the moment to get a handwritten apology letter, pounding yet another nail into the coffin.

In a 2013 *Training Bulletin* published by Third Degree Communications, Inc. (a consulting firm that trains police and other professionals), Paul Francois and Enrique Garcia wrote an article titled "Obtaining a Letter of Apology." After arguing for the strategic benefits of getting this letter, they recommended ways to convince the suspect to write it.

- "Sell the letter as a means of showing remorse," they state, "*to convince others* he is truly sorry for his actions."
- Borrowing a technique used by sales professionals, say: "I'm going to give you an *opportunity* that I've given everyone that has sat in the same chair you're sitting in, and they've all taken me up on it . . ." You're planting the seed that if "everyone" else has done this, it's a good idea for him to do it as well.
- Don't ask the subject if he wants to write the letter. "Simply provide the subject with pen and paper."

I don't doubt that a letter of apology reinforces the perception of guilt in fact finders. Just as you cannot imagine admitting to a crime you did not commit, you surely can't imagine apologizing for it. But if a suspect like Wesley Myers has capitulated, even if innocent, he will rather easily be persuaded to follow that confession up with a letter that may bring forgiveness and the kinds of legal benefits that come from accepting responsibility: hence, the presence of apologies in innocent people's false confessions.

Physical Reenactment

Earlier, I described an Israeli case in which a thirteen-year-old girl was brutally murdered in a bathroom stall at her school. After ten days of interrogations, which featured serial presentations of false evidence, a Ukrainian immigrant named Roman Zadorov confessed. The people of Israel and the courts were steeped in controversy. Zadorov was found guilty, but even the victim's mother to this day does not believe he is the killer.

After Zadorov orally confessed, detectives took him to the crime scene and walked him into the school so he could demonstrate his alleged actions. After ascending a flight of stairs, flanked by police, he incorrectly turned to his left, the opposite direction from the murder scene. His escorts nonchalantly steered him right and into the girls' restroom where he "demonstrated" how he locked himself and the victim in a stall.

Although Zadorov's reenactment seemed incriminating, he had endured ten days of interrogation, during which he was told all about the crime—for example, that the stall door remained locked after the murder, so the killer must have jumped over the wall. Based only on his oral confession and this follow-up demonstration, and in the absence of any physical evidence, Zadorov was convicted. Zadorov's demonstration was a form of reenactment: a physical re-creation of some or all elements of a crime. This is a common supplement to the oral confession. It can take the form of a hand-drawn sketch or map, a demonstration inside the interrogation room, or a visit to the crime scene.

In Lake County, Illinois, for example, day care worker Melissa Calusinski confessed to killing a sixteen-month-old boy in a preschool. Afterward, five times, police handed her a doll and directed her to show them how she threw the boy to the ground, which she dutifully did.

In New York City, fourteen-year-old Kevin Richardson was one of the wrongfully convicted Central Park defendants. During his on-camera confession, Richardson stood up and demonstrated how one boy pinned the jogger's arms back while another removed her pants.'

Then there was the wild and crazy story of Kenzi Snider, a nineteen-year-old American exchange student from West Virginia who spent a semester at Keimyung University in Taegu, South Korea. On Saint Patrick's Day, March 17, 2001, Jamie Penich, a fellow American exchange student in the program, from a small working-class town in western Pennsylvania, was brutally murdered. She, Kenzi, and other exchange students had partied at Nickelby's Pub before returning to their rooms in a cheap hotel in Seoul's red-light district, where the murder took place.

Early indications were that an American serviceman might have been involved. Penich had been dancing with GIs at the bar just hours before she was killed, the hotel manager said he saw a young white male with blood on his pants run out that night, and a guest in the room next door reported hearing an angry male voice followed by stomping noises. Jamie's naked body was discovered the next morning. Her face was covered with a black fleece jacket. Korean police investigated locals and U.S. Army suspects stationed nearby, but then the investigation languished and the crime remained unsolved.

About a year later, intense political pressure built to solve the crime. On behalf of the Penich family, Pennsylvania senator Arlen Specter lobbied the Korean police and FBI. Shortly thereafter, agents contacted Snider out of the blue. She was back at Marshall University, in Huntington, West Virginia, taking classes and working part-time as a teacher's aide at a school for troubled teens, when the phone rang: We are trying to tie up a few loose ends, they said. Eager to help, Kenzi agreed to meet.

Enter U.S. Army Criminal Investigation Division special agent Mark Mansfield and two FBI agents, Seung Lee and Marc DiVittis. They checked into the Huntington Ramada and arranged for Kenzi to come in, alone, for questioning. What Kenzi did not realize was that they had already drummed up a baseless but elaborate theory—what they called "the lesbian angle." With that presumption to guide them, they interrogated her on and off for three days—right there in a hotel room, of all places.

On the first day and night, they asked Kenzi how she was doing and expressed an interest in her well-being. "We were joking and laughing, and I started to trust them because they seemed so concerned about me," she said years later to Melba Newsome, a writer for *Oprah* magazine. "They never gave any indication that they suspected me." Years later, in a podcast titled "A Tale of Two Systems: The Story of Kenzi Snider," she recalled how one of the agents said he thought of her as a sister.

Snider was comfortable enough in this situation to let the agents know she had not been sleeping well since the murder and having bizarre dreams of being simultaneously attacked by a train and a shark. In response, Agent DiVittis, impersonating Sigmund Freud, suggested that such dreams often reveal sexual conflict.

The agents asked Snider to meet with them again the next morning with an account of everything she could remember about that night. Dutifully she completed her homework and returned with a handwritten account and homemade ice cream for the group.

Then the tide turned brutal. Agents confronted Kenzi with minor inconsistencies in her original and current memories. They accused her and discussed the possibility of committing such a heinous act and then repressing it from memory. As the session proceeded, Snider, under intense duress, was disoriented. She cried and asked about getting a lawyer. If she did that, the agents warned, they could not later say that she cooperated.

When it was done, Kenzi Snider—a Girl Scout and honors student with no history of violence—hunched over in a chair, closed her eyes, and tearfully confessed to stomping Jamie to her death, savagely, in a drunken sexual encounter. Snider was so confused that she came to internalize the belief and form images of how she actually did it.

On her third day, the agents prepared a written confession, and Snider signed it. According to them, not a minute of their three days of questioning was recorded. When later asked, in the light of day, if she murdered Penich, Snider said, "Not by the memories I hold true."

Three weeks later, Snider was arrested and jailed in Charleston, West Virginia, for ten months. She was then extradited to South Korea to stand trial (in fact, she was the first American sent to South Korea under a new extradition treaty). Once there, she was housed for six weeks in solitary confinement, in a four-by-seven-foot cell in a detention center in Seoul. She was permitted two showers a week, thirty minutes a day of recreation time, and seven minutes a day for outside visitors. She was then transferred to a different cell, which she shared with roughly ten other women, and slept on a blanket on a stone floor.

Interestingly, the criminal justice system in South Korea has a deep-seated distrust of the oral confessions police take privately from suspects. So, when Snider arrived, uniformed police handcuffed her, tied heavy blue ropes around her waist, and drove her to the Kum Sung motel that served as the scene of the crime. They handed her a mannequin and said, "You are going to reenact your crime."

Once inside the motel, police escorted Snider to room 103 and flung open the door. As soon as Snider peered in, she felt a surge a relief. The size and layout of the room did not at all match her recently created "memory." She told author Harriet Ryan, "Any doubts I had . . . as far as did this or didn't this happen was cemented. I did not kill Jamie." Immediately and emphatically, she retracted her confession.

She told police but they continued to instruct her in the reenactment and took still photos as she used the mannequin to pretend to kiss Jamie, then hit, kick, and stomp on her. Police and prosecutors pushed, but she would not repeat the motel confession taken by the FBI.

Snider was tried by a panel of judges who tossed out her original confession and acquitted her. The prosecution appealed the verdict, but the appeals court upheld the ruling—in fact, the chief judge explicitly suggested that a third party likely committed the murder. Yet again, the prosecution appealed the verdict. This time, it was the Supreme Court of Korea that affirmed: *not guilty*.

There is an important lesson to be learned in the story of Kenzi Snider. In some ways, a post-confession physical reenactment at the crime scene presents the ultimate in theatrics. But it is potentially diagnostic. Only the perpetrator, without steerage, can locate the "where" and demonstrate the "what" and "how" of a crime. It's one thing to parrot the words; any contaminated innocent suspect can do that. It's more challenging to go through the motions of a physical demonstration. This is an empirical hypothesis in need of research. Something tells me that would be far easier for the perpetrator than for the innocent.

THE VIDEO SOLUTION

I do not begrudge prosecutors, judges, and juries who refuse to disbelieve the confessions of innocents when all they see is their final, detailed, scripted, and rehearsed statements. When further inflamed by the appearance that the suspect has corrected errors or issued a heartfelt apology, sometimes in a letter to the victim's family, or stood up and physically reenacted the crime they did not commit, no human observer stands a fighting chance.

Just as the first goal of a trained interrogator is to induce the presumed-guilty suspect into confession, the second is to persuade the fact finders in court into believing that confession. People are not stupid—except when they are blinded to the context, when they cannot see how the fatal confession came about. It's the primary reason that the single most essential system reform is the mandatory recording of interviews and interrogations in their entirety, from start to finish. More on that later.

Part Three

Why We Believe False Confessions

6

FORENSIC CONFIRMATION BIAS

How Confessions Corrupt Witnesses and CSI Experts

Innocent people induced into making an admission of guilt have largely sealed their own fate. On paper or on camera, Hollywood-like confessions are compelling. Most are augmented by narrative details about the crime that are vivid and quite accurate. Often the narratives reek of credibility, as when the confessor explains not only what happened but why, and then apologizes to the family and expresses remorse. Sometimes they agree to reenact the crime they did not commit.

And it gets worse. Whether true or false, confessions have a way of multiplying in their impact on criminal investigations. This happens because of confirmation biases—the human urge to seek out, perceive, and interpret new information in ways that confirm existing beliefs. The story of Amanda Knox illustrates this point.

AMANDA KNOX'S STORY

For several summers, my family and I rented a farmhouse in Cortona, a magnificent Etruscan city about seventy miles south of Florence. The locals are warm and friendly, the cathedrals and medieval architecture line steep narrow streets, the piazzas are brimming with life, the food is amazing, the city is surrounded by some of the best Chianti and Sangiovese wineries in the world, and it serves as home to the villa Bramasole, the site of the 2003 film *Under the Tuscan Sun*, based on Frances Mayes's book of the same name. The *pici*, a thick hand-rolled pasta, local to that region, is like nothing of I've ever tasted. Finishing up with a double scoop of gelato to be consumed while people-watching from the steps of the Piazza della Repubblica, and, well, Cortona became our favorite place to get away, hide away, and relax for two or three weeks a year.

In November 2007, British exchange student Meredith Kercher was found raped and murdered in Perugia, an ancient hilltop city north of Rome and southeast of Florence. Perugia, the historic capital of the Umbria region, features a Gothic cathedral, a marble fountain, and regional art from as early as the thirteenth century. Perugia is a forty-minute drive from Cortona, so when the news broke, I paid extra-close attention.

Immediately I heard that police suspected twenty-year-old Amanda Knox, an American student and one of Kercher's roommates—the only exchange student who stayed back and did not flee for home after the murder. Then I heard that Knox had confessed, which led to three arrests. By Italian law, all suspect interrogations are to be recorded, but somewhere I read that the tape was lost. How was that possible? It seemed inconceivable. Then I read that the interrogation was never taped to begin with. That seemed even more inconceivable. At this point, curiosity seized me.

Knox was a happy, free-spirited girl from Seattle, spending her junior year of college abroad as so many American students do. She was just starting to learn the language and had just met a new boyfriend, a native named Raffaele Sollecito. She was disoriented and devastated by what was happening.

But on a hunch, police did not trust her. She had no history of violence and no motive; fake news notwithstanding, they had no evidence—none. The autopsy results were not in. DNA had not been analyzed. Witnesses had not been interviewed. Rudy Guede, whose DNA was scattered throughout the crime scene, was still at large and unknown.

But Edgardo Giobbi, head of Rome's Special Services, thought that Amanda was too calm, not grief-stricken enough. When he took her back into the house/crime scene, he asked her to put on protective paper shoe covers before entering. She struggled a bit, then, according to Giobbi, she got them on, said "voila," and twisted her hips in what he considered a seductive manner.

The next day, the tabloids reported that Amanda and Raffaele went out to buy sexy lingerie. In 2017, I interviewed Amanda onstage at the American Psychology-Law Society's annual conference. I asked her what really happened. "I was locked out of my apartment because it was a crime scene," she said. "And I had my period." To a ballroom audience now rumbling with laughter, "Say no more" was all I could come up with. Amanda needed underwear. So she went to a Target-like store that didn't even sell lingerie.

Two days later, Giobbi learned that Amanda and Raffaele went out for pizza; he found that suspicious, too. She'd been interrogated for hours that day. She was hungry; she was in Italy. Pizza hardly seems like a meal worthy of suspicion.

Armed with this alleged proof of character, Giobbi boasted in a television interview: "We were able to determine guilt, psychologically, without a need for analyzing evidence."

I've heard these kinds of baseless claims so many times I've lost count. Peter Reilly. Marty Tankleff. Michael Crowe. Gary Gauger. Jeffrey Deskovic. And on and on. According to the detectives who took these men's false confessions, none of them exhibited satisfactory forms of emotionality.

Besides, in the footage I saw, Amanda stood outside the crime scene biting her nails and pressing her hands together. At other times, she slapped herself in the head, shook uncontrollably, and sobbed. What investigators described as a lascivious make-out session with Raffaele to me looked like two somber individuals giving comfort to each other. So you'll have to pardon my cynicism at the very suggestion that Italian investigators can tell when someone is lying by taking in a snapshot of their demeanor.

Armed with a prejudgment of Knox, officials interrogated her on and off for over fifty hours in four days. It culminated on the evening of November 5 when Knox was interrogated for eight hours, without a break, all night and into the morning.

In many ways, she was a vulnerable suspect—young, far from home, without family, traumatized, and grilled by a tag team of up to ten officers in a language in which she was not fluent. Worse yet, she was yelled at, called a liar, threatened, and subjected to the kinds of trickery and deceit that can cause psychological whiplash to innocent suspects. Twice she was smacked in the back of the head, which shocked her. She had never been hit before.

During this final night of interrogation, Knox was given no food, no water, no nap, and no bathroom breaks. Falsely, she was told that Sollecito, who was being simultaneously interrogated in another room, disavowed her alibi and that physical evidence placed her at the scene. She was encouraged to shut her eyes and imagine how the gruesome crime had occurred; a trauma, she was told, that she had obviously repressed. Eventually she broke down crying, screaming, and hitting herself in the head.

Two "confessions" were produced in this last session, detailing what Knox called a dreamlike "vision." Both were typed by police—one at 1:45 a.m., the second at 5:45 a.m. She retracted the statements in a handwritten letter as soon as she was left alone ("In regards to this 'confession' that I made last night, I want to make it clear that I'm very doubtful of the verity of my statements because they were made under the pressures of stress, shock, and extreme exhaustion").

Notably, nothing in the confessions indicated firsthand guilty knowledge. In fact, the statements attributed to Knox were factually incorrect on significant core details. She named as an accomplice Patrick Lumumba, a bar owner she worked for part-time, whom police suspected but who had an ironclad alibi; she also failed to name Rudy Guede, whose DNA was scattered all over the crime scene.

Let me pause and drill down on two points. The first is the fact that Amanda named Patrick Lumumba. She has been roundly criticized for doing so, and even charged with slander—as if the statement attributed to her was voluntary. It is an empirical fact that most false confessions contain accurate details not yet known to the public and "false-fed facts" that are consistent with the police theory of the crime but that later prove to be untrue.

This was exactly what happened in this case. Police were intensely interested in Patrick Lumumba, the owner of a small bar she worked in, the night of the murder. The confession she later signed aligned with their theory. Yet this detail proved to be completely wrong. Consistent with so many cases, the police contaminated her confession. To hold her accountable for a statement in which *she also implicated herself* is absurd.

The second point is that the prosecutor failed to record the interrogations, as required by Italian law, or so he claimed, so the confession attributed to her was not admissible in court. This seems inconceivable to me. At that point, police had Knox under twenty-four-hour surveillance; they seized her computer, read her emails and text messages, and wiretapped her phone. Clearly, she was a suspect. Yet her interrogation sessions, conducted in a room equipped for recording, were inexplicably not recorded. In *The Monster of Perugia*, Mark Waterbury refers to this assertion as "conspicuously unbelievable."

Either way, evidence be damned. Based on Amanda's statement alone, Knox, Sollecito, and the innocent Lumumba were all immediately arrested. In a media-filled room, the chief of police took to the microphone and announced: *Caso chiuso* (case closed).

Fast-forward two weeks. Rudy Guede, a local drug dealer and burglar, was known to carry knives. In the month before Kercher was killed, he was caught or seen breaking into a residence, an office, and a nursery school. The day after Kercher's murder, he fled to Germany. Then on November 19, police announced that Guede was a suspect.

The evidence against Guede was substantial. His DNA was found on Kercher's vaginal swab, sweatshirt, bra, and purse; he left his feces in the toilet bowl of her bathroom; his handprints and shoe prints were found in her blood. In a 2016 article on this case, forensic scientist Peter Gill pointed out that Guede had not previously visited this apartment, so there was no innocent explanation for his DNA at the crime scene.

From Germany, Guede, once identified, was recorded in a Skype conversation telling a friend that news reports were wrong, that Amanda Knox was not even there. The next day, German police arrested Guede; a week later, he was extradited back to Italy.

The case against Rudy Guede was rock solid, and there was never any physical evidence to suggest that Kercher's murder involved multiple perpetrators. But it didn't matter. The damage was done. Patrick Lumumba was released, but Amanda and Raffaele remained in jail. Her so-called confession had set into motion a hypothesis-confirming prosecution, viewed with tunnel vision, that just wouldn't stop.

The post-confession corruption of evidence started with Guede himself. After he was recorded unwittingly on Skype absolving Knox, Rudy's story evolved over time. He heard her that night; Meredith complained to him that Amanda was stealing her money, then he put Amanda inside the crime scene. He and Meredith were together, he said. He was in the bathroom when Knox and Sollecito stabbed her. After this "fast-track trial" testimony, he was sentenced to sixteen years, not the thirty years expected. He served a reduced sentence. Believe it or not, he was recently set free.

In the ensuing months, police forensic experts tested a knife they had collected from a drawer in Raffaele's kitchen. Although lead expert Patrizia Stefanoni asserted that this knife, which contained Knox's DNA on the handle, also contained Kercher's blood and DNA on the blade, independent court-appointed experts fully discredited this conclusion on appeal.

Faced with the fact that the knife tested negative for blood, the prosecution could have revised its unsupported "theory." But instead, the prosecutor sought to explain away the lack of blood evidence by claiming that Knox and Sollecito had cleaned the knife, possibly with bleach. From an evidentiary standpoint, this proposition was baseless.

To further account for the fact that Knox's DNA was found nowhere in Kercher's room or on her clothing, the prosecutor advanced a non-sensical "selective cleaning hypothesis"—that Knox cleaned Kercher's room afterward to remove all traces of herself. First of all, DNA is invisible to the naked eye. Second, as Peter Gill puts it, "It is not possible to clean a room to selectively remove all traces of one individual's DNA whilst leaving behind another individual's [Guede's] DNA."

After Knox confessed, several "eyewitnesses" sprang into view. An elderly woman said she was awakened by a scream followed by the sound of two people running; a homeless drug addict said he saw Knox and Sollecito in the vicinity that night; a convicted drug dealer said he saw all three suspects together; a grocery store owner said he saw Knox the next morning looking for cleaning products; one witness said he saw Knox wielding a knife.

All of a sudden, one of Knox's Italian roommates turned on her. Just before Knox was induced to confess, she and Filomena Romanelli had spoken on the phone. Their conversation, which was recorded by police, revealed that Romanelli was friendly and empathetic to Knox and that the two women were planning to look for another house so they could continue to live together. Yet after Knox's confession, Romanelli's opinion soured. Ultimately, she testified as a negative character witness for the prosecution.

The same thing happened with Knox's British roommates. When police first interviewed them, not one reported that there was bad blood between Knox and Kercher. After Amanda's highly publicized confession, however, these girls brought forth new "memories," telling police that Kercher was uncomfortable with Knox and the boys she would bring home.

The pattern by now should be clear. Authorities induced Amanda Knox to confess. From that moment on, they would not turn back—not even when Guede was identified and apprehended. They presented forensic evidence that was fully discredited by independent examiners, they brought in witnesses who made clams that lacked credibility, and they turned character witnesses against Knox. And that all happened in a court of law.

I've spoken to Amanda about all this. She was "shocked" by the parade of witnesses who testified against her. She was innocent. What they were saying was untrue. So how did that happen? In answer to this question, the science is clear.

I've also spoken with Raffaele about this at length. He is to be admired for his conscience. While others were corrupted by Amanda's confession, he resisted the temptation at great personal sacrifice. Over the next four years, Raffaele was the only solid alibi Amanda had for the night of the murder. He came under unrelenting pressure—from his own lawyers as much as the police and prosecution—to change his testimony and stop vouching for Amanda. But he would not roll on her to save his own skin. In a story filled with villains, he was a hero.

In the court of public opinion, lead prosecutor Giuliano Mignini described Kercher's murder to the press as a satanic ritual sex game in which Meredith was killed because she refused to participate. There was nothing to support his imagination—or his calling Knox a "she-devil."

This was not the first time Mignini had cooked up this script or impugned a defendant's character with lies in the press. Mignini himself was convicted of prosecutorial misconduct in a prior high-profile case in which he blackmailed and wiretapped his perceived enemies. For a riveting account of his abuse of power in this case, journalists Douglas Preston and Mario Spezi's 2008 bestseller *The Monster of*

In 2007, twenty-year-old Amanda Knox was on a semester abroad in Perugia, Italy,
when her British roommate Meredith Kercher was found raped and murdered in
their home. Based on a hunch, police suspected Knox and her new boyfriend,
Raffaele Sollecito. After four days of interrogation, Knox confessed. This photo
was taken in court two years later, before she and Sollecito were convicted. In
2011 they were acquitted on appeal and set free, and in 2015 they were fully
exonerated by Italy's highest court. *Photo licensed from Alamy Images.*

Florence is a must-read. As a result of this publication, Mignini arrested and jailed Spezi, who spent twenty-three days in prison before being released and absolved (he continued this vendetta by repeatedly filing charges against Spezi, all of which were dismissed). Preston was also arrested, detained, interrogated, and threatened with an ultimatum that forced him to leave Italy.

I will add to the mix the following heinous experience to which Amanda Knox was subjected. About a month after her arrest, someone visited her in jail posing as a doctor. After drawing blood, this impersonator told Amanda that she tested HIV positive. This was a lie. He then asked her to write down the name of every sex partner she's ever had so they could be notified, tested, and treated. Amanda dutifully did this, a fact that was leaked to the press, which reported that she kept a prison diary detailing her sexual escapades.

In 2009, Knox and Sollecito were convicted of murder and sentenced to twenty-six and twenty-five years, respectively, in prison. They appealed and were acquitted; the prosecutor appealed; they were reconvicted. They appealed again and were re-acquitted. After eight years in dizzying limbo, the two were fully absolved. In 2015, Italy's Supreme Court ruled that the case was wholly without foundation. Citing "glaring errors," "investigative amnesia," "sensational failures," and "culpable omissions," the court declared Knox and Sollecito innocent. (For excellent factual accounts of this case, which was otherwise mired in disinformation, I recommend Nina Burleigh's *The Fatal Gift of Beauty* and Candace Dempsey's *Murder in Italy*.)

The moral of the story and the theme of this chapter is that *confessions corrupt*. When someone confesses, in an ultimate act of self-incrimination, our instinct is to assume that the person is guilty—no ifs, ands, or buts. Then we proceed to twist, turn, discard, and otherwise fit other evidence into that belief. Confessions taint police and prosecutors. They also taint lay witnesses and forensic examiners. The proverbial mountain of discredited evidence used to convict Amanda Knox and Raffaele Sollecito was nothing but a house of cards built upon a false confession.

In November 2010, at the request of Amanda's family, I submitted a report to the Court of Appeals in Italy. I focused my analysis not only on how her confession was taken but also on its ripple effects on other evidence. This was my closing paragraph:

> Basic psychological research shows that lay people and experts have a natural tendency to interpret ambiguous evidence according to existing beliefs. Studies also specifically show that the presence of a confession, because it creates a strong belief, can contaminate latent fingerprint judgments, eyewitness identifications, and interpretations of other types of evidence. In light of these research findings, the courts would be advised to review the case against Ms. Knox with a full awareness that the confession itself—and the perceptions and evidence it may have influenced—should be treated with caution.

THE PSYCHOLOGY OF CONFIRMATION BIAS

There are certain basic tenets of human nature that no psychologist would dispute—like the fact that people all over the world approach rewards and avoid punishment, that memories are constructed over time, and that people are inherently social creatures, which makes us vulnerable to influence from others.

Another core tenet is that people seek out, perceive, and interpret evidence in ways that verify their preexisting beliefs. Call it "seeing what you want to see," "tunnel vision," or "intellectual stubbornness." It is a striking and all too common feature of human nature: once people make up their minds about something—even if they don't have all the necessary information—they become reluctant to rethink their position when confronted with new evidence.

After examining this problem in criminal investigations, my colleagues Itiel Dror, Jeff Kukucka, and I coined the term *forensic confirmation bias* "to summarize the class of effects through which an individual's preexisting beliefs, expectations, motives, and situational context influence the collection, perception, and interpretation of evidence during the course of a criminal case." The consequences can range from trivial to tragic.

The idea that people selectively *seek out information* that verifies existing beliefs has a long history in psychology. In 1960, experimental psychologist Peter Wason gave students a three-number sequence, like 2-4-6, and challenged them to figure out the rule he had used to generate this set. The best way to proceed, they were told, is to make up their own sequences and ask the experimenter to indicate whether or not they fit the rule. Subjects were told they could test as many sequences as they wanted and then to state the rule only if they were certain that they knew it.

The task was straightforward, and the rule behind 2-4-6 was easy: any three increasing numbers. Yet out of twenty-nine subjects, only six discovered the correct rule without first seizing upon one that was incorrect. What happened was this: subjects would start with an initial hypothesis (adding by 2s, even numbers, skipping numbers) and then search only for confirming evidence. Thinking that the rule was "adding by 2s," a subject might test 6-8-10, 50-52-54, 21-23-25, and so on, yet never try disconfirming sets such as 6-8-4 or 3-2-1. When all the sequences fit, the subject would proudly and with confidence announce the wrong rule.

When I complain about a guilt-presumptive interrogation, this is why. The investigator who becomes convinced that a suspect is guilty asks questions aimed at confirming that hypothesis. It's like the classic experiment by Snyder and Swann described in chapter 4 in which people ask alleged introverts what they don't like about parties while asking alleged extroverts what they do to liven up a good party. Closer to home, it's like the experiment in which my colleagues and I found that subjects directed more aggressive interrogations aimed at confession when they were led to believe that the person they were interviewing was likely to have committed the mock crime. This mindset explains the often relentless interrogations that police direct against suspects who waive their rights and show no signs of a guilty conscience.

Beliefs can steer not only how people search for information but also how they perceive and interpret that information. Imagine you're in a psych lab staring at a computer screen. You're looking at an image slide that is completely out of focus. Gradually, it becomes more focused and less blurry. At this point, the experimenter asks, Can you recognize the picture? The response you're likely to make is interesting. Whether the image is one of a dog, a car, or a fire hydrant, subjects in experiments like this have more trouble identifying the object if they watch the gradual focusing procedure than if they simply view the final, still somewhat blurry, image. In the mechanics of perception, people form interim impressions that interfere with their ability to "see straight" once the evidence has improved.

Or imagine a two-dimensional ambiguous figure that can be seen as the face of a man or as the figure of a kneeling woman. Classically what people "see" is framed by their prior experience or "perceptual set." Those who are first shown a drawing that highlights the man's face see a man's face in the ambiguous figure; those who are shown a kneeling woman first see a woman in the same ambiguous figure. Again, perception is subjective. People tend to see what they expect to see.

Like inkblots, many events in life, even outside the visual-perception laboratory, are ambiguous enough to support contrasting interpretations. In a study that mimics the kind of bias I worry about in the wake of a confession, Italian researchers Paola Bressan and Maria Martello had people rate from photographs the extent to which pairs of adults and children resembled each other. I realize that people often tell mothers and fathers how much their children look just like them. Yet in a result the parent in me would not have predicted, subjects did not see more resemblance in parents and their offspring than in random pairs of adults and children. Yet subjects who were told that certain pairs were parent and child did "see" a resemblance, even when that genetic relatedness information was false.

Closer to home, Nick Lange and others conducted an experiment on speech perception that reinforces the point. In their study, subjects listened to noisy, more or less "degraded" tape recordings filled with static of two people talking—not unlike what you hear in 911 dispatch recordings. Some subjects were told ahead of time that the person being interviewed in the recording was a crime suspect; others were told that he was a job applicant. When the speech recordings were somewhat degraded, subjects for whom the interviewee was purported to be a suspect were more likely to "hear" incriminating words in his speech (for example, "the *gum*" became "the *gun*," and "*chill* them" became "*kill* them").

Even closer to the point: using materials from a federal case in Boston, Jeff Kukucka and I recruited subjects online to evaluate pairs of handwriting samples—one purportedly taken from the defendant, the other from the robbery note handed to the bank teller. Did these defendant and perpetrator handwriting samples match? Before examining the materials, which we had different individuals create in the lab, subjects were told that the defendant had previously confessed to police or denied involvement. Either way, he was now pleading not guilty. As we feared, subjects who were told that the defendant had confessed were more likely to see the two handwriting samples as a match—and, therefore corroborative of the confession.

That human perception can be unwittingly tainted by expectations is beyond dispute. But the criminal justice system is different, you are thinking. Even after police, prosecutors, judges, and juries start to form an impression about a defendant, additional evidence may come to them—and evidence is everything. Or maybe not.

Consider what happens when new information contradicts an expectation you have formed. In one of my all-time favorite experiments, with implications I find particularly pertinent, John Darley and Paget Gross (1983) asked research subjects, students from Princeton University, to evaluate the academic potential of a nine-year-old girl named Hannah. Some subjects were led to believe that Hannah came from an affluent community and that both of her parents were well-educated professionals. Others were told that she lived in a run-down urban neighborhood and that both parents were uneducated blue-collar workers. In light of common stereotypes that link social class and intelligence, and lacking any personal information about Hannah herself, it is not particularly surprising that subjects in the first group thought she had greater potential than those in the second group.

Then Darley and Gross added a second set of high- versus low-class conditions to the experiment. In these third and fourth groups, the subjects also watched a video recording of Hannah taking a scholastic achievement test. As the researchers had scripted, what they saw was a fairly average performance. Hannah correctly answered some difficult questions but missed others that were relatively easy. Most important, all subjects saw exactly the same girl and the same test performance. The objective evidence in both conditions was identical.

One would think that this objective evidence, common to both groups, would override the stereotype. Subjects should lower their ratings of high-class Hannah and raise their ratings of low-class Hannah, thereby erasing the difference. That did not happen. In fact, her test performance had the opposite effect. It widened the gap. Even though all subjects saw the same tape, they assigned Hannah much lower ratings of ability when she was poor and higher ratings when she was affluent. Evidence is subject to interpretation—and interpretation is guided by expectations. Presenting an identical body of mixed evidence did not extinguish subjects' stereotyped beliefs; rather, it reinforced these beliefs. When subjects were asked to explain, those with high expectations pointed to the problems Hannah was able to solve; those with low expectations cited her failures.

People see in evidence what they expect to see, even when they have no skin in the game. But in the context of America's adversarial criminal justice system, where police are aligned against suspects, where prosecutors are aligned against defense lawyers, where experts are hired by one side or the other, and where careers are made or broken by winning and losing in a zero-sum game, the stakes are real and motivational temperatures run high.

The way people interpret evidence can be biased not only by *cognitions* but also by their *motivations*. To quote Julius Caesar, "Men freely believe that which they desire." (The screaming-at-the-TV sports fanatic in me knows all too well how an umpire's close call in a big game can yield wildly divergent perceptions from the fans of opposing teams.)

In an ingenious program of research on "wishful seeing," Emily Balcetis and David Dunning wondered if people would judge objects that they want to be physically closer than more neutral objects. In one study, college students who were fed pretzels without water and were thirsty, compared to those who drank as much water as they wanted and whose thirst was quenched, estimated that a bottle of water across a table was on average three inches closer to them.

In a second study, students in a room estimated their distance from a $100 bill as eight inches closer when they thought they could win it than when they thought they could not. In a third study, subjects took part in a beanbag toss in which they tried to hit a target on the floor that was thirteen feet away. When the target was said to be worth $25 compared to when it had zero value, subjects underthrew the beanbag by an average of nine inches—as if they perceived the target to be closer than it was.

FORENSIC **CONFIRMATION BIASES**

On March 11, 2004, a coordinated series of bombs exploded in four commuter trains in Madrid. The explosions killed 191 people, wounded 1,800 others, and set off an international investigation. Based on a latent fingerprints lifted from a bag containing detonating devices, the FBI positively identified Brandon Mayfield, an American Muslim who practiced law in Oregon. After 9/11, in part because of his conversion to Islam, Mayfield was put on an FBI watch list. Following standard protocol, a number of examiners "independently" concluded that the print was definitely Mayfield's—that the print was "100% verified."

Soon thereafter, however, the Spanish authorities concluded that the prints on the bag were not Mayfield's and that they unequivocally matched the real bomber, an Algerian national named Ouhnane Daoud.

The FBI maintains the world's largest database of fingerprints, with more than seventy million samples. Although it uses sophisticated algorithms to help match samples lifted from crime scenes, the identification ultimately is one of human judgment. Following an internal FBI investigation and a 2006 report by the Office of the Inspector General, "confirmation bias" was listed as a contributing factor to the erroneous identification. At that point, the U.S. government issued a formal apology and paid Mayfield two million dollars in compensation.

Confirmation bias is common to human nature. What makes it so relevant to the subject matter of this book is the automatic belief that confession equals guilt. I'm not just speculating here. Two sources of evidence indicate that confessions unleash a set of processes, as in the Amanda Knox case, that biases the reports of lay witnesses and forensic analysts, which in turn, provides illusory corroboration for the confession itself. I first noticed the problem in cases I was working on in which defendants were proved innocent even after their confessions were "independently" corroborated by evidence that also turned out to be wrong.

I didn't know for sure, but I formulated a hypothesis to be tested—that when police take a confession, they increase the odds that the case will be tainted by other errors of evidence. To test this "corruptive confessions" hypothesis, Daniel Bogart, Jacqueline Kerner, and I examined a sample of wrongful convictions in which actual innocence was not in dispute. For this purpose, the Innocence Project's population of DNA exonerations was perfect. We posed three questions: (1) Do cases in which the exoneree had confessed contain more *other* evidentiary errors? (2) If so, what kinds of other errors were most common? and (3) which came first, the confession or the other errors?

In an archival analysis published in *Psychological Science*, we compared the number, kind, and timing of errors made in wrongful-conviction cases containing a false confession with those without a confession. If confessions have a tendency to corrupt other evidence, we reasoned, then false-confession cases should contain more errors than other cases. As expected, we discovered that multiple types of errors were present in 78 percent of all confession cases, compared to only 47 percent in other cases.

Within that 78 percent subsample, two additional findings caught our attention. First, with regard to these other errors: the false confessions were accompanied, in order of frequency, by invalid or improper forensic junk science (63 percent), mistaken eyewitness identifications (29 percent), and snitches or informants who lied (19 percent). Second, we found that in two-thirds of these cases, the confession came first rather than later in the investigation.

Although troubling, these results do not enable us to know how or why confessions were so often followed by other evidence errors. One possibility is that subsequent witnesses, laypeople and experts alike, were unwittingly influenced just by knowing about the highly incriminating confession. A second possibility is that the confession inspired witnesses to help police and prosecutors convict the presumed-guilty suspect. Without delving into hearts and minds, which I cannot do, it's not possible to tease apart these cognitive and motivational sources of influence.

The Confession Effect on Forensic Examiners

Firearms, tool marks, and ballistics. Fingerprints. Shoeprints. Tire marks. Bite marks. Blood spatter. Toxicology. Handwriting analysis. Arson analysis. Hair and fiber analysis. Forensic pathology. Ponder for a moment the horrifying reality that the most common form of corroboration for false confessions comes from the forensic sciences—or should I say, in some cases, junk sciences.

It's bad enough that the lay witness can be corrupted into seeing or hearing something that did not occur because it implicates a suspect believed to have confessed. Laypeople are inherently imperfect. But objective scientists, trained in validated, state-of-the-art methodologies? How can 63 percent of cases featuring a hotly disputed false confession contain bad science also corrupted by confirmation bias? This scandal used to be one of the system's dirty little secrets. TV forensic dramas notwithstanding, it's not a secret anymore.

In an 1894 treatise on how to distinguish between authentic and forged signatures, William Hagan wrote: "There must be no hypothesis at the commencement, and the examiner must depend wholly on what is seen, leaving out of consideration all suggestions or hints from interested parties. . . . Where the expert has no knowledge of the moral evidence or aspects of the case . . . there is nothing to mislead him." Ahead of his time, Hagan knew the perceptual judgments made by forensic examiners were subject to contextual bias.

In 2009, the National Academy of Sciences (NAS) published a scathing critique titled *Strengthening Forensic Science in the United States: A Path Forward*. This report left no stone unturned in its criticism of crime laboratories across the country and the alarming frequency of errors that have steered innocent people into prison. Although some areas of specialization are better than others, the report acknowledged, the whole gamut of forensic sciences was implicated. With the exception of DNA testing (which was developed in university science labs), the NAS found "no forensic method has been rigorously shown to have the capacity to consistently, and with a high degree of certainty, demonstrate a connection between evidence and a specific individual or source."

Contextual Bias

This report came down particularly hard on the pattern-matching disciplines in which an examiner tries to determine whether a bloody fingerprint, shoe print, tire mark, bite mark, or handwriting sample found at a crime scene matches a sample belonging to a suspect. The response from the inside has ranged from concerned to hostile and resistant to change. Many latent-fingerprint experts have sought to develop objective comparison methods so they can determine error rates; yet many forensic odontologists who make bite-mark judgments insist that nothing is wrong or needs to be changed.

Anyone trained in scientific methods understands the need, and NAS demand, for *standardization*, which means that different examiners in different labs should use the same protocols; *reliability*, which means that an examiner should make the same judgment of the same stimulus on different occasions and that different examiners should agree in their assessments; *accuracy and error*, which means that agreed-upon assessments should be valid in relation to reality; and insulation from *contextual bias*, which means that forensic examiners should not be exposed to outside information or subject to outside pressure. To solve these problems, said the NAS, "These disciplines need to develop rigorous protocols to guide these subjective interpretations and pursue equally rigorous research and evaluation programs."

In real life, contextual bias runs rampant. Forensic experts work on actual cases, which puts them into contact with prosecutors and detectives, who sometimes want a re-examination of non-supportive results. They may also communicate with other examiners, informally or as part of a mandated "peer review" process. And often they have exposure to extraneous information in the case file—such as whether the suspect whose print they are evaluating had confessed, or was on an FBI watch list for having converted to Islam, as in the Madrid-bomber debacle.

In laboratory and field settings, controlled experiments show that the cognitive biases that afflict everyday judgment have the same effect on the high-stakes forensic world. Consider the groundbreaking work of Itiel Dror, an Israeli-born cognitive psychologist with a PhD from Harvard, who lives and works in London. In numerous studies, he and his colleagues have shown that forensic examiners are no different from other humans, subject to the same inadvertent biases, whether they know it or not. In a style that is both witty and forceful, he makes this point repeatedly in workshops he is invited to give all over the world.

In a sobering demonstration of this point, published in 2006, Dror and Charlton recruited six highly experienced latent fingerprint experts from the United States, England, Israel, Australia, and the Netherlands. Dror and Charlton customized a different set of prints for each examiner, tailored for each of the participants. Each set contained four pairs of prints that the specific fingerprint examiner had judged to match the suspect in a prior case and four pairs they had judged to exclude the suspect. This time, the prints were presented on their own; or accompanied by the "fact" that the suspect had confessed, suggesting a match; or accompanied by the "fact" that the suspect was in custody at the time, suggesting exclusion. Results showed that the contextual information produced an overall change in 17 percent of the originally correct match decisions.

If contextual information can lead latent fingerprint experts to change their visual judgments, what about other areas of forensics? In a 1994 study involving polygraph examiners, researchers asked examiners from the Israeli Police Force to evaluate and interpret charts that were previously deemed inconclusive. Some examiners, but not others, were told that the suspect had ultimately confessed. Results showed that those in the confession condition rated the charts as significantly more deceptive than those in the control condition.

Other research shows the same types of contextual bias. In a 2018 study, Claire van den Eeden presented fifty-eight Dutch CSI professionals with panoramic photographs of a mock crime scene in which a female victim depicted by a mannequin hanging in the stairwell had either committed suicide or was murdered. Some investigators were led to believe that the victim had a history of depression; others were told of prior reports of domestic violence at that address. Ultimately, despite the complexity of evidence presented—like blood on a doorknob and hair of a different color on the victim—CSI subjects with a domestic violence mindset were more likely to conclude that the victim had been murdered.

All this illustrates the operation of forensic confirmation biases. Other researchers have reported similar effects on arson investigations, bloodstain-pattern analysis, scent detections in dogs, bite-mark analysis, forensic anthropology, and complex DNA mixtures. That is why, in 2015, the National Commission on Forensic Science stated that task-irrelevant information includes any information about a case—a suspect's criminal history, confession, or alibi—that supports a conclusion that is derived by means other than the physical evidence. Stated otherwise, forensic examiners "should draw conclusions solely from the physical evidence that they are asked to evaluate . . . and not from any other evidence in the case."

You may be thinking, if contextual information is probative of guilt or innocence, doesn't that lead the forensic analyst toward a more accurate judgment? Sometimes yes, maybe; sometimes no. Certainly no forensic examiner should blindly accept and factor in a confession when evaluating a fingerprint, shoe print, bite mark or whatever. Examiners are hired to analyze an item of *physical evidence*. When they testify in court, juries assume that their "match" judgment was based exclusively on the stimulus patterns they compared—and hence that this judgment *independently* corroborates the defendant's confession. If examiners factor in this other information, however, then the confession is double counted, the expert doesn't corroborate anything, and the jury, not aware of the influence, is misled.

The simplest surefire way to ensure that forensic examiners are not corrupted by outside influences: they should be blinded to the case files, shielded from extraneous information—in the same way that in clinical drug trials neither the patients *nor their doctors* know if the patient is receiving an active drug or a placebo, and in the same way that psychology researchers blind not only the subjects but their experimenters to what behaviors will be coded. Double-blind protocols are basic to science; when feasible, it should also be basic in the *forensic* sciences.

The Bias Blind Spot

One would think that double-blinding forensic examinations would be not just an easy fix but an easy sell. It's a protocol used in science—enough said. But resistance has proved fierce in some circles. And my colleagues and I discovered one reason why: most forensic examiners don't believe that cognitive bias is a problem.

In 2017, social psychologist Jeff Kukucka and others surveyed four hundred–plus forensic examiners from twenty-one different countries. Averaging fourteen years of experience, these respondents were experts in fingerprints, handwriting, toxicology, and firearm/tool marks. Most of these examiners worked in large laboratories; others worked alone or in very small laboratories. First, they were asked to estimate the accuracy of their judgments. Then: In your opinion, is cognitive bias a cause for concern (1) in the forensic sciences as a whole, (2) in your specific domain, and (3) in your own judgments?

The results were telling. For starters, respondents estimated that they were 96 percent accurate in their judgments. Remarkably, 148 respondents (37 percent of the sample) stated that their accuracy rate was 100 percent. If forensic examiners believe themselves to be near perfect, they must see themselves as invulnerable to cognitive bias. In fact, that's what they reported. Although 71 percent of respondents saw cognitive bias as a cause for concern in the forensic sciences as a whole, that number dropped to 52 percent with regard to their own domain and to only 26 percent with regard to their own personal judgments. Illustrating "a bias blind spot," these survey respondents could not be clearer: cognitive bias is something that afflicts other people, not me. "I'm a trained professional," one told us. "My decisions are purely objective." This explains why so many respondents believed that they could prevent biasing influences through sheer force of willpower.

I am not just picking on the forensic science community. Along with clinical forensic psychologist Patricia Zapf, we also conducted a companion survey of eleven hundred mental health professionals from thirty-nine countries, mostly psychologists who conduct forensic evaluations for the courts or other tribunals. Most respondents acknowledged the phenomenon of cognitive bias, but they too exhibited a blind spot: Eighty-six percent agreed that cognitive bias is a cause for concern in forensic evaluations as a whole; 79 percent agreed that it was a cause for concern in their own specific domain; and only 52 percent agreed that they personally were subject to cognitive bias. As with the forensic scientists, they too believed that they could overcome cognitive bias through willpower.

I have only scratched the surface when it comes to the problem inherent in the forensic sciences. Consistent with human nature, people are unwittingly subject to contextual bias, which is precisely why double-blind procedures are universally accepted in science. This principle applies to all people—hence, an article that Dror, my colleagues, and I published in 2018 titled "No One Is Immune to Contextual Bias—Not Even Forensic Pathologists."

We wrote this article as part of an exchange with forensic pathologist William Oliver, who argued for, not against, the medical examiner's use of *nonmedical* information. Oliver argued that the forensic pathologist should be free to consider any and all information—such as confessions or testimony from eyewitnesses and informants. He argued that access to outside information increases the consensus among experts and their confidence. But consensus and confidence do not ensure accuracy. If the nonmedical information is incorrect, like a false confession—which

I challenge a medical examiner to sniff out based on his own common sense—the effect will be to mislead pathologists, consensus or not, confident or not.

The Adversarial Allegiance Effect

The problem is even worse than I've let on. People are subject to bias not only because they see what they *expect* to see but also because they see what they *want* to see. The problem is not just cognitive; it's motivational. And it doesn't just afflict forensic science experts; it also afflicts mental health experts who testify in court. University of Virginia psychologist Daniel Murrie calls this partisan bias the *adversarial allegiance effect*.

To test this possibility, Murrie and others recruited ninety-nine forensic psychologists and psychiatrists for a two-day seminar and randomly assigned them to either a prosecution or defense team. For incentive, they were paid $400 a day to score "risk assessment" scales for up to four sex offenders. Each subject met with an attorney. For those assigned to the prosecution, the lawyer noted the importance of proving that the offenders they bring to court are at high risk to reoffend. For those assigned to the defense, the lawyer noted a desire to let the court know that not every sex offender is at high risk to reoffend. At that point, subjects were presented with the same files taken from actual cases and scored the same tests. The findings showed a strong adversarial allegiance effect. All forensic expert subjects read through the same case files and scored the same tests. Yet those working for the bogus prosecution unit assigned higher scores based on the risk-assessment measures than did those working for the defense.

The research on cognitive bias and the allegiance effect on forensic judgments is not a mere exercise in abstract theory testing. It's an explanation for tragic past mistakes and a warning that there are more to come unless the criminal justice comes to grips with the problem.

The Story of Tyler Edmonds

To appreciate just how egregious the influence of a confession can be on a so-called medical opinion, consider the case of Tyler Edmonds. On May 12, 2003, Joey Fulgham of Longview, Mississippi, was shot to death in his sleep. Kristi Fulgham, his ex-wife, was a strong suspect.

While being questioned, Fulgham said that her thirteen-year-old half-brother, Tyler Edmonds, killed her ex by shooting him with a rifle.

Later that day, the sheriff's office asked Sharon Clay, Tyler's mother, to bring the boy in for questioning—which she did. Initially questioned with his mother in the room, Tyler said he didn't know anything about the shooting and that Fulgham was alive when he and Kristi left the house that morning. Asked if he killed Joey, Tyler said: "No, I would not have the heart to do that. I could never kill somebody else."

After several hours, police told Tyler that Kristi implicated him. As the session tensed up with this accusation, Tyler's mom would have no more of it. You need to "stop right there," she said. "Y'all are not going to intimidate this child, not while I'm in this room." At that point, a young deputy with a flat-top haircut pulled Sharon out of the room, separating her and Tyler.

To make a long story short, an officer brought Kristi into the room, and she convinced her young half-brother to confess—which he then repeated on camera. While his mother paced around, upset, knocking on doors and looking for Tyler, who was hidden from view, Tyler was confessing. He said he and Kristi woke up in the middle of the night and went into Fulgham's room with a rifle. "She was behind me and she put her hand on the trigger and I put my hand on the trigger and she kind of squeezed my hand because it didn't work, . . . I just closed my eyes and then it went off."

Four days later, Tyler recanted his confession and explained that Kristi killed Joey, and he did not know about it until she told him and asked that he protect her or she would never see her kids again. It was too late. Edmonds, an honor student at the time, was charged and tried as an adult with capital murder. The state's case rested on Tyler's im-plausible videotaped confession that he and Kristi both held the rifle and squeezed the trigger together.

In support of the state's theory, the trial judge permitted Dr. Steven Hayne, the forensic pathologist who conducted the autopsy, to testify that the path and projectile of the fatal wound corroborated the two-shooter theory "to a reasonable degree of scientific certainty." Say what? He could tell from the wounds that two people pulled the trigger? Other forensic pathologists cringe at the absurdity. Yet on the basis of Tyler's confession and Hayne's assessment, Edmonds was convicted and sentenced to life in prison.

Thankfully, the state appeals court saw this testimony for what it was—an "off-the-cuff opinion" not based in science. "You cannot look at a bullet wound and tell whether it was made by a bullet fired by one person pulling the trigger or by two persons pulling the trigger simultaneously," the court ruled. The Mississippi State Supreme Court agreed and ruled that this testimony was "scientifically unfounded." Edmonds's conviction was overturned in 2007; he was retried and acquitted in 2008.

As for the illustrious Dr. Hayne, that was not his first rodeo, as they say. For a period of over twenty years, he conducted thousands of autopsies and testified all the time. In 2007, Leroy Reddick, a respected medical examiner in Alabama, told author and journalist Randy Balko that "Every prosecutor in Mississippi knows that if you don't like the results you got from an autopsy, you can always take the body to Dr. Hayne." In a 2014 article in the *Washington Post*, Balko put it this way: "Hayne performed the vast majority of autopsies in Mississippi for nearly twenty years precisely because he provided opinions and testimonies that prosecutors found favorable. It was all by design."

Dr. Hayne's work in Tyler's case was intellectually dishonest; there's no other way to put it. And the more forensic pathologists I have spoken to about it, the more I realize that this is among the most indefensible autopsy conclusions. But it does not stand alone.

In 2000 in Virginia, Michael Ledford was charged with setting a fire that burned his wife and killed his one-year-old son. Fire investigators initially determined that the blaze was of undetermined origin. One month later, however, detectives interrogated Ledford at his workplace, through the night, and told him he had failed a polygraph—which was not true (the results were inconsistent). At that point, he confessed. "Before I left," he said,. "I lit a candle and threw it in the chair. I never wanted to hurt my family. . . . I just hope my family and friends and God can forgive me." He would later recant his confession. At that point, however, the arson expert changed his mind: The fire was caused by arson. Rightly or wrongly, Ledford was convicted and is serving a fifty-year sentence.

And then there's the case of Barry Laughman, the young man in Pennsylvania, whom I described briefly in chapter 5. In 1987, his elderly neighbor was raped and murdered in her home, suffocated by a mouth full of pills. Several weeks later, with the case still unsolved, state troopers interrogated Laughman and allegedly produced a meticulously detailed confession. I say "allegedly produced a confession" because what they taped afterward was one trooper reading both the questions and the answers. Laughman sat mute.

What happened next was both surreal and all too common. Once Laughman was arrested, his blood was drawn. Serology tests showed that he had type B blood; yet the semen recovered from the victim belonged to someone who was type A. This "ultimate" exculpatory evidence should have stopped the prosecution in its tracks.

Aware that Laughman had confessed, a chemist for the Pennsylvania State Police went on to propose four "novel" theories, none grounded in science, to explain away the mismatch (at various points she suggested that she tested Laughman before he confessed, or that she was not even aware of his confession—but these revisionist accounts were simply not true).

Perhaps, she suggested, antibiotics that the victim was taking for a urinary tract infection changed the blood type of the rapist's semen. Or bacteria could have formed on the wet vaginal swabs, which could break down the antigen. Or perhaps Laughman did not secrete his B antigen material into his semen. Or maybe because of the victim's position, the semen could have drained from her vagina. You get the idea. The point is, other serologists agree that these theories have no basis in science. For Laughman, this meant that evidence that should have raised a reasonable doubt about his confession had no such effect.

The Laughman case illustrates yet another point about the corruptive effects of confessions on police and how discrepancies can simply be set aside or ignored. After Laughman's arrest, which was reported in the local news, two witnesses—Elwood Bollinger and his girlfriend, Patricia Harrison—said they saw the victim outside at 9 a.m. the morning after Laughman's confessed killing on their way a medical appointment. They insisted they saw her and could prove the date of their appointment. The reaction: police tried to convince these witnesses they were wrong—that they must have seen a ghost.

The Confession Effect on Lay Witnesses

The corruptive effects of confession are not just a forensic sciences problem. After Amanda Knox's confession, eyewitnesses came out of

the woodwork. One heard a scream followed by the sound of two people running; another said he saw Knox and Sollecito nearby that night; a
third saw all three together; a fourth said he saw Knox that night wielding a knife. It's now clear that all of these sightings were figments of
their imagination.

Eyewitnesses

It's no secret that eyewitness memory is imperfect, even in the best of
circumstances; that it is constructed and reconstructed over time; and
that it is malleable in the face of new information. People tend to think
that human memory works like a video camera—that if you turn on the
power and focus the lens, all events will be recorded for subsequent
playback. But it's not that simple. That's why eyewitness identification
error is the leading cause of wrongful convictions, found in a whopping
70 percent of DNA exonerations. It's also why psychologists like Gary
Wells at Iowa State University, and so many others, have conducted
hundreds of studies aimed at identifying best practices for how to administer an eyewitness lineup.

Some eyewitness experiments focus on the conditions of perception,
such as exposure time, lighting, distance, physical disguise, alcoholic
intoxication, stress, sleep deprivation, race, and distraction (did you
know, for example, that the presence of a weapon at the crime disrupts
a witness's ability to identify the perpetrator?). Other experiments focus
on post-perception events and how the information witnesses obtain
after a crime can alter their memory of what they saw. Still other experiments focus on the best ways to construct a fair lineup, instruct the
witness, and ensure that the lineup is double-blind so the officer who
administers it is unable to steer the witness one way or another.

Eyewitnesses should be free from contamination. When they select
someone from a lineup, that identification should reflect what they saw
at the crime scene, not what they heard afterward. The case of Chicago
defendant Michael Evans points to the danger. Evans was convicted for
the rape and murder of a nine-year-old girl because of a lone eyewitness
identification. Then after twenty-seven years in prison, DNA testing
established his innocence. Afterward, the witness revealed that she had
harbored doubts about her identification. "But then I was told there
was a confession," she said. "And that's how they convinced me that
there was more to it than just me."

Can secondhand information about a confession override an eyewitness's memory? To test this hypothesis, Lisa Hasel and I repeatedly staged a theft in front of small groups of college students, 260 in all. At one point, the experimenter left the room, and a white male student entered, poked around for thirty seconds, took the experimenter's laptop, and left. Moments later, a distressed experimenter returned and asked each student to write down a description of the thief and then make an identification decision from a lineup in which he was not included. Some students picked someone from the lineup; others, correctly, rejected all the choices.

The students returned individually two days later, ostensibly to discuss their identification decisions with the experimenter, who was still trying to solve the crime. The experimenter said that she had interrogated some suspects and reviewed eyewitness reports, but had some lingering questions. In Phase 1, some students had mistakenly identified someone; others correctly declined to identify anyone. At this point, the experimenter "revealed" the results of her interrogations and allowed the students to reexamine the lineup. Among witnesses who initially selected someone but were told that a different lineup member had confessed, 61 percent changed their identifications—and did so with confidence. Among those who had correctly rejected the whole lineup but were told that a specific member had confessed, half went on to mistakenly "identify" that confessor.

Alibis

Plowing through wrongful-conviction case files, I am often struck by the absence of exculpatory evidence. If the defendant was innocent and we now know that he was, I'd wonder where the exculpatory evidence was. What was the suspect's alibi to vouch for their whereabouts, whether physical proof of innocence (such as credit card, cell phone, or GPS records) or human alibi witnesses (like a spouse, coworker, friend, neighbor, or waitress)? This question takes me down this deep rabbit hole: just as confessions breed incriminating evidence, they can also abort, distort, and discount exculpatory information.

In Lake County, Illinois, Juan Rivera was induced to confess to the rape and murder of an eleven-year-old girl. It was a confession egregiously taken and maintained even after DNA tests excluded him. On the night of the murder, Rivera was wearing an electronic ankle bracelet, after being arrested for stealing a car stereo. The bracelet, part of a twenty-four-hour home monitoring system, showed he was home at the time, more than two miles from the crime scene. In court, the prosecution variously argued—without proof—that the system could have malfunctioned or that Rivera found a way to disable it, allowing him to leave home without being detected.

In Nassau County, New York, in 1984, Teresa Fusco was raped and strangled. Her naked body was discovered in a wooded area near where she worked. Months later, police interrogated a twenty-one-year-old landscaper named John Kogut for eighteen hours, during which they told him, falsely, that he failed a polygraph. Then he confessed six times. Capitulating to the police theory of the case, he implicated two friends, Dennis Halstead and John Restivo, neither of whom had a criminal record. The three of them, he said, were driving in Restivo's blue van when they abducted, raped, and killed Fusco and then dumped her body in the woods.

On the basis of Kogut's confession, all three men were tried and convicted. In 2003, DNA testing on the vaginal swabs in the rape kit conclusively excluded these defendants. They were innocent; after a collective fifty-four years in prison, their convictions were overturned. Looking back, one wonders: What evidence of innocence existed at the time? At first, Kogut denied any involvement. In fact, he said he was at a birthday party for his girlfriend that night, and bought the cake for the occasion. He named several people who were there and could confirm his whereabouts. Some of these individuals were willing to corroborate his story initially; yet none testified in court. He had alibi witnesses, but they vanished, either because his confession led them to question their memory or because they felt intimidated by police from coming forward.

To vouch for someone, an alibi witness has to recall seeing that person in a particular place at a particular time. Can a defendant's alibi be shaken loose by confession the same way an eyewitness's account can be? In 2016, Stephanie Marion posed this question in an ingenious experiment conducted in my lab at John Jay College. In each session, she brought together individual subject and a female confederate posing as a second subject to work on some problem sets. As soon as they arrived, the experimenter took the two into an office to sign a consent form. There, briefly, they sat at a small, cluttered desk with an open moneybox filled with twenty-dollar bills.

From there, subjects were taken to a testing room next door furnished with two chairs and adjacent desks separated by a wall partition five feet, six inches high by four feet wide. The confederate always took the seat at the desk nearest the door to the office, which forced the real subject to sit on the other side of the divider, unable to see that door. The subject could hear the confederate, however, and "feel" her presence behind the divider (periodically the confederate would move about in her chair, sigh, shuffle papers, or click her pen).

Several minutes after the two subjects started work on their problems, the experimenter burst into the room to announce that money was missing from the adjacent office. In a concerned tone, she asked subjects if they saw or heard anyone in the office. The confederate immediately said no and assured the experimenter that they never left the room. The experimenter then separated the subject and confederate and contacted security. Privately, she asked the subject, who lacked access to the door, if the confederate had stayed in the testing room the whole time. The subject's response was recorded by a concealed microphone.

Ten minutes later, the experimenter returned and asked the subject to help her complete the security officer's "incident report form." As indicated on the form, subjects were told that (1) the confederate denied taking the money; or (2) she confessed but then changed her mind and refused to sign the incident report form, insisting again that she had not left the room; or (3) she confessed and refused to sign, which makes the subject's alibi for her "suspicious." At that point, all subjects were asked to confirm whether the confederate had not left the testing room. Again, their response to this question was recorded.

At the outset, sixty out of sixty-five subjects (92 percent) corroborated the confederate's alibi when first asked ("Yes, I think I would have heard her leave," "Yes, I heard her coughing," "Yes, I'm sure"). Out of those sixty, 95 percent maintained the alibi when told that the confederate denied involvement. Among those told that the confederate confessed but recanted, that number plummeted to 45 percent. Among those to whom it was also suggested that vouching for the confederate was suspicious, implying guilt, that number dropped again. to 20 percent.

In case you're wondering, other researchers in a follow-up study found that word of a confession causes some alibi witnesses to lose confidence in their support for a suspect—even when that suspect is a friend. This result warns of one additional point about how word of a confession can spread like a contagious disease: Confession can also taint defense witnesses who would normally testify favorably about the defendant's character.

Anecdotal support for this hypothesis was apparent among some of Marion's subjects. When asked during the study whether they believed that the confederate stole the money, several subjects in the confession conditions made unflattering spontaneous remarks about her (e.g., "She wasn't really friendly, kept to herself," "She seemed a little nervous," and "She's, like, weird . . . she has, no offense, but, like, a bitch attitude"). These types of remarks were not found in the denial condition even though the confederate's behavior was neutral and consistent across conditions. This type of shift in impressions of an alleged confessor was seen clearly in the wrongful conviction in Italy of Amanda Knox.

Jailhouse Snitches

The wrongful conviction of Juan Rivera is a textbook illustration of so much that is wrong with the criminal justice system. Rivera was innocent. When his ordeal was over, he was granted a Certificate of Innocence and received $20 million in compensation.

Yet based on a false confession that by any standard was egregiously taken, he was convicted by a jury not once, but three times. This happened even though Rivera had recanted his confession; none of the physical evidence linked him to the crime; he was on electronic monitoring at his home more than two miles away; and, before his third trial, he was positively excluded by DNA testing.

The problem for Rivera was that his contested confession did not stand alone. Over defense objections, Judge Christopher Starck admitted testimony from three jailhouse snitches who claimed that Rivera had confessed to them. All these snitches had a motive to lie. One claimed that Rivera referred to the victim as a "little bitch," a "tease" who "deserved everything she got."

After Rivera was convicted and sentenced for the third time, Thomas Sullivan, a former U.S. attorney who represented Rivera, decried the trial. At Rivera's sentencing, he asserted that Rivera had only "the trappings and semblance" of a trial. In his fifty-seven years as a prosecutor and defense lawyer, Sullivan said, "I do not recall a case in which so many rulings, in my opinion, were wrong."

I got a firsthand glimpse at his frustration. Rivera's attorneys had asked me to give expert testimony with regard to his confession. After reading through Rivera's extensive case file, I was incredulous. I flew into Chicago for what I anticipated would be a Frye hearing, in which a judge evaluates whether a proffered expert's testimony has "general agreement" within that expert's scientific community. When I arrived, I learned that Judge Starck refused even to hold this hearing to consider my testimony. Assistant state attorney Michael Mermel had adamantly objected to my presence in court, arguing that the judge has excluded a similar expert ten years earlier, in 1998, so there was no need to revisit the question. The defense argued that the new DNA test results excluding Rivera changed the issue and that the science of confessions was better developed than it was ten years ago.

Back to the snitches. I can run through an extensive list of wrongful convictions in which false confessions were "corroborated" by one or more snitches who lied, claiming that the defendant had privately and without pressure confessed to them. Sometimes they report details consistent with the defendant's actual false confession. The archives of wrongful convictions are filled with horrific tales of jailhouse informants who report that the defendant had confessed to them.

The empirical reason that this presents a confessions problem is that snitches are most likely to enter or be pulled into the fray in cases where the innocent defendant had confessed to police but later recanted. This statistic tells the tale: according to the Innocence Project, 17 percent of the first 375 DNA exonerations involved jailhouse snitches or other incentivized informants who lied. In cases that also contained a false confession, that number is 29 percent, compared to only 12 percent within the population of *non*-confession cases. These contributing factors are not random or independent events.

Snitching is a commonplace, clandestine, and insufficiently regulated "dirty little secret" in the criminal justice system. For a hair-raising exposé on this all-too-common practice in the U.S. criminal justice systems, I recommend Alexandra Natapoff's 2009 book, *Snitching: Criminal Informants and the Erosion of Criminal Justice*.

Jailhouse snitches testify not for moral reasons but because they are incentivized by personal gains ranging from cigarettes and cash payments to improved conditions and release or reduction of sentences. Although jailhouse informants are incentivized to lie, the terms of their "deals" with police and prosecutors often come in the form of an implicit, seldom disclosed "wink and nod."

Two areas of recent research confirm one's worst fears about this practice. First, in a series of laboratory experiments, where the personal stakes pale in comparison to release from prison, Jessica Swanner and others have found that incentives increased the rate at which subjects were willing to allege, falsely, that their lab partner had confessed to causing the experimenter's computer to crash. Many people are corruptible. Second, and to make matters worse, Jeffrey Neuschatz and others time and again have found that the "secondary confessions" that informants report (as with a defendant's firsthand confession) increase the likelihood that a mock jury will find a defendant guilty. Incentives or not, secondary confessions are, first and foremost, confessions in their impact.

The use of snitches in North America has a long and sordid history. In fact, the first documented wrongful conviction in the United States involved a snitch. In Manchester, Vermont, in 1819, police suspected brothers Jesse and Stephen Boorn of killing Russell Colvin, their sister's husband, whom they detested. Both men confessed under pressure. Jesse was put into a cell with Silas Merrill, a forger who testified that Jesse confided to him that Stephen clubbed Colvin to the ground during an argument, that their father happened along, saw that Colvin was still alive, and slit his throat with Stephen's penknife. The three men then buried Colvin in a cellar. In exchange for his testimony, Merrill was immediately released. Fearing execution, Jesse cooperated and confessed. The Boorn brothers were convicted, imprisoned, and sentenced to death—until victim Russell Colvin turned up alive in New Jersey.

INNOCENT MISTAKES, GROSS NEGLIGENCE, OR WORSE?

In the Laughman, Rivera, Kogut, Edmonds, and many other wrongful conviction cases I have worked on, it took me a while to come to this harsh realization: the exculpatory evidence that was twisted or explained away, the alibis that were ignored or vanished, the eyewitnesses who were biased and pressured, and the informants who perjured themselves for personal gain did not always come about through innocent mistakes.

The Story of Anthony Wright

Consider the plight of Anthony Wright. In Philadelphia, on October 19, 1991, police found the body of seventy-seven-year-old Louise Talley—naked and bloodied from stab wounds and other injuries. A blood-stained metal knife was found on her bathrobe. Ms. Talley had also been raped. A stained sheet from her bed tested positive for semen; rape kit samples were inconclusive.

The next day, Detective Manuel Santiago, ostensibly acting on a tip, visited twenty-year-old Anthony Wright at his mother's home. It was early on a Sunday afternoon. Wright, a full-time construction worker and the father of a baby boy, was watching football with a girlfriend when two cops handcuffed him and dragged him off to the police station.

Once there, Detectives Santiago and Martin Devlin say they Mirandized Wright, who immediately confessed. Neither the interrogation nor the confession was recorded. Instead, the confession appeared handwritten in a nine-page question-and-answer statement that Devlin authored up and demanded that Wright sign.

Police then obtained a search warrant and found in Wright's bedroom three blood-stained items of clothing that were detailed in the signed confession: a black Chicago Bulls sweatshirt, a pair of blue jeans with black suede patches, and black Fila sneakers. Both Wright and his mother insisted that this clothing was not his.

Although Wright's attorney urged him to plead guilty to avoid the death penalty, he refused and went to trial. Wright testified that he signed the statement detectives handed to him without an opportunity to read it. "Just sign the paper and you'll go home," he would later recall to ABC News. He signed it, he testified, because he feared for his life after detectives handcuffed him to a chair and threatened to "rip his eyes out" and "skull-fuck" him. "I wanted my mother," he said. "I had no idea what these people would do to me." Of course, detectives chose to record none of the process, so it was Wright's word against theirs. The trial judge chose to disbelieve Wright and ruled that his statement was voluntary and admissible.

At trial, the confession attributed to Wright, in all its exquisite detail, captured center stage. This confession was buttressed by the blood-stained clothing and four supporting actors. Two were suspects-turned-informants named Roland James, a crack dealer, and Buddy Richardson, both of whom claimed that Wright had confessed his planning; both men were released after implicating Wright. The other two were purported eyewitnesses who testified that they saw Wright near the victim's home at the approximate time of her death.

Wright testified at trial that he was never in the victim's house and did not know alleged informants James and Richardson. He said that he worked that day and returned at around 5 p.m., then went to a club and returned home. He insisted that the clothing was not his and in fact that the sizes were not even close to his own. None of this mattered. In June of 1993, Wright was convicted and punished with a mandatory life sentence.

Wright appealed his verdict but to no avail. Then in 2004, Wright hit the jackpot—not by luck but by his own efforts. He wrote to the Innocence Project to plead his case and IP agreed to take it. Peter Neufeld, along with staff attorney Nina Morrison, worked with local counsel. The first order of business: DNA testing. Like forty-four other states at that time (all fifty states are now on board), Pennsylvania law had established an inmate's right to post-conviction DNA testing to prove claims of actual innocence. Yet the Philadelphia DA's office steadfastly opposed Wright's request and the lower court agreed. Basically, the court ruled that Wright was not entitled to DNA testing as per statute—because he confessed.

Setting aside the absurdity of this catch-22, you have to ask yourself a simple human question: Why would a DA's office or a judge refuse the request for DNA testing? Were they exercising the principle of finality, preserving the state's budget, or protecting their pride? Did they believe that confessions prove guilt no matter what, or were they acutely aware of exceptions to that rule? The concept of a false confession is hardly foreign to the courts, especially in the Commonwealth of Pennsylvania, where false confessions had been taken from Bruce Godschalk, Barry Laughman, and others exculpated by DNA.

I had only limited involvement in this case. As IP prepared to appeal to the Pennsylvania Supreme Court, Neufeld called to asked me if the American Psychological Association (APA) might consider submitting an amicus curiae friend-of-the-court brief on behalf of Wright. For many years, the APA had advocated on a number of topics, carefully vetted, in which psychological science is solid and can inform the courts on a particular matter. Up to then, the APA had not weighed in on false confessions but was prepared to do so. The fact that the Pennsylvania courts had barred Wright from DNA testing *because he confessed* demanded a brief on false confessions.

I spoke with the APA's general counsel, Nathalie Gilfoyle. It was clear to her that the principle to be argued was straightforward and firmly grounded in science. But she was troubled by the facts of this particular case. Wright was convicted not only by confession but also by physical evidence, informants, and eyewitnesses. I can't recall exactly how she put it, but she wished that the APA's foray into this area were attached to a case of actual innocence. I'd seen this before, and while I admitted that the state's case seemed strong, with false confessions, you just never know.

Principled as she is, Gilfoyle brought in outside counsel, with whom we worked, and on November 13, 2008, the APA submitted its first-ever amicus brief on false confessions. The APA's point in a nutshell: "A confession that may be considered 'voluntary,' and therefore admissible into evidence, does not conclusively establish actual guilt." At the same time, an APA press release communicated its agnosticism regarding Wright's culpability: "APA has no position with regard to whether Mr. Wright's confession was false or not," attorney Gilfoyle said. What unfolded next was hard to script or predict.

In 2011, the Pennsylvania Supreme Court ruled that a confession does not bar DNA testing and sent the case back to the trial court.

In 2013, retesting of the rape kit revealed the DNA profile of Ronnie Byrd, a crackhead and dealer who lived near the victim at the time. After a lifetime of criminal offenses, Byrd had just died in a South Carolina prison. Tests on the infamous clothing also revealed the victim's DNA inside the sweatshirt and jeans. The clothing was hers, not Wright's. That evidence was planted in his house.

In 2014, the Philadelphia District Attorney's Office begrudgingly vacated Wright's conviction but claimed without any proof whatsoever that Wright committed the crime with Byrd.

In 2016, the DA tried Wright for a second time on the newly concocted theory that he and Byrd were accomplices. This theory made no sense. The two men were twenty years apart in age, and strangers. Besides, the two-perpetrator theory rendered Wright's confession factually incorrect. At this point, informants James and Richardson were dead, so their original testimony was read to the jury. The two "eyewitnesses" from his original trial said their earlier testimony was a lie; they were coerced by police.

In 2016, after about an hour of deliberation (in which most of the time was spent eating lunch; the actual decision-making process took five minutes), the jury acquitted Wright, gifting him, in his words, "the greatest day of my life." As detailed in the *Philadelphia Inquirer*, several jurors wiped away tears as foreperson Grace Greco read the verdict. The next day, Wright was released from prison, met there by his attorneys, friends, and his father, son, and one-year-old granddaughter (his mother had passed away). Back at the courthouse, he and the jurors who had decided his case came together in an emotional "reunion," crying, hugging, exchanging names, and taking pictures.

At a highly attended press conference, foreperson Greco, speaking on behalf of her unanimous peers, said: "I'm angry that this case was ever retried, but thrilled that we were able to release Tony from this nightmare of twenty-five years." Neufeld referred to the DA's decision to retry Wright as "absolutely unconscionable and unacceptable." In a rebuttal comment that speaks for itself, the DA stated: "The verdict only shows that the jury did not find his guilt was proven beyond a reasonable doubt."

In 2018, resulting from a lawsuit filed against the city of Philadelphia and its police department, Wright was awarded $9.85 million.

Shortly after the new DNA results were ready, Neufeld and I appeared together at a World Science Festival event on science and justice. Afterward he blew me away with the news that Wright had been fully and multiply excluded by all DNA tests, that CODIS identified the killer, and that the prosecutor may well be digging in for a retrial.

I immediately contacted attorney Gilfoyle of the APA to let her know what had happened. I don't know which of my conversations that

The story of Anthony Wright of Philadelphia illustrates the cascading effects that often follow from a false confession—from tainted police, witnesses, and prosecutors to appellate judges who bar confessors from exercising the right to DNA testing. In 2016, after a twenty-five-year ordeal, Wright was acquitted at a retrial and freed. Here he holds his granddaughter for the first time. *Photo courtesy of Kevin Monko / Innocence Project.*

day was more animated. As I said to her, "Once again, a confessor whom everyone believed to have been a killer was excluded by DNA and is likely innocent." She was hooked; the APA has gone on to submit several more amicus briefs on false confessions.

All of this brings me back to the question I raise about cases in which a false confession appeared fully and multiply corroborated: Innocent mistake, gross negligence, or worse? When detectives hauled Wright in and forced him to sign a statement they had authored, surely that's no innocent mistake. Nor was it an innocent mistake to fabricate physical evidence by planting the victim's clothing in his house. These are acts of misconduct, plain and simple. What about incentivizing two unsavory informants and accepting their "secondary confessions" at face value?

To answer these questions, it might help to know that in 2019, Willie Veasy was exonerated of a wrongful murder conviction in Philadelphia resulting from a false confession taken by Devlin and fellow detective Paul Worrell; or that in 2020, Walter Ogrod of Philadelphia was exonerated and released from death row, where he had been because of a false confession taken by these detectives.

Finally, what about the prosecutors in this case—first in 1993, then in 2016? One can imagine an innocent mistake attribution in 1993, the year after the Innocence Project was founded, shedding light on DNA exonerations involving false confessions, and several years before the science had fully developed. But for Seth Williams, Philadelphia's district attorney who retried Wright in 2016, after he was excluded by DNA that identified the perpetrator and indicated that the victim's clothing must have been planted, and after the original eyewitnesses admitted they were coerced: Was that still an innocent mistake? (One year later, Williams pled guilty to bribery; he was then disbarred and imprisoned for three years.)

To answer these questions, it might also help to know that in 2018, Wright's legal team filed a complaint with the State Disciplinary Board against the second trial prosecutor, Bridget Kirn, accusing her of allowing two police witnesses to give false testimony in Wright's second trial. These officers testified that they knew almost nothing about the post-conviction DNA testing. Yet the record showed that Kirn had briefed them extensively about the DNA evidence before the retrial. "It is difficult to conceive of a more textbook violation," the complaint asserted, than when a prosecutor stands mute knowing that one of her key witnesses is perjuring himself in this way.

The Ultimate Question

I say this all the time: I am not a mind reader, which is why I am generally reluctant to make attributions of intentionality based solely on overt behavior. With all that I know about the prevalence and naturalness of cognitive bias and blindness, I always start with an assumption that bad behaviors are the product of inadvertent mistakes. Sometimes, however, as contradictory information compounds, I cannot help but shift to an attribution that is more nefarious.

There is a reason why confession cases in particular should sound alarm bells. The first has to do with the nature of confession evidence itself. If an eyewitness identifies the wrong person in a lineup, everyone shrugs their shoulders in the acknowledgment that humans are imperfect; that people make mistakes. No one takes the eyewitness error personally or feels the need to cover it up.

But when police take a confession, which a suspect recants and which later appears to be false, all hell breaks loose. Fundamentally, we all know that innocent people don't just confess, so they must have been threatened or otherwise coerced, tricked, and misled. Critical eyes turn toward the detectives who took that now disputed confession and were not forthcoming about how they did it. In this way, confessions arouse defensive, self-protective impulses in police—and, by unfortunate extension, in prosecutors who fail to serve as a safety net to catch bad confessions. Too often this happens because they perceive themselves to be on the same "team." In fact, in many jurisdictions they are part of the confession-taking process. To this day, I will not forget how, right after a South Carolina jury convicted Bill Wayne Cope, Cope's prosecutor declared to the local press that "the verdict vindicated police."

More often than I'm comfortable knowing, authorities were well aware, or should have been, that they were trafficking in misinformation for adversarial gain—often to avoid admitting to themselves or others they had already coerced an innocent person to confess. Viewed in the best possible light, these were acts of gross negligence.

There is no other reasonable way to interpret the actions taken by the Bronx detectives who tricked sixteen-year-old Huwe Burton into confessing to the murder of his mother. Six days later, Emanual Green, a convicted violent felon who had just moved into the Burtons' building, was pulled over driving Keziah Burton's car. Yet rather than arrest him and reinvestigate the crime, which they would have done if not for Burton's prior confession, they converted Green into an informant against Burton. As soon as Green testified before a grand jury, he was released.

For a relentless barrage of examples, the interested reader should visit the web pages of the Innocence Project and the National Registry of Exonerations. Read through the case summaries, and you'll see that too many of these wrongful convictions were preventable by mere reasonable precautions. But police and prosecutors routinely resist reasonable precautions. Often they obstruct reform efforts, too—whether it involves best practices to eyewitness identifications and forensic crime labs, mandatory video recording of interrogations, or ways to ensure the reliability of jailhouse and other incentivized informants. That's not a secret.

In 2018 and 2019, I served on the New York State Bar Association Wrongful Conviction Task Force. The subcommittee I was on was tasked with proposing reforms with regard to suspect confessions and informants. One proposal, which was already working its way through other states, was to recommend a statewide tracking system that would help the government keep tabs on informants to see whether they had snitched in the past, where, and how often—to help evaluate their credibility.

A second proposal was also pitched that I see as essential. For the same reasons that interrogations should be video recorded in their entirety, so too should every interaction between police and prosecutors and informants. These recordings would show what incentives were offered and where the details for the informant's often-elaborate secondary confession originated.

To anyone interested in procedural fairness and transparency, this does not seem like a controversial proposal. Yet when the subcommittee discussed this proposal in a conference call, a DA from upstate New York chimed in right away, "It's not gonna happen." "Why not?" I asked. "It's not logistically feasible," he said. Even though we were not in the same room, I reflexively reached for the cell phone in my pocket. "I don't understand," I pressed. "*Everyone* carries a video and audio recorder in their pocket." "It's not feasible," he repeated. "But why?" I said. "Because it's just not." It was like listening to a four-year-old's "I don't want to . . . *because I don't want to.*"

After several seconds of awkward silence, the subcommittee chair interceded to note that we would need to have a "consensus" on this proposal. It was my first experience on this task force. What I didn't realize was that this same recording-of-informants idea had failed to gain traction ten years earlier and that, for all practical purposes, this prosecutor had veto power and was sure to kill it. And not for reasons pertaining to truth and justice.

7

WHY FALSE CONFESSORS PLEAD GUILTY—OVER AND OVER AGAIN

On the morning of November 30, 2001, an eighty-three-year-old woman in Clarksburg, West Virginia, the widowed mother of a police officer, was awakened by a lone male intruder brandishing a large knife and a flashlight. "This is a robbery, I need your money," he said. The intruder then forced her out of bed and walked her downstairs and through the house, looking for cash. He then took her back upstairs, where he raped and sodomized her repeatedly before tying her hands behind her back and fleeing. Twenty minutes later, the victim freed herself and telephoned her son.

After police arrived, the victim was taken to the hospital, where a rape kit was collected, as were her semen-stained clothing and bedding. She gave a lucid and highly detailed tape-recorded description of the perpetrator, the flashlight he carried, the bandanna he wore, and his bare white legs. Step-by-step, she described her prolonged and horrific encounter with him. She said she paid close attention so she could describe him to her son. She indicated that her assailant may have ejaculated and did not wear a condom. Asked if there were multiple assailants, she said no, just the one.

One week later, nineteen-year-old Joseph Buffey and a friend were arrested for breaking into a Salvation Army store. Buffey admitted to it. Although there was no evidence to connect him to the rape half a mile away, three detectives pressured him from 7 p.m. to 4 a.m. During that time, Buffey repeatedly denied any involvement. He agreed to take a polygraph, after which he was told that he failed the test. More accusations followed.

After more than eight hours, without food or drink, and with a tape recorder running, Buffey capitulated: "I broke into this old lady's house." When pressed for details, however, he could not deliver. As if he were guessing, some of what he said was strikingly at odds with the facts about the crime, the victim, and the setting. Within minutes, he blurted out: "You really want to know the truth? I didn't do it." At that point, click—the tape recorder was turned off.

Buffey was charged, nevertheless, and assigned public defender Thomas Dyer. Buffey insisted he was innocent. At some point thereafter, Lieutenant Brent Myers of the West Virginia State Police Forensic Laboratory completed DNA testing on the rape kit, which showed that Buffey was conclusively excluded, a fact that the prosecutor did not disclose to Dyer, who had repeatedly asked about the results.

Six weeks after these test results were in, and even though the victim failed to identify Buffey when shown his photograph, attorney Dyer advised Buffey to accept a time-limited "exploding" plea offer. In light of his youth, Dyer suggested, Buffey might serve only fifteen years. On the other hand, because he had confessed, he would be convicted if he risked going to trial. It was a tough spot to be in. When asked later if he would have advised a guilty plea had he known the DNA results, Dyer was unequivocal: "Of course not."

Allocuting to the charges in open court, Buffey said that he "broke into an elderly lady's house and robbed her and forced her to have sex with me." In exchange for his plea to sexual assault and robbery, he was promptly sentenced to serve at least seventy years in prison.

In 2011, with the intervention of the Innocence Project, additional DNA testing using newer methods conclusively excluded Buffey—again. Shortly thereafter, despite unfathomable resistance from the prosecutor's office, and in defiance of a judge's order, the DNA was run through CODIS, the national DNA database. Boom. The profile identified Adam Derek Bowers, a prison inmate with multiple felony convictions—including breaking into a house and robbing and assaulting another woman. In 2001, Bowers lived in the victim's neighborhood.

In a questionable lack of common sense, the prosecutor refused to vacate Buffey's conviction. Instead he speculated that Buffey must have been present with Bowers as an accomplice, taking turns, whispering,

Joe Buffey of Clarksburg, West Virginia, confessed to a rape he did not commit three times—first during a late-night police interrogation, then two months later when he pled guilty in court, and then again fourteen years later when he accepted an Alford plea to avoid a retrial, after his conviction was overturned by DNA.
Photo courtesy of Kyle Jenkins / Innocence Project.

and communicating through hand gestures. To explain the absence of Buffey's DNA at the scene, he added to the story that Buffey had used a condom. This new fictional account contradicted the state's own original theory of the case; it contradicted Buffey's so-called confession, which said nothing about an accomplice; it contradicted the victim's own lucid account of her harrowing experience with a single perpetrator; and there was no evidence whatsoever that Buffey and Bowers were friends.

In August of 2013, at the request of Buffey's defense team, I flew to West Virginia to give testimony in a videotaped deposition to be played in court. From 9:30 a.m. to 3:38 p.m., armed with a PowerPoint presentation, I sought through direct and cross examinations to educate the court about the science of false confessions—dispositional and situational risk factors, types of internal and external corroboration, and the subject of this chapter: why an innocent man would not only confess, but *plead guilty* to a crime he did not commit.

In 2015, the West Virginia Supreme Court considered the case and ruled that Buffey's constitutional rights were violated by the state's failure to disclose the completed favorable DNA test results before plea negotiations. After fourteen years in prison, Buffey was permitted to withdraw his guilty plea—which he did in February 2016.

If you think the story ends with this ruling, think again. The same prosecutor's office that forced Buffey's guilty plea after the DNA results came in would not submit the results to CODIS, refused to overturn Buffey's conviction despite the DNA, and declined to drop the home-invasion charges part of the crime—based on his confession. It also threatened to try Buffey for statutory rape stemming from consensual sex he had with his underage girlfriend when he was a teenager (this girlfriend/woman adamantly opposed this; as a result of their consensual relationship, the couple had a daughter together).

Put yourself in Joe Buffey's shoes. You just spent fourteen years in prison for a crime you did not commit. First you were picked up and accused of a heinous act—and nothing you said stopped the badgering. You were pressured to confess in the middle of the night, but then you recanted, literally, within the body of the confession itself. You were then relieved to hear that a rape kit was collected for DNA testing because you knew it would exonerate you—but then the results were never revealed, and your lawyer was warned that you had to plead guilty now or lose the opportunity. The next thing you know you're in prison, all appeals are failing, and no one believes in your innocence.

Suddenly, at last, the Innocence Project gets involved, the DNA is retested, the state Supreme Court gets involved, and you are permitted to withdraw your guilty plea—which does not happen lightly or often. But the prosecutor has no sympathy, no apologies in waiting, just what feels like a vengeful threat to retry you for the burglary part of that crime. And if that isn't bad enough, he threatens to prosecute you for an old statutory rape conviction involving your then-underage teen girlfriend.

If you plead guilty, you will be released immediately, sentenced to time already served, and spare yourself further punishment. If you refuse, you risk another trial and re-incarceration at the hands of a system you have learned cannot be trusted. The thought of pleading guilty, and confessing yet again, to things you did not do is galling. But here's an option: Would you accept the plea offer if you could proclaim your innocence at the same time?

This option is one that I find galling because it has the potential to target and pressure innocent people. In West Virginia, it's called a Kennedy plea. Everywhere else, it's called an Alford plea, whereby defendants can plead guilty, thereby acknowledging that there is sufficient evidence for conviction at trial, while publicly affirming their actual innocence. I'll say more on that later.

In October 2016, on the eve of his next trial, that was the option offered to Buffey that he could not refuse. An innocent man pressured into confession, then pressured into pleading guilty, and then threatened into accepting an Alford plea. For the record, the prosecutor chalks up a win and Buffey remains a convicted felon—not an exoneree to be embraced and compensated for his wrongful imprisonment. Barry Scheck, cofounder of the Innocence Project, referred to the plea deal as bittersweet. "It is unfortunate that he will have to live with a conviction for a crime he didn't commit," he said. "But he is putting an end to a fifteen-year legal battle and can focus on building a new life with his daughter and other family members."

Two more points about the Buffey case. First, in ruling that he could withdraw his guilty plea, the West Virginia Supreme Court was unanimous and emphatic that the prosecutor violated Buffey's constitutional rights by forcing a plea decision without disclosing the exculpatory DNA results. In a landmark 1963 ruling, *Brady v. Maryland*, the U.S. Supreme Court established that a prosecutor must turn over any exculpatory evidence that tends to show that the defendant did not commit the crime or that witnesses who testified against that defendant lacked credibility. The failure to disclose this information violates the defendant's due process right to a fair trial.

Although the courts have wrestled with what constitutes exculpatory information for this purpose (DNA testing of a rape kit that conclusively excludes a defendant is a no-brainer), *Brady* has proved essential to ensure a level playing field. In *Buffey*, the West Virginia Supreme Court became the first state court in the country to declare that the prosecution also has a duty to disclose before trial—during plea negotiations. Now that roughly 97 percent of all criminal cases in the United States are resolved by guilty pleas, not trials, this opinion broke new ground.

PLEADING GUILTY IN LIEU OF TRIAL

You may have the constitutional right to be presumed innocent, to face
your accusers in a speedy and public trial, in front of an impartial jury of
your peers that, on the basis of evidence, not hearsay, sets a high bar for
finding guilt beyond a reasonable doubt. But that ideal has eroded into
a rare if not fantastical exception to the rule.

In *Brady v. United States* (1970), the Supreme Court described the
guilty plea as "a grave and solemn act to be accepted only with care and
discernment." Operationally, this means that judges should accept a
plea only if they are satisfied that the defendant made the decision
knowingly, intelligently, and voluntarily. These are not just words. In
nuts-and-bolts terms, it means that defendants should be of sound mind
to understand and appreciate the law, the rights that they have and
surrender, and the direct and collateral consequences that follow. It
also means that they make the decision of their own free will, not
induced by coercion or improper inducements—such as threatening to
prosecute a family member. Last but not least, it means that judges
should probe into the case enough to be satisfied that there is sufficient
factual evidence of the defendant's guilt.

"Grave and solemn" notwithstanding, plea agreements are typically
hammered out in private, in an office or courthouse hallway, with little
or no oversight, at any point after arrest and before trial, and often
before evidence is fully disclosed—as in Buffey's case. Often the negotiation takes but a few minutes. A particularly hard-to-fathom reality is
that many defendants meet their lawyer for the first time on the day
their plea agreement is reached.

As to how the U.S. criminal justice system has become a system of
pleas, legal scholars and social scientists point to the prosecutor's power
to use strong-arm tactics that everyone now takes for granted (I will not
use the term plea "bargaining" to describe this lopsided process because the word implies a negotiated transaction between relatively bal-
anced parties—which this is not). These tactics include charge-stacking,
which means adding more and/or more serious crimes to the charge
than an offense merits; detaining defendants behind bars without af-
fordable bail, which pressures them to accept a plea offer; and threatening defendants with the so-called trial penalty (which some refer to as
the offer of a "sentence discount") as measured by the difference be-

tween the sentence offered for a plea, now, and the harsher sentence to be sought upon conviction at trial. I should add that guilty pleas also unleash a cascade of collateral consequences, beyond a prison sentence, that can limit a defendant's later employment opportunities, eligibility for public housing, and student loans, to name just three of the forty-five thousand "invisible punishments" recently inventoried by the American Bar Association.

The Innocence Problem

Nowadays, approximately 97 percent of cases in the criminal justice systems of the United States are resolved by plea bargains, as opposed to trials. This percentage is higher than it has ever has been. So it's not surprising that a growing number of judges, legal scholars, and researchers are concerned about the "innocence problem"—the fear that some unknown number of innocent suspects, like Joe Buffey, fearing conviction and a life or death sentence—plead guilty, as Judge Stephanos Bibas put it, "outside the shadow of trial." This percentage has risen so high that it prompted the Supreme Court, in *Lafler v. Cooper* (2012), to acknowledge that "criminal justice today is for the most part a system of pleas, not a system of trials."

In a 2014 article titled "Why Innocent People Plead Guilty," Federal Judge Jed Rakoff laid bare the rational decision-making basis for this problem: "If the defendant wants to plead guilty, the prosecutor will offer him a considerably reduced charge—but only if the plea is agreed to promptly." According to Rakoff, "The defense lawyer understands this fully, and so she recognizes that the best outcome for her client is likely to be an early plea bargain." The unintended and grave result: "The prosecutor-dictated plea bargain system, by creating such inordinate pressures to enter into plea bargains, appears to have led a significant number of defendants to plead guilty to crimes they never actually committed."

As an empirical matter, I have no idea how many Joe Buffeys in the United States have been forced into pleading guilty to crimes they did not commit. No one does. But logic dictates that as the percentage of cases resolved by guilty pleas climbs, as it has, the number of wrongful pleas climbs with it—probably at a higher rate.

An interesting statistic in the IP and NRE databases is that 80 to 85 percent of those in their archives who were wrongfully convicted went to trial against the advice of counsel. In their hearts and minds, these innocent men, women, and children naïvely banked on their innocence to set them free. They opted for their day in court, believing, perhaps, that the world is fundamentally a just place and that the reality of their innocence would be obvious to any jury paying attention. Consistent with common sense, actual innocence *should* serve as the blockbuster deterrent to the false guilty plea.

Phenomenology of innocence notwithstanding, plea-bargaining researchers caution that the wrongful convictions we know about do not fully capture the extent of an innocence problem.

There are two issues. First, existing databases almost exclusively involve serious felonies in which sentences are long enough for the appeals process to play out and yield results. These same data do not bring to the surface the iceberg of false guilty pleas to lesser criminal charges, including misdemeanors. In these cases, many defendants plead guilty in exchange for a reduced sentence, leaving them little time or incentive to pursue exoneration. The second limitation stems from the ironic fact that many innocents who plead guilty, even if they want to fight for their exoneration, are prohibited from doing so precisely because they pled guilty, which often means waiving the right to appeal. The sad but true fact of the matter is that the innocence problem cannot fully be estimated.

One other sad but true point to consider is this: the initial wave of exonerations that now occupy the archives primarily involve innocent defendants convicted in the 1980s and into the early 2000s. In 1980, the guilty-plea rate nationally hovered at or above 80 percent. That number has climbed steadily ever since to its current peak level. That has to mean that innocent defendants who instinctually used to trust their day in court are now feeling the heat to plead guilty or suffer the penalty for daring to exercise their right to trial.

If one in five wrongfully convicted defendants of that generation got there by plea agreement, what will the rate be among future generations of exonerees who make that decision against a backdrop in which almost no one is willing to risk trial? The playing field was never level. But now the path to trial is a steep uphill climb.

As the guilty-plea rate reaches new heights—a fact that the system has embraced because it saves time and money, ensures conviction for prosecutors, and lightens punishment for defendants—it feels like a win-win. But justice by plea should not be measured solely by cost, time spent, winning percentages, or sentencing leniency. The first and most important metric to consider is diagnosticity: Is the ratio of accurate to wrongful convictions increased, reduced, or unaffected by a system of pleas relative to trial? Just how much wrongful conviction error is a criminal justice system willing to tolerate without scrutiny for the sake of efficiency and other objectives?

As with the scientific study of confessions, the newly emerging literature on guilty pleas is getting built on a mixed foundation of lab experiments, including studies involving lawyers; interviews of individuals who already accepted guilty pleas for various crimes; and analyses of real-life data—which tell us for starters that 97 percent of cases today are resolved by plea agreement. The question is, What does this empirical work tell us about the risk?

Using low-impact role-playing "hypotheticals," some researchers have asked naïve participants to imagine themselves accused of a crime. In 1978, Larry Gregory had male college students imagine that they were either guilty or innocent of an armed robbery. They were then informed about the evidence against them and asked to make a decision: Plead guilty or proceed to trial. To no one's surprise, students were more likely to say they would accept a plea when they imagined themselves to be guilty than innocent—83 percent to 18 percent. The 83 percent is the win the system aims for. The bad news is that the innocent number was a far cry from zero.

Other researchers using Gregory's hypothetical approach involving different crimes, probabilities of conviction, and sentencing options have also found the dual result that imagined-guilty subjects are more likely to say they would plead guilty but that the false guilty-plea rate was far greater than zero. These types of studies are provocative, but they suffer from the fact that the subjects merely projected how they would behave on the basis of hypothetical scenarios with zero stakes attached to their decision. For decades, social psychologists have known better than to trust the results from these types of role-playing exercises. So let's turn to a more straightforward approach: interviews with real-life defendants.

A number of researchers have gone straight to the source by interviewing individuals in detention who had accepted a guilty plea. There's no good reason for these individuals to misrepresent the past to researchers once incarcerated. Still, there's no guarantee that their self-reports are accurate and honest. Even with that disclaimer in place, the number of guilty pleaders asserting actual innocence is substantially greater than zero.

In a 2016 study of youths and adults who pled guilty to felonies in New York City, Tina Zottoli and others found that a sizable portion—27 percent of juveniles and 19 percent of adults—claimed to be completely innocent. In other similar studies, Lindsay Malloy found that 18 percent of juveniles who pled guilty said they were innocent; Allison Redlich found that 37 percent of guilty-pleading defendants with a diagnosed mental illness said they were innocent. Whatever the precise percentage may be, again, the extrapolation to absolute numbers is sobering.

A skeptic might still balk. If you want to know how someone will behave, you can't just ask; you have to closely mimic the decision-making situation and record their *actual behavior*. Researchers Lucian Dervan and Vanessa Edkins did just that. In a study involving seventy-six students, they induced some, but not others, to "cheat" on a solo task by planting a confederate in the room who posed as another student and asked for help. Regardless of whether they cheated or not, the experimenter accused everyone and offered them a choice: plead guilty to cheating and lose their compensation for the study or later face an academic review board at something resembling a trial at which most students historically get convicted and punished to varying degrees. Once again, the dual pattern emerged: A whopping 89 percent of subjects who cheated accepted the plea offer—that's the good news. But 56 percent of those who were innocent of cheating also accepted that offer—again, a far cry from zero.

A Confession That Springs the Trap

My interest in guilty pleas is twofold. First, they are confessions in a different venue. Confessions are taken "inside the box," where the suspect is alone with police and under the bright lights of a closed-door interrogation. Guilty pleas are typically negotiated in the presence of lawyers and formalized in front of a judge within the grandeur of an open and public courtroom.

Despite the surface differences, these forms of self-incrimination by suspects and then defendants are like two peas in a pod. In a 2017 article titled "The Psychology of Defendant Plea Decision Making," Allison Redlich and others note that both come about through the processes of human decision making under pressure; both are subject to the same cognitive, developmental, and social influences. And just as innocent people can be tricked or bullied into a false confession, so too can they be induced to plead guilty to crimes they did not commit.

The second reason I am interested in guilty pleas stems from a hypothesis that almost has to be true. If a defendant's decision to plead guilty is made in the shadow of a trial and based on an intuitive calculation of the probability of conviction weighted by the gravity of the sentence, then it stands to reason that innocent suspects who confessed to police, even if they later recanted that confession, are later more likely than other defendants to feel the heat and plead guilty.

Confessions are brutally potent in court—and all lawyers know it. Boatloads of studies have shown that confessions are so powerfully persuasive that neither juries nor judges will discount confessions even when recanted, coerced, and flat-out contradicted by exculpatory evidence. So, as in Buffey's case, the confessor's own lawyer will almost certainly advise them to avoid trial. For an innocent defendant, the false confession springs the trap. It's the first nail in the coffin; the guilty plea is the last.

To test this hypothesis, I turn to real-world statistics. In September of 2020, Vanessa Meterko, research analyst at the Innocence Project, tallied up the first 375 DNA exoneration cases and found that in 44 of them (12 percent) defendants had pled guilty. I asked her to separate out exonerees who were implicated by a confession (whether their own or someone else's). As I had anticipated, these exonerees were far more likely to plead guilty than everyone else—26 percent versus only 6 percent, more than a fourfold increase. Looking at the larger population of wrongful convictions at NRE, and after statistically controlling for type of crime and other factors, the presence of a confession also predicted an increased false-guilty-plea rate—23 percent compared to only 9 percent.

Also on point, Allison Redlich and her colleagues conducted an on-line plea-recommendation study in which they presented judges, prose-cutors, and defense lawyers with a hypothetical case file. The file con-sisted of thirty-one labeled folders containing assorted types of evi-dence (such as DNA, crime scene analysis, eyewitness accounts) and other factors (like the victim's account, the defendant's past record, community sentiment). Two results tell a powerfully suggestive story. First, 94 percent of these legal professionals across all groups opened the folder titled "confession"—which exceeded the number of those interested in any other folder. Second, the presence of a confession increased their tendency to recommend the plea option, especially among defense lawyers.

All this research lines up behind the hypothesis that false confessors are more likely to plead guilty than others wrongfully convicted. To make the case even stronger, the social psychologist in me would want to test the causal hypothesis in a controlled high-stakes experiment in which the pre-plea situation is *identical* for two groups of subjects ex-cept for the fact that some, but not others, were induced first to confess.

For ethical reasons, it is hard to run the necessary controlled three-phased experiment. Ideally, researchers would entrap some subjects but not others into committing a crime-like act, badger or trick some but not others into confession, and then urge them all later to sign a guilty plea. We could then record the percentage of subjects who ac-cept the plea agreement as a function of whether they were guilty or innocent, and whether or not they had previously confessed.

Without ethical constraint, one could bring college students into the lab, leave them alone to fill out a questionnaire, plant a stack of not-so-hidden bills on the floor, and unobtrusively record as some subjects but not others pocket the money without reporting it to the experimenter. I would then question everyone by deploying tactics from the interroga-tor's playbook, invariably causing some but not others to confess. After-ward, an "administrator" would swoop in to offer a guilty plea. It sounds easy. But creating a "gotcha" situation followed by a hard-core interro-gation would violate the researcher's obligation to respect the rights and dignity of research participants and minimize the risk of harm. Of course, these sessions would be followed by a careful debriefing to ensure the subjects' well-being. But to lure people into stealing would embarrass them; to deploy harsh, even if lawful, methods of interrogation would scare the hell out of them.

An Underpowered but Powerful Experiment

To test the hypothesis that confessions precipitate guilty pleas, Jennifer Perillo and Will Crozier (graduate students at the time, now PhDs in psychology), Cynthia Pollick (a practicing lawyer), and I sought to mimic the high stakes attached to a defendant's real-world decision making.

We recruited second- and third-year college students at John Jay College and offered to pay forty dollars for their time. Knowing that part of each session could prove stressful, we prescreened interested students online using the Beck Anxiety Inventory and excluded those with high scores. We also excluded students with low GPAs to ensure that no one we accused of cheating would fear academic suspension. After several rounds of pilot testing aimed at calibrating the protocol, our final sample consisted of twenty-nine students—twenty-one women and eight men. For those who participated, this experiment proceeded in two phases. Phase 1 consisted of the "crime" and "interrogation," culminating in a signed statement. Two days later, Phase 2 consisted of the threat of "prosecution" and offer of a plea agreement.

For the students, the experience started when they signed up for a "social intelligence" study. Those who survived the screening process were scheduled to come into my lab on the tenth floor of John Jay's newest building, overlooking the Hudson River. The lab itself is a windowless four-room complex consisting of a waiting room, two soundproof interview rooms equipped with concealed cameras and microphones, and a control room furnished with computers, recording equipment, intercoms, and one-way mirrors that peer into the interview rooms.

When individual students entered the waiting room, they met Jen, the experimenter, and Will, posing as a fellow student. After some getting acquainted conversation, Jen brought the students into an interview room and explained that they would fill out an alternating series of questionnaires—some alone, others jointly. The purpose of the study, she said, was to determine if dyads score higher on a test of social intelligence than individuals. Modeled after the TV game show *Family Feud*, the questionnaires asked students to list the most popular four answers per category—"Things That Fly," "Famous Captains," and so on. Before starting, Jen reminded the pair not to collaborate on solo questions, or it would invalidate the results.

Let the games begin. Jen left, and the students proceeded. The first couple of rounds passed uneventfully. In the experiment we had planned, Will would pretend anxiously to struggle on a solo question in half of the sessions and ask for help: "I'm totally blanking on answers for these," he said. "What did you get?" We knew from prior research in our lab and others that most students humanely accommodate this plea for assistance. In this way, we were able to induce "cheating" that violated the experimenter's rule. The students were rendered guilty without being cast in a bad light. In other sessions, no request was made; no one was induced to cheat; everyone was innocent.

Shortly thereafter, Jen collected the responses, administered the next questionnaire, but then returned moments later to inform the students that there was a problem. She pulled the subject into a separate room and said, "It appears that the two of you collaborated on the last individual question series. Statistically, there is no way you could have gotten so many of the same answers without working together." She accused the student of collaborating on solo questions, terminated the session, and asked the student to sign one of two statements for documentation purposes.

In half the sessions, by a flip of the coin, she handwrote a denial and asked the student to sign it; in the other sessions, she handwrote a confession: "The experimenter told us not to share information on individual trials. I admit that I did share information on an individual problem series. I understand the session was terminated early. I am signing this statement voluntarily." To induce compliance with this more demanding request, she made light of the transgression—a common interrogation ploy. If the student refused to sign, she restated her need for documentation and pressed twice more for a confession.

If the student continued to refuse, she crossed out the confession and handwrote a denial statement. After taking a signature to one of the two statements, Jen terminated the session, paid each student twenty dollars of the forty offered for a full session, and took their contact information, allegedly so she could call them to complete the study at a later date.

Two days later, we emailed Phase 1 students an invitation to complete the study in exchange for the balance of their payment. When they arrived, however, Jen said a "project supervisor" wanted to talk about the previously aborted session. She escorted the student to a supervisor's office for a plea negotiation that was covertly recorded for later analysis. Dressed in business attire, the project supervisor, attorney Pollick, greeted and seated the student, produced a copy of that student's signed confession or denial, confirmed that the signature at the bottom was authentic, and asked the student to read the statement aloud. She then explained that the principal investigator wanted to file charges with the Academic Integrity Board but that she managed to strike a possible compromise.

As for the terms of the agreement, the project supervisor explained that if the student *accepted* the guilty plea, he or she would have to do forty hours of community service with the university's custodial staff and that the plea would remain in the student's academic file. If the student were to *decline* the offer, she continued, then the case would be turned over to the board, and the student would be called to attend a half-hour "trial" to try to prove his or her innocence. She assured the student that although that she was unsure what penalty would follow, this was not the type of case that would lead to expulsion and that historically the review board convicts about one out of every four or five students. Those were the choices.

At that point, attorney Pollick printed out a guilty plea agreement which stated the date and charge, an agreement to waive a hearing, and the term of the penalty upon acceptance: "Performance of forty hours of community service to be coordinated with the Department of Facilities Management." The bottom of the form provided space for a printed name, signature, and date.

If students declined, she repeated the offer. "Are you sure? This is your last chance." If they continued to decline, she asked them to sign a plea refusal. If students failed to make a decision within five minutes, the session was terminated. To protect the students' well-being, she also terminated a session early if a student started to cry or became overly stressed out.

Right after the plea or denial was signed, Jen returned, walked the student to another room, offered a bottle of water, and inquired as to what happened. She then asked the student to fill out a brief questionnaire, after which she debriefed them about the true purpose of the study. She then brought each student to my office for a second debriefing session. At that time, I asked them about the experience and how they were feeling, apologized for the various manipulations, and explained why it was necessary and why the study was important. Many students expressed an interest in the project, so I gave them readings on the subject of false confessions and guilty pleas. At that point, we paid each student the second twenty dollars they were promised.

That was the setup: a laboratory experiment, where the stakes felt real, that closely mimicked the decision-making dilemma confronting defendants in the criminal justice system. Having run dozens of experiments at that point in my career, I wondered at first whether any student would actually bend and break, pleading guilty to something they didn't do that would cost them forty hours and a mark on their academic record.

Now let me backtrack and explain how we finalized the details of this study. When social psychologists devise a new paradigm for testing a hypothesis, they often bring in pilot subjects for preliminary testing that enables them to refine various aspects of the protocol. That's exactly what we did. We started by offering a plea deal that carried a hefty twenty hours of community service as a penalty. Then the first handful of guilty and innocent pilot subjects all accepted that deal like it was a no-brainer. They either pleaded guilty or became so visibly upset that we had to terminate the session. In post-session debriefings, these early subjects couldn't be more articulate. They were so fearful of conviction at a hearing that they couldn't take a chance.

We discarded the guilty condition altogether and limited our test to falsely accused innocent subjects. We then fine-tuned the relative choices. We doubled the guilty plea sentence from twenty hours to forty—that's a whole workweek! We also made it less attractive by redefining "community service" as custodial work, not time in a research lab that some had seen as a résumé entry.

On the other end, we reduced the uncertainty of outcome at trial, first, by noting that they would have an opportunity to air their defense. Some said they feared expulsion from school, so we assured them that this "academic death penalty" was not a possible outcome. To further mitigate their fear of trial, we lowered the historical conviction rate from 50 percent to "one out of every four or five students." Only after all these changes were made, and after we burned through twenty-one pilot sessions, did at least some innocent subjects reject the offer of a guilty plea. I will admit, I was shocked by how slow I was to predict what would happen. Making a high-stakes decision in a state of uncertainty, college students exhibited extreme aversion to risk.

Our final experiment consisted of twenty-nine subjects. Despite their innocence, a total of eleven pled guilty, for a false-guilty-plea rate of 38 percent. To test the confession-effect hypothesis, we compared the innocent students who confessed in Phase 1 to those who signed a denial. Among innocent deniers, 59 percent had the fortitude to reject the guilty plea; 35 percent pled guilty, 6 percent had to be terminated. Among innocent confessors, however, only 8 percent rejected the offer; 42 percent pleaded guilty, 50 percent had to be terminated. Feeling duped by his prior confession, one subject lost all trust in the promise of a fair trial: "I don't know if I want to sign this because I signed this shit and y'all doing this nonsense to me. I don't understand. I just don't understand what the benefit is of the hearing if you're already pinning this on me. You're on the school's side."

I could not have put it better myself. In the lab, as in real life, confessing to police is a trap that can later force even innocent people to plead guilty.

The Alford Variant—Pleading Guilty "But I Didn't Do It"

On the evening of November 22, 1963, the day John F. Kennedy was assassinated, Nathaniel Young, who operated a "party house" in Winston-Salem, North Carolina, responded to a knock at the door. He opened it and was shot at point blank range and killed.

Earlier that evening, a man by the name of Henry Alford had visited, accompanied by a young woman described as a prostitute. They purchased several drinks, after which Alford paid Young to rent him a room for a short period of time, which was all the time he could afford. Alford wanted the woman he was with to leave with him, but Young invited her to stay. An argument ensued and Alford ran off with her coat. A few minutes later, there was that knock on the door followed by the gunshot.

Two weeks later, Alford was indicted by a grand jury for first-degree murder, a capital offense. He was appointed counsel, a young attorney who proceeded to investigate the case on behalf of his client. Alford named several witnesses, but when his attorney spoke with them, they contradicted his client's account. Although no one actually saw him pull the trigger, several witnesses said they saw him retrieve his shotgun, which he owned, and four shells, shortly before the murder; heard him state that he was going to kill Nathaniel Young; and heard him state afterward that he executed his plan. As if these accounts were not convincing enough, Alford's attorney learned that his client had a lengthy criminal history, which included a prior conviction for murder. Henry Alford was hardly a sympathetic character.

Shortly thereafter, on the advice of counsel, Alford entered a plea of guilty to second-degree murder, not first, which carried a maximum punishment of thirty years imprisonment, not life or death. The court heard from witnesses, the state presented a summation of its evidence, and then the judge turned to Alford for his admission of guilt. But instead he took the stand himself and proclaimed his innocence. "I ain't shot no man," he said. "I'm not guilty but I plead guilty." Despite his refusal to make an admission, the judge accepted Alford's guilty plea and sentenced him to thirty years.

Alford appealed his conviction, stating that his plea was coerced by fear of execution. After failed attempts within the state, his conviction was overturned by a federal appeals court—but then reaffirmed by the U.S. Supreme Court in *North Carolina v. Alford* (1970). In that ruling, the court held that "an individual accused of a crime may voluntarily, knowingly, and understandingly consent to the imposition of a prison sentence even if he is unwilling or unable to admit his participation in the acts constituting the crime." As long as a judge is satisfied that there is "sufficient factual basis of guilt," the court added, a judge may accept the plea despite a defendant's proclamation of innocence. In that opinion, the Alford plea was born (Alford himself died in prison five years later). Today, fifty-plus years later, it is accepted in forty-seven states and the District of Columbia.

Commentators are quick to note that Henry Alford was not a particularly sympathetic defendant, which is why it is important to disentangle Alford the person from the Alford plea itself. This brings me back to West Virginia's Joe Buffey. Police took a late-night confession from him that he recanted on tape. Allegedly, off tape, he re-confessed. Not only was there no other evidence against Buffey, but the prosecutor's office was in possession of exculpatory DNA tests, which was never disclosed, on purpose or by inadvertence, at the time they pressured Buffey into pleading guilty.

Years later, new DNA testing once again conclusively excluded Buffey and identified the rapist, a serial sex offender from the victim's neighborhood. The West Virginia Supreme Court allowed Buffey to withdraw his guilty plea. But not so fast. Under threat of re-prosecution, and the risk of re-incarceration, Buffey agreed to an Alford plea in exchange for his freedom. Principled as I might be, I suspect I would have done the same if I were in his shoes.

A proponent of the Alford plea might point to this as an argument for it, not against. But looking through a pinhole in this way misses the broader perspective of justice. The prosecutor notched a victory for convicting, again, an innocent man, even after a *Brady* violation so egregious that it caused the state Supreme Court to become the first in the land to assert that Brady rules are in effect not just before trial but during plea negotiations. The prosecutor's alternative was not to try Buffey but instead to dismiss the charges and apologize profusely. Admitting to their mistakes and apologizing—that's what adults do. That's what we want real offenders to do.

The Alford proponent will shrug and say, no harm, no foul. Buffey is back home with no more time behind bars, and he got to proclaim his innocence. Again, this pinhole of a perspective is missing some key points.

First of all, what happened to the Supreme Court's precondition that judges should accept an Alford plea only when the defendant's proclamation of innocence is paired with a strong and sufficient evidence of guilt? That criterion was not met when Buffey pled guilty in 2001, much less fifteen years later after DNA results were disclosed.

Second, a "no harm no foul" sensibility is just plain wrong. An innocent Joe Buffey may have been given an opportunity to salvage some virtue in court, but it means that he is not an exoneree. On the record, he remains a convicted felon with all the limitations and stigma attached to that status. And it means—and this is no small matter—that he is now prevented from seeking financial compensation for his fifteen years behind bars in a civil suit against the government.

Third, on a larger scale, what kind of criminal justice system accepts guilty pleas in the absence of sufficient evidence from individuals who proclaim their innocence? Apart from undermining the public's trust, there is also this hard consequence: if an innocent person is convicted by an Alford plea, then the case is closed. That means that the true perpetrator will not be sought or brought to justice and is free to reoffend. Explain that to the friends and family members of the offender's next victims.

When Henry Alford entered his famous plea in 1963, and when the Supreme Court signed off on it in 1970, the presumed baseline of wrongful convictions hovered over zero. "Once in a blue moon" is the phrase I kept hearing. Since that time, thousands of wrongful convictions have been uncovered, all of which represents a mere fraction of an unknown total. Many of these cases, shockingly, appear to be based on a mountain of evidence. Across samples, autopsies of these wrongful convictions have shown large percentages of them contain eyewitness identification errors, invalid forensic science evidence, false confessions, and testimony from informants who lied. In fact, in 2012 my colleagues and I noted that 55 percent of all IP cases were caused, not by one, but by two or three erroneous forms of evidence. With all this, fifty-plus years later, the courts need to reconceptualize the Alford pleader and rethink the wisdom of plowing over a defendant's in-court proclamations of innocence without substantial—and I mean *substantial*—evidence.

Let's be clear about the scope of the problem. It's not just about Henry Alford and Joe Buffey. In 1997 and then again in 2004, the Department of Justice surveyed thousands of inmates in state facilities and found that 6 to 7 percent had entered an Alford plea. The percentage was particularly high for murder and other serious offenses. From these data, Allison Redlich and Asil Özdoğru estimated that approximately seventy-six thousand individuals in state prisons got there via an Alford plea.

The West Memphis Three

Long before Netflix's 2015 smash hit *Making a Murderer* or *Amanda Knox* and long before *The Confession Tapes*, *The Staircase*, *The Central Park Five*, or the podcast *Serial*, HBO aired *Paradise Lost*, a 1996 documentary about three teen defendants known as the West Memphis Three. Directed by Joe Berlinger and Bruce Sinofsky, this film was followed by two sequels released in 2000 and 2011 as well as *West of Memphis*; *Devil's Knot*, a dramatization starring Colin Firth and Reese Witherspoon; and a handful of other films, podcasts, and books about the case.

West Memphis is a city in Crittenden County, Arkansas. As part of a larger metropolitan area, it is located directly across the Mississippi River from Memphis, Tennessee. On a warm day in May 1993, three eight-year-old cub scouts rode off on their bikes, never to be seen alive again. The next day, their naked, hogtied, bruised, mutilated bodies were recovered from a creek in Robin Hood Hills. Everything about this crime was heinous; everything about it would trigger the primal human instinct for retribution-style closure. Almost immediately, a rumor spread that these killings were satanic, the work of devil worshippers. Certainly no one "normal" could have perpetrated acts so malevolent.

Three times over the next few days, juvenile officer Steve Jones questioned Damien Echols, an eighteen-year-old high school dropout who lived in a trailer park, who liked to dress in black and had a history of depression and other mental health problems. One social worker with whom he met regularly recalled that he once said he might become another Charles Manson or Ted Bundy. Jones noted that although Echols denied knowing anything about the murders, he liked to read books by Stephen King and had the word *evil* penned across his knuckles. Echols agreed to take a polygraph test; the examiner concluded he was deceptive.

Next police focused on sixteen-year-old Jason Baldwin, a friend of Echols. Baldwin was still in high school, a strong student who loved heavy metal music and was gifted with such artistic talent that one of his teachers encouraged him to study graphic design in college. They also focused on seventeen-year-old Jessie Misskelley Jr., a high school dropout like Echols, a party animal known for getting into fistfights. Misskelley also denied involvement and although he was told that a $35,000 reward was available for information leading to convictions, he denied any knowledge. He agreed to take a polygraph, but Detective Bill Durham, who administered the test, concluded that he, too, was deceptive or, more specifically, "lying his ass off." An estimated twelve hours of badgering ensued until Misskelley agreed to state that he, Echols, and Baldwin killed the boys.

Misskelley's "confession" was riddled with mistakes and inconsistencies. In response to leading questions, he said they tied the boys up with rope. That was wrong. The boys' shoelaces were used. He said they committed the murders during the day. That too was wrong. The boys were seen during the day; it had to be at night. Five hours later, after correcting Misskelley's story, police turned on a tape recorder and taped a confession that can only be described as chilling.

Based on this confession and the testimony of Vicki Hutcheson, who claimed to have seen these teens at a gathering of witches (she would later admit that she totally fabricated the story), all three were immediately arrested and charged with capital murder.

No physical evidence ever linked these teens to the murders. In fact, investigators had trampled through the crime scene and removed the bodies from the creek before the coroner arrived. Blood found at the site was never tested. Echols himself had an alibi for the time of the murders—he was at home with family members and had made three phone calls that evening. None of this mattered. At a press conference one month later, the deputy prosecutor announced the arrests. Asked how confident in the case he was, on a one-to-ten scale, he did not equivocate: "Eleven," he said.

In two trials, the three defendants were found guilty of first-degree murder. Echols was sentenced to death by lethal injection. Baldwin and Misskelley were sentenced to life. In the ensuing years, their convictions were upheld by both the state and U.S. Supreme Courts. Then HBO aired *Paradise Lost* and then its first sequel.

In 2003, Vicki Hutcheson testified that she had lied ten years earlier about the gathering of witches. Four years later, DNA testing conclusively excluded the three defendants. In 2010, with the public squarely focused on this case, and suspicious of the result, the state Supreme Court ordered the trial court to reconsider the original verdict in light of the new DNA tests. For the prosecutor's office, this was a moment of truth. They could have moved to overturn the convictions, knowing they would likely fail in a retrial. Or they could hold back and take the coward's way out.

Refusing to relinquish three convictions, the prosecutor would not move to overturn. Then attorney Steven Braga, from the Echols defense team, proposed the Alford plea as a compromise. In a conversation with a writer from *The Jeffersonian*, a publication of the Thomas

Jefferson School of Law, Braga said: "The Alford plea was the only compromise I could come up with to try to bridge the gap between the State's absolute refusal to drop the charges and the Three's absolute demand to maintain their innocence of crimes they did not commit."

When presented with the deal, prosecuting attorney Scott Ellington, not the original prosecutor in this case, saw an opportunity. As he put it, "The state would get the guilty plea that it wanted and the defendants could continue to assert their innocence as convicted felons."

And so it was. The state agreed to an Alford plea—or else, no deal. The West Memphis Three were all still behind bars. In fact, Echols was confined twenty-three hours a day, alone, in a small cinderblock cell on death row. So the two sides agreed. Judge David Laser, who had replaced the original judge, accepted their plea, sentenced the men to eighteen years and seventy-eight days—the precise amount of time they had already served—and called what happened a tragedy on all sides. *New York Times* writer Kim Severson called it a "legally awkward deal." Mara Leveritt, author of the bestseller *Devil's Knot*, called it a "cynical and unsatisfactory end to a sinister prosecution." On the back of this Alford plea that left many observers frustrated, thirty-seven-year-old Jessie Misskelley, Jason Baldwin, and Damien Echols were released back into the world to start new lives.

The West Memphis Three are free, first and foremost, but they desperately want to clear their names. "This was not justice," said Baldwin, a holdout who accepted the plea for Echols's sake. He's right, of course. The deal struck ensured that these men remain felons under the law. It means that police and prosecutors will not investigate new leads or try to bring the real killers to justice because the case is closed. Period. End of story. And it means that Misskelley, Baldwin, and Echols cannot pursue wrongful conviction lawsuits compensating them for their eighteen years in prison.

The Alford plea enables compromise, and often compromise is the mature way to resolve disputes. But lacking sufficient evidence to retry these men, the mature and just thing for the prosecutor's office to do would have been to surrender, overturn the convictions, dismiss the charges, compensate the wrongfully convicted defendants, as provided for in thirty-six states (Arkansas is not one of them) and the District of Columbia, and reopen the investigation of these heinous murders for the sake of the victims' families.

In a 2013 scholarly article critical of Alford pleas, Sydney Schneider quotes Dan Stidham—Misskelley's trial lawyer, who is now an Arkansas district court judge. Stidham told a local reporter that it took the state eighteen years to get it right. And even then, as he put it, it did so "in a cowardly fashion with no honor."

Like the story of Joe Buffey, this case should stir up this provocative, answerable but yet unanswered question. For whom is the Alford plea built? Offenders trapped by substantial evidence who are lured into a traditional guilty plea because they fear trial, or innocents against whom there is no substantial evidence and who often refuse to accept a traditional plea? Although data collection is pending, I have a strong sense of the answer to this question. Horrific stories of innocent men and women wrongfully convicted and incarcerated, whose convictions were so egregiously wrongful they had to be overturned, but who were then threatened with re-prosecution unless they agreed to an Alford plea, are hardly limited to Buffey and the West Memphis Three.

Google the name Christopher Conover of Baltimore, Maryland. Conover spent eighteen years in prison for a double murder before he was excluded by DNA testing. The state vacated his conviction, and he was released. Yet despite the DNA and despite numerous alibi witnesses who said they were with Conover at a birthday party during the murders, the prosecutor vowed to retry him. Desperate to avoid re-incarceration, Conover accepted the offer of an Alford plea in exchange for time served, a deal that the *Baltimore Sun*'s Dan Rodricks referred to as "an arrangement [that] seems to defy logic." Desperate to maintain his freedom, Conover explained, "It would not have been worth it to put my mother and my loved ones through another trial."

Upon release, Conover married his high school sweetheart, and the two moved to North Carolina. Having accepted an Alford plea, he remained a convicted felon and thus not eligible to be exonerated or compensated. He struggled financially. According to his wife, Sue, he suffered from depression, panic attacks, and anxiety. In 2015, at sixty years old, Conover took his own life.

There are others, too. Search for the name Belynda Goff of Berryville, Arkansas; Darrell Edwards of Newark, New Jersey; Leroy Harris of New Haven, Connecticut; Paul Hildwin of Hernando County, Florida; Perry Lott of Pontotoc County, Oklahoma; or Raymond Tempest of Woonsocket, Rhode Island. In each and every one of these cases, a prosecutor shamefully leveraged an Alford plea by vowing to retry an innocent person who had already been punished unjustly and enough.

One might argue that the offer of an Alford plea does defendants whose wrongful convictions are overturned a favor. They get their freedom in exchange for pleading guilty and avoid the uncertainty of trial. That's a false choice, a Hobson's choice. Prosecutors in a system built on integrity should, as many do, offer a third alternative. Dismiss the charges, and move on.

CONFESSIONS FROM PRISON—ARCHAIC CUSTOMS FROM A LESS INFORMED ERA

The guilty plea and its Alford variant is one mechanism by which defendants confess in court to avoid a conviction at trial and a harsh sentence. Once they have accepted a plea, they are carted off to a correctional facility, where at some point they are asked to confess yet again.

Confessions to Parole Boards

After he was wrongfully convicted in 1989 of killing his mother, based on a police-induced confession, Huwe Burton was sent to the Downstate Correctional Facility, a maximum-security prison in Fishkill, New York, where he would start to serve a fifteen-years-to-life sentence. He was sixteen when he confessed; seventeen when he was convicted. He would become eligible for parole fifteen years later.

When his moment of opportunity arrived in 2005, Burton was denied parole. The likely reason: standing before his first parole board, he would not confess, accept responsibility, express remorse, or utter any other requisite words of repentance. He was innocent, he said. Having spent all those years locked up with other inmates, he knew well what the drill was. But he would not play the role: "They tricked me into confessing when I was sixteen," he told me and the graduate students in my lab. "I wasn't going to let them do it to me again at thirty-two."

Burton's father visited him in prison ahead of his next parole hearing and urged him to cooperate. "Huwe, we all know you didn't do this," he said. "Just tell them what they want to hear so you can come home." In 2009, twenty years after his mother was murdered, Huwe capitulated, uttered the magic words, and received his release (sadly, his father died before he was freed).

How parole boards make decisions, the factors they consider, and how they weight those factors, is not fully understood or subject to oversight by the courts. The purpose of parole and the need to make good decisions is a noble one, an act of grace. To the extent that prisoners who have served their minimally sentenced time have shown that they are worthy of release, without posing a threat to the community, especially at a time when correctional facilities are overcrowded, parole is both merciful for the individual and cost-efficient for the state. No one seriously questions this objective; but the criteria used in making the decision are less clear.

Trying to determine if a convicted felon is rehabilitated and no longer a dangerous recidivist, parole boards consider a host of background factors like the nature of the crime for which the inmate is incarcerated, history of other crimes committed, history of substance abuse, the inmate's record while in prison, his or her physical and mental health, and the results of any clinical risk assessments conducted that are aimed at predicting future violence. Parole boards can access all of this information from an inmate's files.

The point of the in-person interview is so the parole board can determine whether an eligible inmate is prepared to be reintegrated into society in a way that ensures public safety. When Timothy McVeigh was executed in 2001 for bombing a federal building in Oklahoma City, which killed 168 people, reporter Kevin Fagan described him as "stone faced." Despite the opportunity to do so, McVeigh uttered no words of regret. Common sense would suggest that prisoners who do express remorse are less likely to offend upon release. In a 2020 law review article, Nicole Bronniman overviews that research, however, and concludes that the correlation is inconsistent and modest.

One problem, as Bronniman correctly notes, is that all prospective parolees know through the grapevine that remorse and responsibility are essential to winning a get-out-of-jail card. They know, as Daniel Medwed put it in a must-read 2008 law review article, "that remorse is essentially a quid pro quo for release." But it's not clear whether parole board officials, through live interviews, can use an inmate's verbal and nonverbal behavior to distinguish between genuine remorsefulness and mere feigned expressions. All over the world, controlled experiments on deception detection, reviewed in chapter 2, have shown that people in general, including experts, cannot accurately distinguish between truths and lies. Overlaid on that foundation of incompetence is that parole boards, in particular, interview some number of psychopathic inmates who are particularly talented at shedding crocodile tears and charming others for personal gain.

What little empirical research has been published is not encouraging. In 1986, Barry Ruback and Charles Hopper reported on a study of parole interviewers in Georgia. Based on prison files, four parole board members predicted how well 103 inmates would do on parole. Then they interviewed the candidates and predicted again how well they would do. Three years later, the researchers went back and tracked what had happened to each inmate. The results showed that the board members were not more accurate in the predictions they made after the interviews than before; in fact, they were somewhat less accurate.

It's not clear that an inmate's in-person interview demeanor, which is used to assess remorse, enables parole decisions that are predictive. It's not even clear that legal professionals agree on what remorse even looks like. In a study of twenty-three Connecticut state judges, for example, Rocksheng Zhong found that some judges saw silence as an indication of shyness, or fear; yet to others, silence meant *callous* or *disengaged*. To some, putting one's head down was a sign of respect, like bowing; to others it was an act of disrespect.

Parole board interviews may or may not have diagnostic value. From what I've read, more research is needed before a strong conclusion can be drawn. Either way, however, it leaves wide open the elephant-in-the-room question: What about prisoners who are innocent, for whom having to confess after a wrongful conviction and incarceration is perhaps the most galling indignity of all? What happens to the innocent prisoners who stand before the parole board, knowing that it's in their best interest to lie even as they proclaim their innocence?

The first time he was eligible, Huwe Burton could not bring himself to confess yet again to killing a mother he loved no matter what the price. He could not bring himself to utter yet another false confession—not until his father urged him to get the words out at later parole board appearances.

Years later, something that escaped public notice happened that was remarkable, forward looking, and admirable. In its 2019 recommendation to overturn Burton's conviction, the Bronx District Attorney's Office hit the nail on the head in a lengthy footnote. "The inculpatory statements that Burton made before the parole board do not, under the circumstances here, suggest that Burton's original confession was true and accurate." Quoting from Medwed's incisive innocent prisoner's dilemma article, the DA noted, "Given the stark reality of prison life—its everyday brutality and ample deprivations—the yearning to escape can overwhelm even the strongest and most stoic of people and prompt an innocent prisoner to surrender to the lure of admitting guilt before the parole board."

Research is clear: A prisoner's acceptance of responsibility is virtually necessary for parole boards to grant an inmate's release. Yet Burton is by no means the only exoneree who has had to confront this dilemma. Edwin Chandler of Louisville, Kentucky, was convicted of manslaughter and robbery in 1995. After repeated interrogations and denials, police falsely told Chandler that his fingerprints were found at the scene, that he failed the polygraph, that neighbors identified sunglasses and a stocking cap as his, and that if he did not confess they would arrest his sister. Chandler steadfastly maintained his innocence for years until he relented and confessed during a parole board hearing. In 2009, he was exonerated by newly discovered DNA evidence.

Bruce Dallas Goodman of Beaver, Utah, was convicted of murder, kidnapping, and rape in 1986 and spent eighteen years in prison. He always maintained his innocence, even after his conviction. But then, appearing before the Utah State Board of Pardons and Parole in 2000, Goodman "admitted" his culpability. Four years later, he was exonerated by DNA.

Garr Keith Hardin of Louisville, Kentucky, was convicted of murder in 1995, the result of a false confession, misleading forensic evidence, and police perjury. After twenty-three years in prison, he was exonerated and released. Along the way, Hardin confessed and accepted responsibility at a hearing before the parole board. Judge Bruce Butler, who vacated Hardin's conviction, noted that Hardin confessed while seeking parole. He ruled that those statements had no bearing on his decision. "The court finds that there is reason for candidates for parole to believe that failing to admit culpability or otherwise take responsibility for the crime(s) for which they are imprisoned, will adversely affect the likelihood of obtaining parole," he said.

Henry Murray of Brooklyn, New York, was another such victim. A jury convicted him of murder in 1979 (the trial judge believed his alibi witnesses but felt compelled to respect the jury's verdict). Although eligible for parole, Murray maintained his innocence over the course of four parole hearings. On his fifth try, "I said what the hell, let me tell these people what they want to hear." "I felt like I sold my soul to the devil," he said. Even then, his parole was denied. He had not fully internalized responsibility for his action, he was told. Finally, after Murray had spent twenty-nine years in prison, Medwed's Second Look Clinic, dedicated to the release of innocent prisoners, assisted in his eighth parole board hearing, and he was released.

The list of innocents who were wrongfully convicted, only to admit guilt and responsibility to a parole board years later, goes on and on: Eddie Lowery, a soldier stationed in Fort Riley, Kansas, spent nine years in prison for rape before gaining his release on parole. In an interview with National Public Radio, Lowery recounted his decision to participate in sex-offender therapy in order to get parole: "I'd had to lie to get out of prison," he said. In 2003, Lowery was ultimately exonerated by DNA.

Then there were the cases of Robert Hill, Sundhe Moses, and Sharrif Wilson, in three separate cases in Brooklyn; Jimmy Ray Bromgard, from Yellowstone; Kirk Odum, from Washington, DC; Jeffrey Clark, of Louisville; Clifford Jones and Korey Wise, the eldest of the Central Park five, both in Manhattan. And these are just some of the "lucky" ones we know about.

Parole boards are not trained or equipped to re-litigate factual questions of guilt and innocence. I get it. But if their ability to distinguish between sincere remorse and feigned expressions is in question, as is human deception detection in general; if the psychopaths within the prison population are particularly adept at lying, a proposition supported by research in other domains; and if wrongfully convicted innocents appear at parole hearings on a non-quantifiable but regular basis, then the system is broken.

At some point, when a prisoner chooses the more difficult path of pleading innocence rather than expressing remorse, all but ensuring failure, parole boards should have another mechanism they can turn to. Expanding the scope of their investigative powers is not feasible, or perhaps even desirable, but referring these cases to organizations that analyze actual innocence claims for a living makes great sense. A network of innocence projects can be found in cities all over the country, along with Centurion Ministries, the Center for Wrongful Convictions, the Exoneration Project, and the Exoneration Initiative. Reviewing cases referred by parole boards would fit squarely within their mission and expertise.

Today, many district attorney's offices contain an in-house but independent Conviction Integrity Unit (CIU) or Conviction Review Unit (CRU). These departments conduct extrajudicial reviews of past convictions to investigate allegations of actual innocence. Some of these reviews are triggered by the discovery of new evidence. Others arise when prior exonerations indicate a particular detective's misconduct—as with NYPD detective Anthony Scarcella, responsible for framing well over a dozen innocent men by coercing confessions, pressuring witnesses, and planting evidence. (One thousand miles away, between 1972 to 1991, Chicago PD detective Jon Burge was involved in the torture of over a hundred suspects into confession.) As the dominoes on the Scarcella and Burge convictions fell one by one, more and more of their prior cases were scrutinized.

At the start of 2021, the National Registry of Exonerations had listed sixty-five CIUs in the country. Over the past few years, I have occasionally consulted with CIUs. Some are better resourced than others; some have a better track record than others. But all are capable of tapping into their office's case files, hiring investigators, and consulting with defense attorneys. New evidence, bad cops, and a prisoner's dogged insistence—I cannot think of one good reason why a prospective parolee's claims of actual innocence should not serve as a third basis for referring an old case to an appropriate CIU.

Post-Release Therapy Confessions

The system's fixation on confession does not stop at the prison gate. For an innocent person who was wrongfully convicted, the stigma and indignity of the experience can persist even after their release.

Take the 1980 case of nineteen-year-old Daniel Andersen, of Chicago, which I describe elsewhere. Based on a coerced confession that he recanted, Andersen was convicted and sentenced to prison. Thirty-five years later his conviction was vacated, and all charges were dismissed.

The Circuit Court of Cook County then granted Andersen a Certificate of Innocence, which the state's attorney did not oppose.

In 2016, Andersen filed a civil suit against the City of Chicago and police officers involved in his case. "A teenager when he was arrested, Mr. Andersen's wrongful conviction forced him to endure nearly three decades in Illinois' most dangerous prisons, and his life has been forever damaged," the complaint stated. It proceeds: "Plaintiff now seeks justice for the harm that the Defendants have caused and redress for the loss of liberty and the terrible hardship that Plaintiff has endured and continues to suffer as a result of the Defendants' misconduct."

The city and the other defendants contested Andersen's complaint. They did not argue that Andersen's wrongful conviction resulted from innocent mistakes, as opposed to acts of misconduct. Despite his exoneration and Certificate of Innocence, they argued that his confession was not false and his conviction not wrongful. At this point, you may be scratching your head, as I did, at this turn of events. Then in June of 2021, a Chicago jury found in favor of Andersen and awarded him $7.55 million.

Full disclosure: I was retained by Andersen's attorneys to review his confession—what caused it, and what rippling effects it had. I've read through thousands of pages in his case file. From this material, I learned that from 2007 to 2010 Andersen was required to attend sex-offender therapy sessions as a condition of his parole. His therapist testified that during these treatments, Andersen had reiterated his confession to attempted rape and murder and expressed remorse (which he had not done in his twenty-seven years in prison).

On the one hand, this would seem to contradict Andersen's many vigorous recantations over the years and the Certificate of Innocence he would later be granted. He was not, after all, in a coercive "bright lights" interrogation room bombarded by promises, threats, or the fear of bodily harm. On the other hand, Andersen feared the parole consequences of refusing to confess, take responsibility, and express remorse. "I had to go through this program. I had to comply with everything," he testified at a deposition. In his mind, the therapist "had the authority to incarcerate me on his own opinion." Andersen's fear was not unreasonable. The therapist himself conceded that although he had no *formal* power to send parolees back to prison, he did make risk assessments and recommendations—including for re-incarceration—and that he spoke regularly with his clients' parole officers (who themselves would sometimes attend the therapy sessions).

To my knowledge, there is no research on the specific question of whether innocent parolees in a sex-offender program would re-confess to crimes for which they were wrongfully convicted. But there are relevant data, cited elsewhere in this book, that address the broader issue in other contexts. I don't know how to put it any more clearly than this: *one-hundred-plus years of basic psychology have shown that people make all sorts of high-stakes decisions that aim to avoid punishment and loss.*

That's why innocent people confess to police behind closed doors and under pressure. It's why they plead guilty in the light of day, in open court, in the presence of counsel, and often under oath, even while proclaiming their Alford plea innocence. It's why innocent prisoners, caged behind bars and desperate to gain their freedom, accept responsibility in front of parole boards. And it's why Daniel Andersen, terrified of being re-incarcerated after twenty-seven years, stated that he accepted responsibility to his sex-offender therapist. And these other confessions, I might add, are not ever reevaluated according to the corroboration criteria described elsewhere in this book.

On the surface, the police interrogation room, the public courtroom, inside prison, and in therapy may seem like four wildly different venues. But at a deep, structural, core level, the process of human decision making under pressure in all cases is absolutely the same. I did something in my consultant's report on the Andersen case I had never done before. I got personal. "I would like to believe that I would have the fortitude after twenty-seven years of wrongful incarceration to assert my innocence without regard for consequence," I wrote. "The laws of human behavior and decision making, however, as embodied in cases I have worked on in which innocent people confessed or pleaded guilty, lead me to realize that I could not be so certain."

SUMMATION—A SYSTEM OBSESSED WITH CONFESSION

At every step of the way, our system is *obsessed* with confession—even when it is recanted, even when it is contradicted by physical evidence, at the police station during interrogation; in court, during a guilty plea,

even among Alford defendants who simultaneously proclaim their innocence; in prison, before the parole board; and after release, as in sex-
offender therapy.

This obsession may have made sense, way back when, at a time when
the presumed base rate of wrongful convictions was at or near zero.
Today, in this post-DNA era, in which thousands of wrongful convictions have been uncovered, revealing the mere tip of an iceberg, it
makes no sense—other than the fact that obsessions are self-perpetuating. With the recognition that must accompany twenty-first-century exonerations, it is time for the system to cure itself of this addiction.

8

CONFESSIONS AT TRIAL

Why Little Else Matters to the Judge and Jury

The National Center for State Courts estimates that 1.5 million people serve on a state jury during the course of a year. Roughly fifty thousand people annually serve on federal juries. To some, jury service means sacrificing time and money. Like paying taxes, it is a duty compelled by government. For others, it offers a welcome disruption from their daily routine, a source of temporary employment, fulfillment of a citizen's obligation, and a source of intrigue. The ambivalence people feel about serving on juries is matched by a constancy of mixed reviews about how effectively the system works.

The jury is an extraordinary concept and institution. I can think of no other venue in which a group of ordinary citizens, strangers to one another, politically unorganized and naïve about their case, are brought together and empowered to make decisions of major consequence on behalf of their community. At the same time, criticism of juries as a decision-making body is a historical constant. Some arguments are pragmatic; the system is too costly, time consuming, and burdensome to those called into service. Other arguments concern the jury's questionable effectiveness as a lay arbiter of justice. Jurors are amateurs, not vetted for intelligence and untrained in the law; they are also gullible, too often driven by prejudice and other emotions.

In 1966, Henry Kalven and Hans Zeisel published *The American Jury*, a classic book in which they surveyed 555 judges who had presided over 3,576 criminal jury trials nationwide. While each of their juries was deliberating, the judges filled out a questionnaire in which they indicated what their verdict would be. A comparison of these responses to the actual jury verdicts was telling in two ways. First, judges and juries agreed on 78 percent of all their verdicts (in a separate study of civil cases, typically involving disputes over money, they exhibited exactly the same agreement rate). Second, within the sample of cases in which they disagreed, it was almost always because the jury voted to acquit a defendant that judges perceived to be guilty. In general, criminal juries are more lenient than judges.

Kalven and Zeisel's project inspired a generation of jury research and consulting that has continued to this day. By analyzing existing court records, interviewing real jurors after trial, bringing "shadow juries" into the courtroom, and presenting mock jurors with trial summaries or simulations, psychologists have dissected the three stages of jury decision making—from the process of selecting individual jurors; to the presentation of evidence, arguments, and instructions in court; and through the jury's deliberation to a verdict.

One particular focus of jury research concerns how they react to confessions—widely considered the most damning of all evidence. In *Jackson v. Denno* (1964), the U.S. Supreme Court ruled that when a suspect recants a confession and goes to trial, the judge must first determine at a pretrial suppression hearing, without the jury present, whether the confession was voluntary and hence admissible as evidence.

There are no simple criteria for making this judgment. Over the years, the courts have ruled that while confessions cannot be produced by physical violence, threats of harm or punishment, explicit promises of leniency or immunity, or interrogations conducted in violation of a suspect's Miranda rights, various highly manipulative forms of trickery and deceit are permissible—including presentations of false evidence and minimization tactics that imply leniency.

In *Jackson*, the court did not specify what standard of proof judges should use to make this pivotal determination (the highest standard is "proof beyond a reasonable doubt," followed by "clear and convincing evidence"; the lowest standard is "preponderance of the evidence"). Then came *Lego v. Twomey*. In that case, Don Richard Lego sought to have his confession suppressed on the grounds that it was not voluntary. He testified that police clubbed him into confessing because the victim was the police chief's friend. Although Lego admitted scuffling with the victim, his coercion claim was supported by a photograph taken the day after his arrest showing his face swollen and bloody. Concluding that the police chief and officers who testified were credible and that Lego was not, the trial judge ruled the confession voluntary and admissible (the judge did not indicate what standard of proof he used, but Illinois law had permitted a preponderance standard at a voluntariness hearing). Armed with the confession, the jury voted to convict, and Lego appealed.

In *Lego v. Twomey* (1972), the Supreme Court ruled in a four-to-three vote that a judge, as in Illinois, may find a confession voluntary by the lowest of standards, a preponderance of the evidence. The majority reasoned that the sole purpose of a pretrial suppression hearing is to exclude evidence that was illegally obtained—not to ensure that the evidence sent to the jury was reliable. In fact, the court assumed out loud that jurors can be trusted to use potentially inaccurate confessions cautiously. "Our decision was not based in the slightest on the fear that juries might misjudge the accuracy of confessions and arrive at erroneous determinations of guilt or innocence. . . . Nothing in Jackson questioned the province or capacity of juries to assess the truthfulness of confessions." In a sentence that still leaves me shaking my head, the court put it bluntly. "That case was not aimed at reducing the possibility of convicting innocent men."

The majority's decoupling of a judge's voluntariness ruling and the reliability of jury verdicts was in my opinion a profound and foreseeable, even then, error in judgment. Certainly in light of twenty-first-century sensibilities with regard to wrongful convictions, what a yet-to-be-corrected mistake that was. To this day, the federal courts use this low preponderance standard. Many but not all states have followed suit. Whatever the criteria, and whatever the standard of proof, once the judge deems a confession voluntary, it becomes the feature presentation of the trial. Front and center and in the spotlight. "Ladies and gentlemen of the jury," the prosecutor will state at the outset, "the defendant admitted his crime to the police. Freely and in his own words, he waived his Miranda rights. Then he told us exactly what he did, how he did it, and why. Sure, he claims now he was coerced. But if you were innocent, would *you* have done that?"

Confronted with a defendant's own alleged words, the jury has to determine guilt beyond a reasonable doubt. To do this, a jury must determine, first, whether police pressure was so overbearing that the situation was "coercive" and, second, whether that coercive situation produced a false confession from an innocent defendant. The wrongful convictions we know about today suggest that the anecdotal answer is a screaming no. So do controlled experiments, which show that confessions have a devastating impact, almost no matter what. The reason for this overwhelming effect can be explained by one of the basic principles of social psychology.

THE COMMON SENSE OF CONFESSIONS IN COURT

Particularly in light of a guilty-plea rate now approximating 97 percent, and in light of the fact that the presence of a confession leads many defense lawyers to recommend that that their clients accept a plea offer, one has to wonder what characteristics unite individuals who confess but then recant and opt for trial. To be sure, some unknown number of them have actual innocence in common.

Archival analyses of cases involving confessors ultimately proved innocent indicate that when they pled not guilty and proceeded to trial, roughly three-quarters to four-fifths were convicted. These figures led Steven Drizin and Richard Leo in 2004 to describe confessions as "inherently prejudicial and highly damaging to a defendant, even if it is the product of coercive interrogation, even if it is supported by no other evidence, and even if it is ultimately proven false beyond any reasonable doubt." At trial, where guilt must be proven beyond a reasonable doubt, the question is why wrongful conviction is the most likely outcome.

A Social Psychology Framework

Social psychology is built on a foundation of three cardinal principles. The first is that humans are inherently and universally social creatures, starting at birth and extending through the life span. The need to belong is a basic human motive. This is why people cling to social acceptance and approval; it's why we try mightily to avoid rejection.

The second principle follows from the first. Precisely because people are socially oriented, they are vulnerable to conformity pressures, subtle and overt, as well as explicit efforts to gain their compliance, obedience, and persuasion. Inside and outside the interrogation room, people can be induced by others to change their behavior and their minds, sometimes in profound ways.

This third principle does not logically or necessarily follow from the second. When people try to explain what causes other people's behavior, which is the subject of "attribution theory," they tend to focus on personal factors and overlook the causal impact of situational forces. This bias is so pervasive and sometimes so misleading that in 1977, social psychologist Lee Ross called it the *fundamental attribution error*.

In the first demonstration of this point, in 1967 Edward Jones and Victor Harris had subjects read an essay presumably written by a college student. Everyone read an essay that staked out a strong position on a then-controversial issue—for example, whether marijuana should be legalized. Some subjects were told that the student had freely chosen to argue this position; others were told that he was assigned to that position by his professor. Afterward, subjects were asked what they thought was the student's true attitude. Consistent with the logic of attribution theory, subjects were more likely to assume that the student's speech revealed his true attitude in the free-choice condition than when it was assigned.

Score a point for logic. But a quick second look at these studies also revealed something not particularly rational or anticipated. Even subjects who thought the student had no choice believed that the essay indicated his true attitude. Whether the essay topic was nuclear power, abortion, drug laws, the death penalty, or matters of foreign policy, the results were always the same.

This effect is hard to prevent. In one experiment, subjects were themselves assigned to argue for a position that may or may not have aligned with their own and write an essay. Afterward, they swapped essays and rated each other. Remarkably, these subjects also showed the effect. In another experiment, the subjects themselves personally assigned the student to argue for a position; they too inferred that the essay reflected his true attitude. No matter how you slice it, the tendency is clear: *even when someone is forced to make a personal statement, we believe that statement to be true.*

Why do lay perceivers consistently fail to appreciate the sometimes-obvious impact of situations? The tendency to draw conclusions about a person without sufficient regard for situational context begins with the fact that people reflexively accept information at face value. In a 1991 article titled "How Mental Systems Believe," Daniel Gilbert distinguished between two Western philosophical views on the acquisition of beliefs.

French philosopher René Descartes suggested that people are neutral in the way they react to new assertions—first acquiring and comprehending an idea and then accepting it or not according to logic or extrinsic evidence. In contrast, Dutch philosopher Baruch Spinoza argued that people automatically accept as true every assertion they hear—and must then, later, correct for that belief if it proves not to be credible. In this view, credulity, acceptance, and belief precede skepticism, doubt, and disbelief. As William James put it his classic 1890 treatise *The Principles of Psychology*, "All propositions, whether attributive or existential, are believed through the very fact of being conceived."

According to Gilbert, the problem stems in part from how we make attributions. Attribution theorists used to assume that people observe someone's behavior, scan for other evidence, and then decide on a causal explanation. Instead, it now seems that social perception is a two-step process: First, people identify the behavior and make a personal attribution; then they correct or adjust that inference to account for situational influences. The first step is simple and automatic, like a reflex; the second requires attention, thought, and effort. Or, as Gilbert put it, "The first step is a snap, but the second one's a doozy."

This tendency for people to accept what they see and hear at face value, and sometimes mindlessly, also manifests itself in other aspects of human behavior. In chapter 3, I reviewed a large body of studies showing that people are inept at lie detection, exhibiting an overall accuracy rate of just over 50 percent. Part of the reason for this finding is that people are notoriously gullible, exhibiting a "truth bias" that contributes to their lackluster performance at identifying deception.

A recanted confession is by its very nature a behavior shrouded in attributional ambiguity. Taken at face value, a defendant's admission of guilt is incriminating and believable, especially when accompanied by a detail-filled narrative. The most parsimonious causal explanation for this statement against self-interest is a personal attribution: the confession betrays the defendant's guilt. I would imagine that many jurors mentally stop right there and either tune out or process all subsequent evidence through a distorted lens. However, the defendant who recants, pleads not guilty, and proceeds to trial offers the jury an alternative causal explanation, a situational attribution: The confession was coerced and does not indicate guilt. To evaluate this less intuitive claim demands a jury's more careful attention and analysis.

At the foundation of *common sense*, people in general are quick to trust what others say, without much scrutiny, and people underappreciate the stranglehold that social situations can have on others. Perhaps an even more relevant question concerns *common knowledge*—what people specifically know about what it is like to become a suspect in a police interrogation.

In recent years, several researchers have assessed people's common knowledge in surveys and questionnaires. These studies have produced some consistent results. First, most people assert that they would never confess to a crime they did not commit. Second, most people are poorly informed about Miranda rights and how to exercise them, how police conduct interrogations, the tactics they are permitted to use, and the psychological effects of these tactics. Most people don't know and are shocked to learn that police are permitted to lie to suspects about fingerprints, DNA, the polygraph, and other evidence. In two recent surveys, Fabiana Alceste, Jeffrey Kaplan, and their colleagues found that laypeople in general underestimate the coerciveness of various interrogation tactics relative to what social science experts know to be true.

Poorly armed by common sense and lacking common knowledge, it is no wonder that juries are so hard on defendants who confessed to police, whether they recanted or not.

Revelations from Mock Jury Studies

In 1952, the Ford Foundation funded what would become known as the University of Chicago Jury Project, directed by law professor Harry Kalven Jr. Kalven was accompanied by a team of social scientists, including sociologist Hans Zeisel. The two would go on to produce *The American Jury*, the study described earlier in which they compared judges' would-be verdicts to the actual verdicts rendered by their juries.

This was a brilliant study. But it was not the method they started out using.

Aiming to shed light on how juries make decisions, the Chicago group took the most direct approach. They sought to spy on the deliberations of real juries. In the fall of 1953, they gained consent from a federal judge in Wichita, Kansas, to bug the jury room—in civil cases only and with approval from the trial judge and attorneys (the juries were not informed). So that no one eavesdropped on deliberations in real time, the tapes were secured until the case was decided, and the identities of all jurors were protected. With these precautions in place, microphones were hidden behind the heating system of the jury room, and five civil juries were recorded. It was the first time in history this happened—and it would be the last.

When the project was discovered, it stirred a public uproar. Newspaper editorials appeared nationwide. Without belaboring the details of the chain of events that followed, a federal law was passed in short order making it illegal for anyone to invade the privacy of a federal jury by observing or eavesdropping on their deliberations. Many states followed suit. With this window shut tight, the Chicago group—and subsequent generations of jury researchers—had to find less direct approaches.

Over the years, jury researchers have found that individual jurors differ in their predispositions to favor a particular prosecution or defense, which is why trial consultants are often hired to help lawyers select jurors. For the most part, however, research has focused on the psychology of evidence and trial procedure—namely, how jurors evaluate confessions, eyewitnesses, experts, forensic science, and judges' instructions; the extent to which they are tainted by pretrial publicity, testimony ruled inadmissible, a defendant's race, or physical attractiveness, and other extralegal factors; and the social dynamic by which individual jurors come together to deliberate as a group and reach a common verdict.

In the first mock-jury study I ever published, Larry Wrightsman and I looked at judges' instructions on the requirements of proof (that the defendant is presumed innocent, the government has the burden of proof, and guilt must be proved beyond a reasonable doubt). This set of instructions is required. Typically judges recite these instructions, along with others of specific relevance to the case, after the evidence is presented. Yet we found that timing is critical. Our jurors started to form their opinions at the outset, as we tend to do in life, so a requirement-of-proof charge not delivered until the case has been presented might as well not be delivered at all.

These results brought to mind an article that Judge E. Barrett Prettyman had written in the *ABA Journal* years earlier on the timing of judges' instructions: "It makes no sense to have a juror listen to days of testimony only then to be told that he and his conferees are the sole judges of the facts, that the accused is presumed to be innocent, that the government must prove guilt beyond a reasonable doubt, etc. . . . Why should not the judge, when the jury is sworn, then and there tell them the rules of the game." These results also speak to the presentation of confession evidence. When prosecutors have this evidence to present, they don't keep it a secret. They build it into their opening statements. At trial, the confession comes in early and often.

Coercion Be Damned

The law on confession evidence is deceptively simple on this point: If jurors find that a confession was voluntary, they are free and likely to weight it heavily in their verdicts. But if jurors believe that a confession was coerced, they are supposed to discount it in their decision making. In light of the ubiquity of the fundamental attribution error, however, it is possible that juries will weight even a coerced confession in their decision making.

To assess what happens in these situations, my colleagues and I, and others, run mock-jury studies. We bring college students or community members into a mock courtroom or classroom, or these days, we'll have national samples of adults log into a password-protected website and participate online. All subjects are presented with a video or transcript of an abbreviated trial containing opening statements, testimony from witnesses, closing arguments, and judges' instructions. Our questions: What effect does adding a confession to a baseline case have on verdicts, and what if that confession had been induced through high levels of pressure?

In one study, we had mock jurors read one of three transcript versions of a double-homicide trial. The transcript we presented, which was adapted from an actual case, involved a male defendant charged with the murder of his estranged wife and male neighbor. The district attorney charged that the defendant, Charles Wilson, stabbed his wife and neighbor in a fit of jealous rage after finding them together. The defendant claimed that he found the bodies when he returned to his former home to get some documents he needed.

In a baseline "control" version of the transcript, the state's evidence was purely circumstantial (no murder weapon was found but, consistent with the medical examiner's report on the wounds, Wilson was left-handed; before calling the police, Wilson phoned his attorney). This version was so weak that only 19 percent of subjects voted guilty

In a second condition, all of the same evidence was presented, plus the defendant was said to have confessed almost immediately upon questioning. I should mention that the confession we inserted consisted of nothing more than an admission of guilt reported secondhand in court. No written or signed statement was presented, no audio or video recording, and no narrative details, explanations, apologies, or expressions of remorse—and no corroboration. As for the circumstances, Wilson was not handcuffed, verbally abused, or threatened. He conceded that he uttered an admission but explained that "I was really upset and don't remember what it was. I was in a state of shock." The detective who was present conceded that Wilson was stressed but rejected the suggestion that the stress would cause him to confess to a crime he did not commit. "No, I wouldn't say that. I mean he just blurted it out. Nobody twisted his arm."

In a third condition, the defendant was said to have confessed under intense pressure. In this version, Wilson testified that the detective handcuffed him, yelled, and interrogated him aggressively. "My arm really hurt from the handcuffs but he wouldn't remove them," Wilson said. He reported that at one point, the detective picked up his gun and "flung it around and waved it in the air," an experience he described as terrifying. For his part, the detective conceded that Wilson was under stress but rejected the suggestion that Wilson would have confessed to a crime he did not commit.

After reading one of these three transcripts, subjects were asked to indicate what their verdict would be if they were on the jury in this case. In the two confession conditions, they were also asked whether the confession was voluntary or coerced. In the low-pressure confession condition, 88 percent of subjects judged the confession to be voluntary. No surprise there. And even though the "confession" consisted of a mere admission that the defendant later recanted and that jurors did not see or hear and was not corroborated by any details or other evidence, the conviction rate more than tripled, to 63 percent.

The most telling set of results emerged from the high-pressure confession condition. In this situation, only 44 percent of subjects judged the confession to be voluntary—far fewer than in the low-pressure condition (though surprisingly high, we thought, in light of the not-so-subtle aggressive circumstances). Yet 50 percent of subjects in this condition voted guilty—also a significant increase above the 19 percent baseline.

People are powerfully influenced by confession even when they concede that it was coerced. Is this failure to discount a coerced confession an affliction of amateur fact finders? In 2012, Brian Wallace and I tested 132 judges from Massachusetts, Pennsylvania, and Missouri before lectures I was asked to give. Like the subjects of my earlier mock-jury study, we asked judges to read a weak baseline-control version of a murder case, a low-pressure confession version, and a high-pressure confession version.

In the baseline case, only 17 percent of judges voted guilty. In the low-pressure confession condition, 85 percent perceived the confession to be voluntary, a ruling that judges make on a regular basis. It came as no surprise, therefore, that 95 percent of judges in this condition voted to convict the defendant. Once again, the high-pressure confession variant yielded a telling pattern of results. In this condition, only 32 percent of judges saw the confession as voluntary; fully two-thirds said they would have ruled to suppress it. So far, so good—until we examined verdicts. Remarkably, 69 percent of judges in this condition voted guilty—a fourfold increase compared to the baseline conviction rate of 17 percent.

Let's stop for a moment and ponder what this means. The law prescribes, and judges know it, that only voluntary confessions should be weighed in rendering a verdict. As a matter of law, the fact finder should mentally erase any confession deemed involuntary, as though it never happened. Yet a fair number of judges failed to discount the confession that even they saw as coerced. As with lay juries, they did not discount a confession even when it was coerced and they were legally required to do so (and, I might add, even though the defendant recanted and no corroborating evidence was presented).

This takes me back to the fundamental attribution error and those studies showing that people infer a college student's true opinion from an essay he wrote—even when he was specifically directed to advocate for that position. The judges in our study, like mock jurors in other studies, fully grasped the coerciveness of the high-pressure confession. But they voted guilty anyway. Long live the fundamental attribution error—even in the high-stakes decision making of a criminal trial.

Research shows two additional points when it comes to juries and confessions. The first concerns the nature of the inducement that police use. In 1980, Larry Wrightsman and I compared the persuasive impact of confessions induced by explicit promises versus threats. Although the courts view these as equivalent grounds for exclusion, we found that people are more likely to infer guilt from a confession that was drawn by a promise of favorable leniency or immunity than by a threat of harm or punishment. This result is not particularly surprising in light of other research showing that people assume that punishment exerts a greater effect on human behavior than does reward. We referred to this pattern of results as a *positive coercion bias*. In fact, this difference persisted even when the judge instructed subjects that both sets of tactics render a confession involuntary as a matter of law, even when the jurors came together to deliberate in six-person groups.

The second additional point is that once a confession enters the picture, almost nothing else matters. Confession is more powerful than eyewitness identification. Jurors infer guilt from confession not only when it was patently coerced but also when there is no corroborating evidence; when the defendant is a teenager; when the defendant suffers from mental illness or interrogation-induced stress; when a confession is reported secondhand by a jailhouse snitch who has a strong motive to implicate the defendant; and even, at times, when a confession is contradicted by DNA testing that excludes the confessor. Add narrative details to the admission of guilt and the effects are even greater. Once a confession enters into court, it's pretty much game, set, match.

The Forbidden Fruit of an Inadmissible Confession

Although juries are tasked with basing their decisions strictly on the evidence presented in court, extrinsic factors often enter the fray—such as pretrial publicity to which jurors are exposed online or from the news media. Just as jurors can be biased by outside publicity, they may also be exposed to extralegal information within the body of the trial itself. According to the rules of evidence, information is admissible if it is relevant and has probative value—unless it was illegally obtained, inflammatory, prejudicial, misleading, confusing, or redundant. If a witness discloses inadmissible hearsay or blurts out something about the defendant's past that the jury is not supposed to hear, the opposing lawyer will object and the judge will sustain the objection and admonish the jury to disregard the disclosure.

This chain of events is often replayed in the courtroom. The question is whether jurors can strike information from their mind on cue the way court reporters can strike it from the record. The research is mixed. Some studies show that jurors can and will disregard information on cue that is later discredited. Others suggest that they cannot insert the genie back into the bottle and pretend they never heard it.

Classic experiments by Daniel Wegner on the ironic effects of attempted self-control illustrate this latter point. When subjects are told, "Try not to think about a white bear for the next thirty seconds," that very image of a white bear intrudes on their consciousness with remarkable frequency. Sometimes the harder you try to inhibit a thought, feeling, or behavior, the less likely you are to succeed. Consistent with that effect, some studies suggest that a judge's admonishment to disregard may actually backfire by drawing additional attention to the forbidden disclosure.

I don't think it is that simple. Jurors genuinely want to convict the guilty and acquit the innocent. They want to get it right. If probative evidence like a confession spills out, and if that information seems reliable, I suspect they will overlook how that confession was taken. But if jurors have reason to believe that the confession cannot be trusted, and therefore may not indicate guilt, they may well set that information aside.

To tease apart the effect of an inadmissible confession, Sam Sommers and I brought eighty mock jurors to the lab and presented them with a murder-trial summary involving a defendant charged with killing his wife and her lover in a fit of jealous rage. In a skeletal baseline version, the case was weak and purely circumstantial. In three other conditions, a police officer testified that a wiretap from an unrelated case picked up an audiotaped telephone conversation in which the defendant can be heard confessing to a friend minutes after fleeing the scene: "I killed Marylou and some bastard she was with. God, I don't . . . yeah, I ditched the blade." Immediately, in each condition, the defense lawyer objected to the disclosure.

This series of events would never play out in an actual trial, where admissibility questions would have been resolved at a pretrial hearing. But this hypothetical enabled us to learn something about juries, what motivates them, and the role of confessions. In response to the defense objection, one of three things happened. In the second condition, the judge ruled the confession admissible and instructed the jury that it was proper evidence. Permission granted. In the third condition, the judge ruled the confession *in*admissible and admonished the jury to disregard it for due process reasons, noting that it was obtained illegally, without a proper warrant. In the fourth condition, the judge again ruled the confession inadmissible and admonished the jury to disregard it. But this time, the judge explained that the tape was to be disregarded because it was unreliable, barely audible, and difficult to determine what was said.

The results supported our thinking. In the baseline version of the case, only 24 percent of mock jurors voted guilty. That number more than tripled to 79 percent in the admissible wiretap condition. When the confession was ruled inadmissible because it was barely audible, subjects fully adhered to the admonishment to disregard, exhibiting the same 24 percent conviction rate as in the baseline condition. They heard the report of the confession but then they mentally erased it when told it could not be trusted. The interesting twist came when the judge ruled the confession inadmissible because of a legal technicality. In this case, most subjects did not mentally erase the inadmissible information. In that condition, 65 percent voted to convict. This result showed that confession evidence is too potent for jurors to ignore because of a mere legal technicality.

DNA: The Great Equalizer?

Antron McCray. Kevin Richardson. Korey Wise. Raymond Santana. Yusef Salaam. When these defendants in the Central Park jogger case were fully exonerated in 2002, thirteen years after they were duped into confession, vilified in the media, and wrongfully convicted by two juries, the case was back in the news. Five boys were convicted; five men were exonerated.

Over the years, I've had countless conversations with friends, family, strangers, acquaintances, colleagues, and students about this case. From these conversations, I came to realize that many people harbor the misconception that these defendants were "DNA exonerated," that they were exculpated by DNA testing conducted after the fact. But that is not how it happened. In 2002, serial rapist Matias Reyes stepped up from prison to confess in detail to the jogger crime. That is what led the Manhattan DA's office to reinvestigate and ultimately move to overturn the convictions. At that time, the DNA from the rape kit confirmed that semen samples originally recovered from cervical swabs and the jogger's clothing and socks belonged to Reyes.

What many people do not realize is that after the boys confessed in 1989—*and before they were tried*—the lab results that came back from the FBI's testing of the rape kit excluded them all. Think about this: several samples matched each other, indicating that they all originated from a single source; yet that source was not any of the five boys. The prosecutor's office was jolted by these results before setting foot in court. Years later, attorney Harlan Levy would recall that prosecutor Elizabeth Lederer was visibly shaken by the results: "I feel like I've been kicked in the stomach," she said. It didn't matter.

Led by Sex Crimes DA Linda Fairstein, the decision was made to proceed to trial on the assertion that the DNA results were inconclusive—which was not true. Lederer called to the witness stand FBI laboratory special agent Dwight Adams but never asked him the ultimate question. On cross-examination, however, Adams was forthcoming: The DNA samples taken from the jogger conclusively excluded all the defendants.

Perhaps there was a sixth assailant? Setting aside the seeming illogic of the theory that five confessors to rape left zero physical traces, that a sixth assailant left all the traces, and that not a single confession cited this sixth assailant, the point is, the two juries that convicted the teen defendants knew that they were excluded by the DNA. It didn't matter. In the battle between science and confession, the confessions prevailed.

Years later, Ronald Gold, a juror in the first jogger trial who held out in the face of pressure from peers during deliberations, put it this way when interviewed in the documentary, *The Central Park Five*: "I was going nuts. No blood on the kids, nobody could identify them, but if they confessed they confessed and that was that."

In 2019, Victoria Bryers, a juror in the second trial, told ABC's *20/20* that these verdicts were her greatest regret. As for false confessions, she said, "I don't think any of us could completely grasp that idea at that point in time."

Writing for the *Village Voice*, R. C. Baker summarized the events in this way: "In hindsight, the FBI disclosures should have exploded a bomb in the heart of the prosecution case. But the testimony set off no fireworks. The disturbing confessions were what had captured the minds of the jury and the press."

By all accounts, DNA has become the gold standard to which other physical means of proof are compared. Surveys show that people trust the science. Yet the Central Park jogger juries went with the confessions instead. Is this historic case anomalous or does it tell us something about the enormous power of confession evidence once presented to juries?

In 1991, sixteen-year-old Jeffrey Deskovic confessed to the rape and murder of a high school classmate after a lengthy and manipulative interrogation. Subsequent DNA testing excluded Deskovic. There was no soft-pedaling it to the jury. So at trial, prosecutors spun a theory: the victim had prior consensual sex with an *unknown* and unidentified boyfriend and Deskovic tried to rape her and then killed her after failing to ejaculate. Deskovic was released fifteen years later when the DNA was matched to a convicted murderer who eventually pled guilty.

There are other cases, too, in which police induced confessions from suspects later excluded by DNA testing. In many of these instances, prosecutors were not deterred. Rather, they proceeded to trial by spinning even more cockamamie theories to reconcile the contradiction, leading the jury to a guilty verdict.

Take the 2009 retrial of Juan Rivera, in Lake County, Illinois. In 1992, Rivera was badgered into confessing to the violent rape and murder of eleven-year-old babysitter Holly Staker. Rivera was convicted and spent years in prison until new DNA testing fully excluded him. Rather than release Rivera, however, state's attorney Michael Mermel sought a retrial. He theorized in court that the young girl had prior consensual sex with an unknown male, after which Rivera raped her, failed to ejaculate, and then killed the girl when she made fun of him. There was scant evidence to support the claim that the girl was sexually

Juan Rivera served more than nineteen years for the 1992 rape and murder of an eleven-year-old girl in Waukegan, Illinois. A jury found him guilty at a retrial, even though DNA evidence proved that the semen taken from the crime scene ruled him out. Rivera was later fully exonerated and won a federal lawsuit against prosecutors and police. *Photo licensed from Shutterstock.*

active (her surviving twin sister, Heather, said they were not). Still, the jury voted guilty.

In response to the criticism that followed, Mermel vehemently defended his approach. "We don't fold our tents and run," he said to *New York Times* writer Andrew Martin. "We don't quaver because somebody holds up three letters: DNA." In 2012, however, Rivera's conviction was overturned once again. This time he was granted a Certificate of Innocence, whereupon he received a $20 million settlement in a federal wrongful conviction lawsuit. In the meantime, the semen found inside Holly Staker was later matched, not to a "consensual sex partner" but to a convicted violent felon serving a life sentence for a crime he committed years later.

It gets even worse. In some instances, DNA not only excludes the confessor before trial but also identifies the perpetrator *before trial*. The 2004 case of South Carolina against Billy Wayne Cope is one example that haunts me to this day. Cope woke up one morning to find his daughter strangled to death in her bed. Police isolated Cope from the rest of his family, held him in a cell, and interrogated him until he confessed three days later.

Then the autopsy showed that Cope's daughter was not just strangled but also sexually assaulted. DNA tests on semen and saliva found on her excluded Cope and matched James Sanders, a serial sex offender who had recently moved into the neighborhood and broken into other homes in the area as well. One would think from this series of events that Cope would have been released, freed, and compensated. Instead, prosecutor Kevin Brackett concocted the theory, in the absence of any supportive evidence, that Cope had pimped his daughter out to Sanders, a stranger. There was no proof that the two had ever met. Yet on the basis of this theory, a single jury convicted both men.

Are self-reports extracted under pressure really so powerful as to overwhelm scientific evidence? One wouldn't think so. Yet how many head-scratching cases like these must one encounter before realizing that something is amiss? Are these extreme one-in-a-thousand cases? To put this hypothesis to the test, Sara Appleby and I conducted a series of mock-jury studies that pitted inculpatory confessions against exculpatory DNA.

In our first study, subjects read an online case summary about the rape and murder of a sixteen-year-old girl found dead in the McDonald's where she worked a night shift. As part of their investigation, police questioned the defendant, who then either confessed or denied involvement, both in some detail. Afterward, they commenced testing the semen found inside the victim that either matched or excluded that same defendant. The combination of these variations produced four versions of the case. The results were simple: When the DNA results matched the defendant, subjects voted guilty, even when he denied involvement. When the DNA excluded the defendant, they voted not guilty, even when he confessed. All that mattered in this first experiment was the science.

So far, so good. Modeling actual cases, the next question we asked was, What would happen if the defendant who had confessed and recanted was excluded by DNA, suggesting innocence, and the prosecutor presented a "theory" aimed at reconciling the contradiction, as in the cases described earlier? Would anyone convict the DNA-excluded confessor under these circumstances?

Using the same case and procedure, we added a condition in which the prosecutor tried to explain away the exculpatory DNA. As in Deskovic's case, he argued that "the DNA test does not mean that the Defendant is innocent, only that he failed to ejaculate and that [the victim] may have had consensual sex with some other person earlier that day." As in the first study, just about everyone convicted the confessed defendant when the DNA matched; only 10 percent voted to convict when the DNA was exculpatory. But when the prosecutor presented the prior-consensual-sex theory to explain the exculpatory DNA, the conviction rate increased from 10 percent to 33 percent.

In a third study, we knew it was important to replicate this troubling result. This time we brought sixty adults from the community into the lab for live small-group sessions. As per logic, only 15 percent voted to convict the defendant who had confessed but was excluded by DNA. When that exculpatory DNA was accompanied by the prosecutor's two-part prior-consensual-sex-plus-failure-to-ejaculate theory, that number tripled to 45 percent. Once again, a sizable percentage of jurors favored the confession when the prosecutor explained away the DNA. The only question that remains is, Just how outlandish a theory are jurors willing to tolerate when armed with a confession?

CORROBORATION INFLATION—
FINAL NAIL IN THE COFFIN

The wrongful convictions in Italy of Amanda Knox and Raffaele Sollecito for the 2007 murder of Meredith Kercher illustrates why judges and
juries often seem blinded by confession. Amanda's so-called confession
at 5:45 a.m. so powerfully altered the trajectory of that case that the
prosecution proceeded even after police apprehended the perpetrator
whose DNA was littered throughout the crime scene. What is particularly remarkable is that Amanda's confession was ruled inadmissible
because the prosecutor neglected, or claimed he neglected, to video-
record the interrogation, as required by Italian law.

None of that mattered. The panel of judges and jurors who convicted Knox and Sollecito were informed of the confession. The perpetrator whose DNA was found on the victim changed his original story
and implicated the young couple (he was recently set free after serving
even less time than his reduced sentence); police forensic experts cited
DNA evidence allegedly linking the defendants to the crime, conclusions that were later fully discredited by a range of outside experts;
several "eyewitnesses" came forward out of nowhere to tell implausible-
to-impossible stories about that night. One of Amanda's roommates
testified as a character witness against her, even though the two had
planned to find a new place to live together. By the time Amanda and
Raffaele went to trial, her inadmissible confession had triggered all
sorts of other "evidence."

Precisely because confessions are highly trusted as a matter of logic
and common sense, and partly because the admission of guilt is almost
always supplemented by narrative details and other credibility cues,
they can well provide a sufficient basis for conviction. The admission,
the "who, what, when, where, and why" story, the error corrections,
physical reenactments, and the heartfelt apologies and expressions of
remorse—it's all just too hard for a jury to dismiss.

Basic research in social and cognitive psychology points to the possibility of a second, even more troubling mechanism by which confessions exert influence: by tainting eyewitnesses, forensic experts, and
others entrusted to provide independent other evidence to a judge and
jury. Often by the time a recanted confession makes its way to trial, it
appears to be topped off by a mountain of support. The problem is that

that mountain is often nothing more than a house of cards built on the back of a false confession. And, well, as the expression goes, "Where there's smoke, there must be fire."

These effects are not necessarily produced by nefarious motives. Imagine you are shown pictures of pairs of adults and children and asked to rate how much they look alike. When people are misled into thinking that the pair is genetically related, they "see" more resemblance. Or imagine listening to degraded speech recordings filled with static. When people are told that the recorded speaker is a crime suspect, they "hear" more incriminating words. These kinds of laboratory demonstrations have filled the pages of psychology journals for years. Now the new and growing body of research described in chapter 6 shows just how dangerous confirmation bias can be when it afflicts the criminal justice system.

The following trio of statistics that my colleagues and I derived from the Innocence Project hints at the problem: (1) In 78 percent of DNA exonerations containing what proved to be a false confession, one or more other errors were introduced into evidence; (2) in 67 percent of these cases, forensic-science mistakes were made; and (3) more often than not, these other mistakes were made after the confession was taken, not before.

Demonstrating that people seek out, perceive, and interpret evidence in ways that verify preexisting beliefs, experiments show that the presence of a confession can bias professional polygraph examiners, latent-fingerprint experts, DNA analysis of complex mixtures, mock eyewitnesses, mock alibis, and laypeople's judgments as to whether a suspect's handwriting matches that found on a bank robbery note handed to the teller. And the worst part is that crime lab analysts are not, as a matter of policy, shielded from knowing that the owner of a latent print they are trying to match, or a shoe print, or hair, or a bite mark, came from a suspect who had confessed.

The bottom line is that juries are doomed to believe the false confessions of innocent people not only because the phenomenon strongly violates common sense and common knowledge but also because of *corroboration inflation*, a tendency for confessions to procreate an illusion of support from extraneous witnesses whose perceptions, memories, and perhaps even their motivations were tainted by the confession.

To sum up: judges, juries, and others are doomed to believe the false confessions of innocent people not only because the phenomenon is counterintuitive and not only because they are clueless about police interrogation practices, but because of corroboration inflation. This appearance of support can come from the details of the confession itself, which is presented as "proof" of the confessor's guilty knowledge. It can also come from extrinsic evidence presented by lay and expert witnesses whose independence was compromised by the confession itself.

With confessions inherently compelling and bolstered by the appearance of corroboration, it is no wonder that the safeguards that are supposed to protect the accused confessor in court so often fail. It's no wonder policy and practice need to be reformed, in the courtroom and the crime lab.

9

CONFESSION BLINDNESS

Why Does the Stigma Persist?

I am not a clinical psychologist. I don't administer the Rorschach test or the Minnesota Multiphase Personality Inventory (MMPI), diagnose mental health and illness according to the *Diagnostic and Statistical Manual* V (*DSM* V), offer counseling or therapy, or prescribe psychotropic drugs. I am not an expert on anxiety, depression, or trauma. But I have talked to more individuals than I care to count who were manipulated by police, some of whom uttered words of confession, implicating themselves and sometimes others, too, some of whom were wrongfully convicted by those words. The experience haunts them years later.

My inbox is filled with unsolicited stories such as this one, in March of 2018, from a man I have never met:

> Though I was never put on trial or convicted, I went through a horrendous interrogation in December of 1975. I was put in a cold room where I thought I would freeze to death. Every bone in my body was hurting. My jaws would hardly move. I could hardly speak. . . . Cold weather still has a terrible effect on me. I still see a counselor. I still have nightmares. . . . I was never able to work at a job for long because of visits to my employers by the police."

As traumatic as this experience was, this man managed to resist the force of interrogation. His fate could have been so much worse. For innocents who succumb, the struggle from prison and afterward becomes something of a hall of mirrors. Often they cannot shed the stigma that prosecutors, judges, juries, appeals courts, and others attach to them.

The underlying psychology is clear and understandable. As I've noted throughout this book, the concept of a false confession is bluntly counterintuitive. So when someone confesses, whether it's true or false, others reflexively see guilt. That perception becomes hard to extinguish.

In 1946, social psychologist Solomon Asch told one group of subjects about a person who was "intelligent, industrious, impulsive, critical, stubborn, and envious." He presented a second group with exactly the same list but in reverse order. Rationally speaking, the two groups should have felt the same way about the person. But instead, participants who heard the first list, in which the more positive traits came first, formed a more favorable impression. Asch referred to this phenomenon as the primacy effect.

Primacy prevails for two reasons. First, once people form an impression, especially if it's based on evidence as potent as a confession, they become less attentive to subsequent information. 'Nuff said, as they say. Second, people who have formed a strong impression of someone begin to interpret even contradictory information in light of that impression. They are tainted. Back to Asch. When research subjects are told that a kind person is also "calm," they assume he or she is gentle, peaceful, and serene. When a cruel person is said to be calm, however, that same word is interpreted to mean cool, shrewd, and calculating. At times, people will even set aside information that plainly disconfirms beliefs—leading to what social psychologists have called the "belief *perseverance effect.*"

People are so instinctually enamored of confessions that the effect can be blinding and self-perpetuating. When a suspect is induced to self-incriminate, police close the case, sometimes even when the actual perpetrator emerges into full view; forensic examiners and witnesses unwittingly taint their perceptions, interpretations, and memories; prosecutors and defense lawyers work to hammer out a plea agreement, even before all the evidence is in; judges rule that the confession was voluntary, almost whenever defendants have the audacity to demand their day in court; and juries see guilt beyond a reasonable doubt, almost regardless of anything else. The net result: confession begets conviction.

For innocent confessors, the uphill battle does not end there. Efforts to overturn a conviction on appeal, win compensation after exoneration, overcome the social stigma reflected in the eyes of others, and return to

a normal life are particularly challenging for innocents who had confessed.

CONFESSION THWARTS EXONERATION
AND OTHER REMEDIES

After conviction, defendants have a right to an appeal in state courts. If
that fails, they can file a writ of habeas corpus in the federal courts to
argue that their constitutional rights were violated. According to 2015
Bureau of Justice statistics, appellate courts reverse, remand, or modify
a trial verdict 12 percent of the time.

I know of no hard data on the question of whether defendants convicted by confession are less successful at the appellate level than this
12 percent average. But there is reason to fear that the adverse effects
of confession do not stop after a case is adjudicated.

From Pennsylvania to West Virginia—and Beyond

Any number of cases can be used to illustrate how intransigent the
courts can be when it comes to confession. To me, one of the more
shocking cases comes from Pennsylvania, where in 1993 Anthony
Wright was convicted by confession of the rape and murder of an elderly woman in Philadelphia. In the case, more fully described in chapter
6, Wright had always insisted he was innocent. At one point, he asked
the state to test the DNA in the original rape kit to prove it. The state
refused.

Here's some background: in 2002, the Commonwealth of Pennsylvania passed a law stating: "An individual convicted of a criminal offense
in a court of this Commonwealth may apply by making a written motion
to the sentencing court at any time for the performance of forensic
DNA testing on specific evidence that is related to the investigation or
prosecution that resulted in the judgment of conviction." In doing so,
Pennsylvania became the twenty-fifth state to enact a DNA-testing statute (it is now the law in all states).

Three years later, the Innocence Project, with assistance from local
counsel, sought DNA testing on Wright's behalf. After Wright had
signed a confession to the rape and murder, police found blood-stained

clothing in his home, took statements from two drug-addicted informants who said he told them what he did, and two eyewitnesses who said they saw him near the victim's home at the approximate time of her death. Wright pled not guilty but was convicted at trial and sentenced to life. The request to prove actual innocence was based on the fact that technological advances made it possible to test DNA using methods not available during his original trial.

For reasons I will never fully understand, the state opposed the motion for DNA testing. One would think that the state would welcome the opportunity to affirm the integrity of its conviction. But in April 2006, Judge D. Webster Keough sided with the state and denied the motion. Citing Wright's confession, Judge Keough ruled that "the evidence was more than sufficient to prove Defendant's guilt beyond a reasonable doubt. DNA testing would not establish a prima facie case of Defendant's innocence." In plain English, yes, the state may have a DNA-testing statute, but Wright confessed so the possibility of actual innocence be damned—or, as Judge Keough put it, there was no "reasonable possibility."

Wright appealed, but the state superior court upheld the ruling, taking the issue to the commonwealth's Supreme Court. In 2008, the American Psychological Association joined the Innocence Project and submitted an amicus curiae brief stating that innocent people can be induced to confess through processes of interrogation and that Wright's confession, even if voluntary by law, should not bar his consideration for post-conviction DNA testing. In 2011, the Supreme Court of Pennsylvania agreed and overruled the lower courts.

Two years later, DNA testing on the victim's rape kit was completed. The DNA conclusively excluded Wright. In fact, it identified the perpetrator, a crackhead, dealer, and repeat sex offender found in CODIS who lived near the victim at the time. He had since died in a South Carolina prison. And that's not all the tests revealed: the clothing police had allegedly seized from Wright's home was not his; it belonged to the victim.

Wright's conviction was vacated. Yet rather than apologize profusely for what had happened, the Philadelphia District Attorney's Office decided to retry Wright as an accomplice. This time, the jury immediately, unanimously, and angrily returned a not-guilty verdict.

This may sound like a happy ending, but one cannot overlook this fact: as a result of a judge who refused to grant DNA testing, a superior court that later affirmed that ruling, and a prosecutor who dug in years later for a retrial despite the DNA, Tony Wright spent ten extra years behind bars, I would argue, because of his confession.

All this was inexcusable. In 1993, the system's lack of enlightenment was par for the course. In 2006, however, false confessions were no longer a secret, not even close—especially in Pennsylvania, and Philadelphia of all places, where Bruce Godschalk had already been DNA exonerated after falsely confessing to two rapes.

One cannot "prove" that Wright's confession is what distorted the events surrounding his exoneration, but the fact is, Judge Keough cited it as a reason to exclude his eligibility to use the state's DNA-testing statute. He confessed, said the judge, proving guilt beyond a reasonable doubt and barring DNA testing.

In West Virginia, I was dumbfounded to read a 2019 news article by Maia Rosenfeld, and then other articles, pertaining to a case about which I have no firsthand knowledge. This story is like a natural experiment, complete with a control group, on the effects of confession on an appellant's success at getting the conviction vacated.

In 2002, the half-naked body of twenty-one-year-old Deanna Crawford was found in a shed in a rural section of West Virginia. She had been raped and strangled to death. Her leopard-print pants had been removed; her top was pulled up. Five years later, with the crime still unsolved, twenty-six-year-old Brian Dement confessed and then pled guilty, implicating three other men in the process: Philip Barnett, Philip's brother, Nathan Barnett, and Justin Black.

Dement's confession and plea were controversial. Diagnosed with learning disabilities and mental health issues that included depression, anxiety, and bipolar disorder, he was a vulnerable suspect. Yet state police interrogated him at the station for nine hours, through the night, yielding three confessions in which the details kept changing, and changed again when he pled guilty and then testified in court. The "constant" in all of his statements was that he and his three associates took the victim on a car ride, struck her, and dragged her out of the car. Parts of his story were implausible and did not add up. Also troubling was that no DNA, fingerprints, shoe prints, clothing, hair fibers, or any other physical evidence, for that matter, could be traced to Dement or the others.

None of these discrepancies deterred prosecutors from moving forward. In 2007, Dement pled guilty—an unsurprising decision after confession. He told investigators he had manufactured a false confession and wanted to recant, or as he put it, "go against my statement," but the judge and attorney would not allow him to do so. In fact, he said that the prosecutor told him he would be in more trouble and punished more severely if he did not testify. Based largely on his statements and testimony, the other men were also convicted of murder.

Almost ten years later, lawyers for the Innocence Project and the Exoneration Project sought new DNA testing. The state court granted the motion, and the results hit the jackpot. Samples were taken from the victim's leopard-print pants, which had been removed, and from a cigarette butt found nearby, which was in the middle of nowhere. The two samples matched each other; both excluded all four men.

There's more. Submitted to CODIS, those same two samples matched a convicted felon. As reported by the Innocence Project in 2018, he was a sex offender who had served time in an Ohio prison. Married three times, he physically abused all his wives, one of whom recalled the night he came home with blood on his clothing and confessed to killing someone. He lived in Huntington, West Virginia, at the time of the murder.

This is where this story takes yet another odd turn. DNA made a slam-dunk case for vacating the four convictions. In fact, it had only three-quarters of that effect. In 2019, Judge Alfred Ferguson overturned the Barnett, Barnett, and Black convictions. But he would not grant a new trial to Dement himself. Unlike the others, he reasoned, Dement confessed; and he pled guilty under oath. "This Court is not going to give him a new trial," said Judge Ferguson. "I don't think he is entitled to it."

This is exactly what I mean when I refer this case as a natural experiment on the corrosive and blinding effects of confession. Dement's confessions implicated all the men, equally. Their fates were tethered by his words. Yet while the judge acknowledged that the others may have been innocent (I think of these men as the control group), he was not willing to concede the same about Dement (the experimental group). These appellants were bundled together by the same inculpatory evidence—and by the same exculpatory evidence. They all should get a new trial, or they should not. As it turned out, three men did; the confessor did not.

There is a surprising postscript to this story. As I write, the prosecutor in this case is preparing to retry Barnett, Barnett, and Black for Crawford's murder—despite the DNA that excluded them. That same prosecutor has not decided to try the guy, who does not fit into the confessional tale of four associates—despite the match to his DNA and regardless of his history of violence. One can only hope that he does not go on to reoffend while he is free to do so.

It is not just DNA that confession evidence plows over. In chapter 4, I described the case of Melissa Calusinski, who to this day remains behind bars for a crime that quite possibly did not occur. Calusinski was a teaching assistant in Lake County, Illinois, when a sixteen-month-old boy lost consciousness and died. The next day, a forensic pathologist concluded from his autopsy that the boy had a fresh skull fracture and died from blunt-force trauma to the head. Based on that initial assessment, detectives interrogated Calusinski for hours until they got her to say that she threw the boy to the ground in frustration. This confession landed her in prison for thirty-one years.

Three years later, a new coroner was hired by the county. He reviewed the case file and saw scabbing and scar tissue in the boy's skull indicative of an old and substantial head injury. He also saw no evidence of a fresh skull fracture. The original pathologist admitted that he missed it. Armed with histology slides and x-rays, the new coroner changed the cause of death from homicide to "undetermined" and urged that Calusinski be released. But that has not happened. Calusinski had confessed and that was sufficient to uphold her conviction on two state appeals.

The Myth of "Harmless Error"

Confessions can directly impede the process of exoneration because of their unique power to overwhelm DNA, autopsy reports, and other evidence. But they can also wreak havoc on the appeals process because they taint perceptions of the defendant and that other evidence. And the judiciary has no idea.

Historically, U.S. courts have excluded confessions from trial that they ruled to be coerced, not voluntary, out of fear that such evidence would be both unreliable and so persuasive it will prejudice the jury. If a trial judge allowed a confession into evidence that an appeals court later deemed to have been coerced, that error routinely triggered an appellate reversal of the conviction and the order for a new trial—sans confession.

Then in *Arizona v. Fulminante* (1991), the U.S. Supreme Court took a step backward and broke new ground. In that case, Jeneane Michelle Hunt, Oreste Fulminante's eleven-year-old stepdaughter, was murdered. There was no evidence linking Fulminante to the killing. While in prison for an unrelated crime, however, he was befriended by Anthony Sarivola, a fellow inmate who was actually a paid FBI informant posing as an organized crime figure. Sarivola warned Fulminante that other prisoners wanted to beat him up because of a rumor that he was a child killer. Sarivola offered to protect him in exchange for "the truth." Fearing for his safety, Fulminante—who was intellectually limited, small in stature, and not well adapted to life behind bars—confessed. Boom.

Ahead of trial, Fulminante sought to suppress his statement, but the trial judge denied the motion, ruled the confession voluntary, and admitted it into evidence. Predictably, the jury voted to convict, and Fulminante was sentenced to death. On appeal, the Arizona Supreme Court reversed the conviction and ordered a new trial. The confession was coerced, they said; the decision to admit it was erroneous. Then the state appealed.

Enter the U.S. Supreme Court. By a five-to-four majority, the court conceded that the confession was coerced, and the trial judge erred by allowing they jury to hear it. Breaking from tradition, however, the court went on to state for the first time that in certain situations, a wrongly admitted confession may be subject to the "harmless error" doctrine. In other words, while the trial judge was wrong to admit the confession, that error was not prejudicial and had no bearing on the jury's verdict. As they say, no harm, no foul.

The court's opinion in Fulminante was justifiably met with some measure of outrage. In an editorial titled "The Supreme Court's Harmful Error," the *New York Times* stated in no uncertain terms: "In wanton disregard of its own precedents, the Supreme Court has announced that the wrongful use of a coerced confession at a criminal trial need not automatically require the reversal of a conviction." Putting this ruling in historical context, and noting that it would have astonished earlier courts, the *Times* stated: "The injection of the harmless error notion was a wild extension of the otherwise valid principle that minor technical mistakes, which inevitably creep into most cases, should not invalidate a fundamentally fair trial, especially if the independent evidence of guilt is overwhelming."

This ruling was out of step not only with legal precedent but also with research on the effects of confession evidence. First, even a hotly contested confession, standing all alone, will substantially boost the conviction rate. Over and over again, research shows that mock jurors and judges vote guilty when the only evidence is a confession that they themselves perceived to be coerced. Voluntariness technicalities be damned. Innocent people don't confess to crimes they did not commit.

A second glaring myth of the harmless-error doctrine applied to confessions is the notion that an appellate court can review all the evidence, examine the error in the context of the trial as a whole, and determine that the jury would have voted guilty beyond a reasonable doubt anyway, even if the confession could somehow be surgically removed. I would argue that appeals judges are ill equipped by intuition and hampered by hindsight biases to objectively estimate the strength of a prosecutor's case and the cumulative or "harmless" nature of the confession in dispute.

The very notion that a confession error can prove harmless when other evidence is sufficient to support conviction is flawed because it rests on the assumption that the alleged other evidence is independent of that confession. It is not. What wrongful convictions have shown is that the confession becomes the foundation in a house of cards. Upon it, other faulty evidence is built. One cannot later extract the confession and declare the rest of the evidence independently corroborative. *Corroboration inflation* is the term I used to describe this phenomenon in "Why Confessions Trump Innocence," an article published in the *American Psychologist*.

In 2010, law professor Brandon Garrett noted that appellate courts that conducted post-conviction reviews of several exonerees who had confessed had affirmed the convictions by citing the "overwhelming nature of the evidence against them and describing in detail the non-

public and 'fully corroborative' facts they each reportedly volunteered."
Yet the empirical studies described in chapter 6 show that confessions
can taint everything else.

The assumption of independence presumed by a harmless-error
doctrine is baseless. A confession can be mentally "subtracted" from the
trial record, but its influence persists. At some point, the judiciary needs
to educate itself and realize that erroneously admitted coerced confessions can corrupt the very evidence that appeals courts later cite to
make the confessions appear cumulative and hence harmless.

Is Confession a Bar to Post-Exoneration Relief?

In 1996, sixty-three-year-old William Beason was found stabbed to
death in his Rochester, New York, apartment. He had multiple stab
wounds in his neck and chest and defensive wounds on his left hand.
Police found a bloodstained knife, towel, and tissues in Beason's bathroom. They believed he was murdered on New Year's Day.

A few days later, thirty-four-year-old Douglas Warney called the
police claiming to have information about the murder. He said he knew
Beason because in the past he had cleaned his house and shoveled snow
from his driveway. Warney had an eighth-grade education and a history
of serious mental health issues. Suspicious of his unsolicited call, detectives treated Warney as a suspect and interrogated him for twelve
hours. During that time, they say, he gave varying accounts, each more
and more incriminating. At first, he said that his cousin Brian killed
Beason, who owed him money; next he said he helped his cousin kill
Beason; finally, he said that he alone did it. As with almost all false
confessions, detectives claimed that Warney furnished details that only
the killer could know. Warney went to trial and was convicted of second-degree murder and sentenced to twenty-five years to life.

In 2004, DNA from the crime scene was sent for testing to the
Monroe County Public Safety Laboratory. They examined samples tak-
en from the victim's fingernail scrapings, blood flecks from the crime
scene, and bloodstains on a towel and tissues in the bathroom. Across
the board, none of the DNA matched Warney—or his cousin for that
matter. But it did match Eldred Johnson Jr., a New York State inmate
serving a life sentence for other crimes. When interviewed, Johnson
admitted that he killed Beason and that he did it alone. Without any

doubt cast as to his actual innocence, Warney's conviction was vacated, and he was released.

Twenty years earlier, New York State had enacted the Unjust Conviction and Imprisonment Act to compensate individuals victimized by the state's justice system, making it one of thirty-six states to do so (a full chart can be found on the Innocence Project's web page).

It is hard to fathom how much money it would take to compensate someone for the trauma of years lost behind bars. It is different everywhere. Some states affix an amount. Louisiana pays $25,000 per year, not to exceed a total of $250,000. Alabama, Florida, Hawaii, and Michigan pay up to $50,000 per year of wrongful imprisonment. Colorado pays $70,000 per year plus $50,000 for each year served on death row. Illinois pays up to $85,350 for five years of incarceration, $170,000 a year for up to fourteen years, and $199,150 after that. In Iowa and Missouri, it's $50 a day; in California, it's $140. Maine pays up to $300,000 per wrongful conviction; in Massachusetts, that figure is up to $500,000. In New York, the amount is determined on a case-by-case basis.

After his release from prison, Warney sought to recover $400,000 from the state's court of claims for his nine years of incarceration. But he was denied. Judge Renee Minarik dismissed Warney's claim on the grounds that his conviction was brought about "by his own conduct"—which is to say, the fact that he confessed. And while his confession may have been false, it had been ruled voluntary and hence lawful. Of course, that is par for the course.

The issue before this court—whether a false confession elicited from a vulnerable suspect by means of the police interrogation process can fairly be deemed to arise from the suspect's "own conduct" (and thus bar recovery under New York's Unjust Conviction Act, Court of Claims Act § 8-b)—is one that can be illuminated by an extensive body of scientific research that has emerged in the twenty-five years since the act was passed in 1984. For what it's worth, New York does not stand alone. In 2012, Robert Norris surveyed the laws across the country and found that one of out of every five compensation statutes excludes exonerees who had pled guilty or otherwise contributed to their own conviction, most notably, by confession.

The court of claims denial to Warney was appealed. In 2011, by a unanimous seven-to-zero margin, the state's highest court sided with

Warney and overturned the court of claims. Later that year, Warney settled a federal civil rights lawsuit against the city of Rochester for $3.75 million.

THE PSYCHOLOGICAL AFTERSHOCKS OF FALSE CONFESSION

It should come as no surprise that convicted offenders released after incarceration suffer from a range of mental health problems, among them, posttraumatic stress disorder (PTSD), depression, and anxiety. For their innocent counterparts, released after having been wrongfully incarcerated, one might hope for a better outcome. Too often, that hope will be dashed.

In *Rectify: The Power of Restorative Justice after Wrongful Conviction*, Lara Bazelon wrote about the "Myth of Happily Ever After." She points to the jubilant scene that typically accompanies the release of all wrongfully convicted individuals. In courtrooms and outside the walls of prison, they appear with their legal advocates, supporters, family, friends, and the press. At this moment of exhilaration, they cry tears of joy, they thank God, and they walk back into the world. Against all odds, this scene represents what Bazelon calls the ultimate fairy-tale narrative.

But that moment does not, as she put it, portend a happily-ever-after ending. Many exonerees suffer in prison; they come out with serious physical and mental health issues. Family members have died or moved away; once-close friends are now mere acquaintances. And as if all of this isn't bad enough, they often struggle to find work and put a roof over their head. They may have been exonerated, but their history precedes them wherever they go.

In 2020, Amy Shlosberg and others published an article titled "'They Open the Door, Kick You Out, and Say, 'Go': Reentry Challenges after Wrongful Imprisonment." Through twenty-four in-depth interviews they conducted with exonerees, these researchers reified Bazelon's account. The first day of freedom was a day of elation and bliss. "It was surreal," said one exoneree. "I step out of the courtroom and the sky, the blue, not a cloud in sight. The sun was out, sunlight on my face and fresh air. . . . I stepped to the press conference, there was a ton of media there, everything I ever wanted to say."

Then reality set in. Released, sometimes hastily, with little more than the clothes on their back and fifty to one hundred dollars of gate money in their pocket, many of the exonerees reported having no place to live, no job, no plan, no health insurance, one or both parents who had died, and fractured old relationships—sometimes even with their own children, who grew up in their absence.

Difficulty adjusting is the norm. They are innocent yet scarred by incarceration, PTSD and other mental health problems are common, trusting others is difficult, and negative public perceptions are palpable. Sometimes when they apply for a job, background checks reveal the criminal record that was supposed to have been expunged. Even if that doesn't happen, exonerees have to explain the years-long gap in their employment history. Of course, it does not help, as some have noted, that police and prosecutors continued to proclaim their guilt following release, which sowed doubts in the public mind. I am disgusted but not surprised by this last revelation. I have personally witnessed all too much of it.

I have worked on cases involving false confessions but also on some involving innocents who were mistakenly identified by one or more eyewitnesses. I cannot say this as an empirical matter, but my impression has long been that the confessors have a far more difficult time coping with life after prison. And as far as I can tell, again, as a matter of impression, they suffer more for two reasons.

The first is that they blame themselves for being weak, naïve, and malleable. They relive their interrogations, trying to piece together what they were thinking at the time. The second reason is social psychological: exoneration or not, they said they did it. Innocent people may get misidentified in an eyewitness lineup through no fault of their own, we think, because humans are imperfect. But as far most of us are concerned, innocent people just don't confess to crimes they did not commit.

Innocent Victims

As detailed in chapter 6, it took Amanda Knox years to come to grips with the confession she was induced to give, a dreamlike "vision" that she was involved in the murder of her friend and roommate in Perugia, Italy. She thought of herself as weak-willed and weak-minded for having been duped. Only when she started to read about false confessions did she realize that her response in that situation was not atypical—in fact, I would be tempted to attribute it to human nature.

I'm not sure I have ever seen a crueler and more inhumane aftermath to a wrongful conviction. The social media onslaught and hateful blogs, which started when she confessed four days after the crime, never abated—not when the actual perpetrator, whose DNA was found all over the crime scene, was picked up weeks later, and not when she was fully absolved by the highest court of the land. In a 2019 article in *Rolling Stone*, Nina Burleigh looked back at the Knox case as the dawn of the fake news era. She described "vicious social media swarms led by trolls using online pseudonyms" and "accusations of fake news hurled at reputable outlets."

This may also help to explain the experience of Raffaele Sollecito, Knox's Italian boyfriend, who was implicated and convicted only by her false confession. He too was fully absolved. Yet when we met years later, he admitted that he had struggled to find the right job in light of his "reputation." In the epilogue of a book he wrote about his experience, Raffaele reflected: "I was no longer the sweet, innocent, ordinary boy from Giavinazzo, but a scarred, more reflective ex-prisoner who could go nowhere without triggering some sort of conversation or expression of opinion."

The psychological aftershocks of a false confession can be illustrated in almost all of the cases I have seen. Two in particular come to mind, cases I've already described: Peter Reilly and Malthe Thomsen.

Peter Reilly

The first time I read about Peter Reilly's 1973 confession to the murder of his mother, in New Canaan, Connecticut, I had just received my PhD. Trained in basic social psychology, I immediately developed an intense curiosity about confessions—the so-called gold standard of evidence. It was at that time that I read one book, and then another, about Reilly's story, which unfolded about an hour from where I'd spent four years in graduate school.

In chapter 3, I described the polygraph abuse of Reilly, who came home one night and found his mother, and only living parent, Barbara

Gibbons, beaten to death and mutilated on the floor. For no good reason, police lasered in on an exploitable Reilly, interrogated him for hours, convinced him he had failed an infallible lie detector test, and induced a confession.

A kid in high school, grief-stricken by what he saw and subjected to unconscionable lies from police whom he was raised to trust, Reilly had no idea that he would spend more than a year in prison for something so personally vile that he had nothing to do with. The transcripts of his lengthy interrogation revealed something not yet recognized or understood. For me, Reilly became the poster child for what Larry Wrightsman and I would call *internalized false confessions*.

Reilly was fortunate that friends and neighbors who knew him were incredulous. Everyone who took a close look at the case recognized that it was a grave injustice. He had public support from authors Joan Barthel and Donald Connery and strong public advocacy from the legendary playwright Arthur Miller. Reilly was not alone.

He is also acutely mindful of how fortunate he was compared to wrongfully convicted individuals who spent ten, twenty, or thirty years behind bars. In Long Island, New York, seventeen-year-old Marty Tankleff was also induced to confess to bludgeoning his parents to death. For that crime he did not commit, he spent eighteen years in prison before his conviction was vacated. When Tankleff was released, Reilly wrote an unpublished essay he titled "Marty and Me: Two of a Kind." After commenting on the striking similarities of their cases, he breathed a sigh of relief as to how relatively lucky he was.

Still, and understandably, the effect was devastating—not just because he had lost his mother but because Connecticut police who set him up publicly refused to back down. They publicly continued to spread misinformation to defend their actions. I should know. I received a phone call in my Williams College office several years ago from a law enforcement officer involved in Reilly's case. He had moved to Massachusetts; I don't recall his name. But he read something I had written and was eager to pick a fight. Looking back, in 2013, Donald Connery, writing for the *Hartford Courant*, quoted the state's attorney as rejecting the police report as "contrived." Connery himself referred to the investigation as a "cops-gone-wild episode."

Does anyone ever really recover from something like this? After interviewing Reilly in 1993, twenty years after his mother was killed,

Joseph O'Brien described him as divorced, unemployed, and disillusioned. What confounded him most, Reilly said, was not what police did to him but the fact that they never changed their minds in the face of overwhelming proof of his innocence.

In 2006, I invited Peter to visit my Monday evening psychology-and-law class at Williams. He and Don Connery drove up. We talked about his experiences. What came through loud and clear was that he was still angry and resentful, thirty-three years later—and I couldn't blame him.

We spoke again by phone, in the fall of 2020. He sounded much better, more at peace. His life was knocked off course, to be sure, and he never fully recovered. But at sixty-four, he plays guitar in three or four local rock bands. He loves music and that helps to sustain him.

Malthe Thomsen

In contrast to Reilly, Thomsen won't have the time to recover from what authorities did to him. In a case described in chapter 4, in 2014, Thomsen—a twenty-two-year-old Danish man hoping to become a teacher—was on an internship at a preschool in New York City. One day, an assistant teacher with a history of filing false complaints, reported seeing Thomsen touch children inappropriately. After the school investigated and found nothing, she was dismissed. She then filed a complaint with the NYPD.

Thomsen was picked up at the crack of dawn one morning, interrogated for several hours, told that his actions were captured on surveillance video, which was a lie, and brainwashed. An assistant district attorney then came in and put him on camera for a video confession.

Thomsen was arrested, charged with several counts of first-degree sexual abuse, and sent to Rikers Island, where he was incarcerated for thirteen days until he posted bail. Because of threats from other inmates, he was placed in solitary confinement. Local headlines referred to him as "Sex Monster."

Except for his so-called confession, there was no evidence whatsoever. No other teacher observed anything suspicious; not a single child who was questioned reported an incident. Within a few months, the Manhattan DA's Office dismissed the charges. In open court, Thomsen exploded in tears. He promptly flew home to Denmark and was later compensated an undisclosed amount of money.

You can see Malthe Thomsen in Katrine Philp's 2018 documentary, *False Confessions*. I have no training as a clinician, but I don't think special training is necessary to discern that he was clearly traumatized by the experience, seemed depressed, and was unable to smile. He gained weight and never did become a teacher.

On January 19, 2019, he died of a blood clot in his heart. He was twenty-seven years old. I found out about this death through an email from the co-producer of *False Confessions*: "Dear Saul, I don't know if you've heard, but Malthe passed away this Saturday, age twenty seven. It was a heart attack and we all blame the four years of fighting for justice, which was an extreme stress for him. It is so very, very sad." Knowing all too well what Malthe had been through, I was numb. Gitte Thomsen, his mother, described the ordeal in the Danish media as a "grueling case that took a hard toll on both him and his family."

There is no limit to the number of heart-wrenching stories I could tell about the psychological aftershocks of a false confession. After release from prison, sixteen years after his conviction, Wesley Myers, whose case I described in chapter 4, still could not get past the horror of what he let happen to him. "They mind-raped me and made me believe I killed someone I loved," he said to Andrew Knapp, a writer for the *Post and Courier*. "It was all a setup." His girlfriend added, "He came out of prison a broken man. It has ruined his life." On September 23, 2021, in Charleston, South Carolina, Myers died at the age of 62 from diabetes-related complications.

SOCIAL STIGMA—HEY, WHAT'S THAT YELLOW PATCH ON YOUR CHEST?

The ancient Greeks used the word *stigma* to describe the visible mutilations, burns, stains, or tattoos that were branded on criminals, slaves, or other outcasts so that others could identify and avoid them. A stigma is a visible and permanent mark of disgrace.

In more recent usage, the word has been used not in a literal sense but figuratively, to describe marks of disgrace on a person's character. In 1963, Canadian sociologist Erving Goffman introduced the word to social scientists in his classic book, *Stigma: Notes on the Management of a Spoiled Identity*. Goffman wrote that life is like a theater and that each of us assumes a certain face, or social identity, that others help us to maintain. He was also quick to note, however, that people are stigmatized not only on the basis of physical deformity but also by low social class, a diagnosed mental illness, and other attributes.

Research on social stigma points to two effects. First, individuals and institutions ostracize, shun, and ignore stigmatized individuals, a direct effect that disadvantages them in school settings, employment, housing, and other life endeavors. The second effect is psychological. Stigmatized individuals know that others are tainted by their stigma, so it gets into their head.

An old social psychology experiment illustrates this point. In a study involving female college students, Robert Kleck and Angelo Strenta cosmetically applied a large facial scar onto each subject's right cheek before sending her out to meet a fellow student. Subjects watched in the mirror as the experimenter applied the scar. Then just before she was sent out, the experimenter applied a moisturizer "to keep the scar from cracking and peeling off." In fact, he removed it completely— without providing the mirror.

At that point, the subject and fellow student had a five-minute conversation. The point is, no subjects wore a painted scar on their face, and the person they spoke to had no idea that a scar had ever been present. Yet subjects who thought they sported the scar, compared to a control group of others who did not, thought that their fellow student spent more time staring at them, kept a greater distance, and saw them as less attractive. None of that was true.

Understandably, convicted felons are subject to the effects of stigmatization. But what about individuals who were convicted, incarcerated, and treated as criminals, but then exonerated? These are men and women worthy of profound sympathy. But too often they suffer from "stigma by association," so the stain does not disappear.

Ex-marine Kirk Bloodsworth was the first person ever to be DNA exonerated. In 1985, Bloodsworth was convicted of killing Dawn Hamilton in Rosedale, Maryland, on the basis of five mistaken eyewitnesses and a shoe print that a forensic examiner erroneously matched to him. He was exonerated and released in 1993 when DNA testing established his innocence (in an odd twist, that DNA later identified a fellow inmate known to Bloodsworth; that inmate was a serial rapist).

Tim Junkin, author of *Bloodsworth: The True Story of the First Death Row Inmate Exonerated by DNA*, notes that upon his release, and despite the dispositive DNA (which had not yet identified the actual perpetrator), the state's attorney offered no apologies. "I believe he is not guilty," she said. "I'm not prepared to say he's innocent." Later that week, someone left an anonymous note on the pickup truck parked in Bloodsworth's driveway. The note contained two words: "Child Killer!"

The Odyssey of Kenzi Snider Brown

The wild and crazy story of Kenzi Snider Brown, described in chapter 5, points to how particularly hard it is to remove the stain that comes with confession. In March 2001, she was a nineteen-year-old American exchange student in South Korea when Jamie Lynn Penich, a student from western Pennsylvania, was brutally murdered in her downtown Seoul motel room after a night of Saint Patrick's Day partying with friends from the program. Snider, from West Virginia, was one of the friends Jamie was with.

At first, Korean police suspected an American serviceman. Penich had been dancing with GIs at a bar that night, the hotel manager reported seeing a young white male running, with blood on his pants, and a guest next door heard an angry male voice followed by stomping noises. Although police investigated locals and U.S. Army suspects stationed nearby, they did not solve the crime.

About a year later, while Kenzi was back home taking classes at Marshall University and working part-time as a teacher's aide at a school for troubled teens, agents contacted her out of the blue. Three agents—one a U.S. Army investigator, the others from the FBI—paid her a visit in Huntington, West Virginia, and interrogated her for the better part of three days in a local Ramada Inn. Their tactics ranged from gaining her trust to misrepresenting the evidence, lying about the consequences of confession, tinkering with her memory, and convincing her not to call a lawyer.

When all was said and done, Kenzi Snider—a Girl Scout and honors student with no history of violence—hunched over in a motel-room chair, shut her eyes, and tearfully confessed to stomping Jamie to death in a drunken sexual encounter. Although she was innocent, Snider had become so confused that she internalized the belief in her own culpability and formed images of how she would have done it. According to the three agents, not a minute of these motel-room interrogations was recorded.

Three weeks later, Snider was arrested and jailed locally for ten months, then extradited to South Korea. Once there, she was held for six weeks in solitary confinement, in a four-by-seven-foot cell. She was then transferred to a larger cell, shared by fifteen women, all sleeping on blankets on a stone floor. Like all prisoners in South Korea, Snider was required to wear a colored patch on her prison garb—in her case, yellow, signifying murder. In transit to and from the facility she was tied with thickly knotted ropes, also color coded in yellow to indicate her alleged crime.

Snider was tried by a panel of judges who tossed out her original confession and acquitted her. The prosecution appealed the verdict, but the appeals court upheld the ruling—in fact, the chief judge explicitly suggested that a third party likely committed the murder. Yet again, the prosecution appealed the verdict. This time, it went to the Supreme Court of Korea, which affirmed: *not guilty*.

In 2006, finally unencumbered by outstanding charges, Snider was free. She never ever was convicted, wrongfully or otherwise. After the ordeal was put to rest in the Korean courts, she filed a lawsuit in U.S. District Court naming the three agents as defendants. "Other than the coerced false confession, no evidence was developed or introduced tying Ms. Snider to the murder," the lawsuit stated. "In fact, physical evidence and eyewitness statements known to the defendants, but ignored by them at the time of their interrogation, strongly indicated Ms. Snider's innocence."

For various stated reasons, that lawsuit was dismissed in federal court. In his opinion to dismiss the case, Circuit Court judge Paul Niemeyer cited the fact that Kenzi did not immediately retract her confession or unequivocally assert her innocence at her extradition hearing. In fact, he quoted the magistrate who conducted that hearing, who concluded that "the evidence presented does not establish that Ms. Snider's will was overborne or that her capacity for self-determination [was] critically impaired."

What this magistrate failed to understand—and what U.S. courts continue to misunderstand—is that while innocent people can be induced into false confessions by coercive tactics that break their willpow-

After confessing to FBI agents, Kenzi Snider was extradited to South Korea to stand trial for the murder of classmate Jamie Penich. Like all prisoners in South Korea, Snider was forced to wear a color patch on her uniform while awaiting trial. In her case, the patch was yellow, signifying murder. Although fully acquitted and absolved, Snider continues to suffer the social stigma that often shadows people who confess. *Photo licensed from Shutterstock.*

er, drive, motivation, and self-determination, they can also be induced to confess through psychological trickery, deceit, and illusions that weaken their beliefs, memories, and grasp on reality. Sometimes, as in Kenzi's case, the devastating effect is cognitive, not motivational.

Fast-forward ten years. I was preparing to write an article on internalized false confessions—a once controversial but now commonly accepted type of confession in which an innocent person comes to internalize a belief in their own guilt, often confabulating false memories in the process. I had followed the Snider case in the news when it happened. But all I had to go on by now were old secondhand newspaper accounts. So I searched online a bit and found a 2006 book about the case by Harriet Ryan titled *Murder in Room 103*. I checked online and saw that used copies were available.

This is where my perspective on this case takes an odd turn—hence, this detour in the narrative. When American exchange student Amanda Knox was arrested in Perugia, Italy, in November of 2007, after confessing to the murder of her British roommate, the story jumped out at me—in part because Perugia is close to Cortona, a medieval Tuscan city that my family and I had fallen in love with.

As the Knox story unfolded in the press, I had a reflex-like second reaction: it's Kenzi Snider all over again. Yes, Amanda's case is the one that got all the attention. But Kenzi's came first.

Hoping to learn more about Snider's confession, I ordered a copy of Ryan's book. While I was at it, I emailed Amanda for her mailing address so I could surprise her with a copy too. I was pretty sure she had not heard of this case but would of course recognize the parallels to her own. So I ordered two copies—one for me, the other for her.

Three days later, as soon as the books arrived, I received an email from Amanda. Short and sweet: "HOLY SHIT. Have you ever met Kenzi? Is this case very well known?"

I filled Amanda in on this earlier case. The next day, a second email arrived. Amanda found Kenzi on Facebook. They chatted. One week later, I received a third email. Titled "Hello," this one was from Kenzi Brown (formerly Snider).

Kenzi and I spoke by phone three or four times. I was acutely mindful of the fact that the trauma of her friend's murder, her confession, the fifteen months she spent incarcerated, and the years of legal limbo that followed were all in her rearview mirror. Her new name indicated she was married. The last thing I wanted was to take her back in time and dredge up bad memories I assumed she would rather forget.

I was wrong. Kenzi *wanted* to talk about all that happened, especially about her confession, which haunts her to this day, and about the aftermath. Yes, she is married and has tried to move on. She has a son who was six when we first spoke. She got all choked up when she talked about him because, as she put it, "I don't want my past to interfere with his present."

For precisely that reason, she told me, she needed to tell her story in her own voice once and for all. I wondered why. I knew her story from her perspective could help raise public awareness and, hopefully, down the road make for more educated and discerning juries in cases involving confessions. But for her, this need was also personal. She told me this story: she had arranged a new play date for her son. When they arrived and she met the playmate's mother, she told her about her past. From experience, Kenzi learned she could not keep it a secret. Yet that was the last play date her son had with that child.

I invited Kenzi, if she was interested, to fly to New York, attend one of my lab meetings, meet my graduate students, and perhaps even record a podcast about her case. Jason Flom, the founder of Lava Records and a legendary executive in the music industry, is also a founding board member, contributor, and staunch advocate of the Innocence Project, where he started the Life after Exoneration program for exonerees.

Three years earlier, Flom launched a new podcast series titled *Wrongful Conviction with Jason Flom.* He and I had met a while back at the New York premiere of a documentary we were both in called *False Confessions.* He lives in an apartment overlooking Central Park, just a few blocks from John Jay College. With Kenzi wanting to tell her story, his podcast series seemed perfect. I contacted him and described her situation. He was all in. So was my PhD student, Patricia Sanchez, who was gearing up to study, for her dissertation, whether exposure to wrongful conviction stories makes people more discerning as jurors.

On March 25, 2019, Kenzi flew to New York. First she attended a lab meeting with my graduate students. Her presence was emotional and riveting. The next day, we headed over to the recording studio for the podcast. Even more than I had realized from our prior conversations, that yellow patch she had to wear on her prison garb was more than just a distant bad memory. For me, it came to represent the stigma that attached itself to her confession.

When Kenzi returned from Korea, she had trouble finding work. "There was a gap in my work history," she told us. "My credit cards had defaulted, my student loans had defaulted." To make matters worse, she lost friendships because people would google her name and see that she had confessed to murder. Of course, they would also see that she was duly acquitted, and never convicted, but that did not seem to erase the stigma. "People have difficulty getting past the confession," she lamented.

About the stigma wrought by her confession, Kenzi said, "It follows you around so you have to monitor your behavior all the time. You can never get too angry or upset."

As for the impact on her social relationships, "When do you tell this to new people you've met? If you wait too long, they feel like you violated their trust, like why didn't you tell me this before, before you came into my house?" This is what caused the play date fiasco.

Kenzi's podcast was moving, to say the least. She was never wrongfully convicted and she never spent large chunks of her life in prison. But that yellow patch she had to wear in the Korean jail, to signify being charged with murder, that stigma has never fully worn off.

Like Amanda Knox, Peter Reilly, Marty Tankleff, Malthe Thomsen, and just about every other individual I know who was coerced, tricked, or duped into false confession, Kenzi, twenty years later, is still, as she put it, "struggling with forgiving myself for letting it happen."

Recognizing in hindsight, and in light of all the reading she has done, Kenzi now sees the red flags in her situation that she had missed, red flags that "made the odds of me getting out of that hotel room without a false confession incredibly small. I keep blaming myself for being stupid and mad that my brain failed me, but really I was just young, isolated, and so very tired with professions of innocence that my only armor gave out."

The reason these psychological aftershocks of false confession persist for so many years is the social stigma that, as Kenzi put it, "follows you around." Kenzi Brown is smart, gentle, soft-spoken, and genuine, and she cares about other people. She had no history of violence, no predisposition, and was never convicted of a crime. But that confession, which everyone she meets now can google, continues to haunt her.

The Stigma of Confession—Research Evidence

In the hierarchy of social stigma, it is bad to be *convicted* and sometimes not much better if the conviction turns out to have been *wrongful*, especially if it involved a *confession*.

In twin studies published in 2015, Kimberly Clow and Amy-May Leach compared people's perceptions in these different situations. In the first study, subjects were randomly assigned to rate people convicted of a crime they committed, or people wrongfully convicted of a crime they did not commit, or a control group of people in general. While not making judgments about specific individuals, subjects perceived individuals who were wrongly convicted as less friendly, likeable, warm, and respectable than average—but more aggressive. On most dimensions, they did not distinguish between exonerees and actual offenders.

In the second study, Clow and Leach probed into whether some exonerees are stigmatized more than others. They had subjects read a newspaper article about a fictional individual who was DNA exonerated after spending ten years in prison for murder. According to the article, he was originally convicted because he confessed, was misidentified by an eyewitness, or was implicated by a jailhouse snitch.

As I would have predicted, subjects were less sanguine about this exoneree's actual innocence and more unfavorable about his character when he was said to have confessed than in the other conditions. The confession planted a seed of doubt that could not later be uprooted. Validating the perceptions of too many real exonerees, confession triggered a stigma that did not detach itself—even after indisputable DNA evidence led the courts to overturn his conviction.

This stigma can have life-altering consequences. Experiments by Kyle Scherr, Jeff Kukucka, and others have shown that when people read about wrongful convictions, those who were convicted because they had confessed or pled guilty were assumed relative to other exonerees to lack intelligence and suffer from mental health issues. They were also judged to be more responsible for their own predicament and hence less deserving of reintegration support.

For people to doubt the innocence of a confessor even after DNA exoneration makes you wonder if there is anything that can be done to detach that stigma. It's an important question with social, economic, and mental health consequences. My colleagues and I took the wrongful conviction by confession hypothesis one step further. Although I would still consider our results preliminary, with more research needed, it appears to confirm that the stigma does not fully detach when DNA testing merely *excluded* the confessor, an evidentiary status that leaves the crime otherwise unsolved. But people do begin to de-stigmatize the confessor when told that the DNA not only excluded him but also *identified* the actual perpetrator. In this situation, the crime is solved, justice is served, and the DNA-identified perpetrator replaces the exoneree as the villain to be blamed and punished.

THE ONE AND ONLY REMEDY

It is clear that people find it harder to wrap their heads around the actual innocence of individuals who were wrongfully convicted because of a false confession as opposed to those victimized by other types of mistakes. This research shows that the false confession plants a seed of doubt, even after exoneration. It also shows that the cascade of effects is prolonged, devastating, and hard to extinguish.

Anthony Wright could not get the Pennsylvania courts to grant his request for DNA testing, despite the law, because he had confessed. Yet that was the only way to rebut the confession he had disclaimed from the very start.

Brian Dement was exculpated by DNA along with his three West Virginia codefendants. In fact, that DNA also identified a serial sex offender with a history of violence. Yet while the judge overturned his codefendants' convictions, he would not do the same for Dement— because he had confessed and pled guilty.

In New York State, Doug Warney was fully exonerated, and no one disputed his actual innocence. Yet the lower courts would not grant him compensation for his wrongful conviction because it was his fault for confessing after a lengthy interrogation.

In Connecticut, Peter Reilly has spent a lifetime trying to escape the shadow of his false confession, the victim being his own mother—in part because police would not relinquish claims of his guilt.

Malthe Thomsen never recovered from the way the NYPD manipulated him into a humiliating false confession. But he was never the same and died of a heart attack at the age of twenty-seven.

And then there's Kenzi Snider Brown. The effects of her false confession persist despite a trifecta of acquittals right up through South Korea's Supreme Court. Twenty years later, she still has to explain herself to others.

Once a false confession is out of the bag, the damage to the innocent person is done. You may think that we all are protected by our Miranda rights to silence and counsel. Think again. Miranda since its inception has become more of a trap than a protective defense, a safe harbor for police, not suspects. And while scholars and practitioners may disagree over the scope of the issues (Miranda's impotence is good news to some, bad to others), false-confession cases have run amok in the fifty-plus years since the U.S. Supreme Court granted citizens their constitutional right to silence and to counsel. More on this to come.

Part Four

How to Fix America's Broken System

10

YOUR RIGHT TO REMAIN SILENT

Safeguard or Trap?

You have the right to remain silent.
Anything you say can and will be used against you in a court of law.
You have the right to have an attorney present.
If you cannot afford an attorney, one will be appointed to you by the court.
You can decide to exercise these rights at any time.

I'm guessing you have lost count of the number of times you've heard this incantation on TV and in the movies, usually delivered to a villainous thug. You can probably recite these words from memory. The question is, if you are in a jam, steered into the bowels of a police station, and so frightened you can barely breathe, does knowing these words have any value?

When I lecture public and college student audiences about interrogation room shenanigans that break people down to confess, the most predictable first question I get sounds something like this: "Why didn't these people just stop talking and demand a lawyer?"

It's a smart question. There's only one surefire way to guard yourself against an influence process that would trick, cajole, compel, or otherwise force you to confess to something you didn't do: exercise your right to a lawyer and in the meantime keep your mouth shut. But is that right a safeguard or a trap?

On March 13, 1963, Ernesto Arturo Miranda, of Mesa, Arizona, was arrested for kidnapping and rape. Although the victim could not iden-

tify him in a lineup, he handwrote a confession, which led to his conviction at trial. Miranda appealed on the ground that he had only a ninth-
grade education and no understanding of his Fifth Amendment right to
silence and Sixth Amendment right to counsel.

In *Miranda v. Arizona* (1966), the U.S. Supreme Court set aside
Miranda's conviction. By a five-to-four vote, the court delivered a bold
ruling that required for the first time that police apprise all suspects in
custody of their constitutional right to remain silent and have a lawyer
present. Calling the process of interrogation "inherently compelling,"
Chief Justice Earl Warren's court created a remedy: Any statement
taken from a suspect without a knowing, intelligent, and voluntary waiver would be considered unlawful and barred from trial.

It's hard to overstate the attention that this landmark case received.
Here's one data point: According to HeinOnline, an internet database
for legal materials, *Miranda* is the fourth most highly cited Supreme
Court opinion—after *Brown v. Board of Education* (1954), *Roe v.
Wade* (1973), and *Griswold v. Connecticut* (1965). Here's another met-
ric: in 2016, the Global Legal Research Center reported that 108 coun-
tries—in the Americas and the Caribbean, East Asia and the Pacific,
Europe and Central Asia, the Middle East and North Africa, South
Asia, and sub-Saharan Africa—have gone on to implement similar protections.

In criminal procedure, *Miranda* stands as an icon for justice, fair
play, and the protection of defenseless citizens from government abuse
of power. There are three reasons why this opinion has loomed so large.
First, the court embedded the rights to silence and counsel in the
Constitution by declaring that they apply not only to defendants in
court but also to suspects in custody at a police station. Second, the
court came right out and expressed grave concern about the coercive
nature of a psychologically oriented interrogation. Third, it laid out a
roadmap to ensure compliance and enforcement—namely, *custody*
triggers the requirement that police *inform* suspects of their rights;
then they must obtain a *waiver* that is knowing, intelligent, and voluntary; if a suspect *invokes* these rights at any time, the interrogation must
stop; any statements otherwise taken will be *excluded* from evidence.

At the time, this ruling set off an uproar among police, prosecutors,
and "law and order" politicians. Violent street criminals will all lawyer
up, refuse to talk, and escape prosecution, they predicted. Or, cops will

In 1963, Ernesto Miranda confessed to kidnapping and rape without knowing his constitutional rights, and he was promptly convicted. On appeal, the U.S. Supreme Court famously overturned his conviction and ruled that police must apprise suspects of their rights. Retried without the confession, Miranda was reconvicted. *Ernesto Miranda mug shot released to the public.*

fail to utter the right words at the right time, and villains will roam free because of a legal technicality. Either way, the law coddles criminals; violent crime rates will surge.

Miranda became politically charged. Congress tried unsuccessfully to invalidate the ruling; some called for Chief Justice Earl Warren's impeachment. Reflecting on all this fifty year later, preeminent legal scholar Yale Kamisar told Victor Li of the *ABA Journal*, "It was scary how strong the negative reaction to Miranda was."

Notwithstanding all these alarms, the sky did not fall—not by a long shot. For starters, empirical studies reported in the first decade after

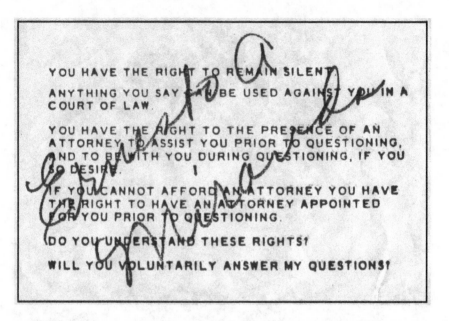

YOU HAVE THE RIGHT TO REMAIN SILENT.
ANYTHING YOU SAY CAN BE USED AGAINST YOU IN A
COURT OF LAW.

YOU HAVE THE RIGHT TO THE PRESENCE OF AN
ATTORNEY TO ASSIST YOU PRIOR TO QUESTIONING,
AND TO BE WITH YOU DURING QUESTIONING, IF YOU
SO DESIRE.

IF YOU CANNOT AFFORD AN ATTORNEY YOU HAVE
THE RIGHT TO HAVE AN ATTORNEY APPOINTED
FOR YOU PRIOR TO QUESTIONING.

DO YOU UNDERSTAND THESE RIGHTS?

WILL YOU VOLUNTARILY ANSWER MY QUESTIONS?

In 1973, Ernesto Miranda was released on parole. To make a living, he auto-graphed and sold Miranda Rights cards—like this image housed at the Phoenix Police Museum—for $1.50 each. In 1976, he was stabbed to death in a bar fight. *Courtesy of the Arizona Police Museum.*

the *Miranda* decision showed that very few suspects invoked their rights once they were warned. Before long, strong opposition subsided; police continued to solve cases by confession; judges continued to allow these confessions in court.

Oddly, thirty years later, after the dust had mostly settled and the opposition had mostly waned, University of Utah law professor Paul Cassell commenced a new assault on *Miranda*. Following an article in the *Wall Street Journal* titled "How Many Criminals Has Miranda Set Free?" he published a 1996 law review article in which he cited pre- and post-*Miranda* clearance rates in support of the claim that confession rates had fallen after 1966.

NYU law professor Stephen Schulhofer immediately countered Cassell's claim by noting fatal flaws in his methodology. He noted, for example, that Cassell violated the introductory statistics dictum that "correlation does not imply causation" by neglecting the fact that violent crime rates rose throughout the 1960s, thereby lowering clearance rates, independent of *Miranda*; that Cassell excluded contradictory data from Los Angeles that he didn't find plausible; and that he obtained pre- and post-*Miranda* samples in New York from different sources, essentially comparing apples and oranges. When all was said and done, Schulhofer detected no significant effect of *Miranda*.

Cassell was not deterred. In 2000, he went on to argue unsuccessfully at the Supreme Court for the repeal of *Miranda* in *Dickerson v. United States*. In affirming *Miranda* in this case, Chief Justice William Rehnquist observed that the warnings had become part of the national culture. He was right, of course. Miranda warnings are such a pop culture trope that fictional depictions of police in TV and movies have to show them for an arrest to look real. Of course, Rehnquist also admitted (assuring *Miranda*'s critics) that "our subsequent cases have reduced the impact of the *Miranda* rule on legitimate law enforcement."

To this day, Cassell remains unconvinced—even though the courts have diluted the original ruling in ways to be discussed shortly; and even while law enforcement groups no longer oppose the requirements, which in itself is telling. Along with economics professor Richard Fowles, Cassell thus greeted *Miranda*'s anniversary with an article titled "Still Handcuffing the Cops? A Review of Fifty Years of Empirical Evidence of Miranda's Harmful Effects on Law Enforcement." Anyone interested in the data presented and their analyses can find it in the *Boston University Law Review*.

In a world of mixed messages, the good news is that *Miranda* is here to stay; the bad news is that it does not work—not in its American birthplace, anyway. It does not protect innocent people; it does not deter the most egregious of police interrogation tactics; it does not prevent false confessions. Think about it. Almost every innocent confessor described in this book, and all others who appear in the wrongful-conviction databases, had waived, or allegedly waived, their rights before confessing. No matter what else had happened in the interrogation room, their confessions were deemed voluntary and hence admissible at trial.

MIRANDA "ON THE BOOKS"

Over the years, highly prominent legal scholars tracking the history of case law have been vocal about their disappointment in the courts. In 2001, Welsh White complained of "Miranda's waning protection" in light of follow-up court rulings that proved narrowing and erosive. In 2003, George Thomas III called *Miranda* a "spectacular failure." In 2017, Yale Kamisar, retired from the University of Michigan Law School and dubbed the "father of Miranda" because of his influential writings on custodial interrogations at the time, lamented how downsized the rule has become. "For those of us who welcomed Miranda," he said, "this turned out to be deeply disappointing." At about the same time, Charles Weisselberg, who had also described himself as an estranged former supporter, pronounced *Miranda* dead and mourned its passing. *Miranda* has failed both "on the books" and "on the ground," he wrote, and now functions as a safe harbor for police.

Over the years, the U.S. Supreme Court has chipped away at *Miranda*, retreating from the mission to protect citizens facing police interrogation. This fifty-plus–year history of case law, in all its complexity, recently led Idaho prosecutor Bryan Taylor to quip, "You Have the Right to Be Confused!" As an alternative to confusion, I would recommend law review articles by White, Thomas, Kamisar, Weisselberg, and others. For now, I will touch briefly on six highlights, better described as lowlights, that have subverted the *Miranda* court's original intent.

1. *North Carolina v. Butler* (1979)

In this case, police apprised the suspect of his rights but he explicitly refused to sign a waiver. Police interrogated him anyway, and he went on to make incriminating statements. The *Miranda* court had imposed on the government a "heavy burden" to demonstrate that suspects knowingly and intelligently waived their rights—and that a valid waiver could not be presumed from silence or from a confession later taken. Thirteen years later, however, Justice Potter Stewart, writing for a five-to-three majority, held that sometimes a waiver can be "inferred from the actions and words of the person interrogated." Introducing the squishy, nonobjective concept of an *implied waiver*, the court held that an explicit waiver of the rights to silence or counsel is not "invariably necessary."

I think Justice William Brennan's dissent put it aptly: "The Court thus shrouds in half-light the question of waiver, allowing courts to construct inferences from ambiguous words and gestures." Thanks to *Butler*, and in an odd step backward, judges now rule over a swamp of subjectivity in which they can attribute waivers to suspects who did no such thing, objectivity be damned. Making an implied waiver determination is like the Rorschach inkblot test: playing mind reader, judges can see in a suspect's actions and inaction whatever it is they are inclined to see.

2. *California v. Beheler* (1983)

The defendant of this case agreed to accompany police to the stationhouse, where officers specifically told him that he was not under arrest and did not Mirandize him. Beheler was interrogated and induced to make a statement. Although he was permitted to then leave the station, police arrested him several days later.

The Supreme Court ruled that Beheler was not in custody. As proof, the court cited the advisement that he was not under arrest. And if he wasn't in custody, police were not required by law to advise him of his rights. In other words, if police tell a suspect that he is not under arrest, which they can do tactically and deliberately, then the suspect may as well be on a park bench, at a Starbucks, or in his own living room—and Miranda does not apply.

There are times when police may legitimately hesitate to Mirandize someone who is not in custody out of fear that the warning itself may create a custody situation and scare a witness and possible suspect into silence. There are also times, however, when officers now go out of their way to "invite" a suspect to the station and deliver what has been called a "Beheler warning." They tell suspects that they are not under arrest, which makes the situation noncustodial in the eyes of the courts, and provides a license to circumvent Miranda. In a 2008 article titled "Mourning Miranda," Charles Weisselberg cited this advice from an officer training course: "At a police station, you should tell the suspect, in a believable way: 'You are free to leave or not answer any questions at any time. Do you understand?' Then you may proceed with interrogation without the need for Miranda warnings."

And that's not all. While telling a suspect he is not under arrest, police will often deploy the various weapons of the Reid technique, from confrontation and the refusal to accept denials, through presentations of false evidence and minimization themes that imply leniency. If it looks like a duck, swims like a duck, and quacks like a duck, then it probably *is* a duck. And so too is an American-style interrogation, which reeks of custody—Beheler warning or not.

3. *Illinois v. Perkins* (1990)

The U.S. Supreme Court broke open a gaping loophole to the requirement that in-custody suspects must be Mirandized. Lloyd Perkins, in jail for aggravated battery, was joined in his cell by an undercover police officer posing as another prisoner. Without Mirandizing Perkins, this officer questioned him about a murder—none of this questioning was recorded, so the tactics used are unknown, the source of any details also unknown; Perkins confessed—that too was not recorded.

It is hard to imagine a more "custodial" situation than being locked in jail, so the trial judge suppressed the confession and an appellate court affirmed. But then the Supreme Court reversed these prior rulings. The court held that Miranda warnings are required to offset the inherent coerciveness of a police-dominated interrogation. Although the undercover agent was in there hunting for a confession, although Perkins was incarcerated, and although no warnings were administered, the confession was voluntary and hence admissible because Perkins was not aware that he was speaking with a police officer.

Writing for the eight-to-one majority, Justice Anthony Kennedy said the point of Miranda was to protect the voluntary nature of police questioning a suspect in ways that are inherently coercive, that no such danger presented itself when an incarcerated person speaks to someone perceived to be a fellow inmate. In a statement that demonstrates the judiciary's inability or unwillingness to grasp the underlying psychology that concerned the *Miranda* court, he added: "Miranda forbids coercion, not mere strategic deception."

The term "mere strategic deception" is potentially misleading. In the case of Roman Zadorov, in Israel, an undercover cop posing as a cellmate reinforced the lies about evidence that police had presented to a disoriented suspect. Police are not permitted to lie, he assured Zadorov. Then there was Oreste Fulminante, suspected of killing his stepdaughter. He was approached in his Florida cell by an undercover FBI agent posing as a fellow inmate. He initially denied killing his stepdaughter. But then the agent offered to protect him from "tough" fellow inmates in exchange for the "truth."

With undercover operations seldom if ever recorded, *Perkins* appears to give police carte blanche to use all manners of trickery, deceit, and yes, possibly classic types of coercion without ever having to Mirandize the already incarcerated suspect. And yes, "mere strategic deception" may not involve old-school "third degree beatings," but duping the suspect can be every bit as dangerous and can also increase the risk of a false confession. The *Miranda* court knew that. Fourteen years later, the *Perkins* ignored it.

4. *Davis v. United States* (1994)

The court next weighed in on a military case in which the defendant agreed to talk with agents. Then, about ninety minutes into his interrogation, he changed his mind and said, "Maybe I should talk to a lawyer." After some discussion, during which agents assured him they had no intention of violating his rights, he agreed once again to talk. Shortly thereafter, he made an incriminating statement. At his court-martial, Davis sought to suppress his statement. He argued that all questioning should have ceased once he asked for a lawyer.

This case made its way to the Supreme Court, where Justice Sandra Day O'Connor, writing for the majority, referred to the defendant's request as ambiguous. "Unless the statement is an unambiguous or unequivocal request for counsel, the officers have no obligation to stop questioning him," she wrote. Raising the bar on defendants to be articulate, she said, "He must articulate his desire to have counsel present sufficiently clearly that a reasonable police officer in the circumstances would understand the statement to be a request for an attorney."

An interesting aspect of O'Connor's majority opinion is the compelling counterarguments to itself that it contained. "We recognize that requiring a clear assertion of the right to counsel might disadvantage some suspects who—because of fear, intimidation, lack of linguistic skills, or a variety of other reasons—will not clearly articulate their right to counsel although they actually want to have a lawyer present."

How can the court concede and yet justify that it has disadvantaged people who are vulnerable? What magical words must a suspect utter, uncluttered by polite hedges born of deference, to be deemed articulate enough? The answer is, it doesn't matter. In O'Connor's words: "But the primary protection afforded suspects subject to custodial interrogation is the Miranda warnings themselves."

Davis paved the way for judges to reject a range of attempts at invocation. Over the years, U.S. courts have rejected statements such as: "I think it's about time for me to stop talking." "I'm not saying shit to you no more, man. You, nothing personal man, but I don't like you. You're scaring the living shit out of me. . . . That's it. I shut up." "I think I would like to talk to a lawyer." "I think I need a lawyer." "Get the fuck out of my face. I don't have nothing to say. I refuse to sign [the waiver form]." "I can't afford a lawyer, but is there any way I can get one?" "I don't got nothing to say." And my favorite, of recent vintage: "Get me a lawyer, dawg."

In *Police: Law Enforcement Solutions*, Devallis Rutledge, special counsel for the Los Angeles County District Attorney's Office, and not a fan of Miranda, advised that these kinds of "wishy-washy" qualifications are ambiguous—so no need to stop questioning.

5. *Berghuis v. Thompkins* (2010)

In this case, the defendant, stone silent, would not speak or answer questions. Detectives read his rights from a form that he refused to sign. Nevertheless, they proceeded to question him for nearly three hours. At that point, they switched gears and queried Thompkins on spiritual matters. "Do you believe in God?" they asked. "Do you pray to God?" and "Do you pray to God to forgive you for shooting that boy down?" Thompkins answered *yes* to all three questions, whereupon he was arrested and charged with murder.

Thompkins's attorney moved to suppress his client's incriminating "yes" response by arguing that he had already invoked his right to remain silent—and that all subsequent exchanges violated his constitutional rights. The judge denied this motion and Thompkins was tried, convicted, and sentenced to life. Ultimately, the case made its way to the Supreme Court where, by a five-to-four margin, the majority held that the mere act of silence is not sufficient; unless a suspect explicitly invokes that right, he has not done so. Reiterating *Davis*, the majority asserted that suspects must invoke their rights affirmatively and un-equivocally.

Common sense normally tells us that actions speak louder than words. Not in this venue. Writing in dissent, Justice Sonia Sotomayor fully appreciated the irony that "suspects must now unambiguously in-voke their right to remain silent—which, counterintuitively, requires them to speak." In a 2012 law review article, Yale Kamisar called *Thompkins* the worst thing that could have happened to *Miranda*.

6. *Salinas v. Texas* (2013)

After two brothers were shot to death in their home in Houston, there were no eyewitnesses but police found six shotgun shell casings at the scene. The investigation led police to suspect Genovevo Salinas, who agreed to submit his shotgun for ballistics testing and voluntarily ac-companied police to the station to answer questions, which lasted for about an hour. Apparently, the situation was noncustodial. Salinas was told he was free to leave so he was not Mirandized.

But then when the police asked the guilt-presumptive question about whether his gun would match the shells recovered from the scene of the murder, he declined to answer. In fact, the officer later described his body language in dramatic terms, stating that Salinas "looked down at the floor, shuffled his feet, bit his bottom lip, clenched his hands in his lap, and began to tighten up." After some moments of silence, police changed the subject and moved on to other questions, which he an-swered. None of this session was recorded to corroborate this account.

Lacking sufficient evidence, police did not immediately charge Sali-nas. Then they obtained testimony from an informant claiming he heard Salinas confess to the killings. On that basis, Salinas was charged. By then, however, he had absconded and was not located until years later. He pleaded not guilty. At trial, the prosecutor cited his refusal to answer the shotgun question as evidence of guilt. During his closing argument, he commented on the fact that Salinas had remained silent when asked about the shotgun. Then the prosecutor added that an innocent person would not have reacted that way, thereby inviting the jury to draw an adverse inference.

Salinas appealed, arguing that this comment on his silence—which preceded both his arrest and Miranda warnings—violated his Fifth Amendment rights. However, by another slim five-to-four margin, however, the Supreme Court affirmed his conviction and asserted that suspects who are not under arrest, have not been Mirandized, and whose presence at the station is voluntary, cannot just sit silent. They must speak up or else suffer the consequence at trial.

So let me get this straight: A suspect must in some unexplained manner articulate the right to silence clearly and explicitly without ever having been apprised of that right? And someone who is under arrest enjoys a right to silence, whereas those who freely answer questions do not?

To sum up: the post-*Miranda* courts have ruled that police may skirt *Miranda* by creating situations ripe for interrogation that are not technically "custodial." They've ruled that police are not required to secure a suspect's waiver before commencing an interrogation. They have also lowered the bar as to what constitutes an adequate warning and raised the bar on what constitutes a clear waiver. So the suspect who falls silent, as provided by the Fifth Amendment, has not technically invoked the Fifth Amendment. And even if police do violate a suspect's narrowed-to-a-sliver rights, thereby excluding the confession from evidence, the state may still use the statement taken to attack a defendant's credibility at trial if that defendant has the audacity to testify.

These are some of the cases that have reduced Miranda to an empty shell of a symbol. The irony is, the courts protected the accused more effectively during the pre-DNA "once-in-a-blue-moon" era, when false confessions were little known and vastly underestimated. Today, in the wake of thousands of newly discovered wrongful convictions, we know better. Yet as the numbers of known false confessions have climbed, the protection of suspects caught in the grip of a police interrogation has waned. It's as if the American judiciary has retreated into a state of denial, oblivious to the facts on the ground and ignorant of Psych 101 principles of human behavior and decision making.

MIRANDA "ON THE GROUND"

For all the angst that *Miranda* has galvanized over the years, one signal emerged early on and has remained constant to this day: Warnings or not, very few American citizens invoke their rights.

Observational studies started to show this pattern almost immediately. In a field study conducted in New Haven, Connecticut, just after *Miranda* became law, Michael Wald and his colleagues reported in a 1967 issue of the *Yale Law Journal* that when the warnings were fully administered, three-quarters of all suspects waived their rights and spoke without a lawyer present. They concluded that the warnings seldom affected the outcome of interrogation.

Thirty years later, criminologist and law professor Richard Leo observed 182 custodial interrogations in Los Angeles and two other California police departments. He observed some of these sessions live; others on videotape. Overall, 78 percent of all suspects waived their rights. In 2007, several colleagues and I approached the question using a less direct type of data set. We surveyed 631 police investigators throughout North America and asked them to estimate from their own experience the percentage of suspects who waive their Miranda rights. Their estimate: 81 percent.

More recent reports from both adult and juvenile interrogations suggest that the waiver rate in the U.S. remains at a high level—and may even have risen. In one study, my colleagues and I analyzed 122 video-recorded interrogations from a mid-sized police department in Rhode Island. With all recording equipment concealed, some suspects, randomly assigned, were told they were on camera; others were not informed. The results showed a 98 percent waiver rate at the outset; 84 percent of suspects continued to waive their rights throughout the interrogation—regardless of whether they knew they were on camera.

After fifty-plus years, there's no question about it. People are inclined to talk to police. The million-dollar question is: Why? Three reasons: Failures of comprehension, police manipulation, and innocence.

Comprehension—"Do You Understand the Rights I Have Just Read to You?"

Miranda warnings may well be iconic within American culture and something we all can recite. But do people know what the words mean and how to execute them? When citizens waive their rights, is their decision to do so, in the Supreme Court's words, "knowing" and "intelligent"? It's a measurable, empirical, and important question that has attracted research psychologists like moths to a flame.

First things first. Comprehension is a more complicated issue than one would think. One of the great misconceptions about Miranda is that the Supreme Court composed the familiar warnings word for word. Actually, while the court dictated the principle that police must inform suspects in custody of their ongoing rights to silence and to counsel, it declined to micromanage the language, leaving that to law enforcement agencies themselves. The question is, would different agencies converge on a common set of words and phrases, or would some degree of chaos ensue?

In studies published in 2007 and 2008, Richard Rogers, a psychology professor at the University of North Texas, compared Miranda warnings from over six hundred jurisdictions across the country. Overall, he and his colleagues collected 945 sets of warnings and found to my astonishment that 888 of them were uniquely worded. Variability was the norm—and the differences were substantial. For example, while the average warning ran 53 words long, they ranged in length from 21 to 231 words.

Differences in wordage were just the beginning. Rogers next measured the complexity of the various warnings using the popular Flesch-Kincaid grade estimate of readability. Calculated on the basis of word lengths and sentence lengths, this metric serves as a proxy for how difficult a passage in English is to understand. On average, Miranda warnings required only a sixth-grade reading level. They ranged, however, from an easy-to-read low of second grade to a difficult post-graduate level—or, to put it another way, from *Goodnight Moon* to the *Harvard Law Review*.

Substantively, all of the warnings presented the mandatory, easy-to-recite first four components regarding the rights to silence and to counsel. But 20 percent failed to include a critical fifth admonition derived from the Supreme Court's opinion—namely, that suspects can choose to invoke their rights *at any time*. This is a serious shortcoming. When I lecture public and student audiences, I often ask something like this: "If police bring you in for questioning and you sign a waiver of your rights to silence and a lawyer, can you invoke those rights later if the situation turns ugly?" My impression, in estimating from a show of hands, is that half of all adults, mostly educated, get it wrong. Maybe it's because signing a waiver makes it feel like a contractual commitment. Whatever it is, this fifth prong of the Miranda warnings is not known to the average person as a matter of common sense.

Miranda Quiz—How'd You Do?

Difficult vocabulary peppered with legal jargon embedded in long sentences is among the barriers to Miranda comprehension. Rogers speculates, too, that because people assume they already know the rights, they don't bother to listen carefully.

It gets worse. Anthony Domanico and other researchers analyzed twenty-nine recorded sessions in Milwaukee and discovered that police sped through their reading of Miranda at a pace that was 31 percent faster than just before or just after the rest of their interviews. A speeded presentation may be tactical, to gain waivers, or it may just flow naturally from the benign fact that the warnings have become so rote that police are on autopilot. Either way, if this tendency exists elsewhere and on a larger scale, the effect would be to impair comprehension.

And there's one more disclaimer. Over the years, psychologists have developed and refined Miranda comprehension questionnaires aimed at assessing what people know of their rights and how to implement them. Performance is always measured under pristine testing circumstances—a quiet room, no distractions, no pressures. That hardly mimics the acute stress of the moment when someone stands accused of a serious crime. For many years, basic research has shown that high levels of stress impair our ability to process information. So it comes as no surprise—but is concerning—that in an experiment in which some subjects, but not others, were accused of cheating, those who were accused moments later scored lower on tests of Miranda comprehension.

Even under optimal circumstances, many American adults are ill informed about their rights. In 2010, Rogers and others published the results of a twenty-five-item "Miranda Quiz" they had created. The items were straightforward single-sentence statements; for each one, examinees indicate whether the statement is true or false. For anyone reading a book on false confessions, the questions should be easy. But when tested, both defendants held in county jails in Texas and Oklahoma and college students from that same region harbored serious misconceptions.

Consider the first prong. Is this true or false: "If you remain silent, your silence can and will be used as evidence against you." In *Miranda*, the Supreme Court stated that "it is impermissible to penalize an individual for exercising his Fifth Amendment privilege." Having the right to remain silent means that you can exercise that right now, freely, knowing that the decision to do so will not come back to bite you later. Yet roughly 30 percent of examinees believed that this statement is true—that to exercise this right can increase the risk of subsequent prosecution and conviction.

Moving on to a related second prong, that anything you say can be used against you—true or false: "If you ask for something to be 'off the record' during an interrogation, it can't be legally used against you." The warning is pretty clear. If you waive the right to silence, *anything* you say can later come back to bite you. Yet 46 percent of examinees Rogers tested incorrectly believed that this statement was true.

Now consider the right to counsel. True or false: "If you ask to speak to a lawyer, the police can ask you questions until the lawyer gets there." Again, the Supreme Court was clear. If a suspect invokes the right to counsel, all questioning must cease on the spot. Yet 35 percent of the examinees in Rogers's study believed incorrectly that police can continue to question suspects until their lawyer is physically present.

As to the words one might need to use to activate the right to counsel, true or false: "In seeking legal assistance, it means the same thing if you say, 'I want a lawyer' or 'I might want a lawyer.'" In the Supreme Court's 1994 ruling in *Davis v. U.S.*, cited earlier, the request for an attorney must be made in language that is unequivocal—no *mights*, *maybes*, or other qualifying words will be taken to communicate an invocation. Yet a whopping 62 percent of examinees Rogers tested erroneously believed this statement to be true.

With regard to the continuing nature of one's ability to invoke one's rights, true or false: "Once you give up the right to silence, it is permanent." The court was clear in *Miranda* and has not wavered since that time that suspects can activate their rights at any time. Many suspects decide to cooperate, thinking they are being interviewed as a witness but then have second thoughts once aggressively accused. In the Rogers study, however, a third of all examinees harbored the perilous belief that any waivers earlier made are permanent even after the situation turns ominous. As noted earlier, in 20 percent of the jurisdictions whose warnings Rogers had sampled, this fifth prong was not included.

Last but not least, Rogers included a couple of items pertaining to police practices of relevance to Miranda. As note earlier, it is lawful for police in the United States to present false evidence to suspects in the effort to elicit confessions. Lawful or not, it is a psychologically coercive tactic that can get innocent people to confess. I would argue that it can also get innocent people to waive their rights.

Imagine you're at the precinct, where a detective accuses you of a fictitious crime, something that never even happened. Personally, I do not know very many folks who can sit silent, lips sealed, in the face of a false accusation. A powerful human self-defense reflex kicks in. Yet consider this statement, true or false: "Police are legally allowed to accuse you of fictitious crimes (crimes that never happened) during the interrogation." More than half of all examinees incorrectly believed that this statement was false. If it happens to them, they may well speak up, thereby waiving the right to silence.

Adolescents and Other Limited Populations

If normal fully formed adults lack a full comprehension of Miranda, one would imagine that teenagers and adults with limited cognitive abilities in particular face an uphill climb.

I do not use the word "pioneer" loosely, but the word aptly describes Thomas Grisso, currently professor emeritus of psychiatry at the University of Massachusetts Medical School. Along with Steven Drizin, Gisli Gudjonsson, Richard Leo, and Allison Redlich, I was fortunate to have convinced Tom to coauthor our 2010 white paper on false confessions for the American Psychology-Law Society. Tom's background was perfect. In 1975, as forensic psychology was coming together as a discipline, he was awarded a research grant from the National Institute of Mental Health (NIMH) to study whether juveniles understood their still-new Miranda rights. Six years later, he summarized this work in a classic book titled, *Juveniles' Waiver of Rights: Legal and Psychological Competence* (he would later publish an update accompanied by a manual, test materials, and scoring guidelines).

Basically, Grisso developed a set of objective instruments that forensic psychologists could use to assess whether individual defendants are competent to waive their rights. At the outset, he determined that two important questions loomed: whether a suspect (1) *understands* the words and phrases used in the Miranda warning and (2) *appreciates* how to implement the rights conveyed by the warning and the consequences that follow from the decision they make.

Drawing on principles of developmental psychology, Grisso, Naomi Goldstein, and other juvenile justice researchers have produced a wealth of research showing that juveniles—particularly those younger than sixteen—have limited Miranda comprehension and appreciation compared to adults (not too surprisingly, the same can be said for individuals with a low IQ and other intellectual disabilities). Most teenagers struggle with various words that are often used in Miranda warnings. Even more, they struggle on measures of appreciation. For example, many teens believe that remaining silent is futile because at some point police and judges can force them to talk. And while many understand that they can have an attorney, they fail to grasp the attorney's role as a private, confidential, personal advocate. If either of these misconceptions was true, of course, then Miranda's constitutional protections would amount to nothing more than hollow promises.

It is hard to overstate the need for using objective measures to determine if young or cognitively limited defendants are competent to waive their rights. The case of sixteen-year-old Brendan Dassey, the "costar" of Netflix's *Making a Murderer*, illustrates why. Dassey was a malleable suspect. He was young, he had a low IQ, he lacked confidence in his own grasp of reality, and he was subjected to a Reid-style interrogation built for adults.

In 2018, the Seventh Circuit Court affirmed his conviction on the ground that Dassey had competently waived his Miranda rights, which constituted prima facie proof that his ensuing statement was voluntary. According to the Seventh Circuit, the proof was in the Dassey tapes, which showed that as the detective read the warning, the boy visibly "nodded in agreement." The naiveté of this ruling should be obvious. Dassey may have nodded, but that gesture may well betray the acquiescence to authority of a low-IQ teen. He might have been too embarrassed to admit a lack of understanding, not agreement with the waiving of one's constitutional rights (of course, every innocent exoneree tricked or pressured into confession had first brushed off Miranda).

Police as Miranda Tacticians

In 1996, Professor Richard Leo observed 182 interrogations, live or on videotape, in three California police departments. Across all sessions, he saw that nearly four out of five suspects waived their rights. In an effort to understand this important result, Leo published a companion article in *Law and Society Review*. The title: "Miranda's Revenge: Police Interrogation as a Confidence Game." In the course of his fieldwork, he noted that several detectives invoked the metaphor of a confidence trick, poker bluff, or skilled salesmanship to describe their approach. "As one police instructor in an interrogation training class I attended proudly declared," Leo reported, "We are con men . . . and con men never tell the mark they've been had."

Confidence games are as old as Western civilization. Maria Konnikova, author of the best seller *The Confidence Game*, agrees. The essence is the exchange of the con's trust for the mark's hope. There are short cons, like the shell game, or three-card monte, dating back to the fifteenth century, in which a shill pretends to align with the mark to cheat the dealer, while in fact conspiring with the dealer to cheat the mark. And there are long cons that can take weeks, months, or years to cultivate, like Ponzi schemes, which lure investors by leading them to believe in the success of a nonexistent venture through quick initial returns peeled from money previously invested by others. The Mr. Big interrogation technique, described in chapter 4, is an "effective" long con aimed at inducing a suspect to confess as an act of hope for a good life in Mr. Big's organization.

Describing a psychological interrogation as a confidence game is hardly a controversial proposition—regardless of whether the final product is a true confession, false confession, or continued resistance. But the first step in cultivating a suspect is to gain the necessary first act of compliance: an apparently voluntary waiver of Miranda rights. Needless to say, it is a whole lot easier to get the waiver than to get a confession.

Drawing on over five hundred hours of interrogations, Leo observed a host of tactical approaches that police used to elicit the high waiver rate. The social psychologist in me cannot help but cringe at the parallels to Robert Cialdini's seminal research on compliance. Professor emeritus of psychology and marketing at Arizona State University, Cialdini has observed salespeople and other masters of influence, leading him and other researchers to test an array of real-life compliance techniques that are based on making two or more related requests. *Click!* The first request sets the trap. *Snap!* The second captures the mark. Once caught in these traps, the unwary victim finds it difficult to escape. In *Influence: Science and Practice*, Cialdini describes these techniques in vivid detail. They go by assorted colorful names—such as the foot-in-the-door, the door-in-the-face, the lure, the one-in-five prize technique, the dump-and-chase technique, the disrupt-then-reframe technique, and the driving-toward-a-goal technique.

In cultivating a suspect, the detective's first order of business is to establish a rapport with the suspect by talking about the neighborhood, food, music, or sports, or anything else that enables them to present as an ally. Upon meeting, the detective might shake hands and inquire as to the suspect's well-being. A simple "Can I get you anything?" goes a long way, so detectives may ingratiate themselves through the offer of water, coffee, cigarettes, or a restroom break. Compliance researchers know that the norm of reciprocity is universal, unspoken but potent: I brought you a bottle of water; now it's your turn to waive your rights.

Every confidence game, short and long, requires a foundation of trust. Once that trust is established, the detective will try to convince the suspect that he or she is inclined to help but cannot do so unless the suspect waives Miranda. Leo described one of many exchanges in this way: "The detective said that he wanted to hear the suspect's side of the story but that he could do so only if the suspect gave us permission to talk to him. The suspect immediately denied any wrongdoing. The detective responded that we could not listen to his side of the story just yet."

In another interrogation that Leo observed, the detective flat-out said to the suspect, "You're implicated. Whether or not you're actually guilty everyone says you did it. Everyone is pointing to you. . . . We need to get your side of the story, but first we have to advise you of your rights."

As for those warnings, many detectives would go on to characterize the process as a mere formality and construct implicit waivers that lead suspects to submit to questioning. One detective prefaced his recitation by saying, "We just need to get this out of the way, it is not a big deal—you probably know these better than I do." If the suspect balks, the detective might exploit the scarcity principle by presenting Miranda as a one-time-only, limited-opportunity, exploding-offer, last chance to tell their side of the story. As reported in *Homicide*, David Simon saw police officers telling suspects, even more explicitly, that they could no longer help them if they were to call a lawyer.

Social psychologists Kyle Scherr and Stephanie Madon devised laboratory experiments involving college students that showed that the tactics of the con may well increase the waiver rate. In one study, they accused innocent students of cheating on an experimental task and told them they would have to discuss the incident with the principal investigator, a professor. Subjects were informed that they had a right to have a student advocate present during that meeting, or they could waive that right. The experimenter led some subjects to believe that their decision could have implications for how the situation would be resolved. Others were told that this decision was trivial. Mirroring the typical crime suspect, very few students asked for a student advocate—and they were more likely to waive that right when the waiver was trivialized. In a similar follow-up study, subjects were also more likely to take a pass on the student advocate when told that most students tend to waive that right.

The Phenomenology of Innocence

Bring to mind an occasion in which you were accused of something you didn't do, maybe by a parent, teacher, employer, friend, or romantic partner. Chances are good, if not virtually perfect, that you did not sit passive and silent without shaking your head, raising your voice, and other otherwise defending yourself. This is human nature, and these reactions are even more likely when the accuser is a detective and the accusation concerns something big like the commission of a violent felony. Silence is not a natural response.

In 2016, I appeared on an episode of CBS's *48 Hours* about the Melissa Calusinski case, which I've described elsewhere. Afterward,

Erin Moriarty—an Emmy-award-winning news anchor who also happens to have a law degree—asked me whether *Miranda* doesn't, after all, serve to protect innocent people who are falsely accused. She was right, of course, that this was the *Miranda* court's fantasy. But, as I put it, "Once we get past people with limited abilities and children, the problem is not that people don't *comprehend* those rights, it's that people who are innocent don't think they *need* them. They may understand what the rights are, they just don't think it applies to them because they didn't do anything wrong."

Since that interview, I've worked on several additional cases in which police induced innocent people to confess, by hook or by crook, and each of these confessions was ostensibly preceded by a knowing, intelligent, and voluntary waiver. Over and over again, I would ask, Why didn't you just stop talking and get a lawyer? And over and over again, the exoneree would shoot me a puzzled look with a shrug of the shoulders as though I had asked the stupidest question: "I didn't need a lawyer," they would say. "I didn't do anything wrong."

In an article subtitled "Does *Innocence* Put *Innocents* at Risk?," I made sense of what false confessors had been saying to me. It was not a fluke; they had all said the same thing in almost the same words. Accompanying the human self-defense reflex, two sets of beliefs, widely held, underlie the innocent person's willingness to speak without a lawyer.

The first is the *belief in a just world* (abbreviated BJW in psych journals) where people eventually, even if not immediately, get what they deserve and deserve what they get. It's a world in which hard work and clean living pay off and where lazy and sinful lifestyles do not. This tendency to attribute a causal linkage between behaviors and consequences enables people to expect moral balance and to maintain a personal sense of security. To believe otherwise is to concede a capriciousness that renders us anxious and vulnerable to the cruel twists and turns of fate.

Individuals differ in the extent to which they embrace just-world beliefs. But the normative tendencies are in place, which is why social psychologist Melvin Lerner in 1980 referred to BJW as "A Fundamental Delusion." Proof of just-world beliefs can be drawn from the English language, with "You get to reap what you sow" on the upside, and "What goes around comes around" on the downside.

Overlaid upon this deep-structure belief in a just world is a more personal, and often incorrect, *illusion of transparency*. Several years ago, Thomas Gilovich and others conducted a series of studies showing that people tend to overestimate the extent to which their thoughts, emotions, and other internal states "leak out," making them transparent to others, even strangers.

In one study, subjects who were asked to tell lies overestimated by a long shot the proportion of observers who would detect their deception. In a second study, subjects were asked to sample a foul-tasting drink without showing their disgust—a situation one might encounter while dining at a friend's place. They masked their revulsion to the foul drink relative to others pretty well. But then they overestimated the number of observers who could identify which of the drinks were foul tasting.

Appreciative of the criminal justice implications, Gilovich opened the report of this research with a passage from Edgar Allan Poe's 1843 short story "The Tell-Tale Heart." The scene involves a guilty protagonist who tries to stay composed while questioned by three police officers investigating a murder. It was not an easy interview; unbeknownst to the officers, they happened to be standing directly above the victim's hidden body. As the protagonist becomes more and more anxious, thinking that the officers know he is lying, he begins to hear what he thinks is his victim's heart beating underneath the floorboards. The sound he hears is his own heart. But he becomes convinced that it's the victim's, that the officers can hear it, and that they know he is a murderer. So he gives himself away. In Poe's words:

> Was it possible they heard it not? . . . no, no! They heard! They suspected! They knew! They were making a mockery of my horror! . . . I could bear those hypocritical smiles no longer. . . . "Villains!" I shrieked, "dissemble no more! I admit the deed! Tear up the planks! Here, here! It is the beating of his hideous heart!"

This scene depicts the criminal who fully appreciates the need for silence—or risk getting busted. But of course, the illusion of transparency works two ways. Just as the perpetrator fears the detection that comes from being transparent, the innocent suspect is comforted by it. Trusting that the world is just and that their innocence is transparent, innocent suspects, having nothing to fear, will err toward waiving their rights to silence and to counsel.

Armed with this backdrop of psychological theory and the self-reports of individuals wrongfully convicted, Rebecca Norwick and I put this hypothesis to the test. Our objective was to create a situation in which subjects who committed a mock crime, or not, were informed that they would be questioned by a detective, and were offered a financial bonus if that detective determined that they were innocent. By random assignment, we inserted one more wrinkle into the procedure: The detective, who was blinded as to each subject's guilt or innocence, presented himself at the outset as neutral, sympathetic, or outright hostile.

Seventy-two college students were recruited for this experiment. One at a time, upon their arrival, Becca greeted each subject outside the lab, explained the situation, and advised that if they found themselves in a difficult spot, they should do whatever was necessary to protect themselves. "You can choose to talk to the police or not, whatever you think will help your cause." To mimic the real-life suspect's incentives, she told subjects that the study might require that they return for a second phase—a "trial" for which they would not be compensated. "Whether there is a trial phase will depend on whether there is sufficient evidence that you are guilty," she said. "So do what it takes in your long-term best interest to either avoid going to trial or to be acquitted."

At that point, Becca handed the subject an envelope containing one of two sets of instructions. The *guilty set* laid out detailed directions on how to steal a $100 bill from a drawer in a nearby classroom; the *innocent set* directed subjects merely to open and shut an empty drawer without stealing anything. After subjects followed their respective directions, they were taken upstairs to an interrogation cubicle furnished with a wooden table, two chairs, a one-way mirror, and a video camera stationed on a tripod.

Each subject waited alone in the cubicle for five minutes. Then a middle-aged man in civilian clothing came in holding a folder, introduced himself as Detective McCarthy, and told the subject that they were under suspicion for stealing money that was missing from the building. The detective (actually a money manager in real life) said that the first order of business was to read subjects their Miranda rights. At that point, one of three variations was administered.

In a *neutral* condition, the detective read the Miranda warning verbatim without added comment and presented a waiver form to the subject for a decision and signature.

In the *sympathetic ally* condition, he encouraged the subject to relax, offered a drink, and described the waiver process as a mere formality. Although you may look guilty, he said, "I think you deserve a chance to tell your side of the story."

In the *hostile—closed-minded* condition, the detective angrily prefaced his reading of the rights. "I am sick of this happening. It's not the first time money's been stolen here. I know you did this and I don't want to hear any lies from you."

Following one of these presentations, the detective handed subjects a rights form and pen and instructed them to reread the rights and sign one of two statements: "I am willing to make a statement and answer questions at this time" or "I am not willing to make a statement or answer questions at this time." Afterward, he asked if they were sure of the decision they made and left the room. At that point, Becca reappeared, told subjects that they would not be interrogated, and administered a questionnaire for them to explain their decision.

The results were telling. Overall, 58 percent of the seventy-two subjects signed a waiver of their rights. More important, as we had predicted, we found a striking effect for guilt or innocence: Eighty-one percent of all innocent suspects waived their rights compared to only 36 percent of those who were guilty. Everything else about their situations was identical, so there was no doubt: innocence increased the waiver rate. In fact, the innocence effect was more powerful than we had anticipated. Even in the uncomfortable condition in which the detective was hostile and closed minded, two-thirds of all innocent subjects decided to waive their rights.

After the experiment was over, Becca asked each subject to explain in writing the reason for their decision to invoke or waive their rights. Interestingly, even when guilty and innocent subjects made the same decision, they articulated different reasons for doing so. Those who had committed the mock crime said they waived their rights for strategic self-presentation reasons: "If I didn't, he'd figure I was guilty" or "I would've looked suspicious if I chose not to talk." Although some innocent subjects were also concerned about how it would look, the vast majority explained that they waived their rights precisely because they were innocent and believed that the truth would prevail: "I did nothing wrong" or "I didn't have anything to hide." They may have been subjects in a lab experiment, but they sounded just like the exonerees I've spoken to.

With tragic results, it reminds me of the case of Peter Reilly, the eighteen-year-old who falsely confessed to killing his mother. When asked by author Donald Connery why he did not invoke his rights, Reilly said, "My state of mind was that I hadn't done anything wrong and I felt that only a criminal really needed an attorney, and this was all going to come out in the wash."

Since we reported on this experiment, other researchers have replicated the finding—especially among innocents who believe in a just world, and in Canada as well as the United States. In fact, innocent people may relinquish other rights too. Shortly after we published our Miranda article, Professor Gary Wells, a good friend and colleague, and the world's leading expert on eyewitness identifications, told me that Louisville police would often ask suspects to waive their right to a full lineup, surrounded by foils, in favor of a one-on-one "show-up." Common sense, empirical research, and the courts have long realized the protective nature of the lineup. Would innocent people sacrifice that protection out of a naïve belief that they are invulnerable to misidentification?

Gary and I tested this hypothesis. We set up a situation in which some college students but not others were directed to steal a package from a mailbox in a crowded public area, toss it into a trash container, and flee to a preset location, where there they were apprehended by a college security officer and "processed." Other students reported to a different location, engaged in a noncriminal act, and returned, also to be apprehended.

All subjects were offered a financial incentive to avoid being charged. The officer then revealed to each subject that there was an eyewitness present and that they fit his general description of the culprit. The officer said that he had to wait for additional photos to arrive before he could assemble a lineup. He then offered a one-on-one show-up as an alternative. "In other words, I can show the witness just your photo to see if he or she identifies you." Among guilty subjects, more than half chose to wait for a full lineup. Yet in the innocent condition, every single subject waived that right. Why? The reason they stated later was clear: they were not even present in the vicinity of the crime; they had no reason to fear identification in a one-on-one show-up.

I should add one particularly unforeseen consequence that can follow from the phenomenology of innocence. It can lead innocent people to confess. I have long known that certain individuals are more vulnerable than others and that certain situations are more perilous than others; these are classic personal and situation risk factors. But innocence is the great deterrent to a false confessions, isn't it?

Then I spoke to an innocent individual in Missouri who agreed to confess after hours of interrogation and resistance. "What finally broke you?" I asked. At first, I could not understand his explanation—that detectives said they had collected physical evidence to be tested. Then he explained further. Knowing he was innocent, he figured he would later be absolved by that evidence. Essentially, and in contrast to everyone's belief that innocence is the great deterrent to confession, this beleaguered man capitulated precisely *because he was innocent*.

A second exoneree whose case I worked on later said the same thing. At sixteen, high school sophomore Jeffrey Deskovic of Peekskill, New York, was wrongfully convicted of the rape and murder of a classmate based only on a confession. After sixteen years, Deskovic was DNA exonerated and released. In an interview with Fernanda Santos of the *New York Times*, who asked why he confessed, Deskovic explained that the police told him they collected DNA and sent it to the lab for testing. "Believing in the criminal justice system and being fearful for myself, I told them what they wanted to hear," he said. "I thought it was all going to be OK in the end." Once released, Deskovic continued his education and earned a master's degree in criminal justice at John Jay College. He also went on to found a nonprofit organization committed to the wrongfully convicted.

Would innocent people really confess to police out of a belief that they will be exculpated by future evidence? Armed with this counterintuitive hypothesis, Jennifer Perillo and I conducted a series of laboratory experiments, published in 2011, in which we accused students of cheating in violation of the university's honor code and urged them to sign a confession. In a control group, not one innocent confessed. But then we said that the session was being recorded by a surveillance camera that would later be examined by a technician, half the innocent subjects signed. Afterward, they cited the prospective evidence as the reason for that decision. To an innocent suspect, the "threat" of proof represents a promise of future exoneration, which paradoxically can make it easier to confess.

Over the years, a diverse array of innocent men and women have confessed to crimes they did not commit. But these individuals also had something else in common: They all waived their rights. Whether you are protected by Miranda depends on how old you are, how smart you are, how the warnings are phrased, and how calm your situation is. It also depends on your mindset, whether you have a consciousness of guilt or a phenomenology of innocence. Research shows that the innocence effect is overwhelming—which means that Miranda does not adequately protect the citizens who need it most: those accused of crimes they did not commit.

Custody—the Courts versus Human Nature

The U.S. Supreme Court ruled that police must Mirandize only suspects who are "in custody" and hence not free to leave. That's more easily said than ruled on. Since then, judges have struggled to define what this essentially psychological construct means.

In *Miranda*, the court defined a custodial interrogation as "questioning initiated by law enforcement officers after a person has been taken into custody or otherwise deprived of his freedom of action in any significant way." Elsewhere in that opinion, the court cited some concrete indicia, such as arrest, police use of intimidation, expressions of hostility, trickery, restriction of personal liberty, and an unfamiliar environment.

In *Stansbury v. California* (1994), the Supreme Court considered a case in which a police officer had failed to Mirandize a suspect because he did not believe the suspect was in custody. In a unanimous ruling, the court held that "an officer's subjective and undisclosed view concerning whether the person being interrogated is a suspect is irrelevant to the assessment [of] whether the person is in custody." Instead, any inquiry into whether a suspect was in custody involves a consideration of the totality of *objective circumstances* of the situation, and hence a determination of whether a *reasonable person* in that situation would feel trapped and unable to leave.

Although no comprehensive list of objective criteria exists, the courts have variously cited as relevant whether police explicitly advised that a suspect was free to leave; whether the suspect was restrained—as in handcuffed, held in a room with the door locked, and stripped of shoes, clothing, cell phone, or car keys; and whether coercive interrogation tactics were used, such as keeping the suspect from friends and family, using physical force or discomfort, making accusations, and using threats, promises, and deceit to elicit a confession. Using these types of factors as a guide, police officers must make real-time assessments of how a reasonable average person would perceive the situation.

Can a police officer, or later a judge, determine whether a reasonable person would feel trapped or free to leave a situation that is potentially in dispute? For starters, classic research shows that actors and observers diverge in their perceptions—specifically, observers (police, judges) will attribute more freedom and responsibility to actors in a situation than the actors (suspects) will attribute to themselves. This phenomenon is so basic that it's called the "actor-observer effect."

Custody may be determined as a matter of law, but it is an inherently psychological construct. While still in graduate school, my student Fabiana Alceste (now a professor at Butler University) was drawn in by this construct, which was essential to Miranda and yet not subject to empirical research. Working in my lab, Fabi spearheaded an intensive two-phased experiment to test the assumption that observers can divine the subjective perceptions of a reasonable person undergoing a police-suspect interaction.

In Phase 1, college students were seated alone in a waiting room when a fellow student (actually a confederate aligned with the experimenter) returned from the testing room to "discover" that her wallet was missing. Visibly distressed, she immediately contacted campus security, which summoned a guard to the lab to investigate. Timothy Luke, an advanced doctoral student familiar with the Reid technique, played the role of guard (he is now a professor at the University of Gothenburg, in Sweden). This situation felt real; as far as the subjects were concerned a theft had occurred, and they were being questioned about it.

By random assignment, the objective circumstances of the situation were varied to model a classic interview versus interrogation. In some sessions, Timothy questioned the subject the way an officer might interview a witness. Fabi, the experimenter, remained in the room, Timothy left the door open, and he asked brief non-accusatory questions. In other sessions, he mimicked the Reid-style interrogation of a suspect. He asked Fabi to leave, made it a point to shut the door, and asked more accusatory questions. The interrogations lasted longer. Unbeknownst to the subjects at the time, these sessions were video recorded with a concealed camera. Afterward, Phase 1 subjects filled out a questionnaire about the experience, indicating in particular whether they felt free to leave. In Phase 2, we recruited a new group of subjects to observe a single interview or interrogation and indicate whether, in their view, the subject was free to leave.

The results were clear. Regardless of whether they were interviewed or interrogated, most Phase 1 subjects *did not feel free to leave*. The "noncustodial" interview condition proved particularly interesting. In contrast to the interrogation, subjects who underwent a benign interview confirmed that they felt like witnesses, not suspects. Yet while Phase 2 observers saw these subjects as perfectly free to pick up and leave, the suspects themselves did not feel that way. Reminiscent of the classic actor-observer effect, this divergence of perceptions calls into serious question the assumption that a reasonable-person standard can be used to determine custody.

A follow-up study was even more telling. Consistently, the courts have asserted that the clearest indication of a noncustodial situation is when police explicitly advise suspects that they are free to go. Enough said. But does this advisement have the assumed effect? Fabi re-created the interview condition of the same paradigm. This time, however, the security guard, at the outset, told some suspects but not others: "Just so you know, you're free to leave. I'm not holding you here. If you don't want to talk to me or need to leave for any reason, you're free to do that." That advisement screams loud and clear. Yet while subjects in that condition knew that they were free to leave, objectively speaking, they did not *feel* any freer compared to the no-advisement control group.

The courts may think they can objectify the custody inquiry, but the potential for ambiguity remains. Without arrest as a custodial bright line, objective circumstances are subject to interpretation by different individuals from different perspectives. Can police officers and judges agree among themselves and with each other on whether a suspect is in custody? To find out, Alceste and I tested 875 people, including police officers and judges, two legally relevant populations; social psychologists, scientific experts on situational influences; and a sample of lay adults, a population of prospective suspects.

Online, the subjects of this experiment read one of three vignettes depicting a high-custody police-suspect encounter, a low-custody encounter, or an ambiguous situation that contained a mix of factors. Afterward, we asked a number of questions starting with, "Was this suspect free to leave?" and "Did the suspect *feel* free to leave?" The results revealed a disparity of perceptions among police, a disparity of perceptions among judges, and the finding that social psychologists were better aligned with lay subjects in their perceptions of what it means to be in custody. In a nutshell, police and judges, but not social psychologists, overrated how free suspects would feel during an interrogation, compared to laypeople. Custody is a squishy concept on which Miranda decisions are made in the police station and later judged in court.

Invoking Rights—the Optics of Silence

People waive their self-protective Miranda rights once advised at an inconsistent rate, and for many reasons—including a lack of comprehension, the tactical con artistry of the presentation, and the naïve phenomenology of innocence. But there's one more factor that rears its ugly head in all sorts of research: the belief that invoking one's rights comes at a steep cost.

Many people harbor the understandable fear that silence and the request for an attorney can be used against them, or even that they could be punished or prosecuted for it. And Miranda warnings seldom contain language to offset this misconception. Analyzing hundreds of warnings from across the country, Rogers found that not a single one assured suspects that exercising their rights would *not* be used against them.

In the 1965 case *Griffin v. California*, the Supreme Court ruled that a defendant had an absolute Fifth Amendment right not to testify at trial. Prosecutors are not permitted to comment on a defendant's failure to take the stand, and judges may admonish the jury not to draw an adverse inference. With regard to a suspect's silence at the police station, the *Miranda* court stated: "In accord with our decision today, it is impermissible to penalize an individual for exercising his Fifth Amendment privilege when he is under police custodial interrogation. The prosecution may not, therefore, use at trial the fact that he stood mute or claimed his privilege in the face of accusation."

As with other aspects of Miranda, the courts have eroded the protection against adverse inference through various exceptions—such as distinguishing among a suspect's silence before arrest, after arrest but before warnings, and after both arrest and warnings. Although the *Miranda* court stated that suspects in custody could exercise their right "in any manner," that is no longer true.

This raises some unsettling psychological questions, the most elemental being: Do people naturally, even without prompting, draw adverse inferences from a defendant's exercise of rights? In 1957, Sidney Hook wrote a book titled *Common Sense and the Fifth Amendment*, in which he argued that invoking the Fifth in court establishes a presumption of guilt. Over the years, research with mock juries has shown that Hook was right. In one study, for example, the defendant who testified but didn't answer specific questions, or who declined to take the stand altogether, was more likely to be judged guilty than one who testified and answered all of the questions.

More recently, we looked at the inferences people draw from silence and the presence of an attorney. Subjects read about a suspect who denied involvement in a burglary while being questioned by police. At one point, that questioning became accusatory, at which point the suspect continued to deny wrongdoing or else said "no comment" to all remaining questions. The difference in perceptions was not subtle: people were far more likely to see the suspect as guilty when he invoked his rights than when he continued to answer questions. In fact, that difference persisted even when we reminded subjects about the right to silence and admonished them not to draw an adverse inference. (While you're at it, try *not* to conjure up an image of a white bear.)

THE NEED TO LOOK ELSEWHERE FOR PROTECTION

After more than a half century, *Miranda v. Arizona* (1966) has failed to fulfill its promise. Two simultaneous sets of developments, in juxtaposition with one another, define the magnitude of this failure. On the one hand, U.S. courts have systematically demolished the Supreme Court's holding, leading its original proponents to pronounce the body dead.

Virtually every aspect of these constitutional protections has been rendered impotent. The courts have set a lower and lower bar, if any, as to what constitutes a sufficient warning—in wordage, presentation, and context; they have set an unimaginably high bar as to what constitutes an invocation of one's rights that police must adhere to; they have set no limits on the tactics police may use to contextualize Miranda in ways that ensure waivers and circumvent the requirements, if invoked; they have offered no concrete, empirically defensible definition of what it means to be "in custody," permitting police, for example, to invite suspects to the station and advise them they are not under arrest, or to deploy the Perkins ruse, by which undercover officers can interrogate unwitting suspects locked in a jail cell without apprising them of their rights. The list of corrosive rulings is extensive, yielding "death by a thousand cuts."

The U.S. judiciary is sadly out of synch with reality. As the courts proceeded to erode Miranda, a revolution at the interface of science and law had begun to use DNA to expose wrongful convictions—many of which involved police-induced false confessions. As the judiciary steadily and repeatedly downgraded Miranda, developments were unfolding that screamed for more protection of suspects, not less. This asynchrony between the courts and the science of wrongful convictions makes you wonder how judges could be so out of touch.

For the purpose of protecting yourself, your children, your friends, and others who stand accused, it's time to learn how to invoke Miranda and to realize that other means of reform are necessary.

11

PROPOSED REFORMS TO POLICY AND PRACTICE

I opened this book by describing my "wall of faces," a glossy poster-sized copy of which hangs in my office and is also on a PowerPoint slide I use when I teach and lecture. This wall presents a matrix of twenty-eight color portrait photos that I update almost annually.

The pictures and the stories they tell are a varied lot. They are men and women; black, brown, and white; children as young as thirteen and fully formed adults; people of different backgrounds, from states all over the country and countries all over the world. A quick glance would suggest that these individuals had little in common. But in fact, each and every one confessed to a crime, often one that was unimaginably monstrous, that they did not commit.

As to the widespread belief that "I would never confess to a crime if I didn't do it," I'd hazard to guess that each and every one of the individuals on my wall would have said the same. These individuals, others whose stories I have touched on, and the many more whose cases I am not even aware of have more in common than just a false confession.

- Innocence notwithstanding, each and every one was targeted for investigation by police and on a hunch that proved wrong.
- Each was isolated and subjected to a modern-day psychological interrogation, a confidence game aimed to stress, confuse, and mislead suspects under intense pressure.

- Each was propped up to handwrite, sign, or recite on camera a confession, coauthored by a detective, rehearsed, and filled with lurid crime details, apologies, and other cues that scream "credible."
- In most cases, the confession corrupted the reports of eyewitnesses, character witnesses, informants, alibi witnesses, forensic examiners, and other evidence.
- In many cases, the confessions led prosecutors to offer, defense attorneys to recommend, and innocent defendants to accept, guilty pleas in court in lieu of trial.
- In all cases, those who refused to accept a plea offer were later convicted at trial by a judge or jury; in many cases, their convictions withstood a challenge on appeal.
- In all cases, the psychological aftershock and stigma attached to the false confessor persisted into, and long after, exoneration.
- Last but not least, these individuals have in common that they waived their Miranda rights—a constitutional "kill switch" that offers, in theory, their only means of protection.

The false-confessions problem is complex and multifaceted—which means that more than one solution is needed to prevent it from happening in the first place and then spreading downstream like a deadly pollutant. First, the system needs to be reformed to prevent police from pulling suspects in on a hunch, using psychologically manipulative interrogation tactics, and eliciting narrative confessions that could have been produced in Hollywood. Second, it is necessary to ensure that prosecutors vet confessions more carefully, that crime lab protocols demand double-blind forensic examiners, and that judges take a more active role in vetting guilty pleas. Third, the system needs to enable smarter fact finding among judges, juries, appeals courts, and parole boards. Fourth, the public, consumers of justice, needs to be better educated about all this, enough to protect themselves, their children, and their communities.

THE JURISPRUDENCE OF CONFESSIONS—
MIXED MESSAGES FROM AMERICA'S COURTS

For me, the highlight of a weeklong trip to Israel was the opening of a lecture by Supreme Court justice Neal Hendel, an American-born justice who had previously cited my work (small world that it is, it turns out we both grew up in Brooklyn at about the same time and attended the same school). I'm glad I had a Hebrew-to-English translator shadowing his words and whispering into my ear. "We used to think of confessions as the *queen* of evidence," he said. "Now we know it's not the queen but the *joker*."

In this one sentence, Justice Hendel captured the conflicting portrayals of confession evidence that have always come from the courts—not just in Israel, and not just today, but over the course of history in the United States. American courts have always treated confession evidence with a bewildering combination of awe and trepidation—as if it were both the queen and the joker.

One the one hand, judges appreciate the power of confessions in solving crimes and locking in convictions. In *Miranda v. Arizona* (1966), an enlightened U.S. Supreme Court acknowledged that confession evidence is inherently powerful—so powerful, in the words of one legal scholar, that "the introduction of a confession makes the other aspects of a trial in court superfluous."

Yet these same courts have shown themselves to be acutely aware that police interrogation is fraught with secrecy and abuse, that it can prey on vulnerable and innocent people, and that judicial oversight is needed to ensure that confessions can be trusted.

The pages of history are clear as to the danger that lurks behind the closed doors of the interrogation room. The Salem witch trials of 1692 warned us long before colonial Americans declared independence from England. In that year, 151 men, women, and children were accused of witchcraft. Sometimes blindfolded, shackled, stripped naked, prodded with pins, beaten, deprived of sleep, and publicly humiliated, fifty-five of them confessed. Twenty who would not confess were executed.

Fast-forward to the 1819 case of Stephen and Jesse Boorn, two brothers convicted and sentenced to death in Manchester, Vermont, for killing Russell Colvin. Both brothers had confessed under pressure and were set to be hanged when Colvin, the alleged victim, was found alive.

They are not the only individuals who have confessed to a crime that was not committed—by anyone.

The U.S. courts have always fundamentally understood that people can be beaten or badgered into confession and that while some individuals are stronger and more resistant than others, everyone has a breaking point.

The courts have also understood that this type of coercion cannot be tolerated for two reasons: accuracy and fairness. First and foremost, coercion compromises the reliability of evidence, causing too many innocent people to confess. Second, coercion does not constitute fair play because it violates our constitutional rights to due process and against self-incrimination.

When it comes to confessions elicited by brute force, the courts have shown little tolerance. The final straw came in 1936 in *Brown v. Mississippi*, where the Supreme Court unanimously reversed the convictions of three black man who had been whipped, pummeled, and tortured into confessing to a murder and declared that confessions taken in these ways would be barred from evidence.

Here's the problem: while judges today understand what was wrong with the *Brown* confessions, they do not understand what's wrong with the subtler psychological tactics that police started to use in the 1940s—and to this day. Incredibly, today's interrogators manipulate suspects into thinking that confession serves their personal self-interest. Using a multitude of techniques, they communicate promises and threats "under the radar" without ever using the words. Suspects know what's being implied, and the courts allow it.

Again, contradictions abound. In *Bram v. United States* (1897), the Supreme Court came down hard on tactics that communicate threats and promises. In the court's words, a confession must "not be extracted by any sort of threat or violence, and not obtained by any direct or implied promises, however slight." Yet many courts went on to disregard and ultimately discard *Bram,* permitting police to communicate promises and threats under the radar, by what cognitive psychologists call "pragmatic implication."

Today's police are thus permitted to tell suspects that what happened was not their fault, externalizing blame, and expressing sympathy—"soft" tactics that imply leniency if not outright immunity from prosecution.

In *Miranda*, the Supreme Court condemned the psychological approach known as the Reid technique, noting that it lacked transparency and that "without proper safeguards the process of in-custody interrogation of persons suspected or accused of crime contains inherently compelling pressures which work to undermine the individual's will to resist."

Yet three years later, in *Frazier v. Cupp* (1969), the same court green-lighted trickery and deceit on the misassumption that these tactics do not put innocents at risk. As a result, today's police are permitted to lie to suspects about the evidence, big lies, brazen lies, repeatedly and without limitation, pretending to have DNA, fingerprints, witnesses, and other incriminating evidence that doesn't exist. To this day, the court has set no boundaries on these fraudulent tactics.

A hundred-plus years of psychological research warns of the risks. But judges are not psychologists; they have not read this literature. Hence, the "joker" often wears the crown of a "queen."

Recognizing that *Miranda* does not protect innocents accused of a crime, I offer a three-tiered model of best practices. I will argue that it is necessary to reform three aspects of the criminal justice system. These remedies have four objectives: (1) to produce confession evidence that is more diagnostic of guilt; (2) to ensure that post-confession safeguards minimize sham corroborations and other cascading effects of false confessions that slip through the cracks; (3) to make judges and juries smarter fact finders; and (4) to educate the public about police investigation practices so they can better protect themselves and their children.

MANDATORY RECORDING OF INTERVIEWS AND INTERROGATIONS

At the request of the American Psychology–Law Society, a division of the APA, a group of top-tiered scholars wrote a white paper on false confessions. Joining me were Professors Steven Drizin, Thomas Grisso, Gisli Gudjonsson, Richard Leo, and Allison Redlich. The paper was published in 2010.

After thoroughly reviewing the relevant literature, we landed on this most important remedy: "Without equivocation, our most essential recommendation is to lift the veil of secrecy from the interrogation process in favor of the principle of transparency. Specifically, *all custodial interviews and interrogations of felony suspects should be videotaped in their entirety and with a camera angle that focuses equally on the suspect and interrogator.*"

This proposal is hardly new. In his classic 1932 book *Convicting the Innocent*, Edwin Borchard expressed concern that police abuses during interrogations led to involuntary and unreliable confessions. His solution, utilizing the technology of the time, was to make "phonographic records [of interrogations] which shall alone be introducible in court." In England, under the Police and Criminal Evidence Act of 1984, the mandatory requirement for tape recording police interviews was introduced to safeguard suspects and the integrity of the process. At first resisted by law enforcement, this requirement to this day has positively transformed the way police interviews are conducted and evaluated.

Don't confuse the call for interrogations to be recorded with the common practice of questioning a suspect off camera and then turning the camera on for a post-interrogation confession. Beginning in 1975, the Bronx County district attorney, Mario Merola, initiated a program to do just that. After officers convinced a suspect to confess, they would take him to the DA's office for an on-camera confession. Compared to the lifeless recitation of written statements reread in court, the theatrics were riveting; the effect was potent. Merola was later quoted in the *New York Times* as saying, "We get a conviction in virtually every case."

The practice of videotaping confessions was adopted in short order throughout New York City, in Chicago, and elsewhere in the country. The result is a Hollywood-style confession, a performance authored, scripted, and rehearsed in ways unknown to the prosecutor, judge, and jury. Yet prosecutors are supposed to vet evidence provided by police in determining probable cause; judges are supposed to rule on whether a confession was taken voluntarily or coerced; and juries are supposed to determine if the details contained within the confession originated with the suspect, indicating guilt beyond a reasonable doubt.

I don't see how any fact finder is sufficiently competent to make these judgments on the basis of such limited information. The best way to increase their competence is to mandate for all cases that *the entire process* of interviewing and interrogation—not just the final production—be video recorded. Importantly, "the entire process" has both a temporal component and a visual-spatial component: from *start to finish*, and from a *"neutral" camera angle*.

Despite repeated calls for the electronic recording of interrogations, it has been the subject of perennial debate. The practice used to draw strong resistance from the entire law enforcement community. Some of the opposition was pragmatic. Before the first portable camcorders came to market in the 1980s, analog videotape cameras were large, bulky, expensive, stationed on a tripod, and connected to recorders of limited storage capacity. Now that the digital revolution has completely altered the financial and logistical calculus, at a time when everyone carries a video recorder linked to the cloud in their pocket, this objection is no longer relevant.

Setting aside these pragmatics, law enforcement resistance is also based on strategic considerations—notably, the fear that recording will inhibit investigators in their quest for confessions; that suspects who know they are on camera will invoke Miranda and refuse to speak, much less incriminate themselves; and that judges and juries may not like the interrogation tactics they see deployed in these tapes.

In their inaugural 1962 edition of *Criminal Interrogations and Confessions*, Inbau and Reid warned that if a law enforcement agency videotapes one confession, raising expectations, "they may find it necessary to do so in all cases" (the most recent edition of the manual does not explicitly oppose the recording of interrogations).

Today, a wide range of professional organizations—including the American Bar Association, American Psychological Association, National Association of Criminal Defense Lawyers, National District Attorney's Association, and International Association of Chiefs of Police—have called for the video recording of custodial interrogations (what constitutes "custodial" in law is an issue for a later time). In a recent op-ed in the *New York Times*, titled "Videotape All Interrogations: Justice Demands It," my coauthor was David Thompson, president of Wicklander-Zulawski & Associates (WZ), a Chicago-based firm that trains in interviewing techniques. WZ recommends that investigators record their work from start to finish.

Thirty states, the District of Columbia, and all federal law enforcement agencies now require the recording of interrogations for some or all felonies. Thanks to Rebeca Brown, director of policy at the Innocence Project, and Thomas Sullivan, a former U.S. attorney, partner at

Jenner & Block, brilliant advocate, and colleague who passed away as I completed this chapter, a listing of those states can be found in the appendix to this book. (For an additional source on state practices, see Bang et al. 2018.)

That thirty states now record interrogations as a matter of policy is the good news. But what about everyone else? In this digital era, in which police in many cities wear body cams, civilians carry video recorders in their pocket, and storage is cheap and plentiful, why doesn't every police and sheriff's department do the same, without exception?

Let's start with the law enforcement perspective. In an article in the *American Criminal Law Review*, Sullivan interviewed hundreds of officers in U.S. police and sheriff's departments that had begun to record interrogations, often despite stiff resistance. Old habits die hard. But almost to a person, Sullivan reported, these officers became "enthusiastic supporters." Typical of this uniformly positive reaction, retired detective Jim Trainum recalls that "when videotaping was first forced upon us by the D.C. City Council, we fought it tooth and nail. Now, in the words of a top commander, we would not do it any other way."

Sullivan's respondents cited multiple benefits. Varying numbers of detectives said that recording full interrogations allows them to focus on the suspect without taking notes; that it allows them to scour the sessions afterward for any fabricated, incriminating, inconsistent, or evasive remarks the suspect may have made; and that they spend less time having to defend their on-camera confession-taking practices in court. In fact, recording deters defendants from making frivolous claims of coercion. One more benefit: the tapes can have enormous educational value. WZ routinely uses interrogation recordings from actual cases to train new investigators.

From a systemic-justice perspective, two arguments support the call for full transparency. The first is that the mere presence of a camera will dissuade police from over-manipulating suspects and encourage instead the kinds of ethical interviewing practices that are starting to reshape modern-day police work. The second is that recording provides an accurate and objective account of what transpired, enabling more accurate fact finding in court. To test these arguments empirically, and to examine the lingering argument that video recording will inhibit suspects, I submitted a grant proposal to the National Science Foundation to fund the following trio of studies.

First, my colleagues and I conducted a field study published in 2014 in which we asked sixty-one officers in a mid-sized Connecticut police department to interrogate suspects in their own interview rooms as part of a mock theft investigation. All sessions were surreptitiously recorded, but only half of the officers were informed of the recording ahead of time.

Later analysis of the recordings showed that our police subjects used the typical tools of the Reid technique. Seventy-three percent sought to establish a rapport through small talk; 65 percent used confrontational tactics, accusing suspects, challenging their denials, and calling them a liar; 65 percent used maximization tactics, threatening suspects with consequences for failing to cooperate; 85 percent communicated leniency, either explicitly upon confession or by minimizing the crime; 95 percent used the false-evidence ploy, suggesting the possibility or outright lying about the evidence.

And here's the punch line: consistent with our hypothesis, camera-informed police were less likely than the others to deploy the kinds of controversial interrogation tactics that can coerce innocent suspects. Through questionnaires we administered after the sessions, we also found that camera-informed police were perceived by suspects (all of whom were clueless as to the camera manipulation) as trying less hard to get them to confess. The mere presence of the camera forced our law enforcement subjects to dial down the intensity of interrogations—and their suspects felt the difference.

The second major argument for recording is that it preserves an accurate and objective memorial account of the tone and exchange between police and suspects. In the Central Park jogger case and so many others I've described, detectives gave one account of what happened; the suspects recollected a wholly contradictory account. Yet from these conflicting secondhand reports, the judge had to rule on whether the statements taken were voluntary; the juries had to determine if the statements were true. Too often everyone gets it wrong.

Is it reasonable to expect that anyone can accurately retrieve from memory hours of unrecorded conversation? No. Research shows that conversational memory is fraught with bias and error. In particular, people often commit source-monitoring errors, remembering what was said but not who said it. Add extraordinary doses of stress to the mix, and memory is further impaired. In a 2004 study that points to this

danger, Charles Morgan randomly assigned trainees in a military survival school to undergo a realistic high-stress or low-stress mock interrogation. Twenty-four hours later, many of those in the high-stress condition could not even identify their interrogators in a lineup.

In 2017, my colleagues and I published our second study, a two-
phased experiment to assess the accuracy and completeness of police
reports of mock interrogations—and the effects of these reports on
people's perceptions. At a different police department in Connecticut,
we recruited sixteen experienced officers to investigate a mock crime
scene, interrogate two innocent suspects, and then submit an incident
report within forty-eight hours. All thirty-two sessions were covertly
recorded; the recordings were later used to score the reports. In Phase
2, naïve observers read a brief summary of the case and then either read
a police report about the session or a verbatim transcript of the session.

The results were telling. First, police and their mock suspects often
disagreed in their recollections of what happened during the interrogations—and these sessions lasted only minutes, not hours. This is precisely why judges and juries are handicapped in court when faced with a
swearing contest between police officers and suspects over what actually occurred. Sometimes these disputes result from ordinary forgetting,
and sometimes they come about through self-serving distortions in
memory and reporting. Either way, fact finders need to see a firsthand
account of the process for themselves to resolve these disagreements.

The second big reveal was that compared to the tapes, our reality
check for what really happened, these reports were filled with errors of
omission, with police understating their use of various tactics. These
errors proved costly. Naïve observers who later read the secondhand
incident reports, compared to those who read the verbatim transcripts
themselves, saw the process as less pressured. They were also more
likely to see guilt in mock suspects who were innocent.

Stop for a moment and ponder the pairing of results in these two
Connecticut studies. In the eye of the camera, police used fewer and
less extreme manipulative tactics, thereby serving as a possible deterrent to false confessions; and naïve observers were less likely to perceive
guilt in innocent suspects, thereby reducing the likelihood of wrongful
convictions.

Despite these very tangible benefits, not to mention the inherent
value that comes with transparency, opponents continue to argue that

recording will distract and inhibit suspects; that some will flat-out refuse to talk. History does not bear out this concern. Still, it's an empirical question to be tested, not left for guesswork; hence the third experiment of our NSF trilogy.

To test this suspect-inhibition hypothesis, Roger Williams University
professor Melissa Russano and I, and others, observed real suspects
caught up in real investigations. With cooperation from the Pawtucket,
Rhode Island, Police Department, a unique opportunity presented itself. Consistent with statewide practice, this department routinely
records its interrogations. And while they may inform suspects of this
fact, they are not required to do so. This combination of practices enabled the first fully randomized field experiment of police interrogations.

In total, we observed 122 adult crime suspects brought into custody
and questioned about crimes ranging from forgery, counterfeiting, and
vandalism to automobile theft, grand larceny, felony assault, and sexual
assault. Fourteen detectives from the Major Crimes Unit were involved. Homicide cases were excluded because some detectives told us
ahead of time that they would be reluctant to abide by random assignment in these investigations. And of course, random assignment of subjects to a condition is the sine qua non of a scientific experiment.

In each case, detectives randomly informed some suspects but not
others that their session would be recorded by concealed cameras and
microphones built into the wall and ceiling (in the camera-informed
condition, detectives were instructed to also point in the direction of
the hidden equipment). After all sessions were completed, we sent the
recordings off to be transcribed and de-identified for objective coding
of the words spoken. The videos were presented to graduate students
who were blinded as to each suspect's condition as they coded various
aspects of behavior. All this enabled us to compare the two groups on a
range of objective measures.

The results of this study were clear. Despite all the fearmongering,
suspects exhibited little awareness or concern about the presence of the
cameras. Very few camera-informed suspects looked in the camera's
pointed direction. Not a single one balked or refused to speak. Statistical comparisons of the two groups further showed that camera-informed suspects spoke as often and as much as those who were not
informed—yes, we counted the number of suspect "utterances" and

CHAPTER 11

found no difference. So it also comes as no surprise that the sessions lasted just as long.

Looking at the first major decision that a suspect has to make, we found that only 2 percent of all suspects invoked their Miranda rights at the outset; only 15 percent did so at some point later. These numbers align closely with waiver rates reported elsewhere. Importantly, camera-informed suspects were no more likely to invoke their rights than those who were uninformed. As to the second important decision a suspect has to make, we found that 45 percent made an explicit admission of guilt and/or a full confession—and camera-informed suspects were just as likely to do so. Their statements also contained similar amounts of detail.

After each session concluded, we asked the lead detective to complete a one-page questionnaire to rate the suspect on a ten-point scale on key behavioral dimensions. Overall, they perceived the suspects to be moderately talkative, cooperative, truthful, and forthcoming. Although detectives also saw the suspects as somewhat anxious and inhibited, no differences emerged between those in the camera-informed and uninformed condition. They also did not perceive the suspects in either group as being self-conscious about being recorded. As far as participating detectives could tell, the camera did not have this inhibitory effect.

Finally, we attacked the bottom line: case dispositions. We tracked what happened to these cases fourteen months later and observed no differences in the rate at which the two groups were ultimately convicted in the form of a guilty plea, conviction at trial, or diversion (a form of sentence involving rehabilitation or other remedy) or set free (via the decision not to charge the suspect, the charges being dismissed and/or expunged, or acquittal at trial).

Of obvious relevance to policy and practice, this study offered no support for the hypothesis that recording—even when it is made transparent, as required in two-party consent states—adversely affects suspects, the process, or case dispositions. As far as I can tell, that last bastion of opposition has been discredited.

Going forward, in light of the false-confessions problem that plagues the system, at a time when just about everyone carries a video camera in their pocket, there are no more excuses. At a time when false confessions taken behind closed doors are a known stark and ugly reality, there are no excuses. Yet too many states still do not implement this simple remedy. And in some states in which it is mandated, you could drive a truck through the loopholes that excuse the failure to do so.

Nothing could be simpler. As soon as a suspect is brought in to be questioned—regardless of whether that suspect is in custody, regardless of whether police characterize the session as an interview or an interrogation—the camera should be turned on along with the lights. Period. No justifications to the contrary should be permitted. The failure to do so should render any statement later taken inadmissible.

I served recently on the New York State Bar Association Wrongful Conviction Task Force. The state had just passed a mandatory video-recording law, and the subcommittee wanted to assess the initial progress by surveying a sample of police agencies from across the state. The response rate was too low to prove informative, but I recall that one small department reported several failures to record custodial interrogations because the suspects refused to go on camera.

In light of our Rhode Island study, where not a single suspect refused, I would like to have seen how those refusals came about. When Bronx DA Mario Merola introduced videotaped confessions in the 1970s, his office told *New York Times* writer Marcia Chambers that only 1 percent of all suspects refused to go on camera—and that was over forty years ago when the equipment was large, obtrusive, and in your face; before surveillance cameras on city streets were an accepted part of life; before police wore body cams to record traffic stops and other street encounters; and before everyone carried a portable video recorder comfortably in their pocket.

A suspect's alleged refusal to go on camera is one loophole used to excuse the failure to record. Others that appear in the New York State law, and other states as well: "equipment malfunction," "unavailability of equipment because it is already in use," and "when an inadvertent error occurs." I've had a smartphone with a camera on it now for years. It is not expensive and not once has it ever malfunctioned.

The biggest loophole in recording laws is the provision that only custodial interrogations must be recorded—not pre-custodial interviews. Research now shows that police and lay adults do not agree as to what constitutes custody, which is in the eye of the beholder. Too often police claim that what they failed to record was merely a pre-interrogation interview from which, lo and behold, a confession was sprung loose. As per past practice, the confession is on camera; the process is not. In the digital twenty-first century, there is no good reason for mandatory recording laws to limit the requirement to so-called custodial situations.

There is also a visual-spatial aspect of what it means to record the entire process. Thirty years after the Central Park jogger case, Andrew Novick—the cameraman hired by the Manhattan DA to videotape the confessions—spoke out about the physical conditions. He described the room they chose as tiny, a small space that resembled a broom closet; poorly lit, making for grainy footage; and in a noisy location, with bad acoustics. He also complained of being told to leave his bright lights on between sessions, which made the room hot and uncomfortable.

Now retired, Novick told me by phone what he said to Rich Schapiro of New York's *Daily News*, that while he does not think that this room was deliberately chosen for effect, "They just created a very dark picture of these defendants."

I'm not aware of any research that has tested the effects of lighting or resolution on people's perceptions of others, but social psychologists have examined camera perspective effects. Research has long shown that when people watch others have a conversation, they see the person they are visually focused on as the more influential or "causal" agent. Everyone else constitutes background. Directors in the entertainment business know this. Perhaps prosecutors do too.

When DA Merola started to videotape confessions, the setup was always the same: After initial introductions that spanned everyone in the room (typically, an assistant district attorney, the suspect, and one or two detectives), the camera would settle in on the suspect, seated in front of a clock on the wall to mark time. While the judge and jury could later hear both the suspect and questioners, only the suspect was visible.

Enter social psychologist Daniel Lassiter. In studies spanning over twenty years of research, Lassiter staged and taped mock interrogations from three different camera angles so that either the suspect or the interrogator, or both, were visible. He would show one of these tapes to groups of lay observers and ask them afterward about the exchange.

Consistently, subjects who saw only the suspect—which is typical—judged the situation as less coercive, and the statement as more voluntary and credible, than those who saw the interrogator or both. By directing visual attention toward the accused, the camera leads jurors to underestimate the amount of pressure exerted by the audible but hidden detective. Remove the interrogator and, well, out of sight is out of mind. In one study, even experienced trial judges were influenced by this variation in camera perspective.

Whether the camera is built into a wall or ceiling, or stationed on a tripod old-school style, it should be positioned in a way that puts all participants in view. From both a temporal and spatial perspective, it is time to lift the veil of secrecy from the interrogation room so that everyone can see how true and false confessions are produced.

HOW TO ELICIT CONFESSIONS THAT ARE MORE DIAGNOSTIC OF GUILT

Time and again, wrongful convictions have shown that once citizens are brought into a police station for questioning, they face an uphill battle, resulting in what my colleagues and I have called a "cumulative disadvantage."

This disadvantage starts the moment detectives determine that a person they are questioning should be considered a suspect. That suspect is then pressured to make an admission of guilt followed by a full confession. That confession unleashes a torrent of consequences. It corrupts eyewitnesses, informants, alibis, and forensic examiners in a way that provides illusory corroboration; and it sets into motion the forces that press the suspect, now defendant, to plead guilty or face conviction at trial. This chain of events makes it difficult later to win a new trial on appeal. Even after exoneration, a social stigma attaches itself to the confessor like glue. Through it all, Miranda—the one and only "kill switch" the system affords the accused—does not work.

All this means that remedies are needed to achieve two objectives: First, minimize the risk that innocent people will be induced to confess. Second, limit the momentum that builds to corrupt both the evidence and the truth-seeking process. Let's start with the first objective.

Micro Remedies: Repair the Reid Technique

U.S. law enforcement culture is inherently adversarial, so it comes as no surprise that American interrogations are confrontational in their approach. Once a suspect is identified, the goal is to make an accusation, stated with confidence, bolstered by disclosures of evidence already gathered, and shutting the door to denial—all aimed at thrusting offenders into a state of despair and incentivizing them to cooperate. Apart from mandating the video recording of interviews and interrogations, four reforms are needed to repair the problems spawned by the Reid technique.

Retract Pseudoscience Claims about Lie Detection

Right out of the gate, American-style interrogations are built upon a paradigm of confrontation. Like it or not, that alone is not what causes problems. I have often said that the Reid technique would be terrific if everyone hauled into the room was guilty. But therein lies the first serious problem: contrary to their claims, Reid's Behavioral Analysis Interview does not arm investigators with superhuman lie-detection abilities. The science on this point could not be clearer. Sometimes the person targeted for suspicion is the offender; often that person is innocent.

It is important that Reid investigators be taught that suspects do not prove themselves to be liars because their voices quaver, because they avoid eye contact or get fidgety in their chairs (demeanor that is particularly ingrained in adolescents). They should understand that science does not support the claim that they can be trained up to an 85 to 90 percent level of accuracy; it never did. They should understand that they are not crackerjack lie detectors but highly flawed observers, like the rest of us—and too self-confident. The data on these points are clear to anyone not stuck in the 1940s. Reid-trained investigators should get with the program, read up on the science, and find training in approaches that are more diagnostic.

By instilling cockiness in police about their mind-reading abilities, Reid & Associates has inadvertently created an interrogation process that is *by definition* guilt-presumptive—and hence, dangerous to innocent suspects. The tunnel vision that this process sets into motion and the confirmation biases that follow makes this a fatal structural flaw.

One way or another, the lie-detection myths need to be dispelled. One way or another, police should be retrained to form impressions on the basis of evidence they have gathered and science-based cognitive interviewing strategies, not gut instincts.

Ban the False-Evidence Ploy

The second desperately needed repair concerns the most lethal weapon in the interrogator's arsenal, a weapon banned in most civilized countries: lying about evidence. If detectives want to bolster the positive confrontation by disclosing *real evidence*, that is fine. As nature would have it, real evidence will point far more often at perpetrators than at innocents. This will result in more diagnostic outcomes: confessions from perpetrators, seldom from innocents. But as soon as police are permitted to concoct lies about fingerprints, hair, blood, a witness, or a polygraph exam, they run roughshod over nature and pressure all suspects equally, guilty and innocent alike. And of course once they do that, the innocent suspect will become visibly anxious, thereby "confirming" the judgment that he or she is a liar.

There is no dispute as to the danger of this tactic. False evidence has singlehandedly precipitated countless proven false confessions, resulting in thousands of years of wrongful incarceration. All too many real-life tragedies described in this book came about through such lies. A hundred-plus years of psychological research is crystal clear. Misinformation renders people vulnerable to manipulation in all sorts of domains, including false confessions—and just about every psychologist knows it. To that end, I would propose a list of commandments. Along with "Thou shalt not physically harm or threaten a suspect or deprive a suspect of food, water, sleep, or contact with a loved one, for an extended period of time," I would add "Thou shalt not lie to a suspect about the evidence."

Only the courts and state legislatures can stop this madness. The law enforcement community has embraced the use of trickery and deceit. Feign sympathy, gain the suspect's trust, and then assault that suspect with brazen lies that dupe them into confession. The U.S. Supreme Court has not revisited this issue in over fifty years, since its 1969 opinion in *Frazier v. Cupp*. Since then, both the behavioral sciences and the explosion of wrongful convictions have warned of the risk. Since then, false-confession experts have testified under oath about it in courtrooms everywhere; the American Psychological Association has done the same in amicus briefs filed all over the country. Ignorance is no longer an excuse.

Ban Minimization Themes That Imply Leniency

At the heart of the Reid technique is the sympathetic presentation of minimization themes that can communicate promises of leniency indirectly through pragmatic implication. The courts have long prohibited the use of explicit promises of leniency. They recognize that innocent people feeling trapped and told they have nothing to lose may be tempted to confess to things they didn't do. But judges have mostly permitted the use of minimization themes that *imply* leniency. As a result, the friendly detective might downplay the offense by suggesting to a suspect that his or her actions were spontaneous, accidental, provoked, seduced, peer pressured, alcohol or drug induced, caused by stress or raging hormones, or otherwise justifiable by external factors.

In the Central Park jogger case, every boy gave a false confession that placed his cohorts at center stage and minimized his own involvement. Each jogger defendant thought he would go home after cooperating in this way.

In North Charleston, South Carolina, Lieutenant McHale started to shape a theme for Wesley Myers even before interrogation had formally commenced: "It's so easy to kill somebody when you're angry," he said. "Sometimes you don't know how strong you are." He even went so far as to plant this seed: "If you're guilty and it's an accident . . ."

In Manitowoc County, Wisconsin, Brendan Dassey's interrogators let him off the moral hook in no uncertain terms. After befriending Dassey and assuring him, "I promise I will not leave you high and dry," Detective Fassbender said that Avery, not Dassey, was to blame: "It's not your fault, remember that." "You've done nothing wrong."

Controlled research shows that statements like these lead people to infer leniency *as if an explicit promise had been made*—and to confess to something they did not do. For suspects under strain, the unstated pragmatic implication offers an escape hatch. This tactic may sound calming and sympathetic, but it's the ultimate con. As for the courts, I would suggest that what should matter is not the words used but the measurable implication of those words to just about any reasonable person who is listening.

Protect Child Suspects

Over the years, the Supreme Court has cautioned that juveniles should be treated with "special care." Kids are vulnerable, which is why they are statistically overrepresented in false-confession cases. They are more easily manipulated than adults, more compliant, more suggestible, and more myopic in their focus on the present. Citing developmental neuroscience, the National Institute of Mental Health has described the teenage brain as "a work in progress."

There are two ways to protect juveniles, an inherently vulnerable population. First, they should be entitled to the mandatory presence of an attorney. It almost never happens. When law professor Barry Feld observed the interrogations of over three hundred juvenile suspects, he found that 90 percent were interrogated alone; a few had a parent present, but the number of attorneys present was zero. When a sample of defense lawyers were interviewed recently about their presence during juvenile interrogations, most reported that they had never been asked to do so, ever.

In some states, the presence of a parent, guardian, or other interested adult is required to protect young suspects who face interrogation. Yet research shows that the presence of an interested adult does not lead juveniles to invoke Miranda and other constitutional rights.

Too often the parent who sits idly through their child's interrogation has been rendered passive. Reid & Associates is complicit in making this happen. Even in the newest edition of their manual, they caution that some states provide for the presence of a parent during a juvenile interrogation—as in the case of four of the five Central Park jogger defendants who were under the age of sixteen. When that happens, they recommend pulling the potentially protective parent aside to encourage the interrogation to proceed—for example, by implying they have evidence and normalizing the situation: "All children at one point or another have done things that disappoint their parents," they point out, and "everyone has done things as a youth that should not have been done."

Paying lip service to the need to be sensitive while questioning kids is nice. But Reid & Associates offers interrogation training courses to school administrators. When it comes to the parents of a child whom administrators want to interrogate, the manual advises this: "A parent who is present during the interrogation should be advised to refrain

from talking, confining his or her function to that of an observer. . . .
The investigator should then proceed with the interrogation as though
he were alone with the suspect." This advice on how to neutralize the
parent is shameful and should be stopped.

If I did not know better, the protective parent in me would think
that the single best way to defend a kid is to ensure the physical presence of a mother, father, or other guardian in the room. Sometimes this
works; but too often it does not. In fact, these adults typically sit pas-
sively and sometimes urge their sons and daughters to "cooperate." The
Central Park jogger case fully illustrates the gamut of possible outcomes.

At fifteen, Yusef Salaam was the only one of the five boys who would
not agree to give a videotaped confession. What empowered him to
resist was that his mother, Sharonne Salaam, a remarkably strong woman, demanded to see her son and then halted the interrogation.

Yet in that same case, Antron McCray, also fifteen, managed for
several hours to resist the pressure to confess with his stepfather, Bob-
by, in the room. Then at one point, McCray told his son to sign a
confession. "I was trying to get my son to lie," Mr. McCray lamented
afterward. "I told him to go along with them. Otherwise he'd go to jail."

You can actually see this counter-protective effect in the videotape
of fourteen-year-old Lorenzo Montoya, interrogated by Denver homicide detectives one evening in January of 2000. The video shows Montoya's mom, Mary Torres, in the room while police badgered her son.
With Lorenzo slumped back in his chair, police misled him about the
evidence and called him a liar.

At one point, the lead detective entered, slipped on a pair of latex
gloves, took the boy's shoes, and suggested, falsely, that prints matching
them were found at the crime scene. Duped by this performance,
Torres chimed in: "Lorenzo, were you there?" "No, I swear to God,"
Montoya replied. "Oh, as God is my witness, Lorenzo, you'd better tell
them something," Torres implored.

Moments later, the detectives asked if Lorenzo would speak to them
alone, so Torres agreed to leave. "You tell them exactly what they want
to hear so we can get out of here," she said to him. "Do you understand?"

There is no dispute as to the proposition that kids should not be
interrogated using psychologically manipulative tactics built for adults.

News flash: In 2021, Illinois and Oregon became the first states ever to pass bills to prevent police from deceiving juveniles about evidence. I expect other states to follow. Still, all suspects sixteen and younger should be accompanied and advised by a professional advocate, preferably an attorney trained to serve in this role. As a second means of protection, law enforcement personnel who conduct interviews and interrogations should receive special training on the added risks.

Macro Remedy: Dump Reid for PEACE

One approach to reforming interrogation practices in the U.S. is to tinker with the status quo. Another approach is to think outside the box and adopt a whole new paradigm. Following recent developments in Europe, a new approach would reconceptualize "interrogation" as a process of information gathering, not confrontation.

In the 1990s, in response to public outcry over several alarming high-profile false confessions, police officers in England and Wales teamed up with research psychologists and other academics to develop evidence-based interview techniques that were non-coercive, ethical, and transparent. Stricter controls were introduced, including the rule that all sessions must be recorded. The word "interrogation" was removed from the vernacular; the primary objective is to gather information, not necessarily by confession.

The system reacted with a wholesale paradigm shift. What started in England and Wales was soon adopted in Scotland and Northern Ireland, making it the official model of interviewing throughout the United Kingdom. Police now use this approach in many other countries, including Australia, New Zealand, Norway, and parts of Canada.

Drawing from the cognitive interview, born in the lab, and introduced to psychology in the 1980s by Edward Geiselman and Ronald Fisher, the British team created a five-stage interview model known by the mnemonic PEACE (Planning and preparation; Engage and explain; Account; Closure; Evaluation). Planning and preparation is a critical first step. Before bringing a suspect into the interview room, PEACE investigators are advised to study the crime in question, know what evidence exists or not, talk to witnesses and forensic examiners, and learn what they can about the suspect in order to define their aims for the interview.

This may all sound obvious, but it stands in sharp contrast to a common feature in American false-confession cases, where a detective immediately targets a suspect based on a hunch and proceeds forward, often getting a confession that contradicts the evidence or, worse, contains false facts that police believed to be true when they took the confession but which proved false after further investigation.

Step 2 involves engaging the suspect in order to establish rapport. PEACE interviewers are not encouraged per se to become fast false "friends" with suspects, but rather to treat them in a professional, respectful, and courteous manner. At this stage, the interviewer should ask suspects how they want to be addressed, find out if they need a drink or a restroom break, and find common ground or shared experiences to build on. In the "Explain" part of this step, the interviewer should explain the purpose of the interview and apprise suspects of their rights. Step 2 is vital to PEACE. To quote a retired British police-officer-turned-psychologist I know: "You'd be amazed at how much people will disclose when you are nice to them."

Step 3 is where the substance begins, where the interviewer asks the suspect for a full and detailed account of events—without challenge or interruption. During this phase, the interviewer asks the suspect to think back over the event by asking open-ended questions that elicit long free-narrative responses, not questions that are pointed, leading, or suggestive. The investigative interviewer might pause at times, which often leads suspects to elaborate, and then probe further and challenge the suspect's version of events by citing other evidence. Importantly, these challenges should be pitched as opportunities for clarification, and not be hostile and accusatory in tone.

Step 4 consists of closure. Once the interview winds down, the officer should summarize the suspect's account and offer an opportunity to make clarifications and ask questions. At this point, the suspect is asked to vouch for the accuracy and completeness of the account given and is told that additional questions may follow.

The final step is one of evaluation. After the suspect has been questioned, the investigator reviews the information obtained and how it fits into the investigation as a whole. At this point, the interviewer determines what, if any, additional information is needed and what future action should be taken.

Over the years, PEACE, and variants more generally, has evolved in response to new research. In 1999, Rebecca Milne and Ray Bull published *Investigative Interviewing: Psychology and Practice*. In 2013, Eric Shepherd and Andy Griffiths published their second edition of *Investigative Interviewing: The Conversational Management Approach*. On the shoulders of these academics and practitioners—David Walsh, Gavin Oxburgh, Lorraine Hope, Trond Myklebust, and others—this approach now provides police with an alternative that is both powerful and diagnostic.

Before PEACE was implemented in England, the national confession rate hovered at 50 percent, and reports of false confession had alarmed the public. After PEACE, the confession rate continued to hover at 50 percent—without the false confessions. Laboratory experiments that modeled the two approaches showed the same effect: information gathering produces more diagnostic outcomes than confrontation. Jackpot.

PEACE is one variant of this new paradigm. But others, homegrown, are developing, too. In 1982, Doug Wicklander and Dave Zulawski founded WZ, an interview and interrogation training firm for law enforcement, military, and private-sector investigators. Both had been trained and employed by Reid & Associates, so when they opened for business, their training reflected that influence. Over the next few decades, WZ expanded to include less confrontational approaches. In response to all the false confessions as well as the types of research cited in this book, they continue to evolve.

On March 6, 2017, WZ alerted all of its clients to a press release titled: "Wicklander-Zulawski Discontinues Reid Method Instruction after More than Thirty Years." Citing the risk of false confessions tied to the Reid technique as well as advances in the psychology of interviewing, WZ moved exclusively to PEACE-like approaches. "The Reid Method has remained relatively unchanged since the 1970s," WZ said. "It does not reflect updates in our legal system and does not acknowledge the availability of scholarly work on the subject." WZ does not now present a fully formed alternative to PEACE. But its current president, David Thompson, is committed to an evidence-based non-confrontational paradigm.

A second homegrown alternative has been developed through the High-Value Detainee Interrogation Group (HIG) program, a U.S.

government entity established in 2009 by the FBI, CIA, and DoD. As with PEACE, the mission was to bring together intelligence profession- als and research psychologists to devise lawful, science-based, and ef- fective methods for purposes of national security.

In 2016, HIG published a report that brought together science and practice. The report is extensive. Parts of it could have been produced by PEACE advocates: "Prepare, plan, and support," "Develop and maintain rapport," "Use active listening skills," "Elicit narratives using open-ended questions," to name a few principles. Yet other parts rec- ommend more pressure-filled tactics that draw from research on per- suasion. The term *interrogation* is still used to describe the process.

The point is, there are varying alternatives that American police agencies can now explore. In fact, many city departments have started to do just that. I can think of no more interesting proxy for this ongoing paradigm shift than this: in early 2020, John Reid & Associates an- nounced that they would be offering training in the Reid P.E.A.C.E. Method.

HOW TO CONTAIN THE TOXIC EFFECTS OF A FALSE CONFESSION

Many criminal justice professionals exhibit an unnerving complacency about the false-confessions problem. Even once they acknowledge the possibility, they go on to assume that the system contains layers of safety nets, so "not to worry."

What are those safety nets? It starts with the assumption that police would correctly target offenders for interrogation, not innocents, and that they would know a false confession if they saw one. Next, well- resourced prosecutors will rein in overzealous police by making sure the confession was voluntary and corroborated before plotting a guilty plea offer in lieu of trial; wise judges will limit prosecutors who over- reach by suppressing confessions that were coerced; juries will use their common sense to figure out that the confessor was innocent; finally, appeals courts will review the entire record with the clarity of hindsight and an eye on errors of procedure and fact. That's the theory, anyway.

In 2020, Kyle Scherr, Allison Redlich, and I proposed a five-stage "cumulative-disadvantage" framework that flies in the face of this theory. Firmly embedded in the ideals of American democracy and the presumption of innocence embodied by William Blackstone's declaration "It is better that ten guilty escape than one innocent suffer," one would assume that the criminal justice system is self-correcting in the ways I just described.

If all this were true, then a person's innocence would matter more as the process unfolds. In sharp contrast, we have argued that the system often compounds errors occurring from one stage to the next, with each successive stage tainted by its predecessors. As a result, actual innocence may sometimes matter less and less over time, not more.

The research I describe in this book tells us something about these stages and how this might happen. First, during a pre-custodial interview, police will often misjudge innocent citizens as being deceptive because of their verbal and nonverbal behavior. At the same time, innocent suspects harbor a naïve phenomenology of innocence that leads them to believe they have nothing to hide and that everything will work itself out. So they waive their Miranda rights, setting themselves up for what comes next.

During the second stage, innocent suspects are subjected to a confrontational and guilt-presumptive interrogation. Alone and clueless, they are accused of the crime, their denials are called lies, and they are confronted with the kinds of mind-bending tactics that increase the empirical risk of a false admission accompanied by a detailed narrative. Making matters worse, juveniles and adults with cognitive impairments and mental health issues are particularly vulnerable.

The third stage of cumulative disadvantage kicks in as soon as the innocent suspect is arrested. Beginning immediately, in what one would normally consider a truth-seeking process, the suspect's confession begins to corrupt the course of the ensuing investigation. It can cause eyewitnesses to change their identifications; it can lead alibi witnesses to question and retract their support; it brings forth jailhouse snitches and other informants; and it can skew the way forensic-science examiners interpret physical evidence.

One might expect self-correction to kick in during the fourth stage, when the suspect-turned-defendant retains a lawyer, and the prosecutor commences discovery. Weighed down by a confession that appears intrinsically corroborated by crime details and extrinsically corroborated by lay and expert witnesses, the suspect-turned-defendant is at a cumulative disadvantage during all processes of adjudication. At this point, the case built against the confessor is often so compelling as to virtually ensure a wrongful conviction through a guilty plea or trial verdict.

Finally, the accumulated disadvantages that transited the innocent confessor from a pre-custodial interview into prison persist through post-conviction life, handicapping appeal efforts and thwarting DNA testing. In a new article published in 2022, Kyle Scherr and Christopher Normile analyzed the course of events in more than a thousand homicide cases with the NRE archives and found that the process of official exoneration took longer in those cases involving false confessions, relative to all others. Compounding the problem, research shows that the social stigma attached to these individuals persists even after they are officially exonerated and released back into the community.

Video recording and reforming the processes of interrogation will mitigate the risk of confession errors at the outset. To prevent the accumulation of disadvantages that follows, two additional measures are needed—bring the scientific method into crime labs, and use experts to educate judges and juries.

BRING THE SCIENTIFIC METHOD INTO CRIME LABS

Fixing the system has to extend from the police station into the crime lab. Forensic examiners—whether experts in DNA, fingerprints, bite marks, blood spatter, ballistics, or handwriting—must be "blindfolded," not tainted by the fact that a confession was taken.

This is not a mere abstract science problem. To this day, I am rattled by what I witnessed in Columbia, South Carolina. A toddler had died while in day care. Based on chest X-rays, pediatric records, and other physical evidence, the medical examiner concluded that the cause of death was pneumonia. But then police interrogated the caretaker and induced a confession. In response, the medical examiner revised his autopsy conclusion: The child, he said, was suffocated.

Seventy-eight percent of all false confessions in the Innocence Project's DNA case files contained one or more *other* errors of evidence, most of which were taken *after* the confession was produced and recanted. In particular, 63 percent of false confessions were accompanied by forensic-science errors, 29 percent contained eyewitness mistakes, and 19 percent brought in informants who lied. While it is possible that some of these errors were made independent of the confession, a powerful combination of case studies and laboratory experiments points to a more troubling non-coincidence by which confessions consciously or unconsciously taint forensic examiners and other witnesses.

The National Commission on Forensic Science recently concluded that forensic examiners "should draw conclusions *solely from the physical evidence that they are asked to evaluate . . . and not from any other evidence in the case.*" Fingerprint experts should compare the latent prints from the crime scene to a suspect's fully rolled prints. The same goes for shoe prints, bite marks, tire marks, firearms, handwriting, facial image comparisons, and other pattern-matching judgments. (The same principle should also apply to forensic pathologists and arson investigators, though that is a more complicated argument.) These types of purportedly independent judgments do not require and should not be "facilitated" by extraneous information like "Oh by the way, the suspect whose print you are looking at confessed."

Several reforms are needed to increase accuracy and reduce error in the forensic sciences. To mitigate the stain of a confession, the simplest and most important remedy is to insulate forensic examiners from extraneous information. They should not be subject to pressure from police and prosecutors and should not have access to other evidence in the case file. This prescription is not driven by a lack of trust but, rather, the realization that forensic examiners are human. Professionals or not, their perceptions are subject to bias because, like the rest of us, they tend to see what they expect or want to see.

Double-blind protocols are everywhere. The pharmaceuticals industry knows well that in clinical drug trials, neither the patients nor their doctors should know if the pill a patient gets is an active drug or a placebo. In psychology research, we routinely blind not only the subjects but also our experimenters. In the Rhode Island video study I described earlier, we sought to ensure that someone other than the lead detective administered the camera-informed versus uninformed instructions to the suspects. In this way, the lead interrogating detective did not know whether a particular suspect was in one condition or the other. Double-blind protocols are basic to science; when feasible, they should also be basic to forensic laboratories.

In the related context of eyewitness lineups, researchers similarly advocate a double-blind procedure in which neither the witness nor the administrator knows which individual in the lineup is the suspect. The rationale is the same: the lineup administrator, who stages a lineup and knows which person in it is the presumed perpetrator, may inadvertently steer the witness—perhaps suggesting a second look if the witness balks or interpreting a "maybe it's number four" comment as an identification if it referred to the suspect.

Paralleling research on confirmation biases in psychology, Margaret Bull Kovera and other eyewitness researchers have demonstrated the reasons for a double-blind procedure. Some studies show that witnesses are more likely to pick an innocent suspect out of the lineup when the administrator knows which lineup member is the suspect than when blinded as to the suspect's identity. Other studies show that witnesses are more likely to pick the suspect when the lineup administrator is visible than when standing out of view, behind the witness. In 2020, social psychologist Gary Wells and others published a white paper on eyewitness identifications (I call it White Paper 2.0; an earlier version was published in 1998). Among their unequivocal recommendations: double-blind lineups.

The proposal to shield forensic examiners from confessions and other extraneous aspects of the case file may sound too rational to generate controversy. But when my colleagues and I suggested this in a 2013 article on forensic confirmation biases, the commentaries that followed were not unanimous. Research psychologists were fully on board but practitioners were not.

Commenting on our article, forensic examiner Leonard Butt conceded that analysts are often exposed to potentially biasing stimuli and that some go out of their way to read case reports or talk to investigators. "Perhaps such interest merely provides some personal satisfaction which allows them to enjoy their jobs *without actually altering their judgment*," he suggested. After all, "many tasks performed by forensic examiners can be tedious, mundane, and to many people just not interesting or diverse enough to interest them in doing it." Butt took his argument one half-step further: "As a forensic examiner with nearly thirty years of experience, I can confirm that analysts do face, and are influenced (*not necessarily in a bad way*) by the types of biasing stimuli that are discussed."

Backed by science, I cannot disagree more on both fronts. First, exposure breeds a potential for influence—and a greater likelihood, for example, that a handwriting expert will see a "match" to a suspect's handwriting if that suspect was said to have confessed. Second, Butt's parenthetical "not necessarily in a bad way" implies that extraneous information can increase accuracy. At times this may be true. Faced with ambiguous visual evidence, the examiner whose match judgment is influenced by a confession may well be correct for factoring in that confession (never mind that this expert likely knows nothing about false confessions).

But the forensic analyst's mission is not to integrate all the evidence, as the judge and jury are supposed to do, but rather to make a single, independent, circumscribed, "in a vacuum" judgment. When the fingerprint expert testifies in court to declare a match, the judge and jury assume that this opinion was based on the prints alone—that this visual stimulus, therefore, independently corroborates the confession. For the examiner to suggest otherwise is to misrepresent in court what they did, how they did it, and what it means.

EXPERT TESTIMONY

In May 2006, I made a presentation on false confessions to the Wisconsin Criminal Justice Study Commission, in which I listed the virtues of a mandatory video recording policy. Afterward, attorney Jerry Buting asked this interesting question: If judges and juries can see the defendant's interrogation, "do you think that they, in their common experiences, are going to understand how that leads to false confessions? Or is this something that we're going to need to present expert testimony on, like you or someone, some other psychologist?"

What an interesting question, I thought. I could not assert an empirical answer with any degree of certainty, so I speculated: "Now this is just intuition," I said. "But I think that they will not need an expert when they have access to the tape." I did not realize it at the time, but attorney Buting represented defendant Steven Avery, who was implicated in nephew Brendan Dassey's video confession. I also did not know that Dassey's attorney had agreed to show the jury only a small portion of his client's interrogation—and did so without an expert.

The question of whether exposure to full interrogation videos will make for smarter fact finders remains an interesting empirical question. For two reasons, I am no longer as optimistic as I was fifteen years ago. First, I've seen too many cases in which the jury saw all or part of a highly questionable interrogation yielding a contaminated confession, and yet convicted the defendant. The Melissa Calusinski case described in chapter 6 is one example. Others I know well include the Brendan Dassey, Lorenzo Montoya, and Adrian Thompson cases. Part of the problem is that juries should see not just selected segments, but the entire process, no matter how time-consuming and inconvenient (if watching twelve hours of continuous interrogation is hard on a jury, imagine how hard it is on a suspect). For reasons I will never understand, Dassey's trial attorney agreed to limit what the jury saw to a forty-minute clip that excluded some of the most troubling exchanges.

The second reason I am no longer sanguine about judges and juries without an expert's guidance is that people do not know what happens in the interrogation room and what factors can lead innocent people to confess. Surveys show that people do not see implied promises couched in feigned sympathy as problematic; they are not sufficiently sensitive to how confessions are contaminated by police questions; and, dangerously, they tend to accept at face value an interrogator's negative feedback and innuendo. As data collection in my lab demonstrates, jurors who watch an interrogator chastise a subject ("You're lying to me.") come to believe that the subject is lying.

I am similarly skeptical when it comes to judges. Several years ago, I spoke to Illinois state court judges. At one point, I asked them to indicate by a show of hands how many had ruled on confessions in which the suspect hand-corrected errors to the written statement before signing it. Just about every hand went up. Then I advanced to the next PowerPoint slide, a page from the Reid manual. The key paragraph starts simply enough, advising detectives to deliberately insert factual errors into the written statement that the suspect will spot and correct.

At first glance, this is an interesting way to prove that the suspect has guilty knowledge that an innocent person does not. But then the text continues: "The investigator should keep the errors in mind and raise a question about them in the event the suspect neglects to do so." The judges, some quite experienced, had no idea. Many told me so afterward. Like anyone else, they took the corrected-error trick to be diagnostic of guilt. Yet when we examined a sample of typed and handwritten confessions later proved to be false, we found that 44 percent contained at least one corrected error. I see this all the time in the cases I have reviewed.

Although expert testimony can help to educate jurists, the courts have shown themselves to be reluctant. On January 12, 1906, a Chicago woman named Bessie Hollister was found lying facedown in a trash bin. She had been raped and murdered. A man named Richard Ivens discovered her body and immediately reported it. He was interrogated for hours until he confessed—repeatedly, said police, enriching his story on each successive occasion. Although Ivens had alibis and immediately recanted his confession, the district attorney proceeded to trial.

Ivens, who was intellectually disabled, was badgered in a lengthy and highly suggestive interrogation. His attorney sought expert testimony from Harvard psychology professor Hugo Münsterberg, but the judge refused. Münsterberg, whose 1908 book *On the Witness Stand: Essays in Psychology and Crime* was well ahead of its time, was deeply troubled by the confession itself and how it was taken. "It is a sad story which I am going to report," he said. Solely on the basis of his confession, Ivens was convicted. Within the week, "he was hanged for a crime of which he was no more guilty than you or I." (For a contemporaneous account, I recommend J. Sanderson Christison's 1906 book *The "Confessions" of Ivens: A Character Study and Analysis of the Case.*)

On March 30, 1988, eighty-two years later, social psychologist Elliott Aronson testified as an expert on behalf of a Berkeley student named Bradley Page, who was tried in California for the murder of his girlfriend. The only evidence against Page was a confession that he retracted, saying he became confused during an emotional interrogation that lasted through the night. He was told he had failed a polygraph exam and that his fingerprints were found at the scene, neither of which was true. He was then prompted to imagine what happened, leading him to recite four taped statements, culminating in a confession.

To my knowledge, this was the first time a psychologist testified at trial on the subject of confessions. On the witness stand, Aronson, one of the most prominent social psychologists in history, cited research on conformity, compliance, obedience to authority, and other forms of social influence to explain how someone like Page might be induced to confess to a crime he did not commit. At his first trial, the jury acquitted

Page of first- and second-degree murder but was hung on the charge of voluntary manslaughter; retried on this lesser charge, he was later convicted (for a description of Aronson's testimony, see Davis 2010).

Since that time, psychologists and other social scientists in the United States, Canada, and elsewhere have served as expert witnesses in trials that contain disputed confessions. The precise number of these instances is not known. I have worked on dozens of cases and testified as an expert twenty-five or thirty times. I have colleagues who have appeared in hundreds of trials.

Experts in this field may be psychologists who specialize in child and adolescent development, intellectual disabilities, mental health, personality, social persuasion, and memory. Or they may be forensic psychiatrists, criminologists, or law professors who study police investigation. These areas of specialization are not known to the average judge or juror as a matter of common sense. That's why experts are needed.

Importantly, the scope of such testimony is limited. When I testify at trial, it is not to proclaim a confession "false" and the defendant "innocent." Rather, the goal is to inform the jury about empirical risk factors of relevance to the particular case. Although it is sometimes hard to walk a fine line on the battlefield of an American courtroom, most experts in this field will tell you that their objective is to educate, not advocate.

Despite the voluminous body of research described in this book, U.S. courts are of two minds about this type of testimony. Some judges admit confession experts routinely, especially when the entire prosecution hinges on a confession. Other judges exclude confession experts as a matter of course. Some have claimed that the scientific community lacks consensus as to what is reliable and valid. Others have claimed that the relevant psychology is already within the ken of the average juror and hence not useful.

This last point, that jurors already know about false confessions through common sense, is ludicrous. To the contrary, research shows it's all *counter*intuitive. I have been studying this phenomenon for forty years, and even *I* am still shocked on a daily basis. As I said in a recent email to a law professor colleague in Pennsylvania, "It strikes me as crazy that a court would opine that juries don't need assistance. The problem is, judges don't know what juries don't know because they don't know it either!"

On the question of whether the literature qualifies as scientific, several metrics provide the answer. The theories, methods, and statistics used in the study of confessions are drawn from basic psychological science. Many of the journals in which the research is published are peer and blind reviewed, selective (as measured by rejection rates), and high in impact (as measured by citation metrics). Some of this research is funded by the National Science Foundation, the National Institute of Justice, the Department of Homeland Security, and other agencies that make high-stakes funding decisions.

Prima facie indicators of general acceptance within the scientific community also favor expert testimony in this domain. First, this literature is sufficiently mature that it has served as the basis of a 2010 AP-LS white paper. Second, the APA has submitted seven amicus curiae briefs to state supreme courts on the subject of confessions. Collectively, these briefs assert that innocent people can be induced to confess; that certain dispositional and situational factors increase the risk; and that juries have difficulty assessing this evidence. The APA reiterated these key points in the 2014 "Resolution on Interrogations of Criminal Suspects."

A pairing of two recently published studies indicate, first, that confession experts agree at high levels of consensus about the subject matter of expert testimony and, second, that the average layperson does not possess this knowledge. In the first study, we surveyed eighty-seven confession experts from all over the world. They worked not only in the United States but also in the United Kingdom, Canada, Australia, Sweden, Japan, Spain, Cyprus, and the Netherlands. They all had a PhD; most were highly published; many had extensive courtroom experience. We asked this diverse blue-ribbon sample of experts to indicate, for each of thirty propositions, whether it was reliable enough to cite in court. These items pertained to truth and lie detection, interrogation tactics, confessions, and relevant general principles of psychology.

Overall levels of consensus were high. As indicated by an agreement rate of at least 90 percent, experts agreed that the risk of false confessions is increased not only by explicit threats and promises but also by false evidence and minimization tactics that imply leniency; that sleep deprivation lowers people's resistance to influence; and that misinformation can alter a person's memory for that event. Eighty-five percent agreed that PEACE and other forms of investigative interviewing elicit more diagnostic outcomes than the confrontational Reid technique. At the bottom end, only about 20 percent believed that people can be trained to detect lies by observing nonverbal symptoms of anxiety, or that confessions can be verified by the details they contain.

In the second study, we asked the same questions online to 150 American adults. Compared to the experts, this sample exhibited significantly less agreement about the benefits of investigative interviewing; the risks of false evidence, promises, and minimization; or the heightened risk to juveniles. Compared to experts, these laypeople oversubscribed to the powers of human lie detection, the diagnostic value of confession details, and the power of Miranda to serve as a safeguard. On a common set of propositions, statistical comparisons showed that laypeople do not know what the experts know.

BOTTOM'S UP

My objective is to raise public consciousness and advocate for the repair of a broken system. Influencing policy and practice from the top down is the "official" way to instigate reform. It's why psychologists, social scientists, and legal scholars testify, submit briefs, and advocate in courts and in state legislatures.

An alternative approach is to inform and educate the citizenry, create a groundswell of public opinion, and inspire change from the bottom up. Trained in the model of the "pure scientist," I was not always comfortable with this posture. It's an approach I adopted only recently by giving public lectures, writing op-ed articles in newspapers, talking to journalists and the news media, and working with podcast and documentary filmmakers. It's the reason I wrote this book.

Raising public awareness is important on two fronts. First, people need to know when and how to protect themselves and their loved ones. Whether you are called in for questioning by police trying to solve a crime or by private security investigating a theft in the company where you work, or whether your child is called into the principal's office at school about a theft or act of vandalism, it's important to know what to expect and how to defend yourself.

Second, you may one day find yourself called for jury duty to participate in a rapidly vanishing exercise of the Constitution: a public trial.

Unfortunately, the very processes that can cause innocent people to confess are so counterintuitive that juries cannot fully grasp the perils. Now you know.

APPENDIX

States That Require the Recording of Custodial Interrogations

State	Year	Source	Coverage
Alaska	1985	Court ruling	All crimes
Minnesota	1994	Court ruling	All crimes
Illinois	2003	Statute	Homicides; specified other felonies
New Jersey	2005	Court ruling	All crimes
Wisconsin	2005	Court ruling	All juveniles; adult felonies
New Mexico	2006	Statute	Felonies
Maine	2007	Statute	Serious crimes
North Carolina	2007	Statute	All juveniles; specified felonies
Maryland	2008	Statute	Specified felonies
Nebraska	2008	Statute	Specified felonies
Indiana	2009	Court ruling	Felonies
Missouri	2009	Statute	Specified felonies
Montana	2009	Statute	All crimes
Oregon	2010	Statute	Specified felonies
Connecticut	2011	Statute	Specified felonies
Arkansas	2012	Court ruling	All crimes
Michigan	2012	Statute	Specified felonies
California	2013	Statute	Homicides
Rhode Island	2013	Police policy	Capital offense crimes

Hawaii	Various	Police policy	Serious crimes
Vermont	2014	Statute	Homicides; sexual assaults
Utah	2015	Court ruling	Felonies
Colorado	2016	Statute	Homicides; specified other felonies
Kansas	2017	Statute	All crimes
Texas	2017	Statutes	All crimes
New York	2018	Statute	Specified felonies
Oklahoma	2019	Statute	Homicide; rape cases
Virginia	2020	Statute	All crimes
Ohio	2021	Statute	Homicides; sexual assaults
Washington	2021	Statute	All juvenile cases and adult felonies

Note: All federal law enforcement agencies and the District of Columbia also require the recording of custodial interrogations under specified circumstances.

REFERENCES

Alceste, F., Jones, K. A., & Kassin, S. M. (2020). Facts only the perpetrator could have known? A study of contamination in mock crime interrogations. *Law and Human Behavior, 44*, 128–142.

Alceste, F., & Kassin, S. M. (2021). Perceptions of custody: Similarities and disparities among police, judges, social psychologists, and laypeople. *Law and Human Behavior, 44*(3), 197–214.

Alceste, F., Luke, T. J., & Kassin, S. M. (2018). Holding yourself captive: Perceptions of custody during interviews and interrogations. *Journal of Applied Research in Memory and Cognition, 7*, 387–397.

Alceste, F., Luke, T. J., Redlich, A. D., Hellgren, J., Amrom, A., & Kassin, S. M. (2021). The psychology of confessions: A comparison of expert and lay opinions. *Applied Cognitive Psychology, 35*, 39–51.

Allport, G. W., & Postman, L. J. (1947). *The psychology of rumor.* New York: Holt.

American Psychological Association (2008). *Anthony Wright v. Commonwealth of Pennsylvania.* Amicus Curiae Brief filed November 13, 2008.

American Psychological Association (2010). *Douglas Warney vs. State of New York.* Amicus Curiae Brief filed July 9, 2010.

Appleby, S. C., Hasel, L. E., & Kassin, S. M. (2013). Police-induced confessions: An empirical analysis of their content and impact. *Psychology, Crime and Law, 19*, 111–128.

Appleby, S. C., & Kassin, S. M. (2016). When self-report trumps science: Effects of confessions, DNA, and prosecutorial theories on perceptions of guilt. *Psychology, Public Policy, and Law, 22*, 127–140.

Arizona v. Fulminante, 499 U.S. 279 (1991).

Arthur, R. O., & Caputo, R. R. (1959). *Interrogation for investigators.* New York: Copp.

Asch, S. E. (1955). Opinions and social pressure. *Scientific American,* November, 31–35.

Atkins v. Virginia, 536 U.S. 304 (2002).

August, C. N., & Henderson, K. S. (2021). Juveniles in the interrogation room: Defense attorneys as a protective factor. *Psychology, Public Policy, and Law, 27*, 268–282.

Balcetis, E., & Dunning, D. (2006). See what you want to see: Motivational influences on visual perception. *Journal of Personality and Social Psychology, 91*, 612–625.

Balcetis, E., & Dunning, D. (2010). Wishful seeing: More desired objects are seen as closer. *Psychological Science, 21*, 147–152.

Balko, R. (2007). CSI: Mississippi: A case study in expert testimony gone horribly wrong. *Reason,* November. https://reason.com/2007/10/08/csi-mississippi/

Balko, R. (2014). Mississippi prosecutors say ex-medical examiner can travel through time. *The Washington Post,* July 28.

Banaji, M. R., & Greenwald, A. G. (2013). *Blindspot: Hidden biases of good people.* New York: Delacorte Press.

Bang, B., Stanton, D., Hemmens, C., & Stohr, M. (2018). Police recording of custodial interrogations: A state-by-state legal inquiry. *International Journal of Police Science & Management, 20,* 3–18.

Barthel, J. (1976). *A death in Canaan.* New York: Dutton.

Baumeister, R. F., & Leary, M. R. (1995). The need to belong: Desire for interpersonal attachments as a fundamental human motivation. *Psychological Bulletin, 117,* 497–529.

Bazelon, L. (2018). *Rectify: The power of restorative justice after wrongful conviction.* Boston: Beacon Press.

Bedau, H. A., & Radelet, M. L. (1987). Miscarriages of justice in potentially capital cases. *Stanford Law Review, 40,* 21–179.

Berg, A. J. (2012). *West of Memphis.* Wellington, NZ: Wingnut Films.

Berghuis v. Thompkins, 560 U.S. 370 (2010).

Berlinger, J., & Sinofsky, B. (1996). *Paradise Lost: The Child Murders at Robin Hills.* New York: HBO.

Berlinger, J., & Sinofsky, B. (2000). *Paradise Lost 2: Revelations.* New York: HBO.

Berlinger, J., & Sinofsky, B. (2011). *Paradise Lost 3: Purgatory.* New York: HBO.

Bibas, S. (2004). Plea bargaining outside the shadow of trial. *Harvard Law Review, 117,* 2463–2547.

Bickman, L. (1974). The social power of a uniform. *Journal of Applied Social Psychology, 4,* 47–61.

Blass, T. (2004). *The man who shocked the world.* New York: Basic Books.

Borchard, E. M. (1932). *Convicting the innocent: Errors of criminal justice.* New Haven: Yale University Press.

Brady v. United States, 397 US 742 (1970).

Bram v. United States, 168 U.S. 532 (1897).

Bressan, P., & Dal Martello, M. F. (2002). Talis Pater, Talis Filius: Perceived resemblance and the belief in genetic relatedness. *Psychological Science, 13,* 213–218.

Brignall, Richard (2015). *A police Mr. Big sting goes wrong: The story of Kyle Unger.* Toronto: Lorimer.

Bronnimann, N. (2020). Remorse in parole hearings: An elusive concept with concrete consequences, *Missouri Law Review, 85,* 321–356.

Bronx County District Attorney (2019). *People of the State of New York v. Huwe Burton: Recommendation for Dismissal.* January 22, 2019.

Brown v. Mississippi, 297 U.S. 278 (1936).

Buckley, J. P. (2012). Detection of deception researchers need to collaborate with experienced practitioners. *Journal of Applied Research in Memory and Cognition, 1,* 126–127.

Buffey v. Ballard, No. 14-0642, W.Va. Sup. Ct. (2015).

Burger, J. M. (2009). Replicating Milgram: Would people still obey today? *American Psychologist, 64,* 1–11.

Burleigh, N. (2011). *The fatal gift of beauty: The trials of Amanda Knox.* New York: Broadway Books.

Burleigh, N. (2019). How Amanda Knox's trial was the dawn of the fake news era. *Rolling Stone,* June 13. https://www.rollingstone.com/culture/culture-features/amanda-knox-nina-burleigh-fake-news-italy-murder-847731/.

Burns, S. (2011). *The Central Park Five: A chronicle of a city wilding.* New York: Knopf.

Butt, L. (2013). The forensic confirmation bias: Problems, perspectives, and proposed solutions—Commentary by a forensic examiner. *Journal of Applied Research in Memory and Cognition, 2,* 59–60.

California v. Beheler, 463 U.S. 1121 (1983).

Cash, D. K., Dianiska, R. E. & Lane, S. M. (2019). The effect of statement type and repetition on deception detection. *Cognitive Research, 4,* 38.

Cassell, P. G. (1996). Miranda's social costs: An empirical reassessment. *Northwestern University Law Review, 90,* 387–499.

Cassell, P. G., & Fowles, R. (2017). Still handcuffing the cops? A review of fifty years of empirical evidence of Miranda's harmful effects on law enforcement. *Boston University Law Review, 97*, 685–732.

Chambers, M. (1983). Videotaped confessions increase the conviction rate. *The New York Times*, June 5, p. 30.

Christison, J. S. (1906). *The "Confessions" of Ivens: A character study and analysis of the case* (no publisher; available at Harvard Law School Library).

Cialdini, R. B. (2009). *Influence: Science and practice* (5th ed.). New York: Pearson.

Cleary, H. (2014). Police interviewing and interrogation of juvenile suspects: A descriptive examination of actual cases. *Law and Human Behavior, 38*, 271–282.

Clow, K. A., & Leach, A.-M. (2015). Stigma and wrongful conviction: All exonerees are not perceived equal. *Psychology, Crime & Law, 21*, 172–185.

Cogsdill, E. J., Todorov, A. T., Spelke, E. S., & Banaji, M. R. (2014). Inferring character from faces: A developmental study. *Psychological Science, 25*, 1132–1139.

Connery, D. S. (1977). *Guilty until proven innocent.* New York: G. P. Putnam.

Connery, D. A. (2013). Peter Reilly's hard won justice. *Hartford Courant*, September 27.

Correll, J., Hudson, S., Guillermo, S., & Ma, D. S. (2014). The police officer's dilemma: A decade of research on racial bias in the decision to shoot. *Social and Personality Psychology Compass, 8*, 201–213.

Crane, M., Nirider, L., & Drizin, S. A. (2016). The truth about juvenile false confessions. *Insights on Law & Society, 16*, 10–15.

Darley, J. M., & Gross, P. H. (1983). A hypothesis-confirming bias in labeling effects. *Journal of Personality and Social Psychology, 44*, 20–33.

Davis v. United States, 512 U.S. 452 (1994).

Davis, D. (2010). Lies, damned lies, and the path from police interrogation to wrongful conviction. In M. Gonzales, C. Tavris, & J. Aronson (Eds.), *The scientist and the humanist: A festschrift in honor of Elliot Aronson* (211–247). New York: Psychology Press.

Dempsey, C. (2010). *Murder in Italy: The shocking slaying of a British student, the accused American girl, and an international scandal.* New York: Berkley Books.

DePaulo, B. M., Lindsay, J. J., Malone, B. E., Muhlenbruck, L., Charlton, K., & Cooper, H. (2003). Cues to deception. *Psychological Bulletin, 129*, 74–118.

Dervan, L. & Edkins, V. A. (2013). The innocent defendant's dilemma: An innovative empirical study of plea bargaining's innocence problem. *Journal of Criminal Law and Criminology, 103*, 1–48.

Dickerson v. United States, 530 U.S. 428 (2000).

Domanico, A. J., Cicchini, M. D., & White, L. T. (2012). Overcoming Miranda: A content analysis of the Miranda portion of police interrogations, *Idaho Law Review, 49*, 1–22.

Drizin, S. A., & Leo, R. A. (2004). The problem of false confessions in the post-DNA world. *North Carolina Law Review, 82*, 891–1007.

Dror, I. E., & Charlton, D. (2006). Why experts make errors. *Journal of Forensic Identification, 56*, 600–616.

Dror, I. E., & Hampikian, G. (2011). Subjectivity and bias in forensic DNA mixture interpretation. *Science & Justice, 51*, 204–208.

Dror, I. E., Kukucka, J., Kassin, S. M., & Zapf, P. A. (2018). No one is immune to contextual bias—Not even forensic pathologists. *Journal of Applied Research in Memory and Cognition, 7*, 316–317.

Ebbinghaus, H. (1885). *Memory: A contribution to experimental psychology.* New York: Dover.

Eberhardt, J. L. (2019). *Biased: Uncovering the hidden prejudice that shapes what we see, think, and do.* New York: Viking.

Eberhardt, J. L., Goff, P. A., Purdie, V. J., & Davies, P. G. (2004). Seeing black: Race, crime, and visual processing. *Journal of Personality and Social Psychology, 87*, 876–893.

Ekman, P., & O'Sullivan, M. (1991). Who can catch a liar? *American Psychologist, 46*, 913–920.

Elaad, E., Ginton, A., & Ben-Shakhar, G. (1994). The effects of prior expectations and outcome knowledge on polygraph examiners' decisions. *Journal of Behavioral Decision Making, 7,* 279–292.

Elbein, S. (2014). When employees confess, sometimes falsely. *The New York Times,* March 9, p. BU1.

English, T. J. (2011). *The savage city: Race, murder, and a generation on the edge.* New York: HarperCollins.

Feld, B. C. (2013). *Kids, cops, and confessions: Inside the interrogation room.* New York: New York University Press.

Firstman, R., & Salpeter, J. (2008). *A criminal injustice: A true crime, a false confession, and the fight to free Marty Tankleff.* New York: Ballantine Books.

Flom, J. (2019). *Wrongful Conviction Podcast with Jason Flom: A tale of two systems: The story of Kenzi Snider.* Season 8, Episode 8, March 25, 2019.

Frazier v. Cupp, 394 U.S. 731 (1969).

Freedman, J. L., & Fraser, S. C. (1966). Compliance without pressure: The foot-in-the-door technique. *Journal of Personality and Social Psychology, 4,* 195–202.

Frenda, S. J., Berkowitz, S. R., Loftus, E. F., & Fenn, K. M. (2016). Sleep deprivation and false confessions. *PNAS Proceedings of the National Academy of Sciences of the United States of America, 113,* 2047–2050.

Gansberg, M. (1964). 37 who saw murder didn't call the police. *The New York Times,* March 27, p. 1.

Garrett, B. L. (2010). The substance of false confessions. *Stanford Law Review, 62,* 1051–1119.

Garrett, B. L. (2015). Contaminated confessions revisited. *Virginia Law Review, 101,* 395–454.

Geiselman, R. E., & Fisher, R. P. (1986). Interviewing victims and witnesses of crime. *U.S. Department of Justice, Research in Brief,* 1–9.

Gilbert, D. T. (1991). How mental systems believe. *American Psychologist, 46,* 107–119.

Gilbert, D. T., & Malone, P. S. (1995). The correspondence bias. *Psychological Bulletin, 117,* 21–38.

Gill, P. (2016). Analysis and implications of the miscarriages of justice of Amanda Knox and Raffaele Sollecito. *Forensic Science International: Genetics, 23,* 9–18.

Gilovich, T., Savitsky, K., & Medvec, V. H. (1998). The illusion of transparency: Biased assessments of others' ability to read one's emotional states. *Journal of Personality and Social Psychology, 75,* 332–346.

Goff, P. A., Jackson, M. C., Di Leone, B. A. L., Culotta, C. M., & DiTomasso, N. A. (2014). The essence of innocence: Consequences of dehumanizing Black children. *Journal of Personality and Social Psychology, 106,* 526–545.

Goffman, E. (1963). *Stigma: Notes on the management of spoiled identity.* New York: Simon & Schuster.

Gregory, W. L., Mowen, J. C., & Linder, D. E. (1978). Social psychology and plea bargaining: Applications, methodology, and theory. *Journal of Personality and Social Psychology, 36,* 1521–1530.

Griffin v. California, 380 U.S. 609 (1965).

Grisso, T. (1981). *Juveniles' waiver of rights: Legal and psychological competence.* New York: Plenum.

Grisso, T. (1998). *Instruments for assessing understanding and appreciation of Miranda rights.* Sarasota, FL: Professional Resources Press.

Gudjonsson, G. H. (1984). A new scale of interrogative suggestibility. *Personality and Individual Differences, 5,* 303–314.

Gudjonsson, G. H. (1992). *The psychology of interrogations, confessions, and testimony.* London: Wiley.

Gudjonsson, G. H. (2003). *The psychology of interrogations and confessions: A handbook.* Chichester, UK: John Wiley & Sons.

Gudjonsson, G. H. (2018). *The psychology of false confessions: Forty years of science and practice.* Chichester, UK: John Wiley & Sons.

Guyll, M., Madon, S., Yang, Y., Lannin, D. G., Scherr, K., & Greathouse, S. (2013). Innocence and resisting confession during interrogation: Effects on physiologic activity. *Law and Human Behavior, 37,* 366–375.

Harcourt, B. E. (2007). *Against prediction: Profiling, policing, and punishing in an actuarial age.* Chicago: University of Chicago Press.

Hartwig, M., Granhag, P. A., Strömwall, L. A., & Kronkvist, O. (2006). Strategic use of evidence during police interviews: When training to detect deception works. *Law and Human Behavior, 30,* 603–619.

Hasel, L. E., & Kassin, S. M. (2009). On the presumption of evidentiary independence: Can confessions corrupt eyewitness identifications? *Psychological Science, 20,* 122–126.

Heider, F. (1958). *The psychology of interpersonal relations.* New York: Wiley.

Hill, C., Memon, A., & McGeorge, P. (2008). The role of confirmation bias in suspect interviews: A systematic evaluation. *Legal and Criminological Psychology, 13,* 357–371.

Honts, C. R., Forrest, K., & Stepamescu, A. (2019). Polygraph examiners unable to discriminate true-false juvenile confessions. *Polygraph & Forensic Credibility Assessment, 48,* 1–9.

Honts, C. R., Kassin, S. M., & Craig, R. (2014). "I'd know a false confession if I saw one": A constructive replication with juveniles. *Psychology, Crime and Law, 20,* 695–704.

Honts, C. R., & Kircher, J. C. (1994). Mental and physical countermeasures reduce the accuracy of polygraph tests. *Journal of Applied Psychology, 79,* 252–259.

Hook, S. (1957). *Common sense and the Fifth Amendment.* New York: Criterion Books.

Horgan, A. J., Russano, M. B., Meissner, C. A., & Evans, J. R. (2012). Minimization and maximization techniques: Assessing the perceived consequences of confessing and confession diagnosticity. *Psychology, Crime & Law, 18,* 65–78.

Horselenberg, R., et al. (2006). False confessions in the lab: Do plausibility and consequences matter? *Psychology, Crime & Law, 12,* 61–75.

Horvath, F. S., Jayne, B. P., & Buckley, J. P. (1994). Differentiation of truthful and deceptive criminal suspects in behavioral analysis interviews. *Journal of Forensic Sciences, 39,* 793–807.

Hovland, C. I., Janis, I. L., & Kelley, H. H. (1953). *Communication and persuasion: Psychological studies of opinion change.* New Haven: Yale University Press.

Illinois v. Perkins, 496 U.S. 292 (1990).

Inbau, F. E., & Reid, J. E. (1942). *Lie detection and criminal interrogation.* Baltimore: Williams & Wilkins.

Inbau, F. E., & Reid, J. E. (1962). *Criminal interrogation and confessions.* Baltimore: Williams & Wilkins.

Inbau, F. E., Reid, J. E., Buckley, J. P., & Jayne, B. C. (2013). *Criminal interrogation and confessions* (5th ed.). Burlington, MA: Jones & Bartlett.

Innocence Project (2018). New DNA test results exclude Innocence Project client Philip Barnett and identify alternate suspect in 2002 murder case. June 1, 2018. https://innocenceproject.org/new-dna-test-results-exclude-philip-barnett-and-identify-alternate-suspect/.

Jackson v. Denno, 378 U.S. 368 (1964).

James, W. (1890). *Principles of psychology* (vols. 1–2). New York: Holt.

Jones, E. E., & Harris, V. A. (1967). The attribution of attitudes. *Journal of Experimental Social Psychology, 3,* 1–24.

Junkin, T. (2004). *Bloodsworth: The true story of the first death row inmate exonerated by DNA.* Chapel Hill, NC: Algonquin Books.

Kalven, H., & Zeisel, H. (1966). *The American jury.* Boston: Little, Brown.

Kamisar, Y. (2012). The Rise, decline and fall (?) of *Miranda. Washington Law Review, 87,* 965–1040.

Kamisar, Y. (2017). The Miranda case fifty years later. *Boston University Law Review, 97,* 1293–307.

Kansas v. Marsh, 548 U.S. 163 (2006).

Kaplan, J., Cutler, B. L., Leach, A.-M., Marion, S., & Eastwood, J. (2020). Perceptions of coercion in interrogation: Comparing expert and lay opinions. *Psychology, Crime & Law, 26,* 384–401.

Kassin, S. M. (1997). The psychology of confession evidence. *American Psychologist, 52,* 221–233.

Kassin, S. (2002). False confessions and the jogger case. *New York Times* op-ed, November 1, p. A31.

Kassin, S. M. (2005). On the psychology of confessions: Does innocence put innocents at risk? *American Psychologist, 60,* 215–228.

Kassin, S. M. (2012). Why confessions trump innocence. *American Psychologist, 67,* 431–445.

Kassin, S. M. (2017). The killing of Kitty Genovese: What else does this case tell us? *Perspectives on Psychological Science, 12,* 374–381.

Kassin, S. (2021). It's time for police to stop lying to suspects. *The New York Times* Op-ed, January 30, p. A23.

Kassin, S. M., Bogart, D., & Kerner, J. (2012). Confessions that corrupt: Evidence from the DNA exoneration case files. *Psychological Science, 23,* 41–45.

Kassin, S. M., Drizin, S. A., Grisso, T., Gudjonsson, G. H., Leo, R. A., & Redlich, A. D. (2010). Police-induced confessions: Risk factors and recommendations. *Law and Human Behavior, 34,* 3–38.

Kassin, S. M., Dror, I., & Kukucka, J. (2013). The forensic confirmation bias: Problems, perspectives, and proposed solutions. *Journal of Applied Research in Memory & Cognition, 2,* 42–52.

Kassin, S. M., & Fong, C. T. (1999). "I'm Innocent!": Effects of training on judgments of truth and deception in the interrogation room. *Law and Human Behavior, 23,* 499–516.

Kassin, S. M., Goldstein, C. C., & Savitsky, K. (2003). Behavioral confirmation in the interrogation room: On the dangers of presuming guilt. *Law and Human Behavior, 27,* 187–203.

Kassin, S. M., & Gudjonsson, G. H. (2004). The psychology of confession evidence: A review of the literature and issues. *Psychological Science in the Public Interest, 5,* 33–67.

Kassin, S. M., & Kiechel, K. L. (1996). The social psychology of false confessions: Compliance, internalization, and confabulation. *Psychological Science, 7,* 125–128.

Kassin, S. M., Kukucka, J., Lawson, V. Z., & DeCarlo, J. (2014). Does video recording alter the behavior of police during interrogation?: Mock crime-and-investigation study. *Law and Human Behavior, 38,* 73–83.

Kassin, S. M., Kukucka, J., Lawson, V. Z., & DeCarlo, J. (2017). Police reports of mock suspect interrogations: A test of accuracy and perception. *Law and Human Behavior, 41,* 230–243.

Kassin, S. M., Leo, R. A., Meissner, C. A., Richman, K. D., Colwell, L. H., Leach, A-M., & La Fon, D. (2007). Police interviewing and interrogation: A self-report survey of police practices and beliefs. *Law and Human Behavior, 31,* 381–400.

Kassin, S. M., & McNall, K. (1991). Police interrogations and confessions: Communicating promises and threats by pragmatic implication. *Law and Human Behavior, 15,* 233–251.

Kassin, S. M., Meissner, C. A., & Norwick, R. J. (2005). "I'd know a false confession if I saw one": A comparative study of college students and police investigators. *Law and Human Behavior, 29,* 211–227.

Kassin, S. M., & Norwick, R. J. (2004). Why people waive their Miranda rights: The power of innocence. *Law and Human Behavior, 28,* 211–221.

Kassin, S. M., Redlich, A. D., Alceste, F., & Luke, T. J. (2018). On the general acceptance of confessions research: Opinions of the scientific community. *American Psychologist, 73,* 63–80.

Kassin, S. M., Russano, M., Amrom, A., Hellgren, J., Kukucka, J., & Lawson, V. (2019). Does video recording inhibit crime suspects?: Evidence from a fully randomized field experiment. *Law and Human Behavior, 43,* 44–55.

Kassin, S. M., & Sommers, S. R. (1997). Inadmissible testimony, instructions to disregard, and the jury: Substantive versus procedural considerations. *Personality and Social Psychology Bulletin, 23,* 1046–1054.

Kassin, S. M., & Sukel, H. (1997). Coerced confessions and the jury: An experimental test of the "harmless error" rule. *Law and Human Behavior, 21,* 27–46.

Kassin, S., & Thompson, D. (2019). Videotape all police interrogations—Justice demands it. *New York Times* op-ed, August 1.

Kassin, S., Wells, G., & Holland, L. (2005). Why suspects waive the right to a lineup: A study in the risk of actual innocence. Poster presented at the American Psychology-Law Society, San Diego.

Kassin, S. M., & Wrightsman, L. S. (1979). On the requirements of proof: The timing of judicial instruction and mock juror verdicts. *Journal of Personality and Social Psychology, 37*, 1877–1887.

Kassin, S. M., & Wrightsman, L. S. (1980). Prior confessions and mock juror verdicts. *Journal of Applied Social Psychology, 10*, 133–146.

Kassin, S. M., & Wrightsman, L. S. (1981). Coerced confessions, judicial instruction, and mock juror verdicts. *Journal of Applied Social Psychology, 11*, 489–506.

Kassin, S., & Wrightsman, L. S. (1985). Confession evidence. In S. Kassin & L. Wrightsman (Eds.), *The psychology of evidence and trial procedure*. Beverly Hills: Sage Books.

Kassin, S. M., & Wrightsman, L. S. (1988). *The American jury on trial: Psychological perspectives*. Washington, DC: Hemisphere.

Kidd, W. R. (1940). *Police interrogation*. New York: R.V. Basuino.

Kleck, R. E., & Strenta, A. (1980). Perceptions of the impact of negatively valued physical characteristics on social interaction. *Journal of Personality and Social Psychology, 39*, 861–873.

Konnikova, M. (2016). *The confidence game: Why we fall for it . . . every time.* New York: Viking.

Kovera, M. B., & Evelo, A. J. (2017). The case for double-blind lineup administration. *Psychology, Public Policy, and Law, 23*, 421–437.

Kukucka, J., & Evelo, A. J. (2019). Stigma against false confessors impacts post-exoneration financial compensation. *Behavioral Sciences & the Law, 37*, 372–387.

Kukucka, J., & Kassin, S. M. (2014). Do confessions taint perceptions of handwriting evidence? An empirical test of the forensic confirmation bias. *Law and Human Behavior, 38*, 56–70.

Kukucka, J., Kassin, S. M., Zapf, P. A., & Dror, I. E. (2017). Cognitive bias and blindness: A global survey of forensic science examiners. *Journal of Applied Research in Memory and Cognition, 6*, 452–459.

Lafler v. Cooper, 566 U.S. 156 (2012).

Lange, N. D., Thomas, R. P., Dana, J., & Dawes, R. M. (2011). Contextual biases in the interpretation of auditory evidence. *Law and Human Behavior, 35*, 178–187.

Lassiter, G. D., Diamond, S. S., Schmidt, H. C., & Elek, J. K. (2007). Evaluating videotaped confessions: Expertise provides no defense against the camera-perspective effect. *Psychological Science, 18*, 224–226.

Lassiter, G. D., Geers, A. L., Handley, I. M., Weiland, P. E., & Munhall, P. J. (2002). Videotaped confessions and interrogations: A change in camera perspective alters verdicts in simulated trials. *Journal of Applied Psychology, 87*, 867–874.

Lego v. Twomey, 404 U.S. 477 (1972).

Leo, R. A. (1996). Inside the interrogation room. *Journal of Criminal Law and Criminology, 86*, 266–303.

Leo, R. A. (1996). Miranda's revenge: Police interrogation as a confidence game. *Law and Society Review, 30*, 259–288.

Leo, R. A. (2008). *Police interrogation and American justice*. Cambridge, MA: Harvard University Press.

Lerner, M. J. (1980). *The belief in a just world*. New York: Plenum.

Leveritt, M. (2002). *Devil's knot: The true story of the West Memphis Three*. New York: Atria Books.

Levine, T. R., Asada, K. J. K., & Park, H. S. (2006). The lying chicken and the gaze avoidant egg: Eye contact, deception and causal order. *Southern Journal of Communication, 4*, 401–411.

Levy, H. (1996). *And the blood cried out*. New York: Avon Books.

Lewis, M., Stanger, C., & Sullivan, M. W. (1989). Deception in 3-year-olds. *Developmental Psychology, 25,* 439–443.

Li, V. (2016). 50-year story of the Miranda warning has the twists of a cop show. *ABA Journal,* August 1.

Lidén, M., Gräns, M., & Juslin, P. (2018). The presumption of guilt in suspect interrogations: Apprehension as a trigger of confirmation bias and debiasing techniques. *Law and Human Behavior, 42,* 336–354.

Loudenberg, K. (2017). *The Confession Tapes: A Public Apology.* Netflix S1, E3. https://www.netflix.com/title/80161702.

Luke, T. J. (2019). Lessons from Pinocchio: Cues to deception may be highly exaggerated. *Perspectives on Psychological Science, 14,* 646–671.

Luke, T. J., & Alceste, F. (2020). The mechanisms of minimization: How interrogation tactics suggest lenient sentencing through pragmatic implication. *Law and Human Behavior, 44,* 266–285.

Lykken, D. T. (1981). *A Tremor in the blood: Uses and abuses of the lie detector.* New York: McGraw-Hill.

Malloy, L. C., Shulman, E. P., & Cauffman, E. (2014). Interrogations, confessions, and guilty pleas among serious adolescent offenders. *Law and Human Behavior, 38,* 181–193.

Marion, S. B., Kukucka, J., Collins, C., Kassin, S. M., & Burke, T. M. (2016). Lost proof of innocence: The impact of confessions on alibi witnesses. *Law and Human Behavior, 40,* 65–71.

Martin, A. (2011). The prosecution's case against DNA. *The New York Times Sunday Magazine,* November 27, p. 44.

Medwed, D. S. (2008). The innocent prisoner's dilemma: Consequences of failing to admit guilt at parole hearings. *Iowa Law Review, 93,* 492–557.

Meissner, C. A., & Kassin, S. M. (2002). "He's guilty!": Investigator bias in judgments of truth and deception. *Law and Human Behavior, 26,* 469–480.

Milgram, S. (1963). Behavioral study of obedience. *Journal of Abnormal and Social Psychology, 67,* 371–378.

Milgram, S. (1974). *Obedience to authority: An experimental view.* New York: Harper & Row.

Miller, A. G. (1986). *The obedience experiments: A case study of controversy in social science.* New York: Praeger.

Milne, R., & Bull, R. (1999). *Investigative interviewing: Psychology and practice.* Chichester, UK: Wiley.

Miranda v. Arizona, 384 U.S. 436 (1966).

Mischel, W. (2014). *The marshmallow test: Mastering self-control.* Boston: Little, Brown.

Moore, T., Copeland, P. & Schuller, R. (2009). Deceit, betrayal, and the search for truth: Legal and psychological perspectives on the "Mr. Big" strategy. *Criminal Law Quarterly, 55,* 348–404.

Morgan, C. A., et al. (2004). Accuracy of eyewitness memory for persons encountered during exposure to highly intense stress. *International Journal of Law and Psychiatry, 27,* 265–279.

Mulbar, H. (1951). *Interrogation.* New York: Charles C. Thomas.

Munsterberg, H. (1908). *On the witness stand.* Garden City, NY: Doubleday.

Murrie, D. C., & Boccaccini, M. T. (2015). Adversarial allegiance among expert witnesses. *Annual Review of Law and Social Science, 11,* 37–55.

Murrie, D. C., Boccaccini, M. T., Guarnera, L. A., & Rufino, K. A. (2013). Are forensic experts biased by the side that retained them? *Psychological Science, 24,* 1889–1897.

Nader, R. (2006). A Corporate abuse—coerced confessions. *IndyBay,* May. 20. https://www.indybay.org/newsitems/2006/05/20/18244411.php.

Narchet, F. M., Meissner, C. A., & Russano, M. B. (2011). Modeling the influence of investigator bias on the elicitation of true and false confessions. *Law and Human Behavior, 35,* 452–465.

Nash, R. A., & Wade, K. A. (2009). Innocent but proven guilty: Using false video evidence to elicit false confessions and create false beliefs. *Applied Cognitive Psychology, 23,* 624–637.

Natapoff, A. (2009). *Snitching: Criminal informants and the erosion of American justice.* New York: New York University Press.

National Academy of Sciences. (2009). *Strengthening forensic science in the United States: A path forward.* Washington, DC: National Academies Press.

National Research Council. 2003. *The polygraph and lie detection.* Washington, DC: National Academies Press.

Neuschatz, J. S., Lawson, D. S., Swanner, J. K., Meissner, C. A., & Neuschatz, J. S. (2008). The effects of accomplice witnesses and jailhouse informants on jury decision making. *Law and Human Behavior, 32,* 137–149.

Newsome, M. (2006). Kenzi Snider did not murder her friend, so why did she confess? *O, the Oprah Magazine, 7,* April 1, 235.

New York Times (1991). Editorial: "The Supreme Court's Harmful Error." March 29, p. A12.

Norris, R. (2012). Assessing compensation statutes for the wrongly convicted. *Criminal Justice Policy Review, 23,* 352–374.

North Carolina v. Alford, 400 U.S. 25 (1970).

North Carolina v. Butler, 441 U.S. 369 (1979).

O'Brien, J. A. (1993). Mother's killing still unresolved, but Peter Reilly puts past behind. *Hartford Courant,* September 23.

O'Hara, C. (1956). *Fundamentals of criminal investigation.* Springfield, IL: Thomas.

Oliver, W. R. (2018). Response to Kukucka et al.: Comment on cognitive bias and blindness: A global survey of forensic science examiners. *Journal of Applied Research in Memory and Cognition, 7,* 161.

Owen-Kostelnik, J., Reppucci, N. D., & Meyer, J. D. (2006). Testimony and interrogation of minors: Assumptions about maturity and morality. *American Psychologist, 61,* 286–304.

Pelonero, C. (2014). *Kitty Genovese: A true account of a public murder and its private consequences.* New York: Skyhorse Publishing.

Perillo, J. T. (2015). Precursors of false guilty pleas: An examination of exonerations. Paper presented at the Meeting of the American Psychology–Law Society, San Diego.

Perillo, J. T., & Kassin, S. M. (2011). Inside interrogation: The lie, the bluff, and false confessions. *Law and Human Behavior, 35,* 327–337

Perillo, J., Crozier, W., Pollick, C., & Kassin, S. M. (2014). The effect of prior false confession on guilty plea decisions. Paper presented at the Meeting of the American Psychology-Law Society, New Orleans.

Philp, K. (2018). *False Confessions.* Copenhagen: Good Company Pictures. https://www.goodcompanypictures.com/false-confessions.

Preston, D., & Spezi, M. (2009). *The monster of Florence: A true story.* New York: Grand Central Publishing.

Prettyman, E. B. (1960). Jury instructions—First or last? *American Bar Association Journal, 46,* 1066.

Puddister, K. (2018). Police investigation in Tina Fontaine's murder: Rethinking the Mr. Big method. *The Conversation,* March 13.

R. v. Hart, 2014 SCC 52, [2014] 2 S.C.R. 544.

Rakoff, J. (2014). Why innocent people plead guilty. *New York Review of Books,* November 20.

Redlich, A. D., Bibas, S., Edkins, V. A., & Madon, S. (2017). The psychology of defendant plea decision making. *American Psychologist, 72,* 339–352.

Redlich, A. D., & Goodman, G. S. (2003). Taking responsibility for an act not committed: The influence of age and suggestibility. *Law and Human Behavior, 27,* 141–156.

Redlich, A. D., & Özdoğru, A. A. (2009). Alford pleas in the age of innocence. *Behavioral Sciences & the Law, 27,* 467–488.

Redlich, A. D., Summers, A., & Hoover, S. (2010). Self-reported false confessions and false guilty pleas among offenders with mental illness. *Law and Human Behavior, 34,* 70–90.

Redlich, A. D., Yan, S., Norris, R., & Bushway, S. (2018). The influence of confessions on guilty pleas and plea discounts. Psychology, *Public Policy, and Law, 24*, 147–157.

Reid, J. E., & Arther, R. O. (1953). Behavior symptoms of lie-detector subjects. *Journal of Criminal Law and Criminology, 44*, 104–108.

Rimer, S. (2002). Convict's DNA sways labs, not a determined prosecutor. *New York Times*, February 6, p. A14.

Roberts, M. H., Klatzkin, R. R., & Mechlin, B. (2015). Social support attenuates physiological stress responses and experimental pain sensitivity to cold pressor pain. *Annals of Behavioral Medicine, 49*, 557–569.

Rogers, R., Fiduccia, C. E., Drogin, E. Y., Steadham, J. A., Clark, J. W., III, & Cramer, R. J. (2013). General knowledge and mis-knowledge of Miranda rights: Are effective Miranda advisements still necessary? *Psychology, Public Policy, and Law, 19*, 432–442.

Rogers, R., Harrison, K. S., Shuman, D. W., Sewell, K. W., & Hazelwood, L. L. (2007). An analysis of Miranda warnings and waivers: Comprehension and coverage. *Law and Human Behavior, 31*, 177–192.

Rogers, R., Hazelwood, L. L., Harrison, K. S., Sewell, K. W., & Shuman, D. W. (2008). The language of Miranda in American jurisdictions: A replication and further analysis. *Law and Human Behavior, 32*, 124–136.

Rogers, R., Rogstad, J. E., Gillard, N. D., Drogin, E. Y., Blackwood, H. L., & Shuman, D. W. (2010). "Everyone knows their Miranda rights": Implicit assumptions and countervailing evidence. *Psychology, Public Policy, and Law, 16*, 300–318.

Rosenfeld, M. (2019). Despite DNA evidence of innocence, West Virginia man who pled guilty remains locked up. *Injustice Watch*, September 19. https://www.injusticewatch.org/interactives/trading-away-justice/west-virginia.html.

Rosenthal, A. M. (1999). *Thirty-eight witnesses*. Berkeley: University of California Press (Original work published 1964).

Rosenthal, R., & Fode, K. L. (1963). The effect of experimenter bias on the performance of the albino rat. *Behavioral Science, 8*, 183–189.

Rosenthal, R., & Jacobson, L. (1968). *Pygmalion in the classroom: Teacher expectation and pupils' intellectual development*. New York: Holt, Rinehart & Winston.

Ross, L. (1977). The intuitive psychologist and his shortcomings: Distortions in the attribution process. *Advances in Experimental Social Psychology, 10*, 174–221.

Ruback, R. B., & Hopper, C. H. (1986). Decision making by parole interviewers: The effect of case and interview factors. *Law and Human Behavior, 10*, 203–214.

Russano, M. B., Meissner, C. A., Narchet, F., & Kassin, S. M. (2005). Investigating true and false confessions within a novel experimental paradigm. *Psychological Science, 16*, 481–486.

Ryan, H. (2006). *Murder in Room 103*. New York: Avon Books.

Salinas v. Texas, 570 U.S. 178 (2013).

Santos, F. (2006). DNA frees a man imprisoned for half his life. *New York Times*, September 21, 2006.

Schachter, S. (1959). *The psychology of affiliation: Experimental studies of the sources of gregariousness*. Stanford, CA: Stanford University Press.

Schanberg, S. H. (2002). A journey through the tangled case of the Central Park jogger. *Village Voice*, November 19.

Schapiro, R. (2018). Cameraman who shot Central Park 5 interrogation videos speaks out for the first time. *New York Daily News*, July 22.

Scherr, K. C., & Madon, S. (2012). You have the right to understand: The deleterious effect of stress on Miranda comprehension. *Law and Human Behavior, 36*, 275–282.

Scherr, K. C., & Madon, S. (2013). "Go ahead and sign": An experimental examination of Miranda waivers and comprehension. *Law and Human Behavior, 37*, 208–218.

Scherr, K. C., & Normile, C. J. (2022). False confessions predict a delay between release from incarceration and official exoneration. *Law and Human Behavior, 46*.

Scherr, K. C., Normile, C. J., Luna, S., Redlich, A. D., Lawrence, M., & Catlin, M. (2020). False admissions of guilt associated with wrongful convictions undermine people's perceptions of exonerees. *Psychology, Public Policy, and Law, 26*, 233–244.

Scherr, K. C., Normile, C. J., & Putney, H. (2018). Perpetually stigmatized: False confessions prompt underlying mechanisms that motivate negative perceptions of exonerees. *Psychology, Public Policy, and Law, 24*, 341–352.

Scherr, K. C., Redlich, A. D., & Kassin, S. M. (2020). Cumulative disadvantage: A psychological framework for understanding how innocence can lead to confession, wrongful conviction, and beyond. *Perspectives on Psychological Science, 15*, 353–383.

Schneider, S. (2013). When innocent defendants falsely confess: Analyzing the ramifications of entering Alford pleas in the context of the burgeoning innocence movement. *Journal of Criminal Law & Criminology, 103*, 279–308.

Schulhofer, S. J. (1996). Miranda's practical effect: Substantial benefits and vanishingly small social costs. *Northwestern University Law Review, 90*, 500–564.

Severson, K. (2012). West Memphis Three, a year out of prison, navigate new paths. *New York Times*, August 17, p. A9.

Shapiro, F. C. (1969). *Whitmore*. Indianapolis: Bobbs-Merrill.

Shepherd, E. & Griffiths, A. (2013). *Investigative interviewing: The conversational management approach* (2nd ed.). Oxford: Oxford University Press.

Sherif, M. (1936). *The psychology of social norms*. New York: Harper.

Shlosberg, A., Nowotny, J., Panuccio, E., & Rajah, V. (2020). "They open the door, kick you out, and say, go": Reentry challenges after wrongful imprisonment. *The Wrongful Conviction Law Review, 1*, 226–252.

Simon, D. (1991). *Homicide: A year on the killing streets*. Boston: Houghton Mifflin Harcourt.

Simons, D. J., & Chabris, C. F. (1999). Gorillas in our midst: Sustained inattentional blindness for dynamic events. *Perception, 28*, 1059–1074.

Skoller, C. (2008). *Twisted confessions: The true story behind the Kitty Genovese and Barbara Kralik murder trials*. Bloomington, IN: AuthorHouse.

Slobodzian, J. A., & Rowan, T. (2016). Twenty-five years later, freed by DNA evidence: "It's the greatest day of my life." *The Philadelphia Inquirer*, August 23.

Snyder, M., & Swann, W. B., Jr. (1978). Behavioral confirmation in social interaction: From social perception to social reality. *Journal of Personality and Social Psychology, 36*, 1202–1212.

Sollecito, R. (2012). *Honor bound: My journey to hell and back with Amanda Knox*. New York: Gallery Books.

Solotaroff, P. (2015). Why is this man still in jail? *Rolling Stone*, March 12, 42–49, 67.

Stansbury v. California, 511 U.S. 318 (1994).

Starr, D. (2013). *New Yorker*, December 9, 42–49.

Starr, D. (2016). Why are educators learning how to interrogate their students? *New Yorker*, March 25, 1–5.

Steinberg, L. (2014). *Age of opportunity: Lessons from the new science of adolescence*. New York: Mariner Books.

Sullivan, T. P. (2008). Recording federal custodial interviews. *American Criminal Law Review, 45*, 1297–1345.

Sullivan, T. P. (2019). Current report on recording custodial interrogations in the United States. *The Champion*, April, 54–55.

Sullivan, T. P., Vail, A. W., & Anderson, H. W. (2008). The case for recording police interrogation. *Litigation, 34*, 1–8.

Swanner, J. K., Beike, D. R., & Cole, A. T. (2010). Snitching, lies and computer crashes: An experimental investigation of secondary confessions. *Law and Human Behavior, 34*, 53–65.

Talwar, V., & Crossman, A. M. (2012). Children's lies and their detection: Implications for child witness testimony. *Developmental Review, 32*, 337–359.

Thomas, G. C., III (2004). Stories about Miranda. *Michigan Law Review, 102*, 1959–2000.

Trainum, J. (2008). The case for videotaping interrogations: A suspect's false confession to a murder opened an officer's eyes. *Los Angeles Times*, October 24.

Trainum, J. L. (2016). *How the police generate false confessions: An inside look at the interrogation room*. Lanham, MD: Rowman & Littlefield.

Van den Eeden, C. A. J., De Poot, C. J., & Van Koppen, P. J. (2016). Forensic expectations: Investigating a crime scene with prior information. *Science & Justice, 56*, 475–481.

Vitello, P. (2012). George Whitmore Jr., who falsely confessed to 3 murders in 1964, dies at 68. *New York Times*, October 16, p. A29.

Voigt, R., et al. (2017). Language from police body camera footage shows racial disparities in officer respect. *Proceedings of the National Academy of Sciences, 114*, 6521–6526.

Vrij, A. (2008). *Detecting lies and deceit: Pitfalls and opportunities* (2nd ed.). New York: John Wiley & Sons.

Vrij, A., Fisher, R., Mann, S., & Leal, S. (2008). A cognitive load approach to lie detection. *Journal of Investigative Psychology and Offender Profiling, 5*, 39–43.

Vrij, A., Mann, S., & Fisher, R. P. (2006). An empirical test of the Behaviour Analysis Interview. *Law and Human Behavior, 30*, 329–345.

Wald, M., Ayres, R., Hess, D. W., Schantz, M., & Whitebread, C. H. (1967). Interrogations in New Haven: The impact of Miranda. *The Yale Law Journal, 76*, 1519–1648.

Wallace, D. B., & Kassin, S. M. (2012). Harmless error analysis: How do judges respond to confession errors? *Law and Human Behavior, 36*, 151–157.

Waterbury, M. C. (2011). *The monster of Perugia: The framing of Amanda Knox.* Perception Development.

Wegner, D. M. (1994). Ironic processes of mental control. *Psychological Review, 101*, 34–52.

Wegner, D. M., Schneider, D. J., Carter, S. R., & White, T. L. (1987). Paradoxical effects of thought suppression. *Journal of Personality and Social Psychology, 53*, 5–13.

Weisselberg, C. D. (2008). Mourning Miranda. *California Law Review, 96*, 1521–1601.

Wells, G. L., Kovera, M. B., Douglass, A. B., Brewer, N., Meissner, C. A., & Wixted, J. T. (2020). Policy and procedure recommendations for the collection and preservation of eyewitness identification evidence. *Law and Human Behavior, 44*, 3–36.

Wells, G. L., Small, M., Penrod, S. J., Malpass, R. S., Fulero, S. M., & Brimacombe, C. A. E. (1998). Eyewitness identification procedures: Recommendations for lineups and photo-spreads. *Law and Human Behavior, 22*, 603–647.

White, W. S. (2001). *Miranda's waning protections: Police interrogation practices after Dickerson.* Ann Arbor: University of Michigan Press.

Willis, J., & Todorov, A. (2006). First impressions: Making up your mind after a 100-ms exposure to a face. *Psychological Science, 17*, 592–598.

Withrow, B. L. (2006). *Racial profiling: From rhetoric to reason.* Upper Saddle River, NJ: Pearson/Prentice Hall.

Wrightsman, L. S., & Kassin, S. M. (1993). *Confessions in the courtroom.* Newbury Park, CA: Sage.

Zapf, P. A., Kukucka, J., Kassin, S. M., & Dror, I. E. (2018). Cognitive bias in forensic mental health assessment: Evaluator beliefs about its nature and scope. *Psychology, Public Policy, and Law, 24*, 1–10.

Zelle, H., Romaine, C. L. R., & Goldstein, N. E. S. (2015). Juveniles' Miranda comprehension: Understanding, appreciation, and totality of circumstances factors. *Law and Human Behavior, 39*, 281–293.

Zhong R. (2015). Judging remorse. *Review of Law and Social Change, 39*, 133–172.

Zimbardo, P. G. (1967). The psychology of police confessions. *Psychology Today, 1*, June 17–20, 25–27.

Zottoli, T. M., Daftary-Kapur, T., Winters, G. M., & Hogan, C. (2016). Plea discounts, time pressures, and false-guilty pleas in youth and adults who pleaded guilty to felonies in New York City. *Psychology, Public Policy, and Law, 22*, 250–259.

INDEX

ABOUT THE AUTHOR

Saul Kassin is Distinguished Professor of Psychology at the John Jay College of Criminal Justice and Massachusetts Professor Emeritus at Williams College. He received his BS from Brooklyn College in New York and his PhD from the University of Connecticut, after which he was awarded postdoctoral fellowships at the University of Kansas, the U.S. Supreme Court, and Stanford University.

Kassin has written several college textbooks—including *Social Psychology*, now in its eleventh edition—and scholarly books, such as *Confessions in the Courtroom*, *The Psychology of Evidence and Trial Procedure*, and *The American Jury on Trial: Psychological Perspectives*. Having published roughly two hundred articles and book chapters, he is laser focused on research-based policies designed to prevent and correct wrongful convictions.

Starting in the 1980s, Kassin pioneered the scientific study of police interrogations and confessions. At that time, he distinguished three types of false confessions, a taxonomy that is still universally accepted today. He then developed the first experimental laboratory paradigms for examining how innocent people are duped into confession and the impact these confessions have in duping judges, juries, and forensic examiners. In a trio of studies funded by the National Science Foundation and reported in a *New York Times* op-ed article, he and his colleagues have written extensively on the benefits of video recording interrogations. His work is cited in courts all over the world.

Kassin has received prestigious lifetime-contribution awards from the American Psychological Association (APA), the Association for Psychological Science (APS), the American Psychology–Law Society (AP-LS), and the European Association of Psychology and Law (EAPL). Over the years, his work has been quoted in countless newspapers and magazines. He has also appeared as a media consultant on all major networks in the United States and abroad, on syndicated network programs like the *Oprah Winfrey Show*, and in various podcasts and documentaries—including Ken Burns's 2012 film *The Central Park Five*. He was also featured in a 2019 *Science* magazine article.